Inside AppleTalk®

Second Edition

Gursharan S. Sidhu
Technical Director

Richard F. Andrews
Staff Engineer

Alan B. Oppenheimer
Staff Engineer

Network Systems Development
Apple Computer, Inc.

Addison-Wesley Publishing Company, Inc.

Reading, Massachusetts ■ Menlo Park, California ■ New York
Don Mills, Ontario ■ Wokingham, England ■ Amsterdam ■ Bonn
Sydney ■ Singapore ■ Tokyo ■ Madrid ■ San Juan

Contents

Part I Physical and Data Links

Part II End-to-End Data Flow

Part III   Named Entities

Part IV   Reliable Data Delivery

9   AppleTalk Transaction Protocol / 9-1

10   Printer Access Protocol / 10-1

Part V End-User Services

13 AppleTalk Filing Protocol / 13-1

14   Print Spooling Architecture / 14-1

Appendix A   LocalTalk Hardware Specifications / A-1

Appendix B   LLAP Access Control Algorithms / B-1

Figures and Tables

Acknowledgments

EVEN THOUGH *Inside AppleTalk* was published by Addison-Wesley as recently as early 1989, the needed evolution of technology has already made it necessary to produce a new edition! In fact, even while we were in the final editing and production stages of the first edition, our engineering teams were busy implementing a major extension of the network system, now known as AppleTalk® Phase 2. This extension was introduced in June of 1989, and its various components are now in users' hands. This second edition includes all changes made to the protocols to implement the enhanced capabilities of AppleTalk Phase 2.

It is my privilege to acknowledge the contributions of many of the finest networking engineers in the industry in this endeavour. Jim Mathis, who has been involved with network systems design since the advent of TCP (Transmission Control Protocol) in his university days at Stanford, worked with me on the early architectural design of Phase 2, critiquing and suggesting amendments to the design. The refinement and translation of that design into an actual implementation was done by a team under the leadership of Alan Oppenheimer, who is a co-author of this book. Major contributions were made by several members of Alan's staff—I would like to make special note of Sean Findley, Louise Laier, Kerry Lynn, and Mike Quinn. These engineers *par excellence* have built a new version of the system in the face of the enormous challenge of maintaining compatibility with existing AppleTalk applications. The results have been simply extraordinary. Whereas the original AppleTalk system had a size limitation of at most 254 devices connected to a single network, the new design extends this limit to approximately 16 million devices. The owner of the network system has enhanced flexibility in distributing these devices on the various networks that comprise the internet. Much care has been devoted to minimizing the use of network bandwidth for the system's internal coordination, such as routing table maintenance.

The AppleTalk network system now offers an even greater range of connectivity options than before, encompassing all the most important physical and link-level technologies, such as LocalTalk™, Ethernet®, and token ring. But more importantly, it has established a much-envied level of ease of use, pushing network arcana into the distant background of the user's experience. Although within Apple® this ease of use is now taken for granted, we should take note of what our customers think. They have voted with their pocket books and the result is an installed base that is variously estimated by a variety of independent services at between 2 and 3 million connections. This market place reality might provide sufficient basis for us to view AppleTalk as a *de facto* standard, standing in the company of stalwarts like SNA (Systems Network Architecture) and DECnet™. Even developers, Apple's close partners in the success of our products, have indicated their interest in this system by buying an unexpectedly large number (approaching 10,000) of copies of *Inside AppleTalk,* and this despite its being a deeply technical book. We at Apple are beholden to them for their support.

In the first edition, I acknowledged Apple's deep gratitude to a distinguished line of third-party supporters of AppleTalk. I would like to add a special personal note of thanks to Guy Riddle, recently appointed Bell Labs Fellow, for enthusiastically and single-handedly incorporating AppleTalk into AT&T's product offerings.

I would like to extend my appreciation for the special efforts of the staff in Apple's Networking and Communications Publications department. Thanks go to Judy Helfand, editor; Joyce Zavarro, art director; Debbie McDaniel, production editor; Ron Morton, production assistant; Robin Kerns, film and print supervisor; and Patrick Ames and Rani Cochran.

Don Casey, who joined Apple in 1988 after a long and distinguished career at IBM, has made enthusiastic private and public observations on the AppleTalk network system. Coming from a veteran of the industry, these have been a source of much joy to me. He has my appreciation for his kind thoughts and, somewhat tongue in cheek, my admiration for his good taste.

Gursharan S. Sidhu
January 1990

Acknowledgments to First Edition

THE DEVELOPMENT of the AppleTalk network system spans more than a five-year period. Although the authors of *Inside AppleTalk* were the key players in the system's design, many others helped in numerous ways.

Without a doubt, the genesis of AppleTalk is to be found in the demanding and uncompromising questioning of Steve Jobs. In particular, at the National Computer Conference (NCC) in Anaheim in 1983, he asked me the key question: "Why has networking not caught on?" My awkward attempts to answer his question started us on this venture. Invention always has its instigator, and Steve played this role for AppleTalk as he has for many other wonderful products from Apple. I owe a great personal debt to him for first listening to my fervent but not yet fully formed vision of networks as empowering extensions of the personal computer and for later helping remove barriers from our developmental path.

Bob Belleville, former engineering director of the Macintosh® Division and ever a pragmatist, converted the vision into three succinct memos that put a stop to all argument on this issue at Apple. He provided a focus for this nascent activity, including the general goals for LocalTalk (then known as AppleBus), the LaserWriter® printer, and the system's file server. Although the actual products turned out considerably different from what he indicated in those memos, he summarized the target area with consummate simplicity.

The most exciting activity of the last quarter of 1983 and the first few months of 1984 was the development of the LocalTalk Link Access Protocol (LLAP). This protocol is the basis of LocalTalk and related connectivity implementations from several vendors, including PhoneNET from Farrallon Computing and Fiber Optic Communication Card from Du Pont Electronics. I wish to acknowledge several colleagues at Apple who played key roles in this difficult design activity: Ron Hochsprung and Larry Kenyon for their very creative design participation, George Crow for the superb analog design of the LocalTalk hardware, and Jim Nichols for an uncompromising test harness that proved that the design was efficient and stable.

The AppleTalk protocol architecture almost did not happen. Bob Belleville proposed an external, device-interconnect bus for the then-closed Macintosh personal computer. Creating a network system was my somewhat clandestine idea; when I described the network architecture to Bob on January 24, 1984, about two hours after the Macintosh introduction, I did so with some trepidation. I am grateful to him for his forthright admission that I had made AppleTalk into something much more comprehensive than he had anticipated and for his full support!

In its early days, any new idea is tender and vulnerable. I am especially grateful to Ed Taft of Adobe Systems, one of the most widely known members of the networking community, for his very thorough review and his advice in late 1983 and early 1984. His extremely encouraging comments bolstered my own commitment to build this system; without his encouragement, compromises to "conventionalism" might have crept in.

It was all very well to have the approval of fellow designers of network systems, but the proverbial proof-is-in-the-pudding was still missing: How would users of the system respond to it? Stan Dunton and Rich Brown of Dartmouth College provided a crucial vote of confidence in early 1984 with their decision to install AppleTalk as their campus-wide system. I will be eternally grateful to Stan for standing up at the first AppleBus Developers' Conference and saying: "This is just the system we've been waiting for someone to design."

My biggest debt of gratitude is to Rich Andrews and Alan Oppenheimer, who have been my technical partners in this venture from the beginning. The credit for the outstanding reliability of the Macintosh AppleTalk drivers goes to Alan's meticulous attention to detail in writing them. They are a model of how an efficient and tight implementation of network protocols can be achieved in a difficult environment.

The elegant design of the AppleTalk Transaction Protocol (ATP) exactly-once packet exchange is the contribution of Rich Andrews. Rich listened to my somewhat unconventional ideas about not building a general stream protocol but relying instead on transactions. I then suggested at-least-once and exactly-once service. My exactly-once proposal, however, was considerably clumsier than Rich's modification, which has become integral to millions of Macintosh and LaserWriter ROMs.

One of the impressive services in the AppleTalk system is provided by the AppleShare® file server, which was many years in the making. Rich Andrews has been my partner in this venture throughout. I wish to thank him for his tremendous effort in the face of considerable adversity and public opprobrium. His persistent, dogged work toward the final AppleShare product has earned him the title of Apple Hero.

Rich and Alan join me in thanking all our colleagues in Apple's Network Systems Development (NSD) group; in particular, we would like to mention a few veterans: Pat Dirks, Bruce Gaya, Rick Hoiberg, and Gene Tyacke. Tim Warden and Steve Schwartz made significant contributions to the chapters on the AppleTalk Data Stream Protocol (ADSP) and the Printer Access Protocol (PAP), for which they have my appreciation and thanks.

Since 1985, the NSD group has enjoyed the support and encouragement of Ed Birss and Jean-Louis Gassée. Both have become strong converts to our dream of extending the power of the individual beyond the desk top.

The unsung key contributors to a system such as AppleTalk are the third-party developers who have risked their investment funds to add end-user value. They kept AppleTalk alive when many thought it was just a printer cable. I wish to acknowledge, as representative of this group, the following key entrepreneurs: Evan Solley of Infosphere for the first AppleTalk disk-server product; Andrew Singer, formerly of Think Technologies, for the InBox electronic mail service; Alex Gernert, formerly of Tri Data, for the Netway 1000 SNA connectivity server; Rob Ryan of Hayes Microcomputer Products, Inc. and Tim McCreery of Kinetics for their AppleTalk routers; Reese Jones of Farallon Computing for the PhoneNET implementation of LocalTalk service; and Bob Denny of Alisa Systems for the implementation of Apple's AppleTalk for VMS software.

Lest other good developer friends take umbrage at my not mentioning them specifically, I plead the impracticality of producing an exhaustive list; they know the depth of my gratitude—and that of the users—to all of them. This large body of third-party developers is a measure of the broad acceptance of the AppleTalk system.

Protocol specifications of the AppleTalk system have been provided to developers in several versions starting with the "AppleBus Developer's Handbook" of March 1984. It was my intention to publish it as a book, but we grossly underestimated the effort involved. It was not until August of 1988 that we assembled some of Apple's finest editors, production editors, and desktop publishers to pull together all the pieces that comprise this book. I am indebted to Judy Bligh, editor; Judi Seip, art director; Sheila Mulligan; Ron Morton; Roy Zitting; Debbie McDaniel; Luann Rugebregt; and Patrick Ames.

Finally, I would like to dedicate this book to the patience and understanding of my wife, Elvira, who endured the many nights when I paced the floor while struggling with some protocol problem.

Gursharan S. Sidhu
November 1988

Introduction

C O N T E N T S

■

THIS BOOK PROVIDES the internal design details of the AppleTalk® network system. As such, it is intended for those who are not content merely with being users of the system but who would like to go behind the scenes. *Inside AppleTalk* is designed to meet the needs of those interested in understanding AppleTalk network technology. Distinguished among this group are developers wishing to connect devices to this network system or to write computer programs that use its services.

Readers are not required to have a detailed knowledge of network systems. Those generally familiar with the design of computing systems should be able to grasp the material presented here. ■

Network systems

The basic goal of computer network systems is to eliminate access barriers that result from the geographical and physical separation of various devices and the resources they embody. Network systems are the essential basis of distributed computing.

Computer network systems consist of computing components and connectivity components. *Computing components* include *computing devices,* such as personal computers, minicomputers, and mainframe computers, and special *server devices,* such as file servers and print servers. These devices are connected through a variety of cables, other data channels, and routing and gateway components, which collectively are the *connectivity components* of the system.

Protocols—What are they?

The effective operation of any distributed system, of human beings or of devices, is based on underlying rules that prescribe the nature and form of the permitted and accepted interactions. In the world of diplomacy, these rules are known as protocols.

Similarly, computer networks operate on the basis of carefully designed and scrupulously enforced rules of interaction—also called **protocols**—between the network system's interconnected devices. Internal descriptions of such systems consist mainly of discussion and specification of the protocols, their objectives, and their interactions. This collective of information is known as the *protocol architecture* of the network system.

Inside AppleTalk defines and describes AppleTalk's protocol architecture. To understand AppleTalk's design fully, one must also examine its *topological architecture,* which is concerned with the manner in which the connectivity of the network system is implemented.

Not all aspects of AppleTalk protocols are covered in this book. Some issues, such as network management and gateway protocols, will be examined in companion volumes. Likewise, protocols for database access and for page description are discussed elsewhere.

AppleTalk

AppleTalk is a comprehensive network system designed and developed by Apple Computer, Inc. It consists of many different kinds of computer systems and servers and a variety of cabling and connectivity products.

This system was designed as an integral part of Apple Computer's mission to provide greater power to the individual through computer technology. The ultimate objective was to go beyond personal computers to *interpersonal computing*. The cornerstone of this vision is the Macintosh® family of personal computers. These computers allow users to directly manipulate and use various capabilities and resources through an elegant, aesthetic, and empowering user interface. The AppleTalk network system was envisioned as a natural and seamless extension of the Macintosh beyond the confines of the user's desk top, allowing the individual to gain access to remote resources and to interact with other users through personal computers.

Why did we design it?

When this design activity was initiated in late 1983, many barriers prevented the widespread adoption of network technology. No one doubted networking's vast promise; yet its acceptance was proving slower than anticipated.

It was expensive (approximately $1000 for each computer) to connect a computer to network systems. This high cost, acceptable for minicomputers and mainframes, seemed prohibitive for the personal computer (itself priced around $1000). Furthermore, the services received by users who decided to pay the high initial price were limited.

More importantly, network systems were foreign appendages, conceived independently of computers and then only as an afterthought. Networks appeared to be celebrations of technology designed with more attention to such issues as data transmission speed than to user convenience. Users of network services had to learn the idiosyncrasies of each particular network. Access to resources through the network had to be obtained in a manner different from that used for local resources resident on the user's computer. The network constituted a hindrance when it should have extended the user's reach.

We could not use existing network protocol architectures to achieve our goal of seamlessly extending the user's computing experience. We chose instead to develop our own architecture in which we would utilize standard technology where appropriate and innovate freely where necessary.

Key goals of the AppleTalk architecture

AppleTalk was developed to be a general-purpose network system that pays special attention to the needs of personal computers and their users. In designing AppleTalk's protocol architecture, we had a number of key goals.

Versatility

The system should serve as the basis for a broad variety of applications, ranging from an external bus for attaching a few peripheral devices to a single Macintosh computer, to a network system connecting thousands of computer systems dispersed over a potentially wide area. Our objective of having a general-purpose design for AppleTalk made it imperative that we carefully construct the protocols with an eye to future, as-yet-undefined applications.

Computer networks are among the most promising technologies for bridging the operating system incompatibilities of the diverse types of computers in use today. The most valuable resource in these systems is the information generated by users. Network technology should allow users to exchange and share this information without concern for the special format and internal idiosyncrasies of dissimilar computer systems.

To achieve this goal, the network system must be designed from its inception to allow any type of computer to participate as an equal—and to the best of its ability.

"Plug-and-play" capability

The user should be able to plug a computing device into a network system and use it immediately without any of the complications of configuration. This "plug-and-play" capability, pioneered in AppleTalk, has now come to be a much-sought-after convenience of network systems. Several features of AppleTalk protocols make this possible (for example, the dynamic address-acquisition capability and the use of automatic name lookup to obtain access to network resources).

Peer-to-peer architecture

The network system's architecture should avoid centralized control. Such control would not only increase the initial entry cost of the network system but also create a single point of failure. Furthermore, centralized control can adversely impact efficiency and in several ways reduce the user's personal control over network resources.

AppleTalk protocols are peer-to-peer in structure, and the communicating entities operate as equals when interacting.

Simplicity

The protocols should be simple and easy to implement. Simplicity is essential if small, limited-memory and limited processing-power devices are to operate successfully on the network. Furthermore, simpler protocols can reduce network overhead and thus enhance performance and efficiency.

This simplicity of design and the resultant small size of network software also make it economically feasible to build network software into all computing devices, whether or not the user intends to connect the devices to a network.

Link independence

Each computing device should be able to use future technologies without the major costs of redesigning the protocol architecture and refitting ROMs and system software. Communications technology will continue to advance rapidly, offering new, as-yet-unforeseen interconnect hardware.

The protocol architecture had to be independent of the physical link. This decision has allowed us to include in the AppleTalk system a variety of physical-link options. We have introduced, for example, the use of Ethernet, token ring, and other physical-link technologies without any change to the architecture.

Seamless extension of the user's computer

Although the protocol architecture has not been designed for a particular type of computer, special attention was paid to the integration of the network system with the user's computer. In particular, the Desktop interface of the Macintosh was maintained across the network system. Making the network system transparent is central to a smooth extension of the user interface of the Macintosh, especially its direct manipulation capability.

Open architecture

The protocol architecture should be kept open so that any developer, Apple or third-party, can gain access to the services of any protocol in the architecture. But, more importantly, new protocols can be added to the architecture at any point.

Openness is essential if the architecture is to be extended or modified over its lifetime. Third-party developers can add protocols to build special services not contemplated by the designers of AppleTalk. For example, although AppleTalk has not included standards for electronic messaging/mail, various third-party vendors have been able to design and add such capability independently.

The AppleTalk network system

AppleTalk is a comprehensive network system that runs on a variety of data transmission media using various data-link methods. It facilitates communication between network devices, such as users' computers, file servers, and printers, which may be a mixture of Apple and non-Apple products. Several elements make up an AppleTalk network system: AppleTalk software and AppleTalk hardware; the latter includes computing components and connectivity components.

The AppleTalk software implements the AppleTalk protocols in each device connected to the system.

The network devices and cabling methods comprise the physical or hardware components of an AppleTalk network system. The layout of a network is called its *topology,* that is, the arrangement of the devices and cables of the network system (see *Figure I-1*).

■ **Figure I-1** Network topology

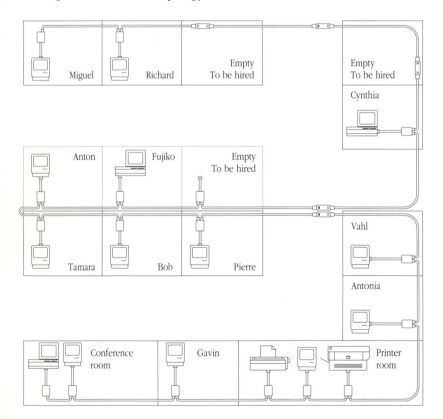

On a typical network, the majority of the devices, known as network **nodes,** will be users' personal computers. Other network nodes could be operating, for example, as file or print servers or as routers and gateways.

AppleTalk connectivity

The first step in designing a protocol architecture is to build its connectivity infrastructure—the communication hardware and the associated protocols for controlling access to the hardware links.

AppleTalk's design allows users to include a variety of data-link and cabling methods in a network system. In fact, an AppleTalk network can be set up using any of the widely available cabling and data-link technologies. Current widely used AppleTalk data-link and cabling methods include LocalTalk™ ; EtherTalk® , using standard Ethernet media; TokenTalk, using token ring; and LANSTAR AppleTalk, using Meridian LANSTAR media.

These different links can be interconnected in the AppleTalk system via routers to build very large local or geographically dispersed **internets.** The different links used in any particular portion of an AppleTalk internet can be chosen by the user according to the expected traffic, distance, and desired response characteristics in that portion of the internet.

Users can install low-cost, twisted-pair LocalTalk cabling when 230.4 Kbits/second bandwidth is sufficient. Higher-cost and higher-speed EtherTalk can be installed when full 10 Mbits/second performance is required and when the increased cost is acceptable. Likewise, wide-area links such as telephone lines can be used to extend the geographical reach of an AppleTalk network.

The cabling used in a particular portion of an AppleTalk network system can be viewed as a data highway shared by the connected network nodes. The associated data-link technology provides the protocols necessary to share that particular highway. This data-link technology consists of two principal portions: the media-specific or physical protocol and the data-link access protocol.

The physical protocol specifies physical aspects of the data link, such as how a data bit is encoded or modulated for transmission on the particular medium. For instance, on a fiber-optic link a bit is to be converted into a pulse of light of specified waveform, wavelength, and duration. In the case of electrical links, the impedance characteristics, signal strengths, and frequencies are specified by the physical protocol.

Data-link access protocols are concerned with the logistical aspects of sending the data packet through the physical medium over a potentially shared link. These protocols have several basic goals, such as addressing, error detection (in some cases, error recovery), and medium access control.

LocalTalk

The Apple LocalTalk product connects local work groups using inexpensive (typically under $100 per computer), easily configurable cabling to link workstations and other computing devices in an AppleTalk network system. LocalTalk is ideal for small, local work groups in which modest data transfer rates are acceptable. It provides a price-performance point unmatched by any other connectivity product in the industry.

Since the transmitter and receiver hardware for LocalTalk is built into every Macintosh and Apple IIGS® computer, LaserWriter® printer, and many peripheral devices, setting up the network is a simple process of connecting the devices with appropriate user-installable cabling and connectors. LocalTalk hardware is also available for Apple® IIe and MS-DOS computers, and for ImageWriter® II and ImageWriter LQ printers.

As shown in *Figure I-2,* LocalTalk is laid out in a bus topology, meaning that all devices are joined in a line with no circular connections. The physical characteristics of the LocalTalk twisted-pair cable allow it to reliably support a recommended maximum of 32 devices. A single LocalTalk network can span up to 300 meters.

The operation of a single LocalTalk network is managed by the **LocalTalk Link Access Protocol** (LLAP). LLAP was developed with the following goals:

- to build a low-cost, physical link
- to allow plug-and-play operation

LLAP is the data-link access protocol used to deliver data packets from any node of a LocalTalk network to any other node on that network. It makes a "best effort" to deliver the packet but does not guarantee its delivery. However, LLAP does ensure that if a packet is delivered it will be free of errors. The detailed specification of LLAP is provided in Chapter 1, Appendix A, and Appendix B.

LLAP includes a dynamic address-acquisition method that is crucial to the plug-and-play nature of the AppleTalk system.

The physical protocol governing the operation of LocalTalk is summarized in Appendix A. Several third-party vendors have implemented data links based on LLAP but have used different

- **Figure I-2** LocalTalk network

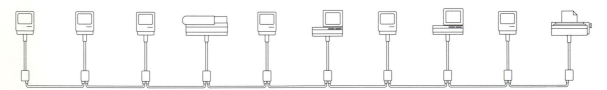

physical media. Notable among these are PhoneNET from Farallon Computing and the Du Pont Electronics Fiber Optic Communication Card for the Macintosh II. PhoneNET is an alternative implementation of LocalTalk functionality on standard, twisted-pair telephone cabling connected in a star topology with a central hub; the Electronics Fiber Optic Communication Card uses LLAP but with a different physical protocol from LocalTalk.

An AppleTalk data link other than LocalTalk is implemented using additional hardware, such as an interface card, and appropriate software. Two commonly used media are Ethernet and token ring. These alternative AppleTalk links do not use LLAP. Since their addressing schemes are different from those expected by the AppleTalk protocols, it is necessary to translate the AppleTalk node addresses into the addresses used by the particular link. This translation is carried out by using the **AppleTalk Address Resolution Protocol** (AARP) specified in Chapter 2.

EtherTalk

The Apple **EtherTalk** product provides high-speed connection of computing devices in the AppleTalk network system. It uses standard Ethernet technology including thick or thin coaxial and twisted-pair cabling with data transmission at 10 Mbits/second. This high-bandwidth medium is desirable for network segments that carry heavy traffic or require very agile response characteristics.

When used in an AppleTalk system, EtherTalk's faster transmission speed results in better performance. Furthermore, EtherTalk can support as many concurrently active AppleTalk devices as can be connected to an Ethernet network.

EtherTalk relies on an extension of the Ethernet data-link protocol that uses AARP. This extended protocol, known as the **EtherTalk Link Access Protocol** (ELAP), is specified in Chapter 3.

TokenTalk

The Apple TokenTalk® product provides connection to industry-standard token ring networks. It uses token ring technology to provide access to token ring networks. TokenTalk is desirable for those environments already using token ring cabling for other purposes, such as access to mainframe computers.

Like EtherTalk, TokenTalk can support as many concurrently active AppleTalk devices as can be connected to the token ring network.

TokenTalk also uses AARP to extend the underlying data link. This extended data link protocol is known as the **TokenTalk Link Access Protocol** (TLAP), and is described in Chapter 3.

Routers and AppleTalk internets

Large and geographically dispersed AppleTalk network systems can be built using the data-link products available for AppleTalk to interconnect the various networks through routers. The resulting system is called an AppleTalk internet, as shown in *Figure I-3*.

■ **Figure I-3** AppleTalk internet

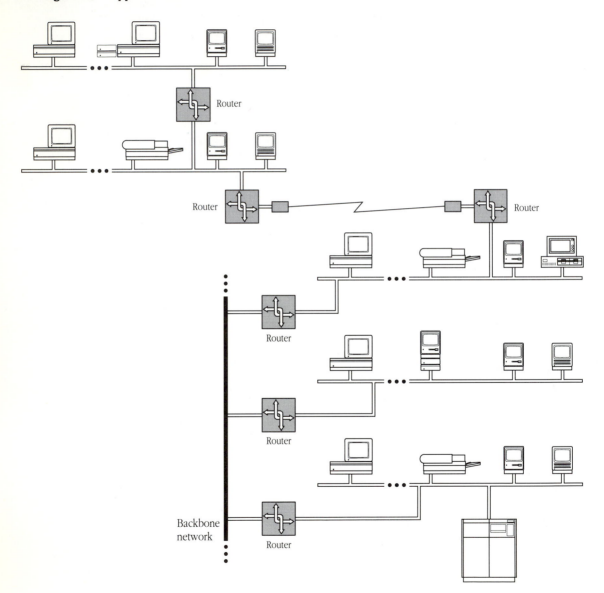

An AppleTalk *router* is a computer that is connected to each of the AppleTalk networks it interconnects. Routers operate as store-and-forward devices. Each network of the internet is assigned a unique range of numbers known as its **network numbers,** and every AppleTalk data packet traveling across an internet includes a network number in the range of the destination network. By consulting this number, routers are able to forward the packet from router to router until it arrives at its destination network. There the appropriate data link delivers the packet to the destination node.

Routers forward data packets by consulting tables of routing information. The initial acquisition of a routing table and its continuous maintenance are carried out by routers using the **Routing Table Maintenance Protocol** (RTMP) specified in Chapter 5.

Datagrams and network visibility

AppleTalk extends the node-to-node packet delivery service of the various individual links and the routers to a process-to-process, best-effort delivery. Thus, the various processes operating in the nodes of an internet can exchange data packets. The basis of this service is the **Datagram Delivery Protocol** (DDP) specified in Chapter 4. DDP provides the processes with addressable entities known as **sockets.** Processes can attach themselves to one or more sockets within their respective nodes and then exchange packets with each other through these sockets. The data packets exchanged through this DDP service are known as **datagrams.** Datagram delivery is the key service of the AppleTalk architecture upon which other value-added services are built.

Once a process has attached itself to a socket, it is then accessible from any point in the AppleTalk network system. It is said to be a **network-visible entity** (NVE).

Names, addresses, routes, and zones

The identification of available network entities is fundamental to the construction of network services and distributed computing applications. Three basic concepts are germane to this discussion—names, addresses, and routes. An entity's *name* can be seen as an attribute that is a location-independent, usually unique identifier of a network entity, much like names in the everyday world. An entity's *address* provides information related to its location, while a *route* is an actual path that data will have to traverse to reach the entity.

Users are comfortable with the use of names, but they prefer that addressing and routing be attended to automatically by the network system. Thus AppleTalk provides a service to let any network-visible entity give itself one or more names. Then the user of the network can discover the existence of that entity through a standard AppleTalk mechanism. The actual conversion of the name into an address is automatically done by the appropriate software in the user's computer, without the user's intervention. Access to the entity is provided by the software by using this address and the routing capabilities of DDP and RTMP built into all nodes. The named-entity discovery and address conversion is provided by the **Name Binding Protocol** (NBP) discussed in Chapter 7.

Very large internets could present the user with long, clumsy lists of network-visible entities. To help organize these long lists, AppleTalk internets can be subdivided into AppleTalk **zones.** Name searching can then be done within one or more user-specified zones. This added organizational convenience is enabled by the **Zone Information Protocol** (ZIP) discussed in Chapter 8. The zone structure and the **name-lookup process** require the close interaction of end nodes and routers. This interaction is governed by NBP and ZIP.

Many network systems provide a naming service through the use of centralized repositories known as *name servers*. Every named entity must register its name and address with the name server. The server then helps other network nodes to discover and address the named entities of the system. An important consideration in the design of AppleTalk was that it not require dedicated name servers. Requiring such servers would dramatically increase the entry cost and installation complexity of the network system. For small network systems, name servers may not add much value. NBP neither precludes the use of name servers nor provides the services needed for their management.

AppleTalk and reliable data exchange—transactions and streams

DDP provides a best-effort packet-delivery service. Datagrams still could be lost or damaged in transit through the internet. To ensure reliable, end-to-end delivery of these packets, AppleTalk includes a variety of protocols, each with different capabilities.

The **AppleTalk Transaction Protocol** (ATP) provides a reliable packet exchange in the form of request-response pairs (see Chapter 9). Packet exchange transactions of this nature are central to the interaction of a user with a server such as a file server. The **AppleTalk Session Protocol** (ASP) extends the ATP service by allowing two processes to exchange a sequence of transactions reliably (see Chapter 11).

The **AppleTalk Data Stream Protocol** (ADSP) allows two processes to open a virtual data "pipe" between their sockets. Either process can write data bytes into the pipe and read data bytes from it (see Chapter 12). Data bytes written into an ADSP pipe are delivered reliably at the other end in the exact same order.

Those readers familiar with network systems have come to expect the key reliable data-transfer service of a network system to be a connection-oriented data stream or virtual circuit. AppleTalk's heavy use of transaction protocols in lieu of stream protocols might surprise them.

  stream services are implemented on packet networks at the cost of considerable protocol overhead. However, stream protocols are a natural extension of physical connections used in most data communication applications. These virtual circuit services emulate familiar capabilities and are readily accessible to and used by programmers. These users often employ such streams, however, to implement a client-server interaction, which is of a request-response transaction nature. The programmer has to add overhead to undo the stream service, in effect, and to convert it back to a transaction service. With ATP/ASP, AppleTalk avoids the double overhead of first extracting stream service from a packet-oriented system and then converting it back to a transaction service.

Stream services of ADSP are included in the architecture for two reasons: first, as a convenience to programmers familiar with such services in other network systems; second, to provide the natural data transport service for implementing capabilities such as terminal emulation and file transfer. ADSP will also prove useful for gateways that provide end-to-end connection services between AppleTalk nodes and nodes on other network systems.

AppleTalk end-user services

AppleTalk was designed to be a foundation for interpersonal computing. Two fundamental end-user services developed for this purpose are shared printing and shared filing. The key AppleTalk printing products are the ImageWriter and LaserWriter families of printers. Further printing convenience is provided by the PrintMonitor and AppleShare® print server spooling capabilities. File sharing services are implemented as a seamless extension of the Macintosh Desktop in AppleShare, which provides AppleTalk file service.

AppleShare is designed to be a sharing platform for a variety of user computers, including the Macintosh, MS-DOS, and Apple II families. In particular, it serves as the basis for Apple's popular classroom network system used by students from kindergarten through the university.

Publication of the protocols on which these products are based has allowed third parties to add other printing and file serving devices that are compatible with Apple's products. This compatibility ensures a uniform user experience across a range of products with different price, performance, and capability characteristics. For instance, AppleTalk users can write documents on their Macintosh computers and use an Apple LaserWriter to print them during the development process. After the document has been fully developed, the user can print it on higher-resolution typeset equipment in *exactly* the same manner as on the LaserWriter.

Likewise, Macintosh users can gain access to files stored on any VAX™-resident, AppleShare-compatible file server such as AlisaShare or PacerShare in *exactly* the same way as files stored on an AppleShare file server (or, in fact, on the user's local disks).

AppleTalk printing services

Printing on an AppleTalk network is possible with several different hardware and software configurations. AppleTalk networks support both direct printing and printing with a spooler.

Direct printing

Direct printing occurs when a workstation sends a print job directly to a printer connected to the network system, as shown in *Figure I-4*.

When a user issues a command to print a document, the application begins a series of AppleTalk calls attempting to establish a connection to the printer. The calls first initiate NBP's name-lookup process to find the currently selected printer and its AppleTalk address. Then the **Printer Access Protocol** (PAP) is used to open a connection with the printer.

Once the connection is established, the workstation and the printer interact over the PAP connection. PAP uses lower-level protocols, such as ATP and DDP, to provide a data-stream service for sending the print data to the printer. For a detailed specification of PAP, see Chapter 10.

Printing services on AppleTalk can also be implemented through ADSP.

■ **Figure I-4** Direct printing

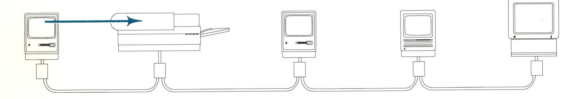

Printing with a print spooler

A **print spooler** is a hardware or software application that interacts with a printer to print documents. When a computer sends a file to be printed, the print spooler intercepts the file and handles all printer interaction, freeing the computer for other tasks. Two types of spooler implementations are used with AppleTalk: a background spooler and a spooler/server.

A **background spooler** is a software application that operates in the user's computer as a background process and spools print jobs to the user's local disk. An example of an application that allows background printing is the PrintMonitor application included with the Macintosh MultiFinder™.

A **spooler/server** is an application that runs on a computer set up to be a print spooler and connected to the AppleTalk network system (see *Figure I-5*). A spooler/server works by setting itself up as a surrogate printer; that is, when the computer tries to print, it sees the spooler/server as a printer and, in fact, cannot distinguish it from a printer. When the user prints, the user's computer produces the print data and sends it to the spooler/server. Since the spooler/server stores the print data in its hard disk, it is able to quickly accept this information from the user's computer, which is freed for other use. The spooler/server then takes charge of the more time-consuming task of getting the data processed by the printer.

■ **Figure I-5** Printing with a spooler/server

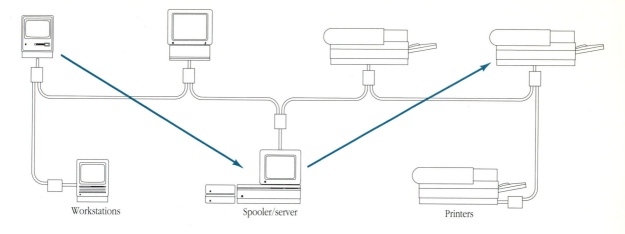

Workstations   Spooler/server   Printers

LaserWriter and other printers accept only one job, or connection, at a time. Spooler/servers can accept several connections at a time, thereby minimizing the contention problems that occur when several workstations try to print simultaneously. AppleShare includes a spooler/server for printing on any Apple-supplied AppleTalk printers and on compatible third-party printers.

AppleTalk print spooling is more fully discussed in Chapter 14.

AppleShare and AppleTalk file service

Within an AppleTalk network system, the AppleShare file server provides a location where a user on the network can store and gain access to common files without disrupting other users' activities.

Using AppleShare File Server software, a Macintosh computer with one or more hard disk drives can become a dedicated file server on the network. Each hard disk attached to the AppleShare file server is called a **volume.**

To be able to use an AppleShare file server, a user is *registered* on the server, given a password, and placed into one or more user groups, as appropriate. Gaining access to the file server involves a login process in which the server asks for the user's identification, consisting of a **user name** and a **password.** Once the server has examined its registered user database and validated the user, the selected server volumes' icons, much like a hard disk icon, appear on the user's Macintosh Desktop.

The login process assures confidentiality; users must be registered and must enter a password before being able to gain access to protected portions of server volumes. Unregistered users can log in as **guests;** that is, they can obtain access to information that is unprotected.

Within a server volume, files are stored in folders. Folders on a Macintosh are analogous to directories on an MS-DOS or UNIX® computer; both folders and directories are named entities that hold files or other folders/directories. Opening and saving files and creating folders are done the same way on a file server volume as on a local disk.

Each AppleShare folder has an owner, who determines which users may have access to the folder and in what fashion. Access privileges control access to information on the file server; a folder can be kept private, shared by a group of users, or shared by all network users. The user information placed in the server's user database allows the server to determine a user's access privileges when he or she tries to gain access to the contents of a folder.

The **access privileges** for a folder or volume let the owner, the group, or guests see folders, see files, and make changes inside the folder. Users can select folders and view their access privileges for those folders. In addition, a folder's owner can examine and change the access privilege information, which includes the owner's name, the folder's associated group, the owner's privileges, the group's privileges, and a guest's privileges (see *Figure I-6*). The owner can transfer the folder's ownership to another user.

■ **Figure I-6** Access privileges

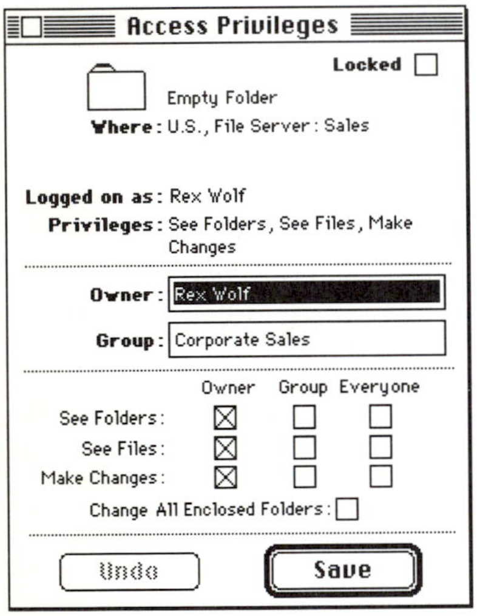

Access to an AppleShare file server is not limited to Macintosh computers. The LocalTalk PC Card allows MS-DOS-compatible personal computers to be connected to a LocalTalk network. Using this card with the AppleShare PC software, MS-DOS personal computer users can print to LaserWriter, ImageWriter II, and ImageWriter LQ printers from within an application. AppleShare PC software also allows these users to work with an AppleShare file server by means of a menu-based user interface. Additionally, AppleShare PC supports various third-party Ethernet and token ring cards, allowing MS-DOS machines to connect to EtherTalk and TokenTalk networks.

Likewise, Apple IIGS and Apple IIe computers can gain access to the printing and filing services of an AppleTalk system. LocalTalk hardware is built into the Apple IIGS, while the Apple IIe requires the use of a plug-in LocalTalk board. In fact, Apple IIe and Apple IIGS computers can operate and even start up in a diskless fashion from an AppleShare server.

The dialog between a user's computer and an AppleShare file server is conducted using the **AppleTalk Filing Protocol** (AFP). AFP was central to the global vision that the AppleShare product serve as the basis for cross-system information sharing between dissimilar computers. For this reason, AFP calls were specifically designed to have enough semantic and syntactic content to allow complete servicing of each of the computer families. Most importantly, these calls provide sophisticated services for managing a shared Desktop view of the file server's volumes. Changes made by the user of one Macintosh computer will automatically be reflected on the Desktop view of any other Macintosh computer viewing the same folder or volume.

The AFP file server environment encourages the development of applications that can themselves be shared as well as those that allow the sharing of data. To use applications within the server's shared storage environment, special considerations are necessary for file management, particularly when the applications allow multi-user and multilaunch capabilities. Multi-user applications let two or more users make changes to the same file concurrently. Multilaunch applications let two or more users simultaneously open and work with one copy of an application. AFP includes calls that allow applications to control the concurrent file access required by such applications. The complete specification of AFP is provided in Chapter 13.

Why did Apple decide to design a new filing protocol? Why did we not use an existing, de facto or industry-standard protocol? The design of AFP was started at Apple in 1984. Two other file service protocols were then in various stages of completion, PC-net's SMB and Sun Microsystem's NFS.

SMB and NFS were each designed to serve a particular computer family. Specifically, MS-DOS was the target system for SMB and UNIX for NFS. SMB was later extended to accommodate some versions of the UNIX file system. NFS is currently being extended for use by MS-DOS computers. On the other hand, AFP was visualized from the very beginning to service equally a variety of computers.

Neither SMB nor NFS is capable of handling several significant aspects of the Macintosh **hierarchical file system** (HFS), such as much longer file and folder names, dual fork files, and the Desktop database. Use of SMB or NFS would not have allowed us to provide a seamless extension of the Macintosh Desktop to the file server.

AppleTalk protocol architecture and the ISO-OSI reference model

The various AppleTalk protocols draw upon the services of some other protocol(s) and deliver an enhanced service either to some other protocol or to an application. In *Figure I-7,* the protocols are shown in a layered configuration, with a protocol in a higher-level layer drawing on the services of one or more protocols in lower-level layers. Layered models for network protocols are inspired by their prior use in describing various concepts (in particular, operating systems) of stand-alone computers. Today, most carefully designed network systems rely on a layered protocol architecture.

The schema shown in *Figure I-7* permits an easier understanding of the complexities of the overall system. It provides a framework for examining the interaction of the different components and for isolating functionality to certain portions of the system. This structure allows a divide-and-conquer approach to designing and building the protocol architecture.

Beyond these general observations, an examination of various network systems reveals a common pattern to the progression of services provided by the layers of these protocol architectures. This progression typically proceeds from the physical management of data communication hardware to the data-link access services discussed earlier. Beyond the data link, network-wide addressing and routing capabilities are added. Reliability of data transfer is usually the next value-added service, involving retransmission disciplines and connection/session management services.

Above the connectivity services, network systems are now beginning to address presentation issues such as data representation incompatibilities. Finally, the protocols for providing various user and application-level services such as filing and electronic messaging are added.

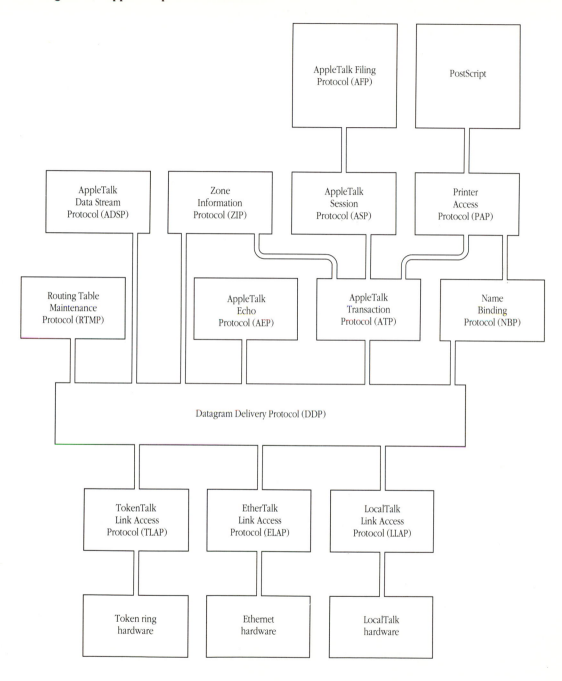

In the 1970s, the International Standards Organization (ISO) developed and published a standard framework known as the Open Systems Interconnection (OSI) reference model (the **ISO-OSI reference model**). This model defines in explicit terms the concepts of a protocol and a service interface. It defines a protocol architectural framework consisting of seven layers: physical, data link, network, transport, session, presentation, and application. The goal of the model was to establish a standard framework and the associated terminology for describing, studying, and comparing the protocols of network architectures. Although the ISO-OSI reference model did not define any standard protocols, it was to serve as the framework in which future activity on protocol standardization would proceed.

Protocol entities populate the layers of the ISO-OSI reference model. A protocol entity located in layer n of the model draws upon the services provided by layer $n-1$, and in turn provides layer n services to protocol entities located in layer $n+1$. A protocol entity gains access to the services of another protocol entity, located in the adjacent lower layer, through a service interface (see *Figure I-8*). Protocol entities located in the same layer of the model communicate with each other through a protocol.

The AppleTalk protocols can now be placed in the framework of this model, as shown in *Figure I-9*. The reader is cautioned not to read from this figure a protocol compatibility of AppleTalk with the OSI protocols currently in various stages of definition, approval, and deployment. This figure merely establishes that the architectural structure fits into the standard framework of the ISO-OSI model.

■ **Figure I-8** Interfaces and protocols

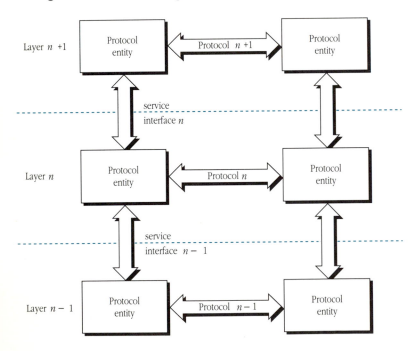

■ **Figure I-9** AppleTalk protocols and the ISO-OSI reference model

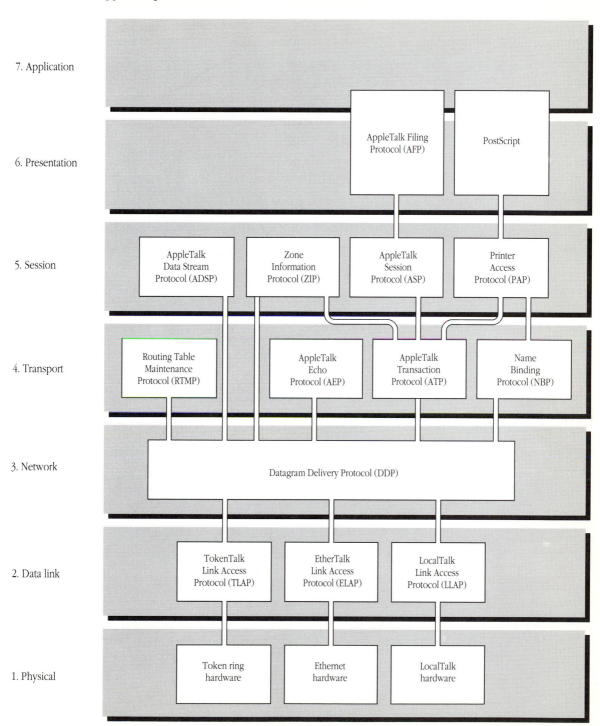

AppleTalk Phase 2

AppleTalk Phase 2, introduced in June 1989, provides compatible extensions to the AppleTalk
network system that enable it to function better in large network environments. Such
environments often include thousands of concurrently active devices and multiple concurrent
network protocols and data links. AppleTalk Phase 2 removed the restriction of a maximum of 254
concurrently active AppleTalk devices on one network. In addition, AppleTalk Phase 2 was designed
to minimize the interference of AppleTalk protocols with other non-AppleTalk devices in the same
environment.

Changes introduced with Phase 2 do not affect non-routing LocalTalk devices. In addition, none
of the higher-level protocols have changed. These include ADSP, ASP, PAP, and AFP. Only one small
enhancement (the TRel timer in exactly-once transactions can be set by the requestor) was added to
ATP. Most of the changes are to ELAP, DDP, RTMP, NBP, and ZIP. These changes need only be
implemented in routers and in EtherTalk devices (TokenTalk was introduced as a part of AppleTalk
Phase 2).

The single most important protocol change in AppleTalk Phase 2 is that a single AppleTalk
network can now be assigned more than one network number. The size of the range of network
numbers assigned to a network determines the maximum number of concurrently active AppleTalk
devices that can be supported on that network (253 devices per network number). LocalTalk
networks are assigned only a single network number, as they need support no more than 254
devices.

A key component of AppleTalk Phase 2 is the AppleTalk Internet Router product. In addition
to serving as the first router to implement the Phase 2 protocols, the AppleTalk Internet Router
allows up to eight AppleTalk networks (of any data-link type) to be interconnected. The router
software runs on a Macintosh and thus provides the familiar Macintosh user interface for router
setup and for monitoring of the internet. The router supports LocalTalk, EtherTalk, and TokenTalk
and can be extended to support other data links as they are added to the AppleTalk network
system.

Thoughts of the future

The initial installation of AppleTalk was spurred on by a trio of products—the Macintosh computer, the LaserWriter printer, and LocalTalk connectivity. AppleTalk played a significant role in the ensuing desktop publishing revolution. In the first place, it provided shared access to an outstanding, but relatively expensive, printing device. The ability to share the printer significantly reduced the per-user cost of the LaserWriter printer to an acceptable price-performance point. Users were able to exploit this technology while focusing primarily on the outstanding quality of the printed page.

A variety of other network services helped broaden the appeal of AppleTalk. Today the AppleTalk network system is used by an installed base of more than 1 million computers and servers in network configurations that range in size from a minimum of two devices to large internets with thousands of devices. A variety of personal computer systems (including Macintosh, Apple II, MS-DOS, and UNIX computers and larger central computers such as VAXs), are connected to AppleTalk systems. A full range of servers and services is available from Apple and other vendors.

All network systems keep growing and changing over their lifetimes. AppleTalk is no exception. In the future, AppleTalk is expected to grow in both scope (size) and reach (variety).

Scope

Large organizations and their subsidiaries are making increasing use of networking technology, thus creating the need for very large network systems. These systems will connect hundreds of thousands of computers of all sizes and types. As organizations span the globe, their networks will be required to extend over wide geographical areas.

Large networks will require more sophisticated routing and management capabilities. Special issues related to slow or intermittently available links will require resolution. Naming and authentication services will become important issues for organizations wishing to provide a more uniform control of these aspects.

Reach

The growing use of network systems has made users aware of the cumbersome integration of networks into their computers. This difficulty is exacerbated by the variety of network technologies and protocol families in use today.

A response to this growing qualitative complexity has been a drive to establish international protocol standards. Notable among these movements are the efforts of various national and international organizations under the auspices of ISO to define and ratify a single family of standard protocols.

This standardization activity will help as these protocols find wider acceptance. However, it appears that the network systems of tomorrow will continue to use a variety of protocol families. This increasingly complex network system, if not properly designed, could be extremely difficult to use. An important goal for AppleTalk is to extend the user's reach into this polyglot environment with an immediacy of service and elegance of interface modeled on today's AppleShare. This will require the use of a variety of new products, such as gateways and entirely new technologies still being developed.

Gateways are software and/or hardware devices that are interposed between two dissimilar network systems. The gateway serves a role akin to that of a simultaneous interpreter between people speaking different languages. This analogy might explain why gateways have long been considered an important networking technology. However, the use of gateways has so far been relatively limited. The complexity of full, seven-layer gateways between dissimilar protocol families has, in general, rendered them impossible to design and build.

Specialized gateways have been quite effective. For instance, gateways between different electronic mail systems are now finding increased use. The development of a variety of application-level gateway services will extend the reach of AppleTalk into non-AppleTalk systems and will bring important resources and services to the desk tops of AppleTalk users.

Companion volumes to *Inside AppleTalk* will be published to provide the specifications of these extensions and modifications.

About *Inside AppleTalk*

Inside AppleTalk is divided into five parts. The book is further divided into fourteen chapters (an in-depth, chapter-specific, table of contents begins each chapter within the five parts) and four appendixes. A glossary of terms and an index complete *Inside AppleTalk.*

Part I covers the physical and data-link alternatives that can be used in an AppleTalk network system. This part includes a summary of the LocalTalk Link Access Protocol (LLAP); procedural details for this protocol can be found in Appendix B. In addition, Part 1 includes a detailed description of the AppleTalk Address Resolution Protocol (AARP) and discussions of how AARP is used by the EtherTalk Link Access Protocol (ELAP) and the TokenTalk Link Access Protocol (TLAP).

Part II describes the AppleTalk protocols that facilitate end-to-end transmission of data across the network, specifying in detail the Datagram Delivery Protocol (DDP), the Routing Table Maintenance Protocol (RTMP), and the **AppleTalk Echo Protocol** (AEP).

Part III covers the AppleTalk protocols that handle naming, providing detailed descriptions of the Name Binding Protocol (NBP) and the Zone Information Protocol (ZIP).

Part IV describes the AppleTalk protocols that guarantee reliable data delivery over the network and includes detailed information about the AppleTalk Transaction Protocol (ATP), the Printer Access Protocol (PAP), the AppleTalk Session Protocol (ASP), and the AppleTalk Data Stream Protocol (ADSP).

Part V describes the protocols that provide end-user services and includes a complete description of the AppleTalk Filing Protocol (AFP). In addition, Part 5 discusses the specification for print spooling in an AppleTalk network.

The appendixes provide electrical specifications, LLAP procedural details, and a summary of the AppleTalk protocol parameters.

Typographic and graphic conventions used in this book

Throughout this book, all numerical quantities are given as decimal numbers, except where otherwise noted. A dollar sign preceding a number (for example, $3E) indicates hexadecimal (base 16) notation. Bit sequences and binary numbers are written as strings of 1s and 0s beginning with a 0.

Words and phrases in **boldface** are described in the Glossary.

In figures depicting packet formats, the following graphical conventions are followed:

- Each simple rectangle represents 1 byte (8 bits). Vertical tick marks or solid lines delineate each bit. The rightmost bit is the least-significant bit and is numbered bit 0. The leftmost bit is the most-significant bit and is numbered bit 7.

- Each rectangle with one or more pairs of horizontal tick marks represents 2 or more bytes. Within the multibyte field, the bottom-right bit is the least-significant bit and is numbered bit 0. The top-left bit is the most-significant bit.

- A pair of vertical ellipses represents a field of variable length.

- In most cases, the figure will show the format of the protocol being described and will omit the formats of the other encapsulating protocols.

Where to go for more information

Readers wishing more detail about networking concepts mentioned in this chapter are encouraged to consult the following references.

AppleTalk

■ **General** (available from Addison-Wesley Publishing Company, Inc.):

AppleTalk Network System Overview

Inside Macintosh, Vol. II, Chap. 10

Inside Macintosh, Vol. V, Chap. 30

■ **AppleTalk system** (available from Apple Programmer's and Developer's Association [APDA]):

AppleShare Programmer's Guide for the Apple IIGS

AppleTalk for VMS Documentation Suite:

   AppleTalk for VMS Architecture and Implementation

   AppleTalk for VMS Bridge Control Program Guide

   AppleTalk for VMS Installation and Operation Guide

   AppleTalk for VMS Protocol Support Library Reference Manual

Asynchronous LaserWriter Driver Developer's Guide

Macintosh AppleTalk Connections Programmer's Guide

LocalTalk PC Card and Driver Preliminary Notes

Software Applications in a Shared Environment

General networking

Tanenbaum, Andrew S. *Computer Networks.* Englewood Cliffs, NJ: Prentice-Hall, Inc., 1981.

Data links

Inside AppleTalk does not specifically address Ethernet or token ring cabling and protocols. For more information on these physical and data-link protocols, refer to:

The Ethernet, A Local Area Network: Data Link Layer and Physical Layer Specifications, Version 2.0, November 1982 [specification document jointly published by Digital Equipment Corporation, Intel Corporation, and Xerox Corporation].

802.2 Logical Link Control. IEEE, Inc., October 1985.

802.3 Carrier Sense Multiple Access with Collision Detection. IEEE, Inc. May 1986.

802.5 Token Ring Access Method. IEEE, Inc. 1985.

Connection-oriented protocols

■ For TCP/IP, please consult:

Cerf, V. G. and Kahn R. E. "A Protocol for Packet Network Interconnection." *IEEE Trans. Commun.* COM-22:637–648 (May 1974).

■ The Xerox Network Systems (XNS) internet protocols are specified in:

Internet Transport Protocols. Xerox Systems Integration Standard X.S.I.S. 028112, December 1981.

■ The X.25 access standard is specified in the following publication of the CCITT:

Data Communication Networks Interfaces: Recommendations X.20–X.32, Red Book, Volume VIII-Fascicle VIII.3. Geneva: International Telecommunications Union-CCITT, 1985.

PostScript

PostScript® is the document representation/page description protocol used for communication with LaserWriter printers. The widely used standard was first made available as a product in the AppleTalk system, in Apple's LaserWriter printers. For a detailed discussion of PostScript, refer to:

Adobe Systems Incorporated. *PostScript Language Reference Manual.* Reading, Mass.: Addison-Wesley Publishing Company, Inc., 1985.

ISO-OSI reference model

Zimmermann, H. "OSI Reference Model—The ISO Model of Architecture for Open Systems Interconnection." *IEEE Trans. Commun.* COM-28:425–432 (April 1980).

Database access

CI/1 Connectivity Language: Language Description, Network Innovations, August 1988.

Part I **Physical and Data Links**

P A R T   I   of *Inside AppleTalk* discusses the protocols used to communicate between the nodes of a single AppleTalk network. These protocols comprise the two lowest layers of the AppleTalk protocol architecture (as shown in *Figure I-9* of the Introduction).

In particular, Part I specifies:

- the LocalTalk Link Access Protocol (LLAP)
- the AppleTalk Address Resolution Protocol (AARP)
- the EtherTalk Link Access Protocol (ELAP)
- the TokenTalk Link Access Protocol (TLAP)

AppleTalk's node-to-node packet transmission is the responsibility of the Datagram Delivery Protocol (DDP). DDP was designed to be data-link independent. This means that DDP can send its packets through any data-link and physical technology.

The Macintosh and Apple IIGS computers, and most LaserWriter printers, have built-in hardware for LocalTalk network connectivity, which is based on LLAP, as specified in Chapter 1, "LocalTalk Link Access Protocol." An important feature of the design of LLAP and DDP is that the node-addressing mechanisms used by these two protocols are identical. Hence, DDP can directly call and use the services provided by LLAP.

For LocalTalk hardware specifications, see Appendix A. Various alternative hardware implementations are available that provide exactly the same service as LocalTalk. These alternative data links directly use LLAP but substitute different hardware for LocalTalk cabling. The use of these links requires no additional protocol.

When using an arbitrary data link below DDP, a fundamental problem of address mismatch can arise. This problem results from the different forms of the node addresses used by DDP and the particular data link. AppleTalk provides an address-resolution capability for mapping between these addresses. This service is provided by AARP and is specified in Chapter 2, "AppleTalk Address Resolution Protocol."

The first use of AARP was made by Apple in the EtherTalk connectivity product, which sends DDP packets over an industry-standard Ethernet local area network. In this situation, the node addresses of DDP are converted, through the use of AARP, into 48-bit Ethernet node addresses. DDP packets are wrapped in appropriate headers and sent through the standard Ethernet data-link services. Furthermore, a node's AppleTalk address is dynamically assigned despite Ethernet's use of statically assigned addresses. These various services, together with the mechanisms used by the Ethernet data link, are referred to as ELAP and are specified in Chapter 3, "EtherTalk and TokenTalk Link Access Protocols."

Apple's TokenTalk product provides many of the same services as EtherTalk. AARP is used to map node addresses used by DDP into the 48-bit addresses used by token ring. DDP packets are wrapped in token ring headers and sent through the standard token ring data-link services. A node's AppleTalk address is dynamically assigned. These services are referred to as TLAP and are specified in Chapter 3, "EtherTalk and TokenTalk Link Access Protocols."

The discussion in Part I is restricted to mechanisms for node-to-node delivery of AppleTalk packets on a single network. Routing extensions in the case of multiple, interconnected AppleTalk networks are discussed in Part II.

In Part I, the term *AppleTalk node address* (or simply **AppleTalk address**) refers to the node address used by DDP and higher levels of the AppleTalk protocol architecture. Likewise, *hardware node address* (or simply **hardware address**) refers to the address used by a particular data-link layer. ■

Chapter 1 LocalTalk Link Access Protocol

CONTENTS

■

THE LOCALTALK LINK ACCESS PROTOCOL (LLAP)
corresponds to the data-link layer of the ISO-OSI reference model and allows
network devices to share the communication medium. This protocol provides
the basic service of packet transmission between the nodes of a single
LocalTalk or compatible network.

The physical hardware offers the connected nodes a shared data transmission
medium, referred to as the **link.** LLAP is responsible for regulating the access
to this shared link by the nodes of the network.

LLAP accepts data from its clients in the node and then encapsulates it in an
LLAP data packet. The encapsulation adds a destination node address to the
packet, allowing LLAP to deliver the data packet to its destination node. The
packet also contains the sending node's address, which is delivered by LLAP to
the data's recipient.

Furthermore, LLAP ensures that any packets damaged in transit are discarded
and not delivered to their destination node. In that situation, however, LLAP
itself makes no effort to ensure delivery of the packet. It provides a best-
effort delivery of the packet.

The main responsibilities of LLAP are to

- provide link access control

- provide a way to address nodes

- perform data transmission and reception ∎

Link access control

The nodes on a given link compete for access to the link. Without a way of controlling their access, data could not be transferred reliably over the link. The different nodes would in a sense "stumble" over each other's transmissions. LLAP provides appropriate link-access management to ensure fair access to all nodes.

LLAP manages access to the shared link by using an access discipline known as **Carrier Sense Multiple Access with Collision Avoidance** (CSMA/CA). There are three parts to the CSMA/CA technique.

Carrier sense means that a node wishing to send a data frame first checks the transmission medium before sending any data. The node is said to "sense" the activity on the link. If the link is in use, then the node defers to the ongoing transmission.

Multiple access refers to the fact that more than one node can obtain access to the link. *Collision avoidance* means that the protocol attempts to minimize the occurrence of collisions on the link. A collision occurs when two or more nodes transmit data at the same time. In the LLAP CSMA/CA technique, all transmitters wait until the line has been idle for a specified minimum amount of time plus an additional random period before attempting to transmit.

The use of random wait periods has the effect of spreading the data transmissions over time. This dispersion is greater when traffic is higher and when more collisions are expected to occur.

It is important to note that LLAP does not require suitable hardware to detect the occurrence of collisions. Instead it has to infer that a collision might have occurred. LLAP uses a "handshake" mechanism to allow it to make this inference. Furthermore, the handshake mechanism reduces the loss of channel bandwidth when a collision occurs because the collision normally occurs in the handshake phase. Since the handshake messages are short in length, only a small amount of the link's time is wasted by a collision.

Node addressing

Node addressing provides a means of uniquely identifying each node connected to the link. LLAP uses a technique called **dynamic node ID assignment,** a method that eliminates a configuration step and also allows easy movement of nodes between networks.

Node IDs

LLAP's node-addressing mechanism consists of assigning an identification number to each node and including that number in all packets destined for that node.

LLAP uses an 8-bit **node identifier number** (**node ID**) to identify each node on a link. A node's ID is its data-link address.

Each LLAP packet includes the node IDs of its sender and its intended destination. These addresses are used by the network hardware to ensure that the packet is delivered only to the correct destination node.

Dynamic node ID assignment

Unlike other network data links, LLAP uses a dynamic node-ID-assignment scheme. With dynamic node ID assignment, a node does not have a fixed, unique address. Instead, a node assigns itself a node ID upon activation.

A key goal of dynamic node ID assignment is to prevent a conflict that otherwise might occur when a node is moved between networks and when the old node ID of the device is already in use on the new network. Other solutions to this problem have relied on building universally unique node addresses into each device when it is manufactured.

LLAP's dynamic address-assignment scheme eliminates what has been a typical part of network configuration. It does so without the need to build a universally unique number into each node or to administer the assignment of such numbers to different vendors.

When a node is activated on the network, the node makes a "guess" at its own node ID, either by extracting this number from some form of long-term memory (for example, nonvolatile RAM or disk) or by generating a random number. The node then verifies that this guessed number is not already in use on that network.

The node verifies the uniqueness of its node ID number by sending out an LLAP **Enquiry control packet,** as shown in *Figure 1-1,* to the guessed node address and by waiting for acknowledgment. If the guessed node ID is in use, then the node using it will receive the LLAP Enquiry control packet and will respond with an LLAP **Acknowledge control packet.** The reception of the Acknowledge control packet notifies the new node that its guessed node ID is already in use. The node must then repeat the process with a different guess. Each Enquiry control packet is transmitted repeatedly to account for cases in which a packet is lost or a node already using the guessed node ID is busy and therefore might miss an Enquiry packet.

■ **Figure 1-1** Under dynamic node ID assignment, a new node tests its randomly assigned ID

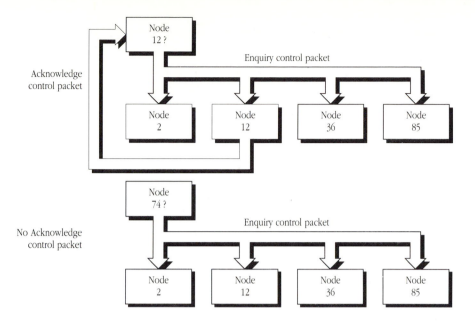

LLAP node IDs are divided into two classes: user node IDs and server node IDs. **User node IDs** are in the range 1–127 ($01–$7F); **server node IDs** are in the range 128–254 ($80–$FE). A destination node ID of 255 ($FF) is called the **broadcast hardware address** (broadcast ID) and has a special meaning. Packets sent with the destination node ID equal to 255 are accepted by all nodes, permitting the **broadcasting** of packets to all nodes on the network. A destination node ID equal to 0 ($00) is not allowed and is treated as unknown.

Node ID range	Description
0 ($00)	not allowed (unknown)
1–127 ($01–$7F)	user node IDs
128–254 ($80–$FE)	server node IDs
255 ($FF)	broadcast ID

The division of node IDs into two groups minimizes the negative impact of a node acquiring another node's ID when the latter is busy and fails to respond to the entire series of Enquiry packets. This situation can occur because some nodes may be unable to receive packets for extended periods of time (for example, if they are engaged in a device-intensive operation such as gaining access to a disk or transferring a bitmap document to a directly connected laser printer). Such a node would not respond to another node's Enquiry packets, which could result in two nodes acquiring the same node ID.

Excluding user (nonserver) node IDs from the server node ID range eliminates the possibility that user nodes (which are switched on and off with greater frequency) will conflict with server nodes. It is imperative that no node ever acquire the number of a node functioning as a server; this would disrupt service not only between the two conflicting nodes but also for users trying to communicate with either of those nodes.

Within the user node ID range, verification can be performed quickly (that is, with fewer retransmissions of the Enquiry control packet), thus decreasing the LLAP initialization time for user nodes. A more thorough node ID verification is performed by servers (in other words, additional time is taken to ensure that they acquire unique node IDs on the link). This scheme increases the initialization time for server nodes but is not detrimental to the server's operation since such nodes are rarely switched on and off.

Data transmission and reception

LLAP uses two kinds of packets: control packets, which are used for internal protocol control purposes, and data packets, which include data provided by LLAP's client.

LLAP packet

An LLAP packet consists of a 3-byte LLAP header followed by a variable-length data field (0–600 bytes). (See *Figure 1-2*.) The LLAP header contains the packet's destination node ID, the source node ID, and a 1-byte LLAP type field. The **LLAP type field** specifies the type of packet. Values in the range 128–255 ($80–$FF) are reserved to identify LLAP **control packets.** LLAP control packets do not contain a data field.

■ **Figure 1-2** LLAP frame and packet format

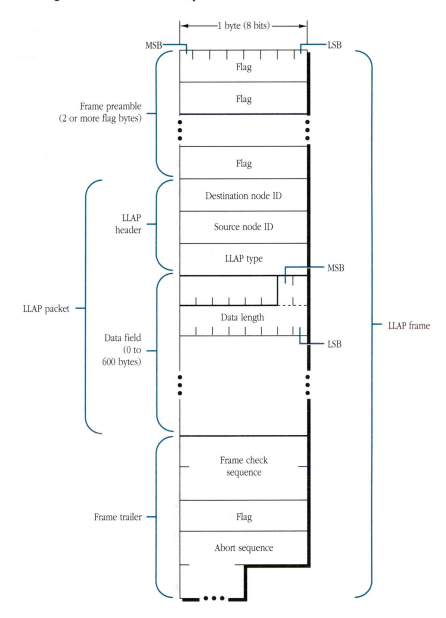

Four types of control packets are currently in use. All other LLAP type field values in the range 128–255 ($80–$FF) are reserved by Apple for future use.

Name	LLAP type field value	Description
lapENQ	$81	Enquiry packet used for dynamic node ID assignment
lapACK	$82	Acknowledgment packet responding to a lapENQ
lapRTS	$84	request-to-send (RTS) packet notifying the destination node that a data packet awaits transmission
lapCTS	$85	clear-to-send (CTS) packet response to lapRTS, indicating readiness to accept a data packet

◆ *Note:* LLAP control packets received with values in the LLAP type field other than those previously listed are currently invalid and must be discarded.

LLAP type fields with values in the range 1–127 ($01–$7F) are used for LLAP **data packets;** these packets carry client data in the data field. In such packets, the type field specifies the LLAP type of the client to whom the data must be delivered. This specification allows the concurrent use of LLAP by several network layer protocols and is crucial to maintaining an **open systems architecture.** The LLAP implementation in the receiving node uses the LLAP type field to determine the client for whom the data is intended. The client, in turn, uses this field to decide how to interpret the LLAP data for use by a higher-level protocol. As an example, Datagram Delivery Protocol (DDP) packets correspond to the values 1 and 2 in the LLAP type field.

LLAP transmits and receives data packets on behalf of its clients. The format and interpretation of the data field are defined by higher-level protocols.

The low-order 10 bits of the first 2 bytes of the data field must contain the length in bytes (most-significant bits first) of the LLAP data field itself. The data length includes the length field itself. The high-order 6 bits of the length field are reserved for use by higher-level protocols.

The LLAP header is 3 bytes long, and the data field can contain from 2 to 600 bytes. Therefore, the smallest valid LLAP data packet is 5 bytes long; the largest is 603 bytes.

LLAP frame

An LLAP frame encapsulates an LLAP packet with a frame preamble and a frame trailer, as shown in *Figure 1-2*.

On the link itself, LLAP uses a bit-oriented link protocol for transmitting and receiving packets. The **frame preamble** precedes the packet and is used to identify the start of the frame. The **frame trailer** has two objectives. First, it includes a 2-byte quantity called the **frame check sequence** (FCS) that is used to detect and discard packets received with errors. Second, the last portion of the trailer, consisting of a flag byte and an **abort sequence** (12–18 1's), serves to demarcate the end of the frame.

The use of a bit-oriented protocol allows the presence of all possible bit patterns between the frame's leading and trailing flags. The frame delimiter for LLAP, known as a **flag byte,** is the distinctive bit sequence 01111110 ($7E). Typically, flags are generated by hardware transmitters at the beginning and end of frames and are used by hardware receivers to detect frame boundaries.

In order for a data-link protocol to transmit all possible bit patterns within a frame, the protocol must ensure **data transparency.** LLAP accomplishes data transparency through a technique known as **bit stuffing.** When transmitting a frame, LLAP inserts a 0 after each string of 5 consecutive 1's detected in the client data; this process guarantees that the data transmitted on the link contains no sequences of more than 5 consecutive 1's. A receiving LLAP performs the inverse operation, *stripping* a 0 that follows 5 consecutive 1's.

The 16-bit FCS is computed as a function of the contents of the packet itself (that is, the flags and the abort bits of the frame are not included): the destination node ID, source node ID, LLAP type, and the data field, using the standard cyclic-redundancy check (CRC) algorithm of the Consultative Committee on International Telephone and Telegraph (CCITT). This algorithm, known as CRC-CCITT, is described in detail in Appendix B.

Prior to transmitting a packet, LLAP sends out a synchronization pulse, a transition period on the link that is followed by an idle period (see "Carrier Sensing and Synchronization" later in this chapter). A frame preamble, consisting of 2 or more flag bytes, follows the synchronization pulse. The frame terminates with a frame trailer, which consists of the FCS, 1 flag byte, and the abort sequence. The abort sequence indicates the end of the frame.

Data packet transmission

The transmission of a data packet by LLAP involves a special dialog consisting of one or more LLAP control frames followed by the data frame. This dialog is based on a CSMA/CA access protocol, some aspects of which were outlined in "Link Access Control" earlier in this chapter.

Carrier sensing and synchronization

LLAP packet transmission dialogs require each node to sense the use of the transmission medium. Two techniques are used by LLAP for this purpose.

First, LocalTalk hardware can detect a flag byte, the distinctive bit sequence 01111110 ($7E). This hardware capability is provided to allow the receiving node to achieve byte synchronization with the sender. LLAP can thus provide a certain measure of link-use sensing capability. The flag byte in the trailer is also detected by LocalTalk hardware and provides an indication of the end of the packet. The abort sequence at the end of the frame also forces every node's hardware to lose byte synchronization, thus confirming the end-of-line use by the current sender.

A drawback of the flag-byte synchronization approach is that synchronization can take 2 or more flag bytes to be achieved; during that time the node could determine the line to be idle when it is, in fact, being used by another node.

LLAP supplements this byte synchronization for carrier sensing with a variant of the hardware's bit-clock synchronization capability. For this purpose, prior to sending a request-to-send (RTS) frame, LLAP transmits a synchronization pulse. A **synchronization pulse** is a transition on the link, followed by an idle period greater than 2 bit-times. The synchronization pulse is obtained by momentarily enabling the hardware line driver for at least 1 bit-time before disabling it, causing a transition on the line that will be detected as a clock by all receivers on the network. However, since the transition is followed by an idle period of sufficient length, all receivers conclude that they have lost the clock. They are said to have detected a missing clock. The hardware can detect this missing clock much more rapidly than it can achieve byte synchronization. With the synchronization pulse at the leading edge of an RTS frame, the detection of a missing clock provides a very quick way to detect use of the line by a sender.

The missing clock allows transmitters to synchronize their access to the line (transmitters become immediately aware if a transmission is about to take place). Synchronization pulses can also be sent at the beginning of other LLAP frames.

Further details of carrier-sensing aspects of LocalTalk hardware are discussed in Appendix A.

Transmission dialogs

For the purpose of transmitting information, LLAP distinguishes between two kinds of data packets and, consequently, two kinds of transmission dialogs. A **directed packet** is sent to a single node and hence is transmitted via a **directed transmission dialog.** Similarly, a **broadcast packet** (destination node ID equals 255 ($FF)) goes to all nodes on the link via a **broadcast transmission dialog.**

Dialogs must be separated by a minimum **interdialog gap** (IDG) of 400 microseconds. The different frames of a single dialog must follow one another with a maximum **interframe gap** (IFG) of 200 microseconds.

◆ *Note:* A frame preamble contains 2 or more flag bytes. If more than 2 flag bytes are transmitted, the source must ensure that the destination will receive the flag bytes and the destination address byte within the interframe gap (IFG). In other words, the IFG is defined as the time from the end of the abort sequence of the previous frame's trailer to the end of the current frame's destination address byte.

The transmission dialog is described separately for directed and broadcast packets. *Figure 1-3* illustrates the frames and the timing used in the dialogs. LLAP transmission dialogs are best understood in the case of directed data packets.

The transmitting node uses the ability of the physical layer to sense if the line is in use. If the line is busy, the node waits until the line becomes idle. While the node is waiting, it is said to *defer.* Upon sensing an idle line, the transmitter waits for a time equal to the minimum IDG (400 microseconds) plus a randomly generated period. During this wait, the transmitter continues to monitor the line. If the line becomes busy at any time during this wait period, the node must again defer. If the line remains idle throughout this wait period, then the node sends an RTS packet to the intended receiver of the data packet. The receiver must return a clear-to-send (CTS) packet to the transmitting node within the maximum IFG (200 microseconds). Upon receiving this packet, the transmitter must start sending the data packet within the maximum IFG.

■ **Figure 1-3** LLAP transmission dialogs

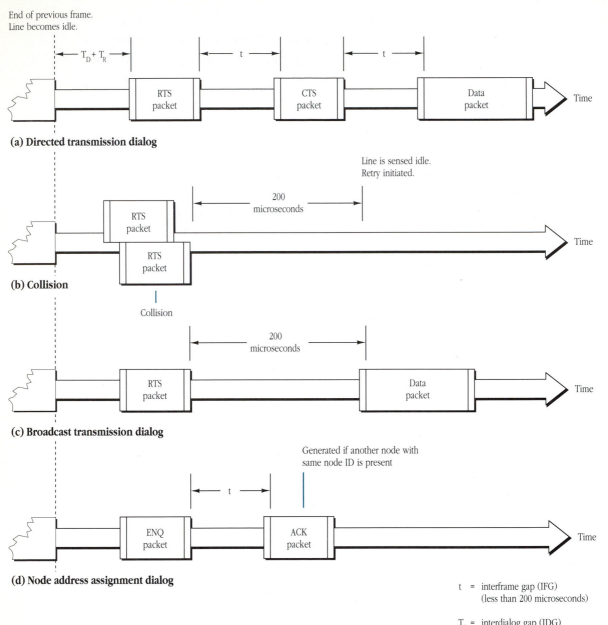

t = interframe gap (IFG)
(less than 200 microseconds)

T_D = interdialog gap (IDG)
(greater than 400 microseconds)

T_R = randomly generated time period

The purpose of this algorithm is to

- restrict the situations in which collisions are more likely to occur (the RTS-CTS handshake); in these situations, a minimum amount of line time is wasted by the collision

- spread out the use of line time among transmitters that are waiting for the line to become idle

The RTS-CTS handshake is said to be successful if a valid CTS packet is received by the transmitter after it has sent out an RTS packet. A successful RTS-CTS handshake signifies that a collision did not occur and that all intending transmitters have heard of the coming data packet transmission and are deferring.

If a collision does occur during the RTS-CTS handshake, then the corresponding LLAP control packet will be corrupted by the collision. This corruption will be detected by using the FCS, and the corresponding packet will be discarded by its receiving node. The net result is that a CTS packet will not be received by the sender of the RTS packet within the maximum permissible time of 200 microseconds, and the sending node will then *back off* and retry. In this situation, the sending node is said to *assume* a collision has occurred.

Two factors are used for adjusting the range of the randomly generated period:

- the number of times the node has to defer

- the number of times it assumes a collision has occurred

This history is maintained in two 8-bit **history bytes,** one each for deferrals and collisions. At each attempt to send a packet, these bytes are shifted left 1 bit. The lowest bit of each byte is then set if the node had to defer or had to assume a collision has occurred, respectively. Otherwise, this bit is cleared. In effect, the history bytes retain the deferral and collision history for the last eight attempts.

The random wait time is generated as a **pseudorandom number.** These numbers (produced through an arithmetic process) are close to a true random sequence. The range of numbers is adjusted according to the current link traffic and collision history. If collisions have been assumed for recently sent packets, it is reasonable to expect heavy traffic and higher contention for the link. In this case, the random wait period should be generated over a larger range, thus spreading out (in time) the different contenders for use of the line. Conversely, if the node has not had to defer on recent transmissions, a lighter offered traffic is inferred, and the random wait period should be generated over a smaller range, therefore reducing dispersion of transmission.

The exact use of the history bytes for determining random wait periods is described in "Algorithms" in Appendix B.

Directed data packet transmission

Directed packets are sent according to the following procedure, as shown in *Figure 1-4:*

1. The transmitter senses the link until the link has been idle for the minimum IDG (400 microseconds).

2. The transmitter then waits an additional random time period.

3. If the link is still free, the transmitter sends an RTS frame to the intended destination node.

4. The destination node responds with a CTS frame.

5. The transmitter, upon successful reception of the CTS frame, sends the data frame (in which it encapsulates the client's data).

The destination node must start sending the CTS frame within the maximum IFG of 200 microseconds. Otherwise, the transmitter will assume that a collision has occurred and will return to step 1. For each attempt, a new random number must be generated in step 2. If the transmitter is unable to send the data packet after 32 attempts, it reports failure to its client.

■ **Figure 1-4** RTS-CTS handshake during a directed data transmission

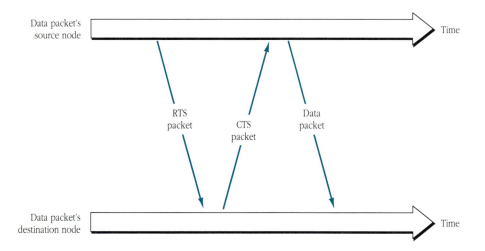

Broadcast data packet transmission

Broadcast packets, which go to all nodes on the link, have a destination node ID of 255 ($FF).
Broadcast packets are sent without collision except if another transmitter attempts to broadcast
at the same time.

Broadcast frames are sent according to the following procedure:

1. The transmitter senses the link until the link has been idle continuously for the minimum IDG
   (400 microseconds).

2. The transmitter then waits an additional random time period.

3. If the link is still free, the transmitter sends an RTS frame with destination address of 255 ($FF).

4. The transmitter checks the line for the maximum IFG (200 microseconds).

5. If the line stays idle throughout step 4, the transmitter sends the data frame.

Although it does not expect to receive a response, the transmitting node sends an RTS frame to
notify all other transmitters of its intent to broadcast. Furthermore, the RTS frame forces a
collision if another transmitter happens to start a directed transmission at the same time, causing
that node to back off.

  If the transmitter detects link activity during step 4, it returns to step 1 to try again. The node
will make 32 attempts, beginning with step 1, before reporting failure to its client.

Packet reception

A node will accept an incoming packet if

- its destination address is the same as the node's ID (or is the broadcast address)
- the frame's FCS is verified to be correct

A receiving node will reject bad frames resulting from one of several error conditions. LLAP handles
these situations internally, without referring them to its client.

Error conditions	Description
packet size	packet length is less than 5 bytes or more than 603 bytes
overrun/underrun	LLAP could not stay synchronized with the incoming data
frame type	the type field does not match a valid LLAP value
frame check sequence	CRC-CCITT has detected an FCS error

The above discussion describes in general terms LLAP's transmission and reception mechanisms. A more detailed specification of these packet transmission and reception disciplines is given in Appendix B.

Also included in Appendix B are detailed algorithms of LLAP's dynamic node ID assignment as well as the CRC-CCITT computation of the FCS.

Chapter 2   AppleTalk Address Resolution Protocol

CONTENTS

■

THE APPLETALK ADDRESS RESOLUTION PROTOCOL
(AARP) maps between any two sets of addresses at any level of one or more
protocol stacks. Specifically, in the AppleTalk protocol architecture, AARP is
used to map between AppleTalk node addresses, used by the Datagram
Delivery Protocol (DDP) as well as higher-level AppleTalk protocols, and the
addresses of the underlying data link that is providing AppleTalk
connectivity. AARP makes it possible for AppleTalk systems to run on any
data link. ∎

Protocol families and stacks

The collection of all the protocols, corresponding to the upper five layers of the ISO-OSI reference model, used in a particular protocol architecture is referred to as a **protocol family.** An instance of a protocol family in a given node is known as a **protocol stack.** This terminology allows us to distinguish between the protocol architecture itself and an instance of that architecture implemented in a particular node.

Protocol and hardware addresses

Figure 2-1 shows a node in which several protocol stacks (for instance, AppleTalk, TCP/IP, XNS) are in simultaneous use. The node is connected to a single data link, and the packets of the different protocol families running in the node are all sent through this same data link. Each of the node's protocol stacks must use its own addressing scheme to specify the address of the node. The node address used by one protocol family will usually not be intelligible to any of the other families. In addition, the data-link layer has its own scheme for assigning an address to the node. Thus, a node can have multiple addresses, each of which is intelligible to one particular protocol family or data link.

The node address used by a protocol stack is said to be the node's **protocol address** corresponding to the particular protocol family. This address identifies the particular stack among its peers on the same network and is used to communicate with these peer entities.

The node address used by a data link is the node's hardware address.

Address resolution

A protocol stack can send a packet through the node's data link to another node in which the same protocol family is resident. For this purpose, when the protocol stack calls the data link to send a packet to its peer stack in another node, it will specify the destination node by using the latter's protocol address. Since this address is not intelligible to the data link, it must first be translated to the equivalent data-link or hardware address of the destination node. This translation of addresses is known as **address resolution.**

■ **Figure 2-1** Multiple protocol stacks using a single link

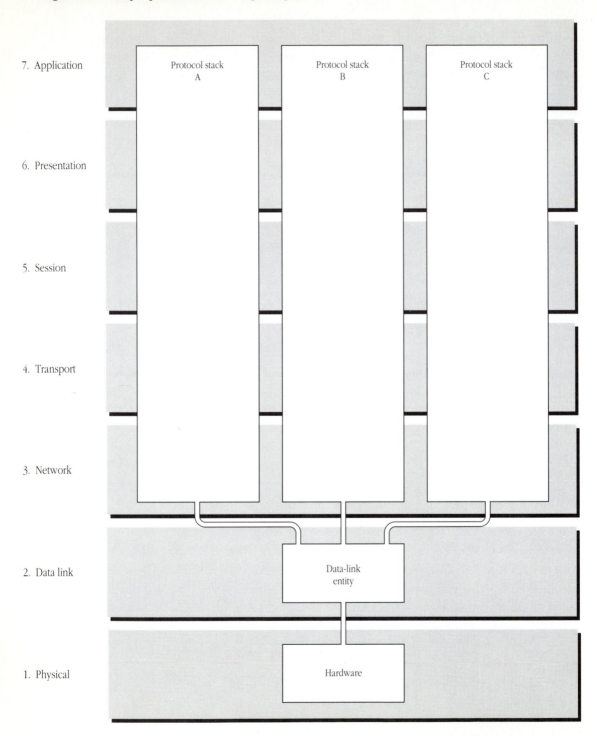

7. Application

6. Presentation

5. Session

4. Transport

3. Network

2. Data link

1. Physical

A *hardware address* is the address used by the physical and data-link layers of a network. Each node must have a hardware address that is unique on the link that it is using.

In addition to receiving packets addressed to its own hardware address, a node will generally accept packets that are addressed to the data link's broadcast hardware address (broadcast ID) or to a **multicast hardware address.**

When a node transmits a packet that has the broadcast hardware address as its destination address, then all nodes on the link will receive the packet. Each data link defines the value of its broadcast hardware address.

A multicast hardware address is similar to the broadcast hardware address. When a node transmits a packet that has a multicast hardware address as its destination address, then only a specific subset of the nodes on the link will receive the packet. Some nodes on the link may *not* have a multicast address; other nodes may have one or more multicast addresses.

In summary, a node on the link receives all packets sent to the node's unique hardware address, to the broadcast hardware address, and to any of the node's multicast hardware addresses.

The *protocol address* of a node is the address that uniquely identifies a protocol stack in that node among all other instances of stacks of that type on the network. A protocol address is used by a protocol stack to identify a peer protocol stack to which packets are to be sent.

In addition to receiving packets that contain its unique protocol address, a protocol stack may also receive packets addressed to a **broadcast protocol address.** Just as the broadcast hardware address causes all nodes on the network to receive the packet at the data-link level, the broadcast protocol address causes all nodes on the network to receive the packet at the level of the protocol stack.

For example, a packet could be addressed to the broadcast protocol address for a protocol stack. If all nodes with instances of that protocol stack belong to a particular multicast hardware address, then the data link would use this multicast hardware address to ensure delivery of the packet to all these nodes.

If a node supports more than one protocol stack and uses a single data link, then the node has a protocol address associated with each stack but has only one hardware address.

AARP services

When a stack calls the data-link layer to send a packet to a particular node, the stack will supply the destination address in terms of a protocol address. This address must first be resolved into the corresponding hardware address of the destination node. AARP provides the services needed to perform this address resolution.

As indicated earlier, AARP can be used to map between any two sets of addresses at any protocol level. Although this chapter discusses AARP's use in mapping between protocol addresses and hardware addresses, the concepts presented here can be applied to the more general case.

An AARP implementation has as its clients the various protocol stacks in a given node. AARP uses the node's data link to

■ **translate a protocol address into a hardware address**

Given a protocol address for a particular protocol family, AARP determines the hardware address of the node that is currently using that protocol address.

■ **determine the node's protocol address**

AARP dynamically assigns a protocol address to a stack in the node. AARP ensures that this address is unique among all nodes on the network of that protocol family.

■ **filter incoming packets**

AARP interposes itself in the packet reception path between the data link and each protocol stack. For all data packets received by the node, AARP verifies that the packet's destination protocol address is equal to either the node's protocol address or the broadcast protocol address for that protocol family. Otherwise, AARP discards the packet.

AARP operation

AARP's key service is address resolution. For this purpose, each node has a cache of mappings between the various protocol addresses and the corresponding hardware addresses. When one of the node's protocol stacks asks AARP to resolve a given protocol address, AARP starts by looking in the cache for the appropriate mapping. In the event that the necessary mapping is not found in the cache, then AARP queries all the nodes on the data link for the desired mapping by using the broadcast or multicast capability of the underlying data link.

The query can be done by using the data link's broadcast capability. In this case, the query packet sent out by AARP will be received by every node on the data link, regardless of whether that node has a protocol stack corresponding to the protocol family of the requested protocol address. The use of an appropriately set up multicast hardware address can help ensure that only the relevant nodes receive the AARP query.

In the description below, various AARP operations require the broadcasting of AARP packets. The word *broadcast* here refers to broadcasting at the protocol stack level; it does not necessarily have to be sent as a data-link broadcast. An AARP broadcast means that the AARP packet is to be delivered to all nodes implementing the protocol family to which the AARP packet refers.

In each node, AARP maintains a cache of known protocol-to-hardware address mappings, known as an **Address Mapping Table** (AMT). Such an AMT must be maintained for each protocol stack that wishes to use AARP services. Whenever AARP discovers a new address mapping, it creates a corresponding AMT entry to reflect the new mapping. If no more space is available in the AMT for the new mapping, AARP purges one of the existing AMT mappings by using some type of least-recently-used algorithm. Likewise, AARP modifies existing AMT entries to reflect changes in address mappings.

Address mapping

AARP queries for address mappings are made by using two types of AARP packets: AARP Request and AARP Response packets.

Request packets

When asked by a client to determine the hardware address corresponding to a given protocol address, AARP first scans the associated AMT for that protocol address. If the protocol address is found in the AMT, AARP reads the corresponding hardware address and immediately delivers it to the client.

If the hardware address is *not* found in the AMT, then AARP attempts to determine the hardware address by querying all nodes supporting the corresponding protocol family. AARP uses the data link to broadcast a series of AARP Request packets. The objective of broadcasting the AARP Request packet is to discover the node that is using the protocol address.

The AARP Request packet carries in it an identifier of the protocol family and the value of the protocol address to be mapped.

Response packets

When a node receives an AARP Request packet, its AARP implementation compares the protocol address from the packet with the node's protocol address for the indicated protocol family. If the addresses match, then the node's AARP returns an AARP Response packet to the requester. This packet contains the hardware address requested by the sender of the AARP Request packet.

Upon receiving this Response packet, the requesting node's AARP inserts the newly discovered mapping into the corresponding AMT. AARP then returns the requested hardware address to its client.

If a Response packet is not received within a specified time interval, then AARP retransmits the Request packet. This process is repeated a specified maximum number of times. If after these retries a Response packet is not received, then AARP returns an error to its client. This error implies that the protocol address is not in use and that no corresponding node exists on the link.

Dynamic protocol address assignment

Each protocol stack in a given node must have a protocol address. This address is usually assigned when the stack is initialized. AARP provides one way of making this assignment. However, a protocol stack may choose to assign its protocol address using a different method and then inform AARP of this address. The only requirement is that the protocol address be unique across all nodes of a given protocol family.

When a protocol stack asks AARP to pick a unique protocol address, AARP first chooses a tentative protocol address for the node. It starts either by choosing an address value from some nonvolatile memory or by generating a random number. If a mapping for that address value already exists in the corresponding AMT, then AARP knows that another node on the network is using this protocol address. It then picks a new random value for the protocol address until it identifies an address that is not in that AMT.

Having picked a suitable tentative protocol address, AARP must then make sure that this address is not being used by any other node on the data link. It does so by using the data link to broadcast a number of AARP Probe packets, which contain the tentative protocol address. When a node's AARP receives a Probe packet corresponding to one of its protocol stacks, it examines the protocol address of that stack. If the Probe's tentative protocol address matches the receiving node's protocol address, AARP sends back an AARP Response packet to the probing node.

If the probing node receives an AARP Response packet, then the tentative protocol address is already in use and the node must pick a new tentative address and repeat the probing process. If the probing node does *not* receive a Response packet after a specified amount of time, then it retransmits the probe. If after a specified maximum number of retries the node has still not received a response, then the node's AARP accepts the tentative address as the node's protocol address. AARP returns this value to its client.

Although it is unlikely, two nodes on the link could simultaneously pick the same value for their tentative protocol addresses. To handle this situation properly, a probing node receiving a Probe packet whose tentative address matches its own tentative address concludes that this address is in use. The node then proceeds to select another tentative protocol address. While it is sending Probe packets, a node should not respond to AARP Probe or Request packets.

Retransmission of AARP packets

As described above, AARP retransmits probes and requests until it either receives a reply or exceeds a maximum number of retries. The retransmission interval and count depend on how thorough a search the client requires.

In general, the retransmission interval and count for probes are determined based on the characteristics of the particular data link. These values are chosen to minimize the possibility of duplicate protocol addresses.

The retransmission interval and count for requests may be optionally provided by AARP's clients.

Filtering incoming packets

For two reasons, it is desirable that AARP examine all incoming packets before they are delivered to the node's protocol stacks. First, AARP can help verify that an incoming packet is actually intended for the corresponding protocol stack. Second, AARP can gather address-resolution information from every incoming packet. This information will help maintain AMTs in the node and may result in fewer AARP packets being sent.

The filtering of incoming packets is an optional aspect of AARP; its use is not required.

In the discussion below, it is assumed that each protocol stack has supplied AARP with the stack's protocol address and with any corresponding broadcast protocol address that the stack recognizes. Furthermore, each stack must provide AARP with a mechanism for extracting the destination protocol address from an incoming packet.

Verifying packet addresses

To verify that an incoming data packet is intended for one of the node's protocol stacks, AARP examines the packet's destination protocol address. If this address does not match the node's protocol address or any of the node's broadcast protocol addresses, then AARP must discard the packet.

Gleaning address information

Since all incoming packets intended for one of the node's protocol stacks contain both the hardware address and the protocol address of the sender, AARP can extract the corresponding address mapping from the packet. This mapping can then be used to update the appropriate AMT.

Obtaining mapping information in this way is known as *gleaning*. The use of gleaning eliminates the need to send an AARP Request packet when the stack itself responds to the packet from which the information was gleaned.

In addition to its basic process of extracting mappings from AARP Response packets, AARP can glean information from every AARP Request packet received by the node. Since these packets are broadcast, every node's AARP receives them. AARP can extract a protocol mapping by reading the hardware and protocol addresses of the packet's sender. AARP can insert this mapping into the corresponding AMT.

It is important to note that AARP should *not* glean an address mapping from an AARP Probe packet. The sender's protocol address in such packets is tentative and hence not reliable.

AMT entry aging

The foregoing discussion has described the mechanisms used by AARP for creating and updating AMT entries in response to the various types of incoming packets.

Any particular entry of an AMT could become invalid, however, if the corresponding node is switched off or otherwise becomes unreachable over the link. More seriously, a new node could later come on line and pick the same protocol address. To ensure that an AMT's entries respond correctly to such events, an AARP implementation should age these entries. AARP provides two methods for AMT entry aging.

The first method is to associate a timer with each AMT entry. Every time AARP receives a packet that causes the entry to be modified or confirmed, AARP resets that entry's timer. If the timer expires, the entry has not been confirmed or updated for that period of time. The entry is then declared to be unreliable, and AARP deletes it from the AMT.

If a client now requests a mapping of the protocol address of the deleted entry, then AARP will have to send out an AARP Request. If an address resolution is achieved, then a new entry will be inserted in the AMT.

The second method prescribes that an AMT entry be deleted whenever AARP receives a Probe packet for the entry's protocol address. The reception of such a probe indicates the possibility that the corresponding address might now be used by a different node; the entry should be considered suspect. Note that this method might unnecessarily remove a valid entry if a new node probes for the same protocol address.

Every implementation of AARP is required to use at least one of these two entry-aging methods.

AARP packet formats

Each AARP packet starts with the data-link header for the particular link in use. The rest of the packet consists of the AARP information. This AARP information consists of fields for the hardware and protocol address pairs. In addition, there are fields identifying the data link and protocol family for these addresses.

Specifically, the AARP information is

- a 2-byte hardware type, which identifies the data-link type

- a 2-byte protocol type, which identifies the protocol family

- a 1-byte hardware address length, which indicates the length in bytes of the hardware address field

- a 1-byte protocol address length, which indicates the length in bytes of the protocol address field

Immediately following these fields is a 2-byte function field that indicates the packet function (1 for AARP Request, 2 for AARP Response, or 3 for AARP Probe). The next two fields are the hardware and protocol addresses of the sending node.

Finally, the last two fields of the packet contain a hardware and a protocol address respectively. The actual values in these two fields depend on the type of the packet (its function field).

For an AARP Request packet, the hardware address is the unknown quantity being requested; it should be set to a value of 0. The protocol address field should contain the address for which a hardware address is desired.

For an AARP Response packet, these fields contain the hardware and protocol addresses of the node to which the response is being sent.

For an AARP Probe packet, the hardware address should again be set to 0, and the protocol address field should be set to the sender's tentative protocol address.

Figure 2-2 presents the generic AARP packet formats.

■ **Figure 2-2** AARP packet formats

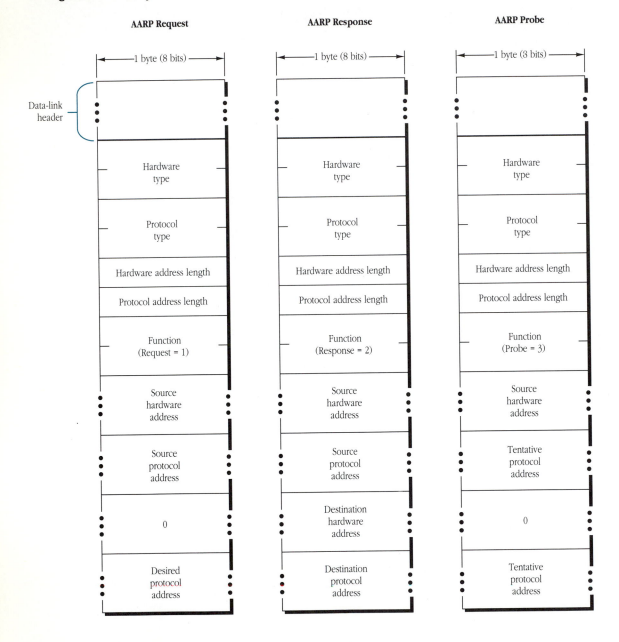

Chapter 3 EtherTalk and TokenTalk Link Access Protocols

CONTENTS

■

WHEN AN APPLETALK PROTOCOL STACK asks the data link to transmit an AppleTalk packet, its objective is to send the packet to the destination node's AppleTalk protocol stack. Consequently, it will provide the data link with the destination's AppleTalk protocol address, a 16-bit network number and an 8-bit node ID. On LocalTalk, which supports no more than 254 nodes, the lower 8 bits of this address can be used directly as the data-link address. Except when AppleTalk uses the LocalTalk data link, the data link will be unable to understand and use the destination's protocol address directly.

In the cases of EtherTalk and TokenTalk, the AppleTalk network system uses industry standards as the underlying data link. Both these data links use 48-bit hardware addresses to identify the network nodes. Thus, EtherTalk and TokenTalk products must translate the AppleTalk protocol address to the 48-bit hardware address before the packet can be transmitted to its destination node.

EtherTalk and TokenTalk were developed by Apple as extensions of these industry-standard data links to allow the use of industry-standard data links and cabling in the AppleTalk network. The extended data-link protocol used by EtherTalk is referred to as the EtherTalk Link Access Protocol (ELAP). The extended data-link protocol used by TokenTalk is referred to as the TokenTalk Link Access Protocol (TLAP). This chapter specifies ELAP and TLAP and also gives an example of the use of the address resolution protocol described in Chapter 2.

ELAP and TLAP use the AppleTalk Address Resolution Protocol (AARP) to map AppleTalk protocol addresses into 48-bit data-link addresses. They then encapsulate the AppleTalk datagram before using the data-link to send the packet. When the AppleTalk protocol stack is initialized, ELAP and TLAP, in combination with DDP, use AARP to acquire the stack's AppleTalk protocol address (node address). ∎

802.2

The Institute of Electrical and Electronics Engineers (IEEE) has specified a standard for Logical Link Control (LLC) for use on Ethernet, token ring, and other data links. This standard, 802.2, involves a set of interfaces, packet formats, and procedures for use on these data links. 802.2 Type 1 specifies a connectionless or datagram service; 802.2 Type 2 is connection-based. ELAP and TLAP use 802.2 Type 1 packet formats. Details of the interfaces and procedures for 802.2 Type 1 are beyond the scope of this book, however it is necessary to understand 802.2 Type 1 packet formats to be able to understand packets as sent by AppleTalk on Ethernet and token ring.

802.2 defines the concept of a Service Access Point or SAP. SAPs are used to differentiate between the different protocol stacks using 802.2 in a given node. A SAP is a 1-byte quantity, and most SAPs are reserved for use by IEEE-standard protocols. One SAP, however, has been reserved by the IEEE for use by all non-IEEE–standard protocols. This SAP, with value $AA, is the SAP to which all AppleTalk packets are sent. However, it is also used by other protocol families. Therefore a way of differentiating the various protocols using the $AA SAP was necessary. For this reason, all packets sent to the $AA SAP begin with a 5-byte protocol discriminator. This protocol discriminator identifies the protocol family to which the packet belongs. Use of the $AA SAP in this way is known as the Sub-Network Access Protocol or SNAP.

Figure 3-1 shows the packet format for an 802.2 Type 1 SNAP packet. The packet consists of four parts. First is the data-link header for the data link on which the packet is sent. Second is the 3-byte 802.2 Type 1 header. This header consists of the destination and source SAPs (both $AA for SNAP) and a control byte indicating that Type 1 service is being used. The 802.2 header is followed by the five-byte SNAP protocol discriminator. Finally, the SNAP protocol discriminator is followed by the data part of the packet.

SNAP protocol discriminators used by AppleTalk include $080007809B for AppleTalk data packets and $00000080F3 for AARP packets.

■ Figure 3-1 SNAP packet format

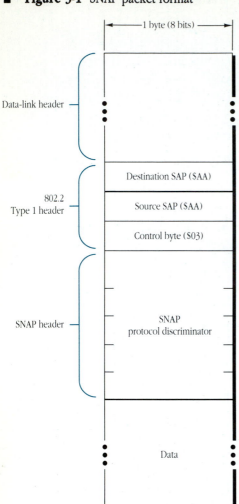

ELAP packet format

Figure 3-2 shows the data packet format for AppleTalk packets on Ethernet. The ELAP header consists of the 14-byte 802.3 header followed by the 802.2 and SNAP headers. 802.3 is an IEEE standard which specifies the format of the data-link header bytes on Ethernet. This header consists of the packet's 48-bit destination and source hardware (Ethernet) addresses and a 2-byte length field indicating the length of the data that follows. 802.3 also specifies that if the total length of the packet is less than 60 bytes (the minimum for Ethernet), pad bytes must be added after the data to bring the packet size up to 60 bytes. Pad bytes are not counted in the 802.3 length field.

■ **Figure 3-2** ELAP packet format

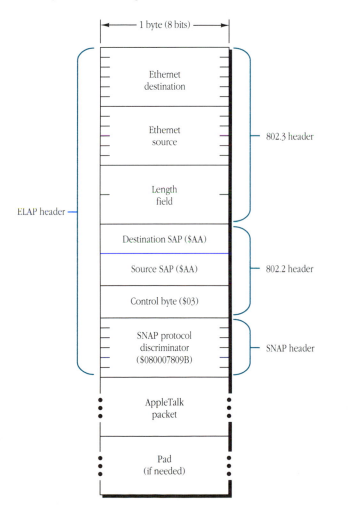

The SNAP protocol discriminator used by AppleTalk is $080007809B. The AppleTalk packet continues, following the ELAP header, with the start of the DDP header.

TLAP packet format

Figure 3-3 shows the data packet format for AppleTalk packets on a token ring network. The TLAP header consists of a 14-byte token ring header followed by optional source routing information and then by the 802.2 and SNAP headers. The token ring header begins with two bytes that are used by the token ring data link. These bytes are followed by the packet's 48-bit destination and source hardware addresses.

The token ring header is followed by variable length source routing information. Source routing is a method used on token ring to surpass the limits on length and number of devices that exist on a single token ring network. Through use of source routing bridges, token ring networks may be combined so as to appear to the upper protocol layers as a single token ring network. The source routing information is used to specify (or in some cases to collect) the route followed by the packet through the source routing bridges. An implementation of TLAP that supports source routing must take into account acquisition and maintenance of source routing information, as this is not performed by the token ring data link.

When source routing information is sent, the high-order bit of the source hardware address is set. (This bit is available because it is never part of a hardware address.) A set bit indicates that between 2 and 18 bytes of source routing information immediately follow the token ring header.

As in ELAP, the SNAP protocol discriminator used by AppleTalk is $080007809B. The AppleTalk packet continues, following the TLAP header, with the start of the DDP header.

■ **Figure 3-3** TLAP packet format

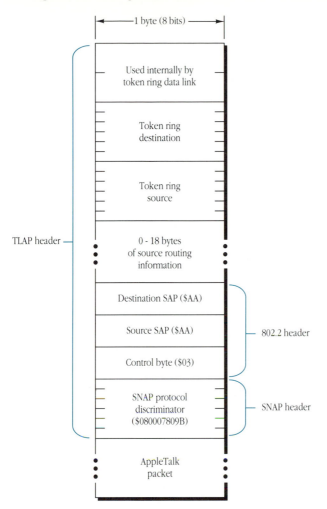

Address mapping in ELAP and TLAP

Ethernet and token ring provide addressing schemes structurally similar to that of LLAP. Nodes on Ethernet and token ring links are identified by unique addresses, and a broadcast capability is provided. These links also provide a multicasting capability, which is used by ELAP and TLAP to minimize the interference of AppleTalk broadcast packets on non-AppleTalk nodes.

However, Ethernet and token ring addresses are different from those expected by the AppleTalk protocol family. Instead of using a dynamically assigned 8-bit node ID, they use a statically assigned 48-bit hardware address. Their broadcast hardware address is also different than AppleTalk's broadcast protocol address of 255 ($FF).

There are conditions under which the AppleTalk protocol family will ask ELAP or TLAP to send a packet directly to a hardware address. If this is the case, no address mapping is performed and the packet is sent directly to the desired address.

Use of AARP by ELAP and TLAP

When the AppleTalk stack is initialized, ELAP or TLAP use AARP's dynamic protocol address assignment to pick an AppleTalk node address unique to the data link on which the node is operating. The network number part of this node address is chosen from within the network number range assigned to the network. The actual use of AARP to choose this address is described in Chapter 4, "Datagram Delivery Protocol."

Unlike the LocalTalk Link Access Protocol (LLAP), ELAP and TLAP make no distinction between server and workstation nodes when they perform this dynamic address assignment. The hardware for those data links provides enough buffering to reduce the chance of an AARP Probe packet being lost by busy nodes. Consequently, the probability of two nodes acquiring the same address is low.

Once an AppleTalk node address has been obtained, AppleTalk operation proceeds in the normal fashion. When ELAP or TLAP is asked to send a packet, it looks at the requested destination address to determine how to proceed. There are three possibilities.

1. If ELAP or TLAP is asked to send the packet directly to a 48-bit hardware address, it calls the underlying data link to perform this operation. Certain operations in DDP require the ability to send a packet directly to a specified hardware address.

2. If ELAP or TLAP is asked to send the packet to an AppleTalk address that is not a broadcast AppleTalk address, it uses AARP to map the packet's destination address into the corresponding hardware address and uses the underlying data link to send the packet to this hardware address. A broadcast AppleTalk address (detailed in Chapter 4), is any address whose node ID (low-order eight bits) is $FF.

3. If ELAP or TLAP is asked to send the packet to a broadcast AppleTalk address, it must send that packet in such a way that all AppleTalk nodes on that data link receive the packet. It is also desirable, however, that non-AppleTalk nodes on the same data link not be interrupted by these packets. The multicasting capability of the Ethernet and token ring data links is utilized to accomplish this goal. A specific multicast hardware address is assigned for AppleTalk broadcasts. ELAP or TLAP, in each AppleTalk node, registers itself with the underlying data link to receive all packets addressed to that multicast hardware address. Packets addressed to a broadcast AppleTalk address are then sent by ELAP or TLAP to this multicast address and received by all AppleTalk nodes on the data link. Since non-AppleTalk nodes will not have registered on this multicast address, they will not be interrupted by the packet.

The multicast address used by ELAP for AppleTalk broadcasts is $090007FFFFFF. The multicast hardware address used by TLAP for AppleTalk broadcasts is $C00040000000. ELAP and TLAP also use these multicast addresses for AARP broadcasts.

AARP specifics for ELAP and TLAP

ELAP and TLAP impose restrictions on the tentative AppleTalk node address that AARP picks when attempting to dynamically choose a unique AppleTalk node address. These node IDs must not be chosen by AARP: Node ID 0 (invalid as an AppleTalk node ID), $FF (AppleTalk broadcast node ID), and $FE (reserved as an AppleTalk node ID on Ethernet and token ring).

In addition, during the address acquisition process, ELAP and TLAP are asked by the AppleTalk stack to choose the network number part of the node address in a specific range. Thus, when picking tentative node addresses, AARP must be sure to pick them in this requested range.

Incoming data packets contain the source data-link address and the source AppleTalk address. Source address gleaning can be performed easily by AARP by obtaining the source's AppleTalk and data-link addresses from the packet and then updating the AMT. This gleaning is not a required part of ELAP or TLAP. For example, some developers might consider the computational overhead of gleaning to be excessive and therefore not include the capability in their implementation.

The AARP probe-retransmission interval and count for ELAP and TLAP is specified as 1/5 second and 10 retransmissions, respectively. For AARP requests, the corresponding parameters are left to the discretion of the specific implementer. AARP request and probe packets are sent to the same multicast hardware address used for AppleTalk broadcasts and thus interrupt only AppleTalk nodes. This address is $090007FFFFFF for ELAP and $C00040000000 for TLAP.

Zone multicast addresses used by ELAP and TLAP

AppleTalk data links should allocate a number of multicast addresses for use in the name lookup process, as indicated in Chapter 8, "Zone Information Protocol." ZIP and NBP use these addresses to minimize the effect of the name lookup process on nodes not in the desired zone. The specific zone multicast addresses defined for use by ELAP and TLAP are illustrated in *Figure 3-4*.

■ **Figure 3-4** ELAP and TLAP multicast addresses

	ELAP	TLAP
AppleTalk broadcast address	$090007FFFFFF	$C00040000000
Zone multicast addresses When used with the address assignment algorithm described in Chapter 8, the first address in each list represents a[0].	$090007000000 *253 addresses* $0900070000FC	$C00000000800 $C00000001000 $C00000002000 $C00000004000 $C00000008000 $C00000010000 $C00000020000 $C00000040000 $C00000080000 $C00000100000 $C00000200000 $C00000400000 $C00000800000 $C00001000000 $C00002000000 $C00004000000 $C00008000000 $C00010000000 $C00020000000

AppleTalk AARP packet formats on Ethernet and token ring

Each AARP packet on Ethernet and token ring begins with the same set of headers used by ELAP or TLAP. The SNAP protocol discriminator defined for AARP is $00000080F3. Following these headers, 6 bytes of AARP information identify the packet as requesting an AppleTalk-to-Ethernet or AppleTalk-to-token-ring address mapping:

- a 2-byte hardware type, with value of 1, indicating Ethernet, or value of 2, indicating token ring as the data link

- a 2-byte protocol type, with value of $809B, indicating the AppleTalk protocol family

- a 1-byte hardware address length, with value of 6, indicating the length in bytes of the field containing the Ethernet or token ring address

- a 1-byte protocol address length, with value of 4, indicating the length in bytes of the field containing the AppleTalk protocol address (The high byte of the address field must be set to 0, followed by the 2-byte network number, and then the 1-byte node ID.)

The rest of the AARP packet contains the source and destination hardware and AppleTalk addresses, the latter always in 4-byte fields with the upper byte set to 0. *Figure 3-5* shows the AARP packet formats for Ethernet or token ring.

Figure 3-5 AppleTalk-Ethernet or AppleTalk-token ring AARP packet formats

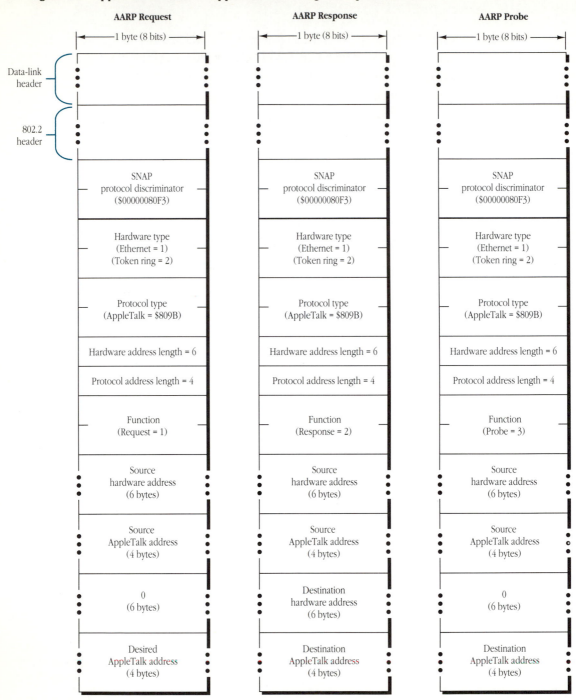

Part II **End-to-End Data Flow**

P A R T I of *Inside AppleTalk* specifies the LocalTalk, EtherTalk, and TokenTalk link access protocols. These protocols govern the operation of local-area data links that can be used to connect network nodes in a geographically restricted area.

In particular, LocalTalk can be used to connect up to 32 network nodes with a maximum cumulative link span of 300 meters. EtherTalk and TokenTalk use standard networking technology to build a local area network (LAN) with a large number of nodes and a cable length of up to several kilometers.

Larger networks than those permitted by these local-area data links can also be set up. This extension can be achieved in two ways:

- by using bridges to extend a single LAN or data link
- by interconnecting several LANs through routers to build an internet

Bridges and routers are intelligent devices that extend network systems by storing and forwarding packets on a path from the packet's source node to its destination node.

A *bridge* operates at the data-link layer (level 2 of the ISO-OSI reference model in *Figure I-9*). It examines the data-link level destination addressing information of packets received by it on the link segments to which the bridge is connected. It then retransmits each packet on the appropriate segment toward the packet's destination node. In effect, bridges extend the effective length and maximum number of nodes limit of a single data link or local area network (LAN). Bridges are widely used in Ethernet-based systems such as DECnet™, and source-routing bridges are widely used in token ring based systems. Since bridges simply extend a particular LAN, their use is transparent to the various protocols of the network system.

Routers are used to interconnect several different LANs or data links situated over a widely distributed geographical area. Routers forward packets by using an address extension defined at the network layer (level 3 of the ISO-OSI reference model).

This address extension, known as a network number, is provided by the Datagram Delivery Protocol (DDP), which is described in Chapter 4, "Datagram Delivery Protocol."

While bridges allow extension of a single data link or LAN, routers can be used to interconnect dissimilar data links into a single internet. In particular, as shown in *Figure 4-1,* routers can be used to enable communication between nodes on LocalTalk, EtherTalk, and TokenTalk data links, thus forming an AppleTalk internet incorporating dissimilar link technologies.

Routers forward packets by consulting routing tables. The Routing Table Maintenance Protocol (RTMP), specified in Chapter 5, governs this table maintenance operation in all AppleTalk routers.

The AppleTalk Echo Protocol (AEP) of Chapter 6 provides the ability to measure round-trip travel times between any two nodes of an AppleTalk internet. This information is useful in a variety of network management functions and for setting retry timers in various transport-level and session-level protocols. ■

Chapter 4 **Datagram Delivery Protocol**

CONTENTS

■

THE LOCALTALK LINK ACCESS PROTOCOL (LLAP) and
other AppleTalk data links provide a best-effort, node-to-node delivery of
packets on a single AppleTalk network. The Datagram Delivery Protocol
(DDP) is designed to extend this mechanism to the socket-to-socket delivery
of datagrams over an AppleTalk internet. Datagrams are packets of data
carried by DDP between the sockets of an internet. An AppleTalk internet
consists of one or more AppleTalk networks connected by intelligent nodes
referred to as **internet routers** (IRs), as shown in *Figure 4-1*.

◆ *Note:* Internet routers should not be confused with gateways. Gateways
   are nodes that separate and manage communication between different
   protocol families.

This chapter specifies DDP. In particular it describes:

■ sockets and their relation to DDP

■ acquisition of a DDP network number and node ID

■ calls at the DDP interface

■ the algorithms used within DDP ■

■ **Figure 4-1** AppleTalk internet and internet routers (IRs)

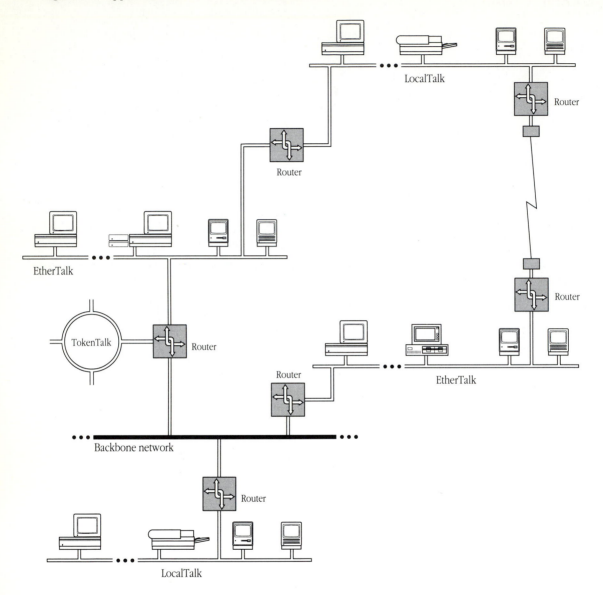

Internet routers

IRs are packet-forwarding agents. Packets can be sent between any two nodes of an internet by using a store-and-forward process through a series of IRs. An IR often consists of a single node connected to two or more AppleTalk networks; it might also consist of two nodes connected to each other through a communication channel. In the latter case, the channel between the two halves of the IR could take any of the following forms:

■ a leased or dial-up line

■ another network (for example, a wide-area packet-switched or circuit-switched public network)

■ a higher-speed broadband or baseband local area network (LAN) used as a backbone

Sockets and socket identification

Sockets are logical entities within the nodes connected to an AppleTalk internet. Sockets are owned by socket clients. **Socket clients** are typically processes (or functions in processes) implemented in software in the node. A socket client can send and receive datagrams only through sockets that it owns.

Each socket within a given node is identified by an 8-bit **socket number.** Socket numbers are treated as unsigned integers. There can be at most 254 different socket numbers in a node. (The values 0 and 255 are reserved and cannot be used to identify sockets.)

Sockets are classified into two groups: statically assigned and dynamically assigned. **Statically assigned sockets** (SASs) have socket numbers in the range 1–127. SASs are reserved for use by clients such as the lower-level AppleTalk protocols (for example, Name Binding Protocol (NBP) and Routing Table Maintenance Protocol (RTMP)). Socket numbers 1–63 are specifically reserved for use by Apple. Socket numbers 64–127 are available for unrestricted experimental use. Use of these experimental SAS numbers is not recommended for released products, since there is no mechanism for eliminating conflicting usage of the same socket(s) by different developers (see "Sockets and Use of Name Binding" later in this chapter). See Appendix C for a summary of socket number usage.

Socket numbers 128–254 are assigned dynamically by DDP upon request from clients in that node; sockets of this type are known as **dynamically assigned sockets** (DASs).

Network numbers and a node's AppleTalk address

Each AppleTalk network in an internet is assigned a range of 16-bit network numbers. These ranges are specified in such a way that no two ranges in an internet have any network numbers in common. An AppleTalk device is identified by a 16-bit network number, chosen from within the range assigned for the node's network, combined with its 8-bit, dynamically assigned **AppleTalk node ID**. The details of choosing this unique network number/node ID combination are discussed in the next section. Combining the socket number with the node's network number and node ID enables any socket on the internet to be uniquely identified. The **internet socket address** of a socket consists of its socket number and the node ID and network number of the node in which the socket is located. As a result, the source and destination sockets of a datagram can be fully specified by their internet socket addresses.

The network number 0 is reserved to mean unknown; by default it specifies the local network to which the node is connected. Packets whose destination network number is 0 are addressed to a node on the local network. This address allows systems consisting of a single AppleTalk network to operate without network numbers. Network numbers $FF00 through $FFFE are reserved for nodes to use during the startup process and at times when an internet router is unavailable. Their use is described in the following sections.

Special DDP node IDs

Certain node IDs are reserved and have special meaning to DDP. These node IDs should never be chosen as a part of an AppleTalk node address. Node ID $FF indicates a broadcast to all nodes with a network number equal to that indicated by the specified network number. As long as this network number is nonzero, the packet is refered to as a **network-specific broadcast.** Although it will be received by all AppleTalk nodes on the data link, it should only be accepted by those with the indicated network number.

If the network number is zero, node ID $FF indicates either a network-wide or zone-specific broadcast. A **network-wide broadcast** is sent to all AppleTalk nodes on the data link and should be accepted by all those nodes. A **zone-specific broadcast** is sent to a particular zone multicast address. DDP should always accept such a packet, however higher level protocols like NBP and ZIP will discard the packet if it is not intended for the node's zone (see Chapter 8, "Zone Information Protocol," for details of zone multicast addressing).

Node ID 0 indicates any router on the network specified by the network number part of the node address. Packets addressed to node ID 0 are routed through the internet until they reach the first router directly connected to a network whose range includes the indicated network number. The packet is then delivered to that router. This facility is used by NBP.

Node ID $FE is reserved on EtherTalk and TokenTalk networks and should not be used as a node ID. This address is a valid node ID on LocalTalk networks.

AppleTalk node address acquisition

DDP is responsible for acquiring a node's AppleTalk address at startup time. This address must be unique throughout the AppleTalk internet. DDP combines with the underlying data link being used by the node, and with internet routers on that data link, to acquire this address. The details of DDP's AppleTalk node address acquisition process depend on the type of network to which the node is connected.

A **nonextended network** is an AppleTalk network on which each node's 8-bit AppleTalk node ID is unique. Thus no more than 254 nodes can be concurrently active on such a network (node IDs 0 and $FF are reserved). Nonextended networks are assigned exactly one network number and exactly one zone name (zones are described in Chapter 7, "Name Binding Protocol"). LocalTalk is an example of a nonextended network.

An **extended network** is an AppleTalk network on which nodes are differentiated by unique network number/node ID pairs. Theoretically, up to 16 million or so nodes can be concurrently active on such a network. Extended networks are assigned a range of network numbers, and all network numbers are chosen from within this range. A second aspect of extended networks is that they can be assigned multiple zone names.

The range of network numbers on an extended network determines the maximum number of concurrently active devices. The maximum number of concurrently active devices on an extended network is equal to the number of network numbers multiplied by the number of possible node IDs. In addition to node IDs 0 and $FF, node ID $FE is reserved on extended networks, and thus there are 253 possible node IDs per network number.

An extended network can be thought of as a number of nonextended networks, each residing on the same physical data link, and each capable of supporting up to 253 nodes. EtherTalk and TokenTalk are examples of extended networks.

Node address acquisition on nonextended networks

The acquisition of an AppleTalk node address on a nonextended network is greatly simplified by the fact that all nodes on the data link have a unique 8-bit AppleTalk node ID. This being the case, the network needs only one network number to guarantee all nodes on it have addresses that are unique in the internet. The underlying data link (LLAP for LocalTalk) is used to dynamically assign this unique node ID. The node's network number is then obtained from a router using an RTMP Request packet. Details of this exchange are specified in Chapter 5, "Routing Table Maintenance Protocol."

If a nonextended network is operating without a router, no reply will be received from the RTMP Request. In this case, the network number is set to zero. If a router later becomes available, the network number is then set to the one specified by the router.

Node address acquisition on extended networks

The acquisition of an AppleTalk network number and node ID on an extended network takes place in two steps. First a **provisional node address** is obtained through the data link for purposes of talking to a router and thereby discovering the network number range that is valid for the network to which the node is connected. Following this, the node's actual network number and node ID are obtained through the underlying data link.

When a node is started for the first time on an extended network, it asks the underlying data link for a provisional node address. The node ID part of this address is chosen at random, and the network number part is chosen from the range $FF00 to $FFFE. This range is reserved for the startup process, and is referred to as the **startup range.**

If the node had been previously started on the extended network, it will have saved the last network number and node ID it used on that network (in non-volatile or disk storage). Upon startup, the node instructs the data link to obtain its provisional node address by trying this "hint" first. If this "hint" is in use, the data link should then try all node IDs with the same network number as the hint. In this way, there is a good chance that the node's provisional node address will include a network number within the network number range for its data link, and there will be no need to obtain another one. If all node IDs with the old network number are in use, the node should proceed to obtain a provisional node address in the startup range. Optionally, it could have saved the entire range of network numbers for the network it was last on and could try other valid network numbers in this range before proceeding to the startup range.

Once a provisional node address has been acquired, the node can proceed to talk to a router to find out the actual network number range in which its network number should be chosen. This is done through a ZIP GetNetInfo request, details of which are described in Chapter 8, "Zone Information Protocol." The response to this request includes the network number range that has been assigned to the node's network. If the node's provisional address contains a network number within this range, it is kept as the node's final network number and node ID. Otherwise, the node instructs its data link to obtain a unique address containing a network number within the range specified by the router. In either case, the node's final network number and node ID are saved in long-term storage for the next time the node starts up.

In the case of an extended network operating without a router, no reply will be received from the GetNetInfo request. In this case, the node's provisional node address becomes its final network number and node ID. Extended networks do not have the concept of a zero network number when no router is available, since that would limit such networks to 253 nodes. If a router does become available later, the node must verify that its network number is within the range specified by the router. This will generally be the case as long as the node was previously started up on its current network.

In the rare case where a router becomes available after the node has started up and the node's network number is not within the range specified by the router, a new address must be acquired before the node can communicate on the internet. However, since the node has been active on its local network for some time, it may already have established network connections. These connections are usually based on the node's address, and thus will probably break when a new node address is acquired. For this reason, the node may continue to operate for some time as if the router had not become active.

During the startup process, the node also acquires information about its zone. Details of this process are specified in Chapter 8, "Zone Information Protocol."

DDP type field

The AppleTalk architecture allows the implementation of a large number (up to 255) of parallel protocols that are clients of DDP. Note that socket numbers are not associated with a particular protocol type and should not be used to demultiplex among parallel protocols at the transport level. Instead, a 1-byte DDP type field is provided in the DDP header for this purpose. See Appendix C for a summary of the use of the DDP type field.

Socket listeners

Socket clients provide code, referred to as the **socket listener,** that *receives* datagrams addressed to that socket. The specific implementation of a socket listener is node-dependent. For efficiency, the socket listener should be able to receive datagrams asynchronously through either an interrupt mechanism or an input/output request completion routine.

The code that implements DDP in the node must contain a data structure called a **sockets table** to maintain an appropriate descriptor of each open socket's listener.

DDP interface

As shown in *Figure 4-2,* the DDP interface is the boundary at which the socket client can issue calls to and obtain responses from the DDP implementation module in the node. The DDP implementation module supports the following four calls:

- opening a statically assigned socket
- opening a dynamically assigned socket
- closing a socket
- sending a datagram

These calls are described in the following sections.

■ **Figure 4-2** Socket terminology

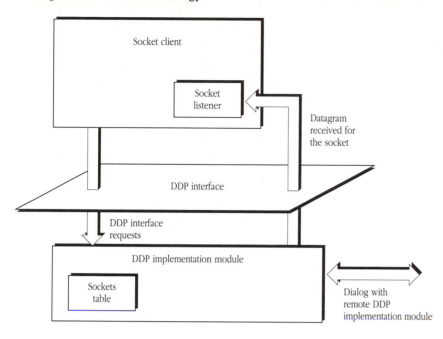

Opening a statically assigned socket

This call specifies the socket number (in the range 1–127) and the socket listener for that socket.
The call returns with a result code, which has the following possible values:

Result code	Meaning
success	socket opened
error	various cases such as socket already open, not a statically assigned socket (outside the permissible range), or sockets table full

Opening a dynamically assigned socket

Opening a dynamically assigned socket is similar to opening a statically assigned socket except that the caller does not specify the socket number. The call returns a result code and, if successful, the opened socket's number (in the range 128–254). The result code has the following possible values:

Result code	Meaning
success	socket opened
error	various cases such as sockets table full or all dynamic sockets in use

Closing a socket

This call specifies the number of the socket to be closed. If the socket is currently open, it is removed from the sockets table. The result code has the following possible values:

Result code	Meaning
success	socket closed
error	no such socket

Sending a datagram

This call specifies the number of the source socket, the internet address of the destination socket, and the DDP type field value. The length and location of the data part of the datagram are also provided in the request. Since DDP includes an optional software checksum in internet datagrams, the caller must specify whether or not this checksum is to be generated. The result code has the following possible values:

Result code	Meaning
success	datagram sent
error	sending socket not open or not valid; datagram too long

Datagram reception by the socket listener

In addition to the four calls just described, a socket listener mechanism must be provided for the reception of datagrams. Although details of the socket listener are not specified (since these are implementation-dependent), some mechanism is needed to deliver datagrams within the node to the destination client. The DDP module should attempt this delivery only if the destination socket is currently open. DDP must discard datagrams if they are addressed to a closed socket or if the datagram is received with an invalid DDP checksum.

DDP internal algorithm

Since DDP is a simple, best-effort protocol for internet-wide, socket-to-socket delivery of datagrams, it does not provide a mechanism for recovery from packet loss or error situations.

The primary function of the DDP implementation module is to form the DDP header on the basis of the destination address and then to pass the packet to the appropriate data link. Similarly, for packets received from the data-link layer, DDP must examine the datagram's destination address in the DDP header and route the datagram accordingly. Details of this operation depend on whether or not the node is an IR (see "DDP Routing Algorithm" later in this chapter).

DDP packet format

A datagram consists of the DDP header followed immediately by the data. The first 2 bytes of the DDP header contain a 10-bit datagram length field. The value in this field is the length in bytes of the datagram counted by starting with the first byte of the DDP header and including all bytes up to the last byte of the data part of the datagram. Upon receiving a datagram, the receiving node's DDP implementation must reject any datagram whose indicated length is not equal to the actual received length. The maximum length of the data part of a datagram is 586 bytes; longer datagrams must be rejected.

Short and extended headers

The DDP header also contains the source and destination socket addresses and the DDP type. Each of these addresses could be specified as a 4-byte internet socket address. However, for datagrams whose source and destination sockets are on the same network, the network number fields are unnecessary. Similarly, for such datagrams on LocalTalk, the source and destination node IDs are found in the LLAP header and would be redundant in the DDP header. Therefore, DDP uses two types of header—short and extended. A **short DDP header** is used on nonextended networks when source and destination sockets have the same network number. An **extended DDP header** is used for exchanging datagrams between sockets with different network numbers. DDP uses the value of the LLAP type field to determine if the packet has a short or an extended DDP header. The LLAP type field value is 1 for the short and 2 for the extended.

A datagram with a short header is shown in *Figure 4-3*. The short DDP header is 5 bytes long. The first 2 bytes of the header contain the datagram length, with the most-significant bits in the first byte. The upper 6 bits of this byte are not significant and should be set to 0. The datagram length field is followed by a 1-byte destination socket number, a 1-byte source socket number, and a 1-byte DDP type field. Datagrams with short headers can be sent only if the source and destination sockets have the same network number. Short headers are used solely for efficiency reasons; in fact, an implementation of DDP is permitted to send datagrams with extended headers even when source and destination sockets are on the same network. Extended headers are required on extended networks; datagrams with short headers should never be used on extended networks.

■ **Figure 4-3** DDP packet format (short header)

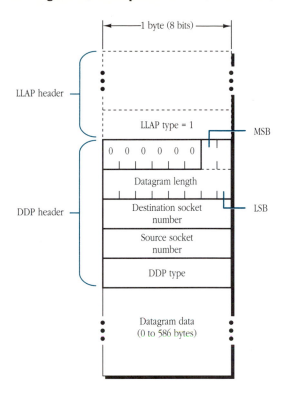

A datagram with an extended header is shown in *Figure 4-4*. The extended DDP header is 13 bytes long. It contains the full internet socket addresses of the source and destination sockets as well as the datagram length and DDP type fields. For such packets, there is a 6-bit hop count field in the most-significant bits of the first byte of the DDP header. See "Hop Counts" later in this chapter. In addition, the extended header may include an optional 2-byte (16-bit) DDP checksum field. See "Checksum Computation" later in this chapter. All 2-byte fields are specified with the high byte first. Datagrams exchanged between sockets on different AppleTalk networks and on any extended network must use an extended header.

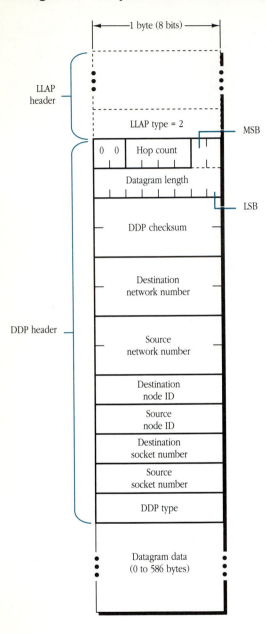

DDP checksum computation

The DDP checksum is provided to detect errors caused by faulty operation (such as memory and data bus errors) within routers on the internet. Implementers of DDP should treat generation of the checksum as an optional feature. The 16-bit DDP checksum is computed as follows:

```
CkSum := 0 ;

FOR each datagram byte starting with the byte immediately following the
Checksum field

REPEAT the following algorithm:
      CkSum := CkSum + byte; (unsigned addition)
      Rotate CkSum left one bit, rotating the most significant bit into the
                      least significant bit;

IF, at the end, CkSum = 0 THEN
      CkSum := $FFFF (all ones).
```

Reception of a datagram with CkSum equal to 0 implies that a checksum is not performed.

Hop counts

For datagrams that are exchanged between sockets on two different AppleTalk networks in an internet, a provision is made to limit the maximum number of IRs the datagram can traverse. Limiting this number is done by including in such internet datagrams a **hop count** field.

The source node of the datagram sets this field to 0 before sending the datagram. Each IR increases this field by 1. An IR receiving a datagram with a hop count value of 15 should not forward it to another IR; if such a datagram's destination node is on a network directly connected to the IR, then the IR should send the datagram to that destination node. Otherwise, the datagram should be discarded by the IR. This provision is made to filter out the internet packets that might be circulating in closed routes. Such a closed route (*loop*) is a transient situation that can occur for a short period of time while the routing tables are being updated by the RTMP. Non-IR nodes ignore the hop count field.

The upper 2 bits of the hop count currently are not used by DDP but are reserved for future use (such as the extension of the maximum value of the hop count beyond the currently allowed value of 15).

DDP routing algorithm

A datagram is conveyed from its source to its destination socket over the internet through IRs. The DDP implementation in the source node examines the destination network number of the datagram and determines whether or not the destination is on the local network. If the destination node is on the local network, the data-link layer is called to send the packet to the destination node. (The short DDP header can be used if the nodes are on a nonextended network.) However, if the destination is not on the local network, DDP builds the extended header and calls the data link to send the packet to an IR on the local network. (If there is more than one such IR, any one will do.) IRs examine the destination network number of the datagram and use routing tables to forward the datagram to subsequent IRs until an IR is reached that is connected to the destination network. (Routers forward datagrams through the data links of intervening local networks.) At the destination network, the datagram is sent to its destination node through the local network's data-link protocol.

Each node on an AppleTalk network maintains (as an internally stored value) the network number range of the local network to which it is attached. The DDP implementation in a datagram's source node determines whether the destination network is the local network by comparing the destination network number to the internally stored network number range. If the destination network number is in the local network number range, the packet can be delivered to a node on the local network. The packet should also be delivered locally if the destination network number is in the startup range ($FF00-$FFFE).

A special case arises on a nonextended network when the internally stored value is 0 (unknown). In this case, if the datagram's destination network number is not 0, then DDP should assume that the packet is intended for a node on the local network. However, DDP must in this case build an extended DDP header and call the data link to send the packet to the specified destination node on the local network. The extended DDP header enables the receiving node to throw away the packet if that node's DDP module determines that it was not the intended recipient (that is, if the destination network number of the packet is not equal to its internally stored local network number).

On an extended network, until a router is heard from, the local network number range should be set to 0-$FFFE. In this way, all packets will be delivered on the local network until a router becomes available.

Using RTMP, IRs maintain routing tables (discussed in detail in Chapter 5, "Routing Table Maintenance Protocol"). For each network number in the internet, the routing tables indicate the node ID (on the appropriate local network) of the next router on the proper route.

Nodes that are not IRs (nonrouter nodes) are not required to maintain routing tables. Such nodes need maintain only the following two pieces of information:

- the network number (THIS-NET) or network number range (THIS-NET-RANGE) of the local network

- the 16-bit network number and 8-bit node ID of any router (A-ROUTER) on the local network

This information can be obtained by implementing a simple subset of RTMP, called the **RTMP Stub,** in each nonrouter node. For nodes on systems consisting of a single network and no router, the values of THIS-NET and A-ROUTER will be 0 (unknown). On extended networks the value of THIS-NET-RANGE will be 0-$FFFE .

The following Pascal-like description specifies the internal routing algorithm used by the DDP implementation module of a nonrouter node on a non-extended network. The sending client issues a call to send a datagram, specifying the destination's internet socket address.

```
IF (destination network number = 0) OR (destination network number = THIS-NET) THEN
    BEGIN
            build the DDP header (it may be the short form);
            call the data link to send the datagram to the destination node
    END
ELSE
    BEGIN
            build the extended DDP header;
            IF THIS-NET = 0 THEN call the data link to send the packet to the destination
                    node
            ELSE IF A-ROUTER <> 0 THEN call the data link to send the packet to A-ROUTER
            ELSE return an error (no router available)
    END;
```

The following is the equivalent algorithm used by the DDP implementation module on a nonrouter node on an extended network. This algorithm is simplified by the fact that if there is no router, THIS-NET-RANGE will always be the full internet range, $0-$FFFE.

```
IF (dest net no. = 0) OR (dest net no. within THIS-NET-RANGE) OR
                        (dest net no. between $FF00 and $FFFE)
    THEN
            BEGIN
              build the extended DDP header;
              call the data link to send the datagram to the dest node
            END
    ELSE
            BEGIN
              build the extended DDP header;
              call the data link to send the datagram to A-ROUTER
            END;
```

For packets received by nonrouter nodes, the routing function simply delivers the datagram to the destination socket in the node. DDP must first verify that the destination network number (in an extended DDP header) is equivalent to that node's internally stored value of its network number. Otherwise, the packet is ignored. (For a precise definition of this equivalence, see "Network Number Equivalence" later in this chapter.) It is also advisable for such nodes to verify that the destination node ID in an extended DDP header matches the node's identifier (or is equal to the broadcast address, 255 ($FF)).

In IRs, the routing algorithm is somewhat more complex (see Chapter 5, "Routing Table Maintenance Protocol").

Optional "best router" forwarding algorithm

The routing algorithm given earlier, combined with the operation of the internet routers, is sufficient to deliver a packet to its destination socket. However this algorithm may result in an extra hop in getting to that destination. This will be the case if the initial router chosen by DDP is not on the shortest path to the destination network (remember DDP picked any router to send the packet to for forwarding). This section details an optional "best router" implementation for eliminating this extra hop under most conditions. "Best router" is highly recommended on extended networks, which often consist of many network segments interconnected by bridges.

When a packet comes in to DDP whose source network number is not within THIS-NET-RANGE (or the startup range), DDP looks at the sender's data-link address. This is the address of the last router on the route from the network the source node was on. Sending packets to this router to get to that network should be the best route in terms of hops. DDP maintains a cache of recently heard from network numbers and the data-link addresses of the "best" router for each of those networks.

When DDP determines that a packet needs to be sent to a router, it examines the "best router" cache to determine if it has an entry for the packet's destination network. If so, DDP calls the underlying data link to send the packet to the data-link address maintained in that cache. Otherwise it calls the data link to send the packet to the AppleTalk address indicated by A-ROUTER — a response will probably come back and an entry will then be made in the cache.

It is recommended that the "best router" cache be aged every 40 seconds or so, so that if a router goes down, an alternate route will be adopted in an expedient manner and network connections will not break. *Aging* in this case means that if no packets are received with a particular source network number for this period of time, the entry for that network should be removed from the cache.

Sockets and use of name binding

Developers of products for AppleTalk should not use SASs except for purely experimental purposes. This restriction is imposed in order to avoid the conflicting use of the same SAS by different developers. Such conflicts are difficult to avoid in the absence of a central administering body.

Instead, developers should use the name-binding technique to allow workstations to discover their server/service socket addresses. As a result, developers must identify their server/service by a unique name. Workstations would then use NBP to bind an address to this name (for details, see Chapter 7, "Name Binding Protocol"). Once the client process has determined the proper destination socket address, it can then proceed to transmit packets to that socket.

This technique requires that developers implement NBP in their servers. While not significant for larger servers, implementation of NBP could pose a problem for smaller, memory-bound devices. Thus, NBP has been designed so that only a subset is required for such memory-bound servers. The NBP subset simply responds to *lookup* packets received over the network. Since the names table of such a server will contain only a single name, the NBP subset need not implement functions such as names table management.

Network number equivalence

The use of network number 0 to indicate unknown introduces some complexity for DDP clients. A DDP client may want to compare two network numbers to determine if they are equivalent. For example, if a request is sent to a node on network 7 and a response is received from a node on network 0, a question arises as to whether the response received was from the same network to which the request was sent. Therefore, it must be clearly defined when two network numbers match (in other words, when they are equivalent). The rule to use is "zero matches anything." As a result, network A is equivalent to network B if A=B or A=0 or B=0. All DDP clients must use this definition of network equivalence.

Chapter 5 **Routing Table Maintenance Protocol**

CONTENTS

■

THE ROUTING TABLE MAINTENANCE PROTOCOL
(RTMP) is used by internet routers (IRs) to establish and maintain the
routing tables that are central to the process of forwarding datagrams
from any source socket to any destination socket on an internet. Chapter 4,
"Datagram Delivery Protocol," introduced the concept of IRs as the devices
by which datagrams are forwarded/routed from any source socket to any
destination socket on the internet.

This chapter describes RTMP and includes information about

- routers and routing tables

- RTMP packets

- RTMP algorithms ■

Internet routers

IRs are the key components in extending the datagram delivery mechanism to an internet setting. *Figure 5-1* shows three basic ways that routers can be used to build an internet. Note that a single router can incorporate all three configurations.

Local routers

A router used to interconnect AppleTalk networks in close proximity is referred to as a **local router** and is shown in Configuration A of *Figure 5-1*. Local routers are connected directly to each of the AppleTalk networks they serve. Local routers are useful in allowing the construction of an AppleTalk internet with a large number of nodes within the same building.

Half routers

Configuration B of *Figure 5-1* shows the use of two routers interconnected by a long-distance communication link. Each router is directly connected to an AppleTalk network. The combination of the two routers and the intervening link serves as a routing unit between the AppleTalk networks. Each router in this unit is referred to as a **half router.** The primary use of half routers is to interconnect remote AppleTalk systems. The intervening link can be made up of several devices (such as modems) and other networks (such as public data networks). Note that the *throughput* of half routers is generally lower than that of local routers, due to the generally slower communication link. Also, these communication links are often less reliable than the local networks of the internet.

Backbone routers

Backbone routers are used to interconnect several AppleTalk networks through a **backbone network** (a non-AppleTalk network). Although these routers might be placed in the local or half router category, they present an important set of properties. Each router could be a local router connected on one side to an AppleTalk network and on the other side to the backbone network. Backbone routers are shown in Configuration C of *Figure 5-1*. Another way of connecting a backbone router to the backbone network might be through a long-distance communication link. Typically, the backbone network either has a much higher capacity than the networks it helps interconnect or is a wide-area network such as a public packet-switched datagram network.

■ **Figure 5-1** Router configurations

Configuration A

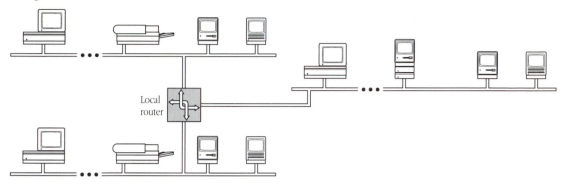

Configuration B

Configuration C

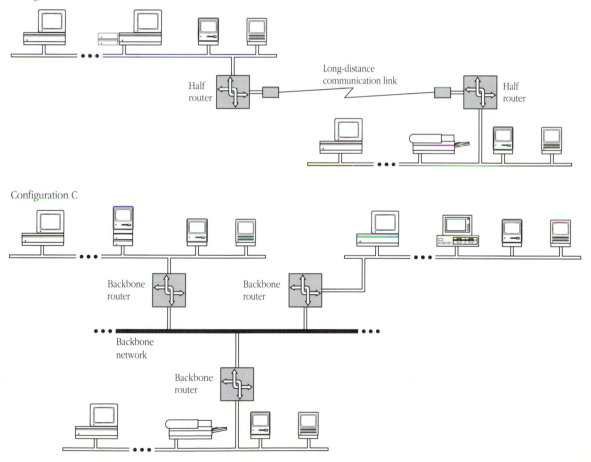

Router model

Figure 5-2 models a router as a device with several hardware ports, referred to as router ports. A router can be connected in any of the three ways previously described (local router to an AppleTalk network, half router to a communication link, or backbone router to a backbone network) or as a combination of all three. In this model, a router can have any number of ports, starting with number 1.

Each router port has associated with it a port descriptor. A **port descriptor** consists of the following four fields:

- a flag indicating whether the port is connected to an AppleTalk network

- the port number

- the port node address (the router's network number and node ID corresponding to the port)

- the port network number range (the network number range for the network to which the port is connected)

- **Figure 5-2** Router model

Router

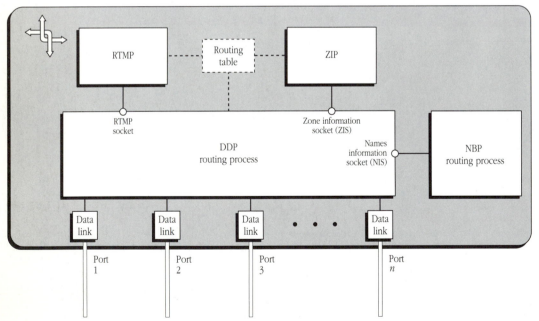

The values of these four fields are self-evident for a port that is directly connected to an AppleTalk network. When a port is connected to one end of a communication link (half router case), the port node address and port network number range are meaningless. When a port is connected to a non-AppleTalk backbone network, the port network number range is meaningless, and the port node address becomes the appropriate address of the router on the backbone network. In this latter case, a provision must be made in the design of the port description for this field to be of any size (possibly variable length) depending on the nature of the backbone network.

◆ *Note:* The AppleTalk node address of a local router is different for each of the router's ports. In other words, for each AppleTalk network to which the local router is directly connected, the router acquires a different network number and node ID.

The router internals include an associated data-link process for each port, a Datagram Delivery Protocol (DDP) routing process, the routing table, and the RTMP process implemented on a statically assigned socket (SAS) known as the RTMP socket (socket number equal to 1). The IR accepts incoming datagrams from the data links and then reroutes them through the appropriate port depending on their destination network number. (The IR makes the routing decision by consulting the routing table.) The RTMP process receives RTMP packets from other routers through the RTMP socket and uses these packets to maintain/update the routing table.

Routers additionally include a Name Binding Protocol (NBP) routing process and a Zone Information Protocol (ZIP) process; the roles of these protocols are discussed in Chapters 7 and 8.

Internet topologies

RTMP allows internets to consist of AppleTalk networks interconnected through routers in any arbitrary topology. A limitation imposed on an AppleTalk internet is that for each router no two of its ports can be on the same network. In addition, nodes on a network that is more than 16 *hops* away (by way of the shortest path) from another network will not be able to communicate with nodes on the second network.

Routing tables

All routers maintain complete routing tables that allow them to determine how to forward a datagram on the basis of its destination network number. RTMP allows routers to exchange their routing tables periodically. In this process, a router receiving the routing table of another router compares and updates its own table to record the shortest path for each destination network. This exchange process allows the routers to respond to changes in the connectivity of the internet (for example, when a router goes down or when a new router is installed).

A routing table that has stabilized to all changes consists of one entry for each network that can be reached in the internet. Each entry provides the number of the port through which packets for that network must be forwarded by the router, the node address of the next IR to which the packet must be sent (network number and node ID for IRs on AppleTalk networks), and the distance to the destination network. The entry in the routing table corresponds to the shortest path known to that router for the corresponding destination network.

The distance to a network is measured in terms of hops, with each hop representing one IR that the packet traverses in its path from the current router to the destination network. This simple measure of distance is adequate for an RTMP that adapts to changes in the connectivity of the network. The distance corresponding to a network to which the router is directly connected is always 0.

◆ *Note:* Other distance measures could reflect the speeds/capacities of the intervening links and therefore try to find the minimum time path. Another method might use current traffic conditions on a particular path to modify the path's contribution to distance. The hop-count measure is selected here for its simplicity. The basic algorithm remains unchanged when more complex measures are used.

Each routing table entry has an entry state associated with it. An **entry state** can take on one of three values: good, suspect, or bad. The significance of the entry state is explained in "Routing Table Maintenance" later in this chapter.

Figure 5-3 shows a typical routing table for a router with three ports in an internet consisting of seven networks. The figure also shows the corresponding port descriptors.

■ Figure 5-3 Example of a routing table

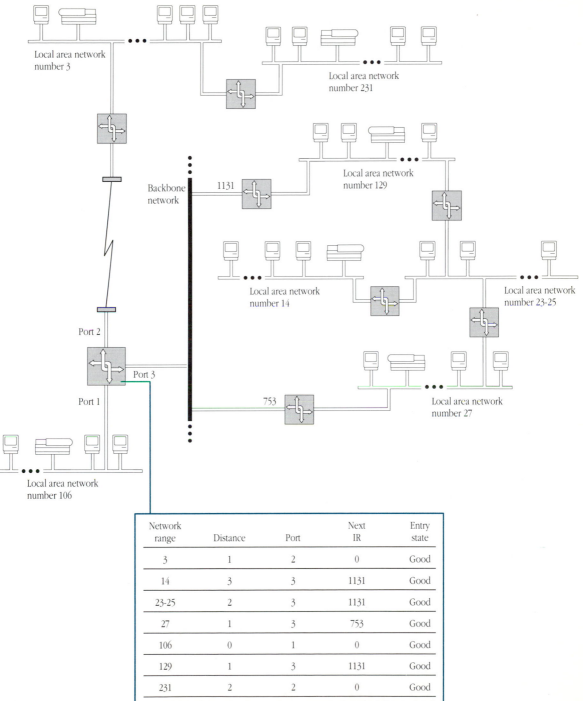

Network range	Distance	Port	Next IR	Entry state
3	1	2	0	Good
14	3	3	1131	Good
23-25	2	3	1131	Good
27	1	3	753	Good
106	0	1	0	Good
129	1	3	1131	Good
231	2	2	0	Good

Routing table maintenance

Routers have no record of the topology or connectivity of the internet. Consequently, RTMP must provide the mechanism for constructing routing tables and for maintaining these tables in the face of routers appearing or disappearing in the internet.

When a router is switched on, it initializes its table by examining the port descriptor of each of its ports. Any AppleTalk port with a nonzero network number range signals that the router is directly connected to that network. In this case, an entry is created in the table for that network number range, with a distance of 0 and with the number of the port. This initial table is called the **routing seed** of the router.

Every router must periodically broadcast one or more RTMP Data packets through each of its ports. The RTMP Data packets are addressed as datagrams to the RTMP socket. Therefore, every router periodically receives RTMP Data packets from all other routers on its directly connected networks, backbones, or communication links. The RTMP Data packets carry the node address of the router port through which the RTMP Data packet was sent, as well as the <network range, distance> pairs (called **routing tuples**) of the entries in the routing table of the sending router. Using these RTMP Data packets, the receiving node's RTMP adds to or modifies its own routing table.

The basic idea is that if an RTMP Data packet received by a router contains a routing tuple for a network not in the router's table, then an entry is added for that network number with a distance equal to the tuple's distance plus 1. In effect, the RTMP Data packet indicates that a route exists to that network through the packet's sender.

Similarly, if an RTMP Data packet indicates a shorter path to a particular network than the one currently in the router's routing table (if the packet's tuple distance plus 1 is less than the table entry's current distance), then the corresponding entry must be modified to indicate that the RTMP packet's sender is the next IR for that network. Even if the paths are of equal length, the entry is modified and routing information remains as up to date as possible. This process allows for the growth and adaptation of routing tables due to the addition of new routes and routers.

Reducing RTMP packet size

The periodic broadcasting of the routing table on each of a router's directly connected data links is fundamental to the routing table maintenance process. Although this broadcasting ensures consistency of the internet's routing tables, it poses some practical problems. In the case of slow data links, such as those used between half routers, the traffic generated by this process can consume a major portion of the available channel bandwidth. This problem is also observed on networks, such as backbones, to which a large number of routers are connected. The overhead is even more notable when the internet has a large number of networks and hence large routing tables.

To address these problems, a technique known as *split horizon* is used by RTMP to significantly reduce the size of RTMP Data packets broadcasted by routers. Referring to *Figure 5-4*, it can be seen that it is never useful for a router B to tell router A that it can get to network n when the path used by B would be to go through A itself (A would just ignore this tuple anyway). Likewise, it is not useful for B to give any other neighbor routers (C,D) this information either. Thus, especially on a backbone, most of the routing table need not be sent at all.

To implement split horizon, routers do not send the entire routing table out each of their ports. Instead, the routers only send those routing tuples that may be used by routers on the network connected to that port. Specifically, all entries whose forwarding port in the routing table is equal to the port out which the entry is being sent are omitted from the RTMP Data packet.

In addition to split horizon, a more economical extension to RTMP could be designed to communicate just the changes to a routing table. Such changes to RTMP have not yet been formulated by Apple Computer.

■ **Figure 5-4** Split horizon example

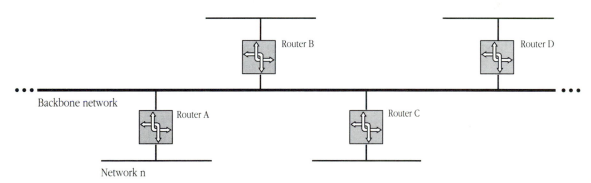

Aging of routing table entries

If routers go down or are switched off, the corresponding changes in status will not be discovered through the previously mentioned process. To respond to such changes, the entries in the routing tables must be aged. *Aging* is the process by which unconfirmed routing table entries are eventually removed from the routing table. In the absence of confirmation through reception of RTMP Data packets, entries are declared suspect and, later, bad. Bad entries are eventually purged from the routing tables.

Each entry in the routing table corresponding to a network to which the router is not directly connected is the result of an RTMP Data packet that was received by the router from the next IR for that network. RTMP considers such an entry to be valid for a limited time only, called the entry validity time. Before starting the validity timer, the router goes through its routing table and changes the state of every good entry to suspect. An entry must be revalidated from a new RTMP Data packet before the timer expires.

If the next IR for a particular entry in a router's routing table goes down, that IR will not send RTMP Data packets. The validity timer will expire, and the router will not have received confirmation of the entry. At that time, the entry's state is changed from suspect to bad. Any other RTMP Data packet received with path information to the network of the entry can be used to replace the entry with the new values from that packet. If no new route is discovered, however, the bad entry will be deleted when the validity timer expires twice more.

This aging process would be sufficient to eventually remove information about a network that can no longer be reached from the routing tables of all routers. The routers that were closest to that network would age the entry out of their routing tables, then routers next to those routers would age the entry, and so on. However to speed up this process (and aid in the more speedy adoption of alternate routes), a technique referred to as *notify neighbor* is used by RTMP. The notify neighbor technique is a method of identifying entries whose state is bad when sending RTMP Data packets. Bad entries are identified in RTMP Data packets by a tuple distance of 31. Routers receiving such a tuple can automatically set the state for that entry to bad and then notify neighboring routers using the same technique the next time they send out RTMP data packets. A tuple identifying a bad entry should only be processed by the receiving router if the router sending the tuple was the one set as the next IR for the network in the tuple (otherwise there is an alternate route to that network). In addition, tuples identifying bad entries should not be sent if they would normally be eliminated by split horizon processing.

Routing table entries whose state is bad are eliminated from the routing table following two further expirations of the validity timer. Until that time, notify neighbor tuples should be sent in RTMP Data packets for those entries.

For a detailed specification of the aging process, see "RTMP Table Initialization and Maintenance Algorithms" later in this chapter.

Validity and send-RTMP timers

Each router has a timer known as the send-RTMP timer. Every time this timer expires, the router broadcasts, through each of its ports, its routing table in the form of RTMP Data packets.

The values for the validity and send-RTMP timers have a significant effect on both the network traffic and on the propagation of routing table adaptations to changes in the internet's connectivity. The exact values of these parameters have been determined through experimentation with actual internets. These values are 10 seconds for the send-RTMP timer and 20 seconds for the validity timer.

RTMP Data packet format

RTMP uses four kinds of packets: RTMP Data, Request, Route Data Request, and Response packets. The routing table maintenance process, discussed in the foregoing, makes use of RTMP Data packets. RTMP Request and Response packets are discussed in "RTMP and Nonrouter Nodes" and "Route Data Requests" later in this chapter.

The format of an RTMP Data packet is shown in *Figure 5-5*. The DDP type field is set to 1 to indicate that the datagram is an RTMP Data packet. The DDP data part of the packet consists of four parts: the sender's network number, the sender's node ID, a version number indicator, and the routing tuples.

 **Figure 5-5** RTMP Data packet formats

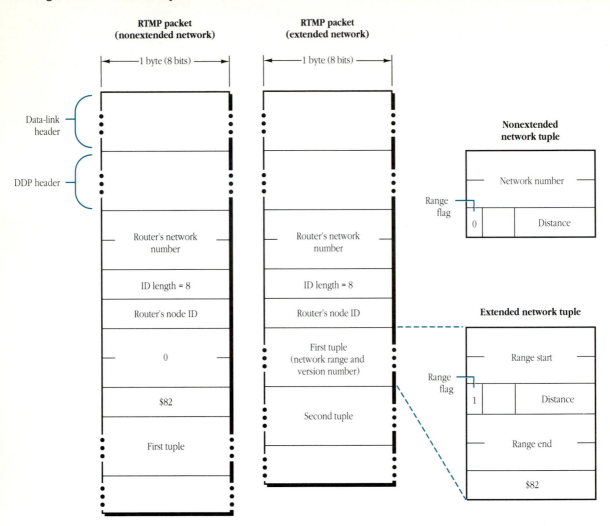

Sender's network number

The first 2 bytes of the RTMP Data packet's DDP data is the router's network number part of the node address of the port through which the packet is sent by the router. On a nonextended network, this field allows the receiver of the packet to determine the network number of the network through which the packet was received. (This is the network to which the corresponding port of the receiver is attached.) RTMP Data packets sent out through ports that are not on AppleTalk networks (for example, over serial lines or a backbone network) should have this field set to 0.

Sender's node ID

The bytes following the sender's network number indicate the node ID of the sender (for the port through which the packet was sent). To allow for ports connected to networks other than AppleTalk networks, this field must be of variable size. The first byte of the field contains the length (in bits) of the sender node's address, with the address itself in subsequent bytes. If the length of the node address in bits is not an exact multiple of 8, the address is prefixed with enough 0s to make a complete number of bytes. The bytes of this modified address are then packed into the sender's ID field of the packet, starting with the most-significant bits. It is from this field that the receiver of the packet determines the ID of the router sending the packet.) On an AppleTalk network this ID is combined with the sender's network number to specify the sender's complete node address.

Version number indicator

Following the sender's node ID, in RTMP Data packets sent on non-extended networks, is a three byte field indicating the version number of the RTMP Data packet. The value of this field is currently $000082. The version number of an RTMP Data packet sent on an extended network is specified in the first tuple, as detailed in the next section.

Routing tuples

The last part of the RTMP Data packet consists of the routing tuples from the sending router's routing table.

There are two types of routing tuples. For tuples specifying information about nonextended networks, tuples are of the form <network number, distance>. The network number is two bytes and the distance is one byte. For tuples specifying information about extended networks, tuples are of the form <network number range start, distance, network number range end, unused byte>. This form is used even for extended networks with ranges of one (for example, 3-3). The network number range start and end are two bytes each. An extended tuple is differentiated from a nonextended tuple by having the high bit of its distance field set. The unused byte in extended tuples is set to the value $82.

The first tuple in RTMP Data packets sent on extended networks serves three purposes. First, this tuple indicates the network number range assigned to that network. Second, the tuple's sixth byte, set to $82, indicates the version of RTMP being used. Third, the tuple serves as the first tuple in the packet. It may, however, also be repeated later in the packet.

For internets with a large number of networks, the entire routing table may not fit in a single datagram. In that case, the tuples are distributed over as many RTMP Data packets as necessary. Tuples are never split across packets. In any event, every time the send-RTMP timer expires, these multiple RTMP Data packets must be transmitted through each router port.

Assignment of network number ranges

Network number ranges are set into the port descriptors of the router ports and are then transmitted through RTMP to the other nodes of each network.

Not all routers on a particular network must have the network number range set into their corresponding port descriptors. At least one router (called the **seed router**) on a network must have the network number range built into its port descriptor. The other routers could have a port network number range of 0; they will acquire the correct network number range by receiving RTMP Data packets sent out by the seed router.

It is a requirement that the routers on a particular network not have in their port descriptors conflicting port network number ranges for that network. The value 0 does not cause a conflict, but otherwise, all seed routers must have the same value for both the start and end of the network number range.

If a router is not a seed router for a particular port and has not yet discovered the network number range associated with that port, it should not send its routing table through that port. In addition, it should not have an entry in its routing table for that particular port until it acquires the port's network number range. However, any IR that is not a seed router must operate with regard to those ports whose network number ranges it does know.

RTMP and nonrouter nodes

Nonrouter nodes do not need to maintain routing tables. As noted in Chapter 4, "Datagram Delivery Protocol," these nodes require only the network number range of the network to which they are connected (THIS-NET or THIS-NET-RANGE) and the network number and node ID of any router on that network (A-ROUTER). Details of the discovery and maintenance of this information depend upon whether the node resides on an extended or nonextended network.

Nodes on nonextended networks

When a node is initialized on a nonextended network, the values of both THIS-NET and A-ROUTER are 0 (unknown). The node can discover the correct values of these two quantities in one of two ways.

The first method is to listen for RTMP Data packets that are being sent out by the routers on the network for the purpose of maintaining their routing tables. Any node relying on this passive listening approach should be sure to wait long enough to receive an RTMP Data packet.

A second, more active approach relies on the use of RTMP Request and Response packets, as shown in *Figure 5-6*. The node makes a request for the network number and any router's node ID by broadcasting an RTMP Request packet. This packet is a datagram with DDP type equal to 5; it can be sent by the node through any socket. The datagram is addressed to destination socket number 1 (the RTMP listening socket). When an RTMP Request packet is received by a router's RTMP process, this process responds by sending an RTMP Response packet to the source socket of the Request packet. This Response packet is identical to a normal RTMP Data packet except that it contains no routing tuples and it is sent as a directed (not a broadcast) packet to the requesting node. The requesting node thus acquires the values of THIS-NET and A-ROUTER from the sender's network number and sender's node ID fields of the Response packet.

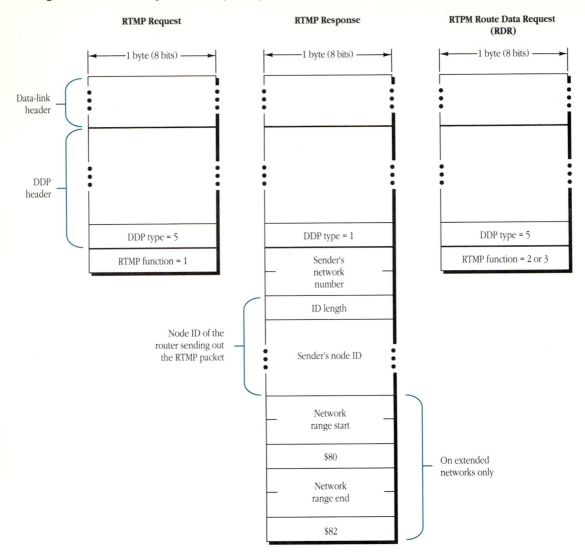

In either approach, nonrouter nodes implement a simple RTMP process, known as the RTMP Stub. This process sits on the RTMP listening socket in that node and, upon receiving an RTMP Data or Response packet, copies the sender's network number and sender's node ID fields into THIS-NET and A-ROUTER. Therefore, THIS-NET and A-ROUTER are set every time an RTMP Data or Response packet is received. While THIS-NET will stabilize to a constant value, A-ROUTER may change continually (if there is more than one router on the network).

Additionally, nonrouter nodes must maintain a background timer for the purpose of aging the value of A-ROUTER. The purpose of this background timer is to handle the case in which all the routers connected to a specific network go down and the network becomes isolated. The value of this timer should be approximately 50 seconds. Each time an RTMP Data packet is received, the timer is reset. If the timer expires, A-ROUTER should be aged, meaning that A-ROUTER should be reset to 0. THIS-NET, however, should not be reset.

◆ *Note:* The RTMP Stub should differentiate between RTMP Data or Response packets (sent by routers) and RTMP Requests (broadcast by nonrouter nodes). The RTMP Stub should ignore RTMP Requests. RTMP Requests can be differentiated from RTMP Data or Response packets because RTMP Requests have a DDP type of 5, whereas RTMP Data and Response packets have a DDP type of 1.

Nodes on extended networks

When a node is initialized on an extended network, THIS-NET-RANGE is set to 0-$FFFE and the network number and node ID of A-ROUTER are both set to 0. The node discovers the correct values of these two quantities and its zone name during the startup process through a ZIP GetNetInfo request, described in Chapter 8, "Zone Information Protocol."

Nodes on extended networks must also implement an RTMP Stub. If A-ROUTER is zero (either due to never being set or due to being aged), the first RTMP Data packet coming in to the RTMP Stub will indicate the presence of the first router. At this time the node can verify that its network number is within the range indicated by the router for the network (by examining the first tuple in the RTMP Data packet) and complete the parts of the startup process it could not complete at startup, setting THIS-NET-RANGE and A-ROUTER from the packet.

Once the node has acquired a value for THIS-NET-RANGE and A-ROUTER, the RTMP process, upon receiving an RTMP Data packet, first verifies that the range specified for the sender's network (in the first tuple) precisely matches the node's value of THIS-NET-RANGE. If the ranges do not match, the packet is rejected and the router aging timer not reset. Otherwise, the sender's network number and node ID are copied into A-ROUTER and the aging timer reset.

If the aging timer expires: A-ROUTER is set to 0, THIS-NET-RANGE is set to 0-$FFFE, and the zone name is aged. The RTMP stub reverts to its initial state.

◆ *Note:* Nodes on extended networks do not generally make RTMP Requests during the startup process. Routers on extended networks must still respond to these requests. RTMP Responses on extended networks should include the first routing tuple, which specifies the network number range.

RTMP Route Data Requests

RTMP Data packets are generally broadcast once every 10 seconds. A node wishing to receive, in a directed manner, an RTMP Data packet can use an RTMP Route Data Request (RDR) packet to obtain this information. This packet has the same format as an RTMP Request packet, except it has a function code of either 2 or 3 (see *Figure 5-6*). A function code of 2 indicates that the router should perform split horizon processing before returning the response; a function code of 3 indicates that the router should not perform split horizon processing (should return the whole table).

A router receiving an RDR packet should send the requested information, in as many RTMP Data packets as required, back to the source internet socket address of the RDR packet. RDRs can be used by a node wishing to have routing information sent to it on a socket other than socket 1 or to obtain routing information from a router that is not on a network to which the node is directly connected.

RTMP table initialization and maintenance algorithms

The following algorithms provide a detailed specification of the initialization and maintenance process of an active router.

Initialization

When switched on, a router performs the following table initialization algorithm:

```
FOR each port P connected to an AppleTalk network
   IF the port network number range <> 0
   THEN create a routing table entry for that network number range with
        Entry's network number range := port network number range;
        Entry's distance := 0;
        Entry's next IR := 0;
        Entry's state := Good;
        Entry's port := P;
```

This algorithm creates a routing table entry for each directly connected AppleTalk network for which the router is a seed router.

Additionally, for each port with a nonzero network number range, the router should attempt to verify that the port's network number range does not conflict with that from another router on the same network. This can be done, for instance, by broadcasting an RTMP Request or ZIP GetNetInfo packet. If a conflict is discovered, the routing seed information should not be used.

Maintenance

The router is assumed to have two timers running continuously: the validity timer and the send-RTMP timer. The router's RTMP process responds to the following events:

- the receipt of an RTMP Data packet
- the receipt of an RTMP Request or RTMP Route Data Request packet
- the expiration of the validity timer
- the expiration of the send-RTMP timer

The following algorithms correspond to these events.

RTMP Data packet received through port P

```
IF P is connected to an AppleTalk network AND P's network number range = 0
THEN BEGIN
    P's network number range := packet's sender network number range;
    IF there is an entry for this network number range
    THEN delete it;
    Create a new entry for this network number range with
        Entry's network number range := packet's sender network number range;
        Entry's distance := 0;
        Entry's next IR := 0;
        Entry's state := Good;
        Entry's port := P;
    END;
FOR each routing tuple in the RTMP Data packet DO
    IF there is a table entry corresponding* to the tuple's network number range
        THEN Update-the-Entry
    ELSE IF there is a table entry overlapping* with the tuple's network number range
        THEN ignore the tuple
    ELSE Create-New-Entry;
```

* See the section, "Tuple Matching Definitions," for definitions of *corresponding* and *overlapping*.

The following three general-purpose routines (Update-the-Entry, Create-New-Entry, and Replace-Entry) are used by this algorithm.

Update-the-Entry

```
IF (Entry's state = Bad) AND (tuple distance < 15)
THEN Replace-Entry
ELSE
    IF Entry's distance >= (tuple distance + 1) AND (tuple distance < 15)
    THEN Replace-Entry
    ELSE IF Entry's next IR = RTMP Data packet's sender node address
            AND Entry's port = P
      { If entry says we're forwarding to the IR who sent us this
        packet, the net's now further away than we thought }
      THEN IF tuple distance <> 31 THEN BEGIN
          Entry's distance := tuple distance + 1;
          IF Entry's distance < 16
          THEN Entry's state := Good
          ELSE Delete the entry
      END
      ELSE Entry's state := Bad;
```

Create-New-Entry

```
Entry's network number range := tuple's network number range;
Replace-Entry;
IF tuple's distance = 31 THEN Entry's state := Bad;
```

Replace-Entry

```
Entry's distance := tuple's distance + 1;
Entry's next IR := RTMP Data packet's node address   { network number and node ID
                                                       on an AppleTalk network }
Entry's port number := P;
Entry's state := Good;
```

RTMP Request packet received through port P

```
IF P is connected to an AppleTalk network and P's network number range <> 0
THEN BEGIN { Prepare an RTMP Response packet }
   Response packet's sender network number := P's port network number;
   Response packet's sender node ID := P's port node ID;
   IF P is connected to an extended network
      THEN Response Packet's first tuple := P's network number range
   Call DDP to send the Response packet through port P to the
         Request's source;
END;
```

Validity timer expires

```
FOR each entry in the routing table DO
   CASE Entry's state OF
      Good: IF entry's distance <> 0
            THEN Entry's state := Suspect;
      Suspect: Entry's state := Bad_0;
      Bad_0: Entry's state:= Bad_1;
      Bad_1: Delete the entry
   END;
```

Send-RTMP packet timer expires

```
IF routing table is not empty
 THEN FOR each router port P DO
    IF the port is connected to an AppleTalk network AND its network number
          range is nonzero
    THEN BEGIN
       Copy-in-tuples;
       Packet's sender network number := port network number;
       Packet's sender node ID := port node ID;
       Call DDP to broadcast the packet to the RTMP socket;
    END

    ELSE IF the port is not connected to an AppleTalk network
        THEN BEGIN
           Copy-in-tuples;
           Packet's sender network number := 0;
           Packet's sender node ID := port node ID;
           Call DDP to broadcast the packet through the port's data link
                to the RTMP socket;
        END;
```

Copy-in-tuples

```
For each entry in the routing table
   IF the entry's port <> P  {split horizon}
      THEN IF the entry's state <> Bad
         THEN copy the entry's network number range and distance
              pair into the tuple (as long as the distance is <15)
         ELSE copy the entry's network number range and distance
              of 31 into the tuple  {Notify Neighbor}
```

Tuple matching definitions

For purposes of routing table maintenence, it is important to define when an incoming RTMP tuple corresponds to and overlaps with an entry in the routing table. An incoming tuple corresponds to an entry in the routing table if the range start and range end of that tuple are the same as the range start and range end of the routing table entry. When comparing ranges where one of the ranges is for a nonextended network (in other words, indicated by just a single network number, like 3), that range should be considered a range of one (that is 3-3).

   An incoming tuple overlaps with an entry in the routing table if any network number in either range is in both ranges. A correctly maintained routing table will contain no overlapping entries.

RTMP routing algorithm

The routing algorithm used by the DDP router in an internet router to forward internet datagrams is shown in *Figure 5-7*. This algorithm applies only to the forwarding of packets received by the router through one of its ports and does not hold for packets generated within the router. The algorithm assumes that when a packet is received through one of the router ports, it is tagged with the number of the port and placed in a queue. The IR removes packets from this queue and then executes the algorithm of *Figure 5-7*. Remember when comparing network numbers that a destination network number of 0 will always match whatever it is being compared to.

■ **Figure 5-7** Datagram routing algorithm for a router

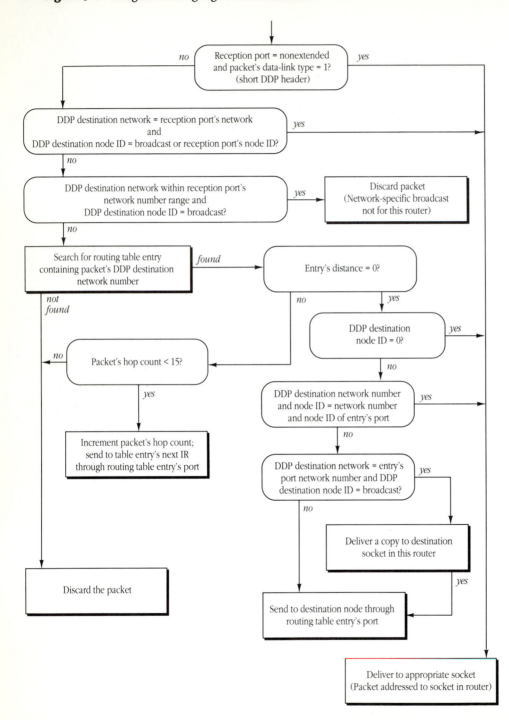

Chapter 6 **AppleTalk Echo Protocol**

THE APPLETALK ECHO PROTOCOL (AEP) is implemented in each node as a process on a statically assigned socket (socket number 4, known as the Echoer socket). The Echoer listens for packets received through this socket. Whenever a packet is received, the Echoer examines its Datagram Delivery Protocol (DDP) type and the DDP data length in the packet to determine if the packet is an AEP packet. If it is, then a copy of the packet is returned to the sender. ■

Figure 6-1 shows the format of an AEP packet. If the DDP type field in a packet is not equal to 4 (the DDP type for AEP) or if the DDP data length is 0, then the Echoer discards the packet and ignores it. However, if the packet has a DDP type equal to 4 and the DDP data length is not 0, then the Echoer examines the AEP header (the first byte of the DDP data). If the first byte, known as the Echo function field, is equal to 1, then the packet is an Echo Request packet. In this case, the Echoer changes the function field to 2, which indicates that the packet is an Echo Reply packet, and the Echoer calls DDP to send the packet back to the sender of the Echo Request packet.

■ **Figure 6-1** AEP packet format

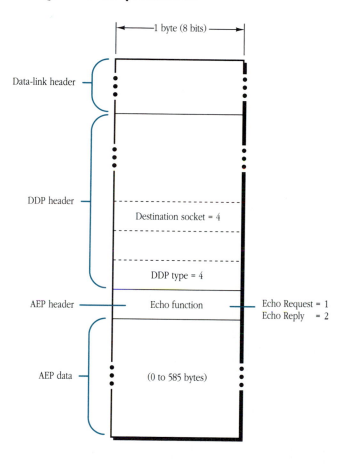

When using AEP services, the client must first determine the internet address of the node from which an echo is being sought (the client process usually uses the Name Binding Protocol (NBP) for this purpose). The client then calls DDP to send an Echo Request packet to the Echoer socket (socket number 4) in that node. The client can send the Echo Request datagram through any socket the client has open, and the Echo Reply will come back to this socket. The client then waits for the receipt of the Echo Reply packet.

◆ *Note:* The client can set the AEP data part of the Echo Request packet to any pattern and then examine the data in the Echo Reply packet (which will be the data sent in the Request packet). The client can use the data in the Reply packet to distinguish between the replies to various Echo Request packets the client has sent.

The client may fail to receive an Echo Reply under the following conditions:

■ The AEP packets are lost in the network system.

■ The target node does not have an Echoer.

■ The target node is currently unreachable or has gone down.

The client should determine how long to wait for the Echo Reply packet before concluding that one of these conditions exists. The client could retransmit the Echo Request packet several times before concluding that the remote node will not respond.

AEP can be used

■ by any DDP client to determine whether a particular node, known to have an Echoer, is accessible over an internet

■ to obtain an estimate of the round-trip time for a typical packet to reach a particular remote node, usually a server (This time estimate is extremely useful in developing certain heuristic methods, for example those used for estimating the timeouts to be specified by clients of the AppleTalk Transaction Protocol (ATP), the AppleTalk Session Protocol (ASP), and other higher-level protocols.)

Part III **Named Entities**

PART III DISCUSSES in detail the Name Binding Protocol (NBP) and the Zone Information Protocol (ZIP).

Part I and Part II described protocols by which AppleTalk conveys packets from one network entity to any other entity on that network or an AppleTalk internet. These protocols use numerical addresses to identify a packet's source and destination entity. From these addresses AppleTalk determines the route the packet uses on its path through the internet.

Although addresses are efficient for internal use, network users prefer names. Names are character strings that can more naturally convey semantic and contextual information to the user. Part III describes the protocols by which names can be converted to addresses. ■

Chapter 7 **Name Binding Protocol**

CONTENTS

■

APPLETALK PROTOCOLS RELY on numeric identifiers, such as node IDs, socket numbers, and network numbers, to provide the addressing capability essential for communication over the network. However, numbers are sometimes hard for users to memorize and are easily confused and misused. For network users, names are a more familiar form of identification. If an entity is referred to by name, the name must be converted into a network address for use by the other protocols. The Name Binding Protocol (NBP) performs the conversion of entity names into addresses.

An AppleTalk network uses dynamic node address assignment; therefore, addresses can change from time to time and cannot be configured into software to gain access to network resources. Name binding provides a way of translating names, which change infrequently, into addresses, which change frequently (see "Sockets and Use of Name Binding" in Chapter 4, "Datagram Delivery Protocol").

This chapter describes NBP and includes information about

■ network-visible entities and entity names

■ name binding protocol services on a single network and on an internet ■

Network-visible entities

A network-visible entity (NVE) is any entity that is accessible over an AppleTalk network system through the Datagram Delivery Protocol (DDP). Thus, the socket clients on an internet are its NVEs.

The nodes of the internet are not NVEs; rather, any services in the nodes available for access over the network system are NVEs. For example, a network print server itself is not the NVE. The print service will typically be a socket client on what might be called the server's request listening socket. The request listening socket is the server's NVE.

The same distinction applies to the users of the network system. They themselves are not network-visible. But a user can have an electronic mailbox on a mail server. This mailbox is network-visible and will have a network address. Although the network does not provide any protocols for conversing directly with the individual user, the protocols communicate with applications and services to which the user can gain access.

Entity names

An NVE can assign itself a name, called an entity name, although not all NVEs need to have names. Entity names are character strings. A particular entity could, in fact, possess several names (aliases).

An **entity name** is a character string consisting of three fields—object, type, and zone—in this order with colon (:) and at-sign (@) separators (for example, Judy:Mailbox@Bandley3). Each field is a string of a maximum of 32 characters.

In addition to a name, an entity can also have certain attributes. For example, a print server's request receiver might have associated with it a list of the printer's attributes such as its type (daisy wheel, dot matrix, laser) and the kind of paper the printer holds. These attributes are specified in a part of the entity name called the **entity type.**

In addition to attributes, some location information about the entity can prove useful for users. For example, a print server might belong to a particular department or building. Users of the network should be able to select a print server on the basis of some appropriate information such as its convenient location. As a result, a zone field has been included in the entity name.

In the entity name, certain special characters can be used in place of strings. For the object and type fields, an equal sign (=) wildcard can be substituted, signifying all possible values. A single approximately equal sign (≈) can also be used to match zero or more characters anywhere within an object or type string. For the zone field, an asterisk (*) can be substituted signifying the default value (that is, the zone in which the node specifying the name resides).

If a network name does not contain special characters, the name is said to be fully specified. For example, Mona:Mailbox@Bandley3 is fully specified. The network name =:Mailbox@* refers to all mailboxes in the same zone as the information requester. The network name =:=@* means all named entities of all types in the requester's zone. Mona:=@*refers to all entities named Mona in the requester's zone regardless of their type. ≈Mona:=@* refers to all entities in the requestor's zone with a name that ends with Mona (e.g. Molly Mona).

Entity names by definition are case-insensitive. Thus, Mona:Mailbox@Bandley3 is considered the same as Mona:mailbox:bandley3 and MONA:MAILBOX:BANDLEY3. For characters in the standard ASCII character set, it is fairly clear what this means: A ($41) is the same as a ($61), B is the same as b, and so forth through Z and z. But the string MAGAÑA should also be considered the same as the string Magaña. ASCII definitions for non-English characters are not standardized. See Appendix D for a complete description of the diacritical matching used in AppleTalk.

◆ *Note:* The character $FF is reserved as the first byte of an NBP object, type, or zone string. This character is reserved to provide flexibility in future development.

Name binding

Before a named entity can be accessed over an AppleTalk network or internet, the address of that entity must be obtained through a process known as name binding.

Name binding can be visualized as a mapping of an entity name into its internet socket address or, equivalently, as a lookup of the address in a large database. For the case of a single nonextended network, the network number field of the internet socket address will always be equal to 0 (unknown).

Name binding can be done at various times. One strategy is to configure the address of the named entity into the system trying to gain access to that entity. This strategy, static binding, is not appropriate for systems such as AppleTalk in which the node ID can change every time a node is activated on the network.

Although entities can move on a network, their names seldom change. For this reason, it is preferable to use names in identifying entities. Services, such as NBP, can then be used to bind names dynamically to internet addresses. This binding can be done when the user's node is first brought up (known as early binding) or just before access to the named entity is obtained (known as late binding). Early binding may result in the use of out-of-date information when the resource is accessed, possibly long after the user's node was brought up. However, since the binding process adds further delay, late binding could slow down the user's initial access to the named entity. Late binding is the appropriate method to use when the entity is expected to move on the internet.

Names directory and names tables

Each node maintains a **names table** containing name-to-entity internet address mappings (known as NBP name-address tuples) of all entities in *that* node. The **names directory** (ND) is a distributed database of name-to-address mappings; it is the union of the individual names tables in the nodes of the internet. The database does not require different portions to be duplicated. The database can be distributed among all nodes containing named NVEs.

Name binding is accomplished by using NBP to look up the entity's address in the names directory. NBP does not require the use of name servers. However, its design allows the use of name servers if they are available.

Aliases and enumerators

NBP allows an NVE to have more than one name. Each of these aliases must be included in the names table as an independent entity.

To simplify and speed up the ability to distinguish between multiple names associated with a particular socket, an enumerator value is associated with each names table entry. The **enumerator value** is a 1-byte integer, invisible to the clients of NBP. Each NBP implementation can develop its own scheme for generating enumerator values to be included in the names table. The scheme developed requires that no two entries corresponding to the same socket have the same enumerator value.

Names information socket

Each node implements an NBP process on a statically assigned socket (socket number 2) known as the **names information socket** (NIS). This process is responsible for maintaining the node's names table and for accepting and servicing requests to look up names from within the node and from the network.

Name binding services

The name binding protocol provides four basic services:

- name registration
- name deletion
- name lookup
- name confirmation

These services are described in the following sections.

Name registration

Any entity can enter its name and socket number into its node's names table to make itself *visible by name* by using the name registration call to the node's NBP process.

The node's NBP process must first verify that the name is not already in use by looking up the name in the node's zone. If the name is already in use, the registration attempt is aborted. Otherwise, the name and the corresponding socket number are inserted into the node's names table. The NBP process then enters the corresponding name-to-address mapping in the ND.

When a node starts up, its names table is empty. When restarted, each NVE must reregister its name(s) in the names table.

Name deletion

A named entity should delete its name-to-address mapping from the ND when it wants to make itself invisible. The most common reason for deleting the mapping is that the entity terminates operation.

To cause a name to be deleted, the entity issues a name deletion call to the node's NBP process. The name deletion call deletes the corresponding name-to-address mapping from the node's names table.

Name lookup

Before obtaining access to a named entity, the user (or application) must perform a binding of the entity's name to its internet socket address. *Binding* is done by issuing a name lookup call to the user node's NBP process. This process then uses NBP to perform a search through the ND for the named entity. If it is found, then the corresponding address is returned to the caller. Otherwise, an *entity not found* error condition is returned by NBP.

The name lookup operation can find more than one entity matching the name specified in the call, especially when the name includes wildcards (= and ≈). The interface to the user must have provisions for handling this case.

NBP does not allow the use of abbreviated names; for example, NBP does not permit reference to Mona:Mailbox. The complete reference Mona:Mailbox@Bandley3 or Mona:Mailbox@* must be provided. Provisions can be made in the user interface to permit abbreviations. The interface must then produce the complete name before passing it on to NBP.

Name confirmation

The name lookup call performs a zone-wide ND search. More specific confirmation is needed in certain situations. For example, if early binding was performed, the binding must be confirmed when access to the named entity has been obtained. For this purpose, NBP has a name confirmation call in which the caller provides the complete name and address of the entity. This call in effect performs a name search in the entity's node to confirm that the mapping is still valid.

Although a new name lookup can lead to the same result, the confirmation produces less network traffic. Name confirmation is the recommended and preferable call to use when confirming mappings obtained through early binding.

NBP on a single network

Name lookup is quite simple on a system consisting of a single AppleTalk network.

When a user issues a name registration (or lookup) call to the NBP process in its node, this process first examines its own names table to determine whether the name is available there. If it is, in the case of a registration attempt, the call is aborted with a *name already taken* error condition. In the case of a name lookup, the information in the names table is a partial response. (Entities in other nodes may match the specified name.)

NBP then prepares an NBP Lookup packet (LkUp packet) and calls DDP to broadcast the LkUp packet over the network for delivery to the NIS. Only nodes that have an NBP process will have the NIS open. In these nodes, the LkUp packet is delivered to the NBP process, which searches its names table for a potential match. If no match is found, the packet is ignored. If a match is found, a LkUp-Reply packet is returned to the address from which the LkUp packet was received. This LkUp-Reply packet contains the matching name-address tuples found in the replying node's names table.

The receipt of one or more replies allows the requesting NBP process to compile a list of name-to-address mappings. If the lookup was performed in response to a name registration call, then the call must be aborted since the name is already taken.

Since DDP provides only a best-effort delivery service, the requesting NBP process sends the LkUp packet several times before returning the compiled mappings to the requesting user. If no replies are received, then no entity is currently using the specified name. For a name registration call, the requested name-to-address mapping is entered into the node's names table. For a name lookup call, the user is informed of a *no such entity* result.

Sending the LkUp packet several times implies that the same name-to-address mapping could be received several times by the requesting node. These duplicates must be filtered out of the list of mappings. One way to filter the list of mappings is to compare the name strings and the address fields with each entry in the compiled list; this method, however, is inefficient. Comparison of the 4-byte address fields is insufficient because of the possibility of aliases. Using the enumerator value together with the address resolves this problem and accelerates the filtering of duplicates.

Name confirmation is similar to name lookup except that the caller provides the name-to-address mapping to be confirmed. The LkUp packet is not broadcast; it is sent directly to the NIS at the specified internet node address. This process can be repeated several times to protect against lost packets or against the target node being temporarily busy.

◆ *Note:* On a single AppleTalk network, there is only one zone, which should be considered unnamed (zone names originate in routers). Any request made by a client to perform a lookup with a zone name other than an asterisk (*) should be rejected with an error.

NBP on an internet

The use of broadcast packets to perform name lookup is impractical in internets because DDP does not allow a broadcast to all nodes in the internet. DDP can broadcast datagrams to all nodes with a single specified network number in the internet. These broadcasts are known as **directed broadcasts.** If NBP were to send a directed broadcast to every network in the internet, the traffic generated would be considerable. Furthermore, in some cases, the excessively large lists of name-address mappings compiled would be cumbersome for the user. For these reasons, the concept of zones is introduced.

Zones

A zone is an arbitrary subset of the AppleTalk nodes in an internet. A particular network can contain nodes belonging to any number of zones (although all nodes in a non-extended network must belong to the same zone). A particular node belongs to only one zone. Nodes choose their zone at startup time from a list of zones available for their network. The union of all zones is the internet. A zone is identified by a string of no more than 32 characters.

The concept of zones is provided to establish departmental or other user-understandable groupings of the entities of the internet. Zones are intelligible only to NBP and to the related Zone Information Protocol (ZIP). (See Chapter 8, "Zone Information Protocol.")

Name lookup on an internet

Internet routers (IRs) participate in the name lookup protocol of an internet. The NBP process in the requesting node prepares an NBP Broadcast Request packet (BrRq packet) and sends it to the NIS of A-ROUTER (see "RTMP and Nonrouter Nodes" in Chapter 5, "Routing Table Maintenance Protocol"). The NBP process in the router, in cooperation with the NBP processes in the other routers of the internet, arranges to convert the BrRq packet into one Forward Request (FwdReq) packet for each network that contains nodes in the target zone of the lookup request. (The exact details of this algorithm are specified in Chapter 8, "Zone Information Protocol.") Each of these FwdReq packets is then sent to the NIS in any router directly connected to the corresponding network. (These packets are addressed to DDP node address zero.) When this router receives the FwdReq, it converts the FwdReq to a LkUp packet and broadcasts it to the NIS in all nodes in the target zone on the destination network. Where possible this broadcasting is done using zone-specific multicast, described in Chapter 8, "Zone Information Protocol." The NBP replies are returned to the original requester.

Since routers on the internet are responsible for generating zone-wide broadcasts, routers must have a complete mapping of zone names to their corresponding networks. ZIP establishes and maintains these mappings, as discussed in Chapter 8, "Zone Information Protocol." Nodes that are not routers do not need to know anything about the mapping between networks and zones. Nodes only need to be able to verify that a lookup is intended for their zone or a zone name of asterisk (*). (Nodes on nonextended networks need not even do this.)

◆ *Note:* On an internet, nodes on extended networks performing lookups in their own zone must replace a zone name of asterisk (*) with their actual zone name before sending the packet to A-ROUTER. All nodes performing lookups in their own zone will receive LkUp packets from themselves (actually sent by a router). The node's NBP process should expect to receive these packets and must reply to them.

NBP interface

The following sections describe the four calls that provide the user with all the functionality of name binding:

- registering a name
- removing a name
- looking up a name
- confirming a name

◆ *Note:* All calls to NBP take an entity name as a parameter. However, the zone name is meaningful only in the lookup call. In all other calls, the zone name is required, for consistency, to be an asterisk (*).

Registering a name

This call is used by an NBP client to register an entity name and its associated socket address. Special characters are not allowed in the object and type fields; the zone name field must be equal to an asterisk (*) or its equivalent.

Call parameters   entity name

                      socket number

Returned parameters   success

                      failure: name conflict; invalid name or socket

Although this feature is not required in NBP, the implementation of the name registration call could verify that the socket is actually open.

Removing a name

This call is made to remove an entity name from the node's names table. Wildcard characters are not allowed in the object and type fields; the zone name field must be an asterisk (*).

Call parameter   entity name

Returned parameters   success

                      failure: name not found

Looking up a name

This call is used to map between an entity's name and its internet socket address. Special characters are allowed in the name to make the search as general as necessary. More than one address matching the entity name is possible. For each match, this call returns the name and its internet socket address. The names returned contain fully specified object and type fields; the zone name, however, may be returned as an asterisk (*), regardless of the zone specified.

Call parameters	entity name
	maxMatches
Returned parameters	success
	failure: name not found
	list of entity names and their corresponding internet socket addresses

The parameter maxMatches is a positive integer that specifies the maximum number of matching name-to-address mappings needed. This parameter is useful if wildcards, such as equal signs (=), are used by the caller in the entity name parameter.

◆ *Note:* All AppleTalk Phase 2 nodes must support the approximately equal sign (≈) wildcard feature. However, some nodes on LocalTalk may not have implemented this feature yet. Such nodes may not respond correctly to lookups containing this character in the object and type fields.

Confirming a name

This call confirms a caller-supplied mapping between entity name and address. Special characters are not allowed in the object and type fields of the name.

Call parameters	entity name
	socket address
Returned parameters	success: mapping still valid
	wrong-socket: net and node number valid and socket number invalid
	failure: mapping invalid
	new socket: returned only in the case of a wrong-socket error

NBP packet formats

NBP packets are identified by a DDP type field of 2. NBP packets are of four types:

- BrRq
- LkUp
- LkUp-Reply
- FwdReq

The format of NBP packets is shown in *Figure 7-1*. The packet consists of an NBP header followed by one or more name-address tuples.

 The following sections describe the NBP packet fields: function, tuple count, NBP ID, and NBP tuple.

- **Figure 7-1** NBP packet format

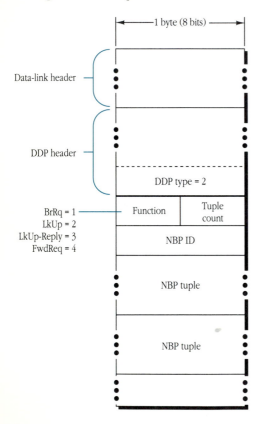

Function

The high-order 4 bits of the first byte of the NBP header are used to indicate the type of NBP packet. The values are 1 for BrRq, 2 for LkUp, 3 for LkUp-Reply, and 4 for FwdReq.

Tuple count

The low-order 4 bits of the first byte of the NBP header contain a count of the number of NBP tuples in that packet. BrRq, FwdReq, and LkUp packets carry one tuple (the name being looked up or confirmed). The tuple-count field for these packets is always equal to 1.

NBP ID

In order to allow a node to have multiple pending lookup requests, an 8-bit ID is generated by the NBP process issuing the BrRq or LkUp packets. The LkUp-Reply packets must contain the same NBP ID as the LkUp or BrRq packet to which they correspond.

NBP tuple

The format of the NBP tuples, the name-address pairs, is shown in *Figure 7-2*. The tuple consists of the entity's internet socket address, a 1-byte enumerator field, and the entity name. The address field appears first in the tuple. The fifth byte in a tuple is the enumerator field. The enumerator field is included to handle the situation in which more than one name has been registered on the same socket. The entity name consists of three string fields: one each for the object, type, and zone names. Each of these strings consists of a leading 1-byte string length followed by no more than 32 string bytes. The string length represents the number of bytes (characters) in the string. The three strings are concatenated without intervening fillers.

◆ *Note:* NBP specifically permits the use of aliases (or, alternately, the use of a single socket by more than one NVE). In this case, each alias is given a unique enumerator value, which is kept in the names table along with the name-address mapping. The enumerator field is not significant in a LkUp or BrRq packet and is ignored by the recipient of these packets.

In BrRq, FwdReq, and LkUp packets, which carry only a single tuple, the address field contains the internet address of the requester, allowing the responder to address the LkUp-Reply datagram. In a LkUp-Reply packet, the correct enumerator value must be included in each tuple. This value is used for duplicate filtering.

■ **Figure 7-2** NBP tuple

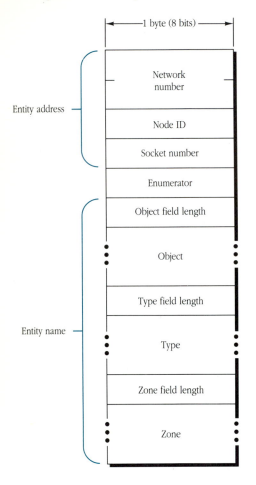

Because normal nodes on nonextended networks (and hence their NBP processes) are sometimes unaware of zone names, including their own zone name, tuples in LkUp-Reply packets may not specify a zone name. The zone names in these tuples may be an asterisk (*), regardless of the zone in which the lookup is performed. Requesters will know the zone name of these responses, because it must be the zone they asked for in the lookup request.

◆ *Note:* In a LkUp, FwdReq, or BrRq request, a null zone name (length byte equals 0) should be treated as equivalent to an asterisk (*).

Chapter 8 **Zone Information Protocol**

CONTENTS

■

ONE OF THE FUNCTIONS of routers is to maintain a mapping between networks and zone names, as mentioned in Chapter 7, "Name Binding Protocol." This network-to-zone-name mapping is maintained by the Zone Information Protocol (ZIP).

This chapter describes ZIP and provides information about

■ network-to-zone-name mapping

■ acquisition of a zone name by a node

■ the structure of a ZIP packet ■

ZIP services

An important feature of ZIP is that most of its services are transparent to nonrouter nodes. Non-router nodes use a small subset of ZIP during the startup process to choose their zone and also to obtain information about the zone structure of the internet. But ZIP is implemented primarily by routers. ZIP provides three major services as follows:

■ maintenance of the network-to-zone-name mapping of the internet

■ support for the selection of a zone name by a node at startup

■ support for various commands that may be needed by nonrouter nodes for obtaining this mapping

The first of these services applies only to routers; the second and third applies to both router and nonrouter nodes.

Network-to-zone-name mapping

Each AppleTalk network has associated with it a **zones list.** This list specifies the zone names that can be chosen by nodes on that network during the startup process and is used by the NBP process in routers to construct a zone-wide broadcast. An extended network can be set up with from 1 to 255 zone names in its zones list; a nonextended network can only contain 1 zone name in its zones list.

The network-to-zone-name mapping service of ZIP is provided by routers. These nodes have a ZIP process that opens the zone information socket and maintains a zone information table (see *Figure 5-2).*

Zone information table

Under stable conditions, each router maintains a complete network-to-zone-name mapping of the internet, known as the **zone information table** (ZIT). This table consists of one entry for each network in the internet. The entry is a tuple of the form <network range, zones list>. The zones list field can be NIL, indicating that the zones list for that network is unknown (this condition is temporary); otherwise, the zones list field consists of a number of a case-insensitive strings specifying the zone names for that network.

◆ *Note:* See Appendix D for a precise definition of case-insensitivity.

The ZIP process in a router recognizes new networks on the internet by monitoring the routing table of the Routing Table Maintenance Protocol (RTMP). (For more information on the routing table, refer to Chapter 5.) When the ZIP process identifies an entry in the routing table that is not in the ZIT, the ZIP process creates a new ZIT entry for that network with a zones list of NIL and initiates an attempt to determine the network's zone list. Likewise, if the ZIP process discovers that the ZIT contains an entry whose network number range is not in the routing table, the ZIP process then concludes that the network is no longer on the internet and removes the network's entry from the ZIT.

Zone information socket: ZIP Queries and Replies

Associated with the ZIP process in routers is a statically assigned socket known as the **zone information socket** (ZIS). During its initialization, the ZIP process opens the ZIS (socket number 6). Requests for zone information must be addressed to this socket. Routers also respond to those requests through this socket. The requests, known as ZIP Queries, contain a list of network numbers whose corresponding zones lists the requesting node wishes to determine. A router receiving such a request responds with a ZIP Reply listing the requested zones lists known to it. (The router does not respond if it does not know any of the requested zones lists.)

ZIT maintenance

In addition to the port descriptor fields used by a router's RTMP (as described in Chapter 5), ZIP requires a field to hold the zones list of the port's network. The zones list field is necessary only for ports connected to AppleTalk networks and only for those ports for which the router contains seed information. One of the zone names in each list in the port descriptors is chosen as the **default zone.** Its use is described later in the section "Zone Name Acquisition." The zones list field can be NIL, indicating unknown, as long as the restrictions specified in "Zone Name Assignment," later in this chapter, are adhered to.

At the time the router is initialized, its ZIT consists of one entry for each directly connected AppleTalk network for which it is a seed router. Both the network number ranges and the zones list fields are taken from the port descriptor for those networks. Additionally, ZIP monitors the routing table for the addition of networks that the router has just discovered. When the router first recognizes such a network, it creates a new ZIT entry with a zones list field of NIL. Whenever a ZIT entry is created with a zones list of NIL (either as just described or at initialization when a ZIT entry is taken from a port descriptor), the router's ZIP process sends a ZIP Query in an attempt to discover the zone list for that network.

This query is sent to the ZIS of the destination node whose address is determined as follows. If the network is directly connected to the router, then the query is broadcast on that network. Otherwise, the query is sent to the router indicated in the next-router field of the network's routing table entry.

A router that receives a ZIP Query should respond to the requesting socket with a series of ZIP Replies indicating the requested zones lists. Routers that are unaware of the requested zones lists or do not yet have complete zones lists should ignore the ZIP Query and need not respond. Upon receiving a ZIP Reply, a router enters the zones lists provided by the reply into the appropriate ZIT entries. For some queries, no reply or an incomplete reply may be received; the query may have been lost, or the queried routers may not have the requested information. For this case, ZIP maintains a background timer for the purpose of retransmitting these queries. Whenever this timer expires, ZIP retransmits one query for each entry in its ZIT whose zones list is still NIL or incomplete.

There are two forms of ZIP Replies. The first form is used when the zones list for a given network (or networks) can fit in one reply packet. This will generally be the case. However if this is not the case, the router replies with a series of **extended ZIP reply** packets. Each packet indicates the total number of zone names for the requested network, and contains as many zone names as will fit. The router receiving the extended ZIP replies adds the zone names to the list for the requested network, and then checks to see if that list contains the indicated total number of zone names. This being the case, the list is said to be complete, and can be used to answer other routers' ZIP queries and for purposes of NBP lookups. If the list is not complete, it should not be used for these purposes until it is completed.

If ZIP's background timer expires and a list is still incomplete (a packet may have been lost), ZIP should retransmit the ZIP Query. It will then receive the entire reply sequence over again, and should be able to complete its list. In this case it will have to filter out names that are already in its list so as to not add them to the list twice.

Through ZIP Queries and Replies zone names will propagate outward dynamically from the named network itself. Those routers that are 1 hop away receive the information on the first query, those 2 hops away may not receive it until the second, and so forth. Eventually, on a stable internet, the ZIT in every router will contain the complete network-to-zone-name mapping and no further ZIP activity will take place.

ZIP also monitors the routing table to determine whether a network has gone down (in other words, to determine whether the network is listed in the ZIT but not in the routing table). In this case, ZIP deletes the corresponding ZIT entry. The network could reappear later with a different zones list, which will then be discovered anew.

Zone name listing

Any AppleTalk node can send ZIP Queries to routers in order to obtain the zones list corresponding to one or more networks, including the network to which the node itself is connected. The routers respond with ZIP Replies, which contain the desired zones list.

However, the use of ZIP Queries for the purpose of compiling zones lists has two shortcomings, especially for nonrouter nodes. First, the ZIP Query and Reply mechanism does not provide a simple way of obtaining a list of *all* the zones in the internet. Second, since ZIP Queries and Replies are datagrams delivered on a best-effort basis, the requesting node has to implement a timeout-and-retry mechanism in order to ensure the reception of a response.

To overcome these limitations, ZIP provides three additional requests, GetZoneList GetLocalZones, and GetMyZone. The purpose of the GetZoneList request is to obtain a list of all the zones in the internet; GetLocalZones is used to obtain the list of all the zones on the requestor's network. The GetMyZone request is used to obtain the name of the zone in which the requesting node is located (only on nonextended networks, since the node knows this information on an extended network).

These functions are typical request–response transactions. The nonrouter node requests some information from a router, and the router responds with that information. For this reason, the AppleTalk Transaction Protocol (ATP), described in Chapter 9, is used for implementing these three functions.

GetZoneList, GetLocalZones, and GetMyZone are sent by ZIP as ATP requests of the at-least-once type (see Chapter 9). The requests are sent to the ZIS in any router on any network (usually the network to which the requesting node is attached). These requests always ask for a single response packet.

The response to the GetZoneList or GetLocalZones request provides a list of all the zones on the internet or the requestor's network. Since this list may not fit in one ATP response packet, each request contains an index value from which to start including names in the corresponding response (zone names in the router are assumed to be numbered starting with 1). To obtain the complete zones list, a node sends a series of GetZoneList or GetLocalZones requests. The first of these requests specifies an index of 1. The user bytes field of the corresponding response contains the number of zone names in that response packet; these bytes also specify whether more zone names exist that did not fit in the response. In that instance, the requesting node sends out another request, with the index equal to the index sent in the previous request plus the number of names in the last response. By repeating this process, the node can obtain the complete zones list from the router.

Additionally, if more than one request is necessary to obtain the complete zones list, then all requests must be sent to the same router because different routers may have their zones lists arranged in a different order. Furthermore, a particular zone name cannot be partitioned between two response packets.

◆ *Note:* A 0-byte response will be returned by a router if the index specified in the request is greater than the index of the last zone in the list (and the user bytes field will indicate *no more zones*). Routers should make every attempt to send a particular zone's name only once in response to a GetZoneList request. A node may receive a particular zone's name more than once, especially during periods when zone names are being changed.

GetLocalZones on a nonextended network should be treated exactly as a GetMyZone—that is the router should return the zone name associated with the requestor's network.

A GetMyZone request is used to obtain the name of the zone in which the requesting node is located. A GetMyZone request asks a router to provide the zone name of the network through which the request was received by the router. This request is essentially a simplified version of the GetZoneList request, in which only one zone name is returned. A 0-byte response is returned if the router does not know the name of the zone (this condition is temporary). This request should only be made by nodes on nonextended networks; nodes on extended networks obtain this information as part of the startup process.

Zone name acquisition

Nodes on extended networks choose their zone during the startup process. The zone name is chosen from the list that has been set up in the routers for their network. The zone name acquisition process is only undertaken by nodes on extended networks; nodes on nonextended networks need not even be aware of their zone name.

Verifying a saved zone name

Nodes save their last zone name in long term storage. When a node starts up, it obtains a provisional node address as described in Chapter 4, "Datagram Delivery Protocol." It then broadcasts a GetNetInfo request containing the saved zone name (or NIL if there is no saved zone name) to the zone information socket (socket 6). Routers receiving the request respond to the requester's internet address with information about the network connected to the port through which the request was received (which is the network on which the node resides). This information includes the network number range (for verifying that the node's provisional address is valid) and an indication as to whether the requested zone name is a valid one for that network. If the requested zone name is valid, it should be used as the node's current zone. If the requested zone name is invalid, the GetNetInfo response also includes the default zone name for that network, which should then be used by the node until another one is chosen.

In cases where a node's provisional address is invalid, routers will not be able to respond to the node in a directed manner. An address is invalid if the network number is neither in the startup range nor in the network number range assigned to the node's network. In these cases, if the request was sent via a broadcast, the routers should respond with a broadcast.

The GetNetInfo request sent by a node during startup should be retransmitted several times to insure that a response is received if a router is available. If no response is received, it should be assumed that no router is available. In this case, the network contains no zone names; only a zone name of asterisk (*) is valid in NBP lookups. If a router becomes available later (as indicated by receipt of an RTMP Data packet), the node can send a GetNetInfo request again.

Choosing a new zone name

In many cases a node may wish to choose a new zone name, for example when the node has no saved zone name at startup or when that saved zone name is invalid. The node can obtain the list of valid zone names for its network through the GetLocalZones request and choose one from that list. At that time, it must also register on a new zone multicast address (see the following section).

It is recommended that changing a node's zone name be done with care if it is performed at any time other than startup, since changing a node's zone name while it has NBP names registered could result in duplicate NBP names in the node's new zone. The node may wish to reregister these names to be safe.

Zone multicasting

A response to the GetNetInfo request also provides the requesting node with the node's zone multicast address. This address, computed in the routers, is a data-link level multicast address used by the node for receiving NBP lookups. NBP lookups are multicasted by routers to the zone multicast address associated with the lookup's destination zone name. The details of this process are described later in the section, "NBP Routing in IRs"; details of the computation of zone multicast addresses are described later in the section "Zone Multicast Address Computation."

Zone multicasting is intended to prevent nodes not in the lookup's destination zone from being interrupted by lookup packets. However, certain data links may not support multicasting or may provide only a limited number of multicast addresses. For this reason, even though registered on a zone multicast address, nodes may receive lookup packets for other zones. Nodes must respond only to NBP lookups for their zone name.

Aging the zone name

Zones lists are defined in routers. If the last router on an extended network goes down, the situation should revert to that in which no routers exist on the network. Details of aging A-ROUTER and THIS-NET-RANGE are specified in Chapter 5, "Routing Table Maintenence Protocol." At the same time as these two quantities are aged, the node's zone name also becomes invalid. Until a router reappears on the network, the node should only respond to NBP lookups with a zone name of asterisk (*). If a router becomes available later, the node's saved zone name should be verified as if a router had never been active before on the network.

Packet formats

Some ZIP packets are identified by a DDP type field of 6. Other ZIP packets use ATP. ZIP packets (described in the following sections) are of three types:

- Query and Reply
- ATP Requests
- GetNetInfo request and reply

ZIP Query and Reply

Figure 8-1 summarizes the formats for ZIP Query and Reply packets. ZIP Queries are always sent to the ZIS of a router (or broadcast to the ZIS); ZIP Replies are always sent from the router to the source socket of the corresponding ZIP Query. The DDP type field in these packets is set to 6 to indicate ZIP. These packets contain a ZIP header that includes a ZIP function byte indicating the following:

- 1 = Query
- 2 = Reply
- 8 = Extended Reply

The ZIP header also contains a network count (n). Queries contain *n* network numbers for which zone lists are being sought. These network numbers indicate the start of the range associated with the desired networks. Replies contain the number of zones lists indicated in the Reply header. Replies (but not Extended Replies) can contain any number of zones lists, as long as the zones list for each network is entirely contained in the Reply packet. Replies consist of a series of network-number/zone-name pairs, with zone names preceded by a length byte. The zones list for a given network must be contiguous in the packet, with each zone name in that list preceded by the first network number in the range of the requested network.

Extended Replies can contain only one zones list. The Extended Reply packet consists of a series of network-number/zone-name pairs, with the network number indicating the start of the requested range (the network numbers in each pair will all be the same in an Extended Reply). The network count in the header indicates, not the number of zones names in the packet, but the number of zone names in the entire zones list for the requested network, which may span more than one packet.

◆ *Note:* Extended ZIP Replies may also be used for responding to ZIP queries with zones lists that all fit in one Reply packet. In this case, the network count will be equal to the number of zone names in the packet.

■ **Figure 8-1** ZIP Query and Reply packet formats

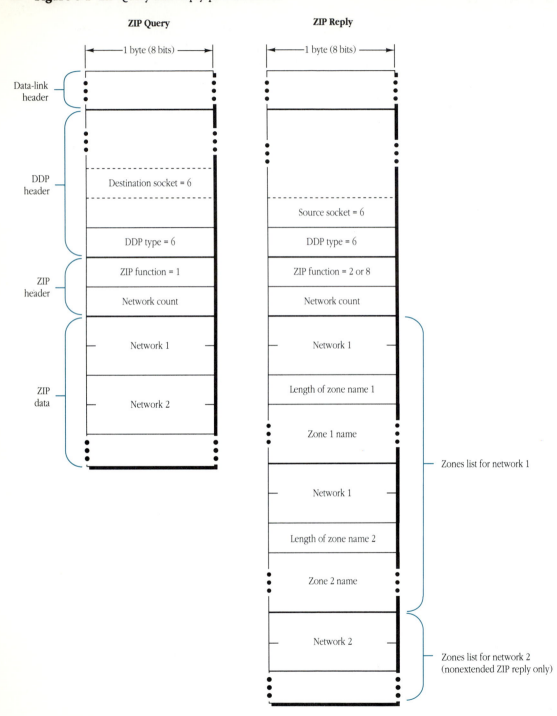

ZIP ATP Requests

Figure 8-2 summarizes the format of the GetZoneList and GetLocalZones request and reply packets. The GetZoneList request contains a function code of 8, indicating GetZoneList, and the desired start index, both in the ATP user bytes field. The GetZoneListReply contains in the ATP user bytes field a LastFlag that is not 0 if the response contains the last zone name in the zone list. A field indicating the number of zones contained in the ATP data part is also in the user bytes field. The GetLocalZones request contains a function code of 9 and is otherwise similar to the GetZoneList request.

Figure 8-2 GetZoneList and GetLocalZones request and reply packets

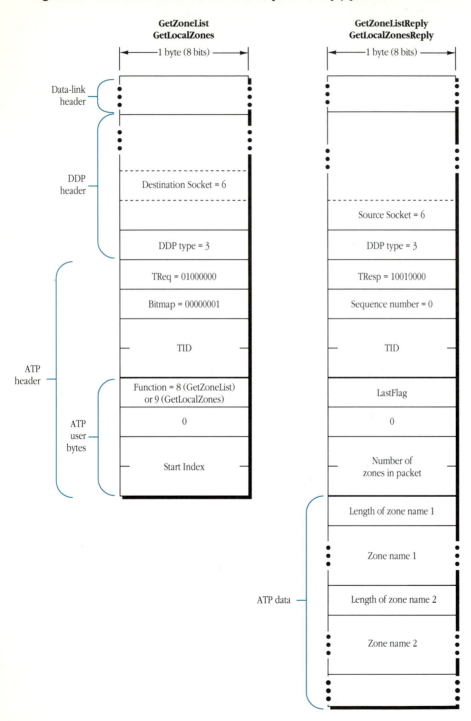

Figure 8-3 illustrates the GetMyZone request and reply packets. The GetMyZone request contains a function code of 7 in the user bytes field. (All other user bytes should be 0.) The response usually indicates one zone name in the user bytes field and contains that zone name in the data field.

■ **Figure 8-3** GetMyZone request and reply packets

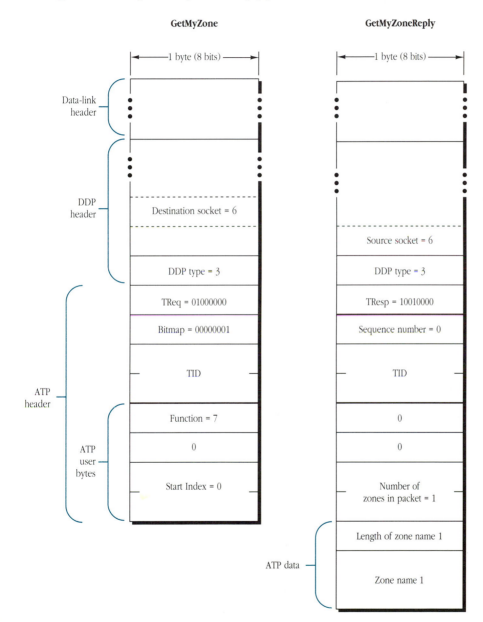

ZIP GetNetInfo Request and Reply

Figure 8-4 illustrates the GetNetInfo request and reply packets. The GetNetInfo request is always sent to the ZIS of a router (or broadcasted to the ZIS); ZIP GetNetInfo replies are always sent to the source socket of the corresponding request. (In the case where the requester broadcasts a request with an invalid node address, the reply may be broadcast.) The function byte in the ZIP header indicates the following:

- 5 = GetNetInfo request
- 6 = GetNetInfo reply

The reply header also contains a byte of flags. These flags provide three pieces of information. The high bit of the byte is set if the zone name in the request is invalid for the network from which the request was sent. The next bit is set for data links that do not support multicast. The third bit is set if the network's zones list contains only one zone name. (In this case, there would be no need to send a GetLocalZones request to obtain the zones list.) All other bits are reserved and should be set to zero.

The GetNetInfo request data consists of 4 bytes of zeros (reserved) followed by the zone name for which information is being requested. The length byte should be set to zero if no zone name is being provided in the packet.

The GetNetInfo reply data begins with the starting and ending network numbers of the network on which the request was made. This range is always followed by a copy of the zone name from the request. Since GetNetInfo replies are sometimes broadcast, nodes receiving such replies should use this zone name to verify that the response is for the zone name that they requested. If not, the reply should be ignored.

The zone multicast address to be used by the node follows the copy of the requested zone name. This is the data-link address on which the node should register to receive NBP lookups. It is preceded by its length in bytes, which should be zero if the data link does not support multicast. In the case where the requested zone name is invalid (as indicated in the flag byte in the header), this zone multicast address is the zone multicast address of the default zone for the requested network, and is followed by the name of that default zone. Otherwise, it is the zone multicast address of the requested zone name, and no default zone name follows.

■ Figure 8-4 GetNetInfo request and reply packets

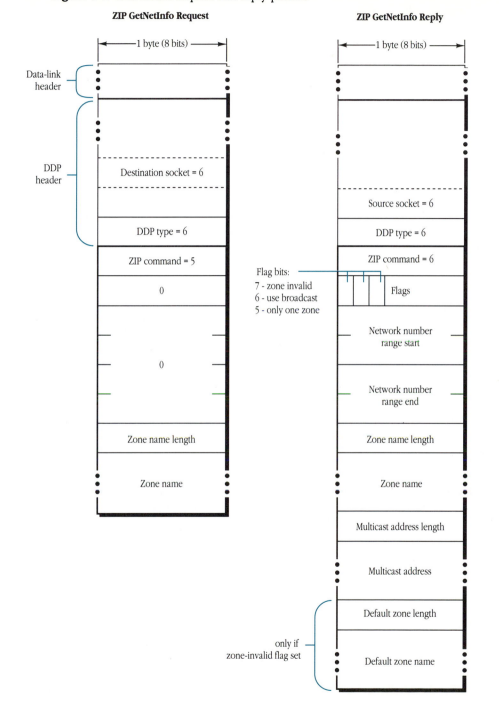

Zone multicast address computation

The zone multicast address associated with a given zone name, on a given data link, is computed by the ZIP process in routers. It is then returned to requesting nodes through a GetNetInfo reply packet. The zone multicast address is based on the bytes in the zone name and the specific data link on which the address is to be used.

To compute the zone multicast address, the ZIP process first converts the zone name to all uppercase characters (since zone names are case insensitive). The details of this conversion are documented in Appendix D. ZIP then converts this string into a number in the range 1-$FFFF by performing the DDP checksum algorithm on each byte of the zone name (not including the length byte). This algorithm, documented in Chapter 4, "Datagram Delivery Protocol," is repeated here:

```
CkSum := 0 ;

FOR each byte in the zone name

REPEAT the following algorithm:
      CkSum := CkSum + byte; (unsigned addition)
      Rotate CkSum left one bit, rotating the most significant bit into the
                  least significant bit;

IF, at the end, CkSum = 0 THEN
      CkSum := $FFFF (all ones).
```

This hashed value, h, is then used as an index into an ordered list of zone multicast addresses associated with the underlying data link. If the data link provides n zone multicast addresses, a[0] through a[n-1], then the zone multicast address associated with index h is a[h mod n]. *mod* is the modulo function, in other words, the remainder when h is divided by n.

NBP routing in IRs

As indicated in Chapter 7, "Name Binding Protocol," routers contain an NBP process that is responsible for the conversion of an NBP Broadcast Request (BrRq) to a zone-wide broadcast of NBP Lookup (LkUp) requests.

The process consists of two stages. In the first stage, the router converts the BrRq packet into a series of FwdReq packets, one for each network which has been set up to include the specified zone. These FwdReq's are sent to the first router directly connected to each of these networks. The second stage of the process consists of the router receiving the FwdReq converting it to a LkUp and sending that LkUp to the correct zone multicast address.

Generating FwdReq packets

The process of converting a BrRq into a series of FwdReqs is straightforward. The router obtains from its ZIT a list of all networks that include the specified zone. The router then uses DDP to send a FwdReq to the NIS of the first router directly connected to each of these networks. To do this, the router sends a FwdReq to node ID 0 of each network. Specifically, each FwdReq is sent to AppleTalk network number nnnn, node ID 0, where nnnn is the start of the range associated with each network.

The DDP data part of a FwdReq packet is the same as that from the NBP Broadcast Request, except that the NBP function field must be equal to FwdReq. If, however, the BrRq originated on a nonextended network, the destination target zone name could be equal to asterisk (*). In this case, the router must substitute the zone name associated with that nonextended network before sending out the FwdReqs. (The router receiving the FwdReq would have no way of knowing this information.) If the router does not know the zone name yet, it should broadcast a LkUp packet on the requesting network, but not send out any FwdReqs.

If the router receiving the BrRq is directly connected to one or more networks that include the specified zone name, these networks will be included in the list obtained from the ZIT. In this case, the router should send out LkUp packets on these directly connected networks as specified in the next section.

Converting FwdReqs to LkUps

A BrRq packet is converted into a series of FwdReq packets, one for each network containing the zone specified in the BrRq packet. The destination of each of these FwdReq packets is the first router directly connected to the destination network. Along the way, routers that are not directly connected to the destination network will forward the packet towards the destination network in the usual manner. When a FwdReq packet is received by the router directly connected to the target network, that router is responsible for converting that packet to a LkUp request and broadcasting it on the appropriate zone multicast address. The DDP data part of a LkUp packet is exactly the same as that from the NBP FwdReq, except that the NBP function field must be equal to LkUp.

If the destination network of the LkUp packet is a nonextended network, the router simply changes the destination node ID to $FF and broadcasts the packet on that network (since a nonextended network has only one zone). If the destination network is extended, however, the router must also change the destination network number to $0000, so that the packet is received by all nodes on the network (within the correct zone multicast address). The router must compute the zone multicast address for the packet, based on the zone name in the packet and the data link on which the packet is to be sent. The router then calls DDP to broadcast the packet to the indicated multicast address. DDP in routers must provide the ability to send a packet directly to a data-link level multicast address.

◆ *Note:* NBP is defined so that the router's NBP process does not participate in the NBP response process; the response is sent directly to the original requester through DDP. It is important that the original requester's field be obtained from the address field of the NBP tuple.

Zones list assignment

The structure of a router's port descriptor is defined in Chapter 5, "Routing Table Maintenance Protocol." ZIP requires an additional zones list field in port descriptors. Zones lists are included in the port descriptors of router ports and are then propagated dynamically through ZIP to all internet routers. Zones lists in port descriptors include an indicator as to which zone name is the default zone.

Only router ports connected to AppleTalk networks need to be associated with zones lists. For each AppleTalk network, at least one router on that network must be configured with the network's zones list; all other routers could have a zones list of NIL in their port descriptor for that network. If, for a given network, more than one router is configured with a non-NIL zone list, these lists must be the same (including the same default zone). In addition, only seed routers used for the purpose of specifying the network number range should contain zones lists that are not NIL. (In other words, if a router is not a seed router for routing information, it should not be a seed router for zone information.) Seed routers should confirm that their zone information does not conflict with that from another router on the same network, for instance through ZIP queries or GetLocalZones requests.

A router having a NIL zone list discovers the names in that list by broadcasting a ZIP query on the network of interest, as described previously. To determine which zone name in the list is the default zone, the router broadcasts a ZIP GetNetInfo request with a NIL zone name on that network (this packet can be sent directly to a router on that network if the address of one is known).

◆ *Note:* The default zone name for a given network is of interest only to routers (and nodes) on that network. Unlike the network's zone list, this information is not propagated to other routers on the internet.

Zones list changing

Under stable conditions, each network's zones list appears in the ZIT of every internet router. Changing a particular network's zones list requires changing that list in every internet router. Indeed, although routers on the stable internet are no longer sending ZIP Queries, each router must still be notified of the change in the zones list. One possible method of notifying all routers of the zones list change would be to send an internet-wide broadcast of the change request. Internet-wide broadcasting, however, is not supported by DDP and is both complicated and expensive in terms of network traffic.

Changing zones lists in routers

ZIP does not specify a way for changing the zones list of a network while that network is active as a part of the internet. It is envisioned that future network management protocols, to be defined by Apple, will provide this functionality. A network management system needs to be aware of all the routers on the internet, and with this knowledge it can implement an all-routers broadcast that notifies all routers on the internet as to the change in a zones list.

Until such network management protocols are defined, the zones list associated with a network can only be changed by temporarily isolating that network from the internet. All the routers directly connected to the network should be brought down and the zones list changed in each of the seed routers. All the routers can then be brought back up. The routers, however, can not be brought back up until the old zones list from that network has disappeared from all the ZITs in the internet. It takes a certain amount of time for the network number range and zone name information about a network to age out of all routers in the internet once that network is no longer connected. Although this parameter is a function of the internet topology, ZIP defines it as a constant known as the **ZIP bringback time.** The exact value of the ZIP bringback time is defined in "Timer Values" later in this chapter.

Changing zone names in nodes

Nodes on an extended network will need to be told if their zone name has been changed. This is so they can register on a new zone multicast address, and so they can perform correct NBP filtering. ZIP specifies a packet, referred to as a ZIP Notify, which accomplishes this function. The format of a ZIP Notify packet is essentially the same as a ZIP GetNetInfo Reply, except the function byte is 7 to indicate Notify (see *Figure 8-5*). The packet specifies the old and new zone names, and the new zone multicast address. It is sent as part of a zones list change operation to the ZIS of nodes on the affected network. It should be sent to the old zone multicast address. Nodes on extended networks should maintain a *ZIP stub* on the ZIS for purposes of receiving ZIP Notifies. Upon receipt of a ZIP Notify (for the zone in which the node resides), the node should register on the new zone multicast address and change its zone name to that specified in the packet. This zone name should also be changed in long term storage.

◆ *Note:* It is not currently a requirement that nodes implement processing of ZIP Notifies. ZIP Notify processing will be required once the network management protocols for changing zones lists are specified.

■ **Figure 8-5** ZIP Notify packet

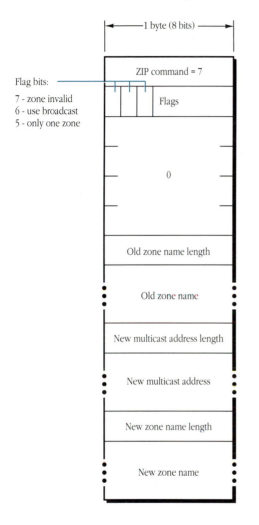

ZIP Notify

Flag bits:

7 - zone invalid
6 - use broadcast
5 - only one zone

Timer values

Two parameter values associated with ZIP must be specified. The first is the value for the ZIP Query retransmission time. This value is equal to the send-RTMP timer, or 10 seconds. The second is the ZIP bringback time. The ZIP bringback time is defined as the minimum time required between bringing a network down and bringing it back up with a new zones list. Since it is desired that this value be a constant, independent of internet topology, the worst-case internet must be used in determining it. Since a network's zone name rarely changes, this value has been conservatively defined as 10 minutes.

Part IV **Reliable Data Delivery**

PART IV DISCUSSES the protocols that add reliability to AppleTalk end-to-end data delivery. Part II described the protocols used to provide end-to-end data flow across an AppleTalk internet. Those protocols do not guarantee the delivery of the data; they merely provide a best-effort service. Two groups of protocols, corresponding to two different models of end-to-end interaction, are discussed in this part.

The first group is based on a data transaction model. The key protocol of this group is the AppleTalk Transaction Protocol (ATP). ATP provides the request–response transaction paradigm on which the session-oriented services of the AppleTalk Session Protocol (ASP) and the Printer Access Protocol (PAP) are based. While ATP is concerned with independent transactions, ASP provides a sequence of transactions guaranteed to be delivered and executed in the order in which the transaction requests are sent. PAP provides a data read/write type of service built with underlying ATP transactions. PAP is the transport/session protocol used by printers of the ImageWriter and LaserWriter families working in an AppleTalk environment.

The second group is based on a more conventional model of reliable data flow—the data stream. This model provides a bidirectional reliable flow of data bytes between any two sockets of the internet. The AppleTalk Data Stream Protocol (ADSP) has been designed for this purpose. ■

Chapter 9 **AppleTalk Transaction Protocol**

CONTENTS

■

THE APPLETALK TRANSACTION PROTOCOL (ATP)
satisfies the transport needs of a large variety of peripheral devices and the
transaction needs for more general networking in an AppleTalk network
system. ATP has been designed to be easy to implement so that maximum
performance can be achieved. Furthermore, nodes with tight memory space
restrictions will be able to support a sufficient subset of ATP.

The fundamental purpose of reliable transport protocols is to provide a loss-
free delivery of client packets from a *source* socket to a *destination* socket.
Various features can be added to this basic service in order to obtain
characteristics appropriate for specific needs.

This chapter describes ATP and provides information about

■   transactions and multipacket responses

■   transaction bitmaps and sequence numbers

■   ATP packet format and service interface ■

Transactions

Often, a socket client must request the client of another socket to perform a particular higher-level function and then to report the outcome. This interaction between a requester and a responder is called a **transaction.**

The basic structure of a transaction in the context of a network is shown in *Figure 9-1*. The requester initiates the transaction by sending a **Transaction Request** (TReq) packet from the requester's socket to the responder's socket. The responder executes the request and returns a **Transaction Response** (TResp) packet reporting the transaction's outcome.

ATP is based on the model that a transaction request is issued by a client in a requesting node to a client in a responding node. The client in the responding node is expected to service the request and generate a response. The clients are assumed to have some method of specifically identifying the data or the operation sought in the request (for example, a disk block or a request to reset a clock).

The basic transaction process must be performed in the face of various error situations inherent in the loosely coupled nature of networks; these error situations include:

- The TReq is lost in the network.

- The TResp is lost or delayed in transit.

- The responder becomes unreachable from the requester.

Several different TReqs could be outstanding, and the requester must be able to distinguish between the responses received over the network. The ability to distinguish between these responses can be built by sending a **transaction identifier** (TID) with each request. A response must contain the same TID as the corresponding request. The TID, in a sense, unambiguously *binds* the request and response portions of a transaction, provided each transaction's TID value is unique.

■ **Figure 9-1** Transaction terminology

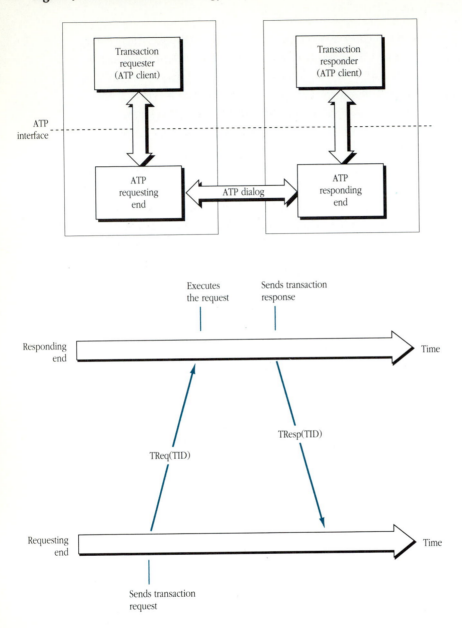

At-least-once (ALO) transactions

In any of the three error situations previously listed, the requester will not receive the TResp and must conclude that the transaction was not completed. The requester must then activate a recovery procedure consisting of a timer and an automatic retry mechanism. If the timer expires in the requester and the response has not been received, the requester retransmits the TReq, as shown in *Figure 9-2*. This process is repeated until a response is received by the requester or until a maximum retry count is reached. If the retry count hits its maximum value, the transaction requester (the ATP client at the requester end) is notified that the responder is unreachable.

This recovery mechanism is designed to ensure that the TReq is executed at least once; the transaction is called an **at-least-once (ALO) transaction.** Such a recovery mechanism is adequate if the request is *idempotent* (that is, if repeated execution of the request is the same as executing it once). An example of an idempotent transaction is asking a destination node to identify itself.

If the ALO service is used, then ATP handles timeouts and retransmission of requests but does not automatically retransmit responses. In this case, it is up to the responding client to handle retransmission of responses to duplicate requests.

■ **Figure 9-2** Automatic retry mechanism

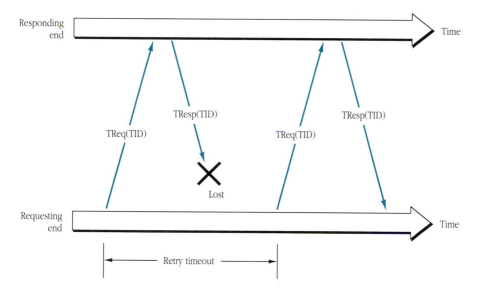

Exactly-once (XO) transactions

When, as previously described, an ATP request is retransmitted, the transaction could be executed more than once. If the request is not idempotent, serious damage could result from the execution of the duplicate transaction request. For nonidempotent requests, a transaction service that ensures the request's execution once and exactly once is essential; the transaction is called an **exactly-once (XO) transaction.** (Whether the ALO or the XO level of service is appropriate can be determined only by the transaction requester.)

Figure 9-3 illustrates ATP's implementation of an XO transaction protocol. In order to implement an XO transaction protocol, the responder maintains a **transactions list** of all recently received transaction requests. Upon receiving a TReq, the responder searches through this list to determine whether the request has already been received (this is known as **duplicate transaction-request filtering**). A newly received request is inserted into the list and then executed; after which the corresponding response is generated by the responder and is sent to the transaction requester. At the same time, a copy of the response is attached to the transaction's entry in the transactions list. Upon receiving a duplicate request for which a response has already been sent, the responder retransmits the response without the intervention of the ATP client. If a duplicate request is received and a response has not been sent out yet (because the request is still being executed), then ATP ignores the duplicate request.

Upon receiving a TResp, the requester should return a **Transaction Release** (TRel) packet to release the request from the responding ATP's transactions list. If this TRel gets lost, then the request would stay in the list permanently. To prevent this situation, the responder *time stamps* a request before inserting it in its list. The list is checked periodically by the responder, and those requests that have been in the list longer than the time specified by the *release timer* are eliminated.

Figure 9-3 Exactly-once (XO) transactions

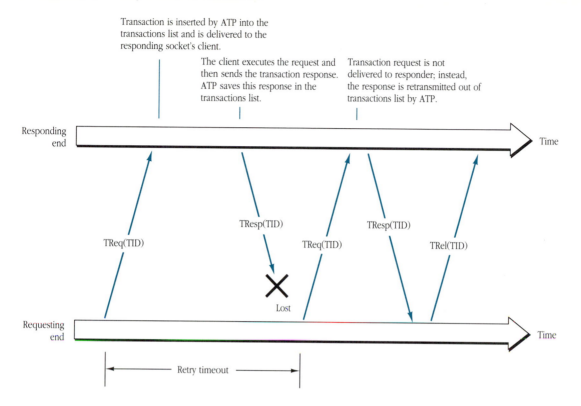

Transaction is inserted by ATP into the transactions list and is delivered to the responding socket's client.

The client executes the request and then sends the transaction response. ATP saves this response in the transactions list.

Transaction request is not delivered to responder; instead, the response is retransmitted out of transactions list by ATP.

This method of filtering duplicate requests by consulting a list of recently received transactions is quite effective in ensuring XO service in most environments. However, it does not guarantee XO service in *all* environments. If packets are guaranteed to arrive in the order in which they were sent (for example, on a single AppleTalk network), then this technique of filtering duplicate requests is completely effective. However, in an internet environment, packets may arrive at their destination in a different order from the one in which they were sent. This out-of-order delivery can occur because of the existence of multiple paths from source to destination and the various transmission delays on these paths. As a result, unusual situations can take place, such as the one shown in *Figure 9-4,* in which the original TResp was delayed long enough in the internet to provoke a retransmission of the request.

■ Figure 9-4 Duplicate delivery of exactly-once (XO) mode

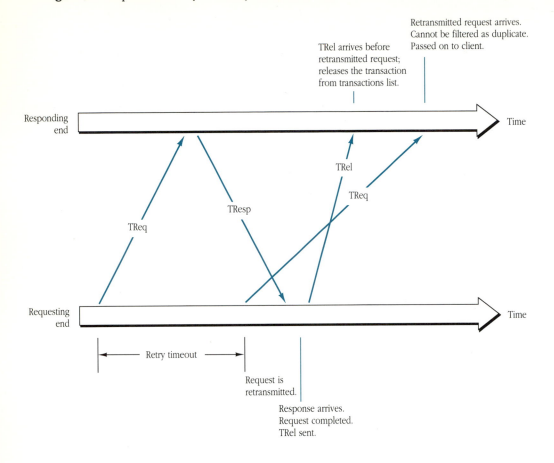

Furthermore, if the TRel sent by the requester (upon receiving the delayed response) arrives before the retransmitted request, the responder (upon receiving the TRel) releases the request from the responder's transactions list. As a result, when the retransmitted request arrives at the responder, it cannot be filtered out as a duplicate. It should be noted that the probability of the occurrence of the situation of *Figure 9-4* is quite low. Furthermore, ATP XO does ensure that if a duplicate request is somehow delivered by ATP to the responder (as in the above example), then the transaction has already been completed and the request can be ignored by the responder. Thus, clients requiring a higher level of guaranteed XO service can obtain it by augmenting the ATP mechanism with some form of simple sequence number checking, which allows a responder to detect delayed duplicate requests. An example of such a sequence number check is detailed in Chapter 10, "Printer Access Protocol."

◆ *Note:* ATP XO should be considered an optional part of ATP. Nodes that do not require XO service need not implement it. Developers should keep in mind, however, that higher-level protocols, such as the Printer Access Protocol (PAP) and the AppleTalk Session Protocol (ASP), may require ATP XO service.

Multipacket responses

This basic ATP model is adequate for most interactions. However, since the underlying network restricts the size of packets that can be exchanged, the TResp may not fit in a single packet. For this reason, the TReq and TResp are looked upon as *messages* (not packets). Although ATP restricts its TReqs to single packets, it allows the TResp message to be made up of several sequentially arranged packets. When the requesting node receives all the response packets (that is, the complete response message), the transaction is considered complete and the response is delivered as a single entity to the ATP client (the transaction requester).

The maximum size (number of packets) of a TResp message is limited to eight packets. The maximum amount of data in an ATP packet (request or response) is 578 bytes. This limit is derived from the Datagram Delivery Protocol (DDP) maximum packet size of 586 bytes minus ATP's header size of 8 bytes.

Transaction identifiers

A transaction identifier (TID) is generated by the ATP requesting end and sent along with the TReq packet. An important design issue is the size of these IDs (16 bits for ATP). Their size is a function of the rate at which transactions are generated and of the **maximum packet lifetime** (MPL) of the complete network system. A basic problem exists because of the finite size of the TID, which will eventually wrap around. Once a TID value is reused, the danger exists that an old packet, with a previous instance of that TID, will arrive and be accepted as valid. Thus, the longer the MPL, the larger the TID must be. Similarly, if transactions are generated rapidly, then the TIDs must again be larger.

For a single AppleTalk network, the time taken for exchanging a TReq and a TResp will generally be on the order of 1 millisecond or greater. Therefore, at most, 1000 transactions can take place per second. From this point of view, a 1-byte TID would ensure a TID wraparound time of about one-quarter of a second.

With network interconnection through store-and-forward internet routers (IRs), however, the impact of an MPL on the order of 30 seconds makes a 1-byte TID inadequate. A 16-bit TID would increase the wraparound time to 1 minute and eliminate concerns about old retransmitted requests and responses being received as a result of TID wraparound.

In "Wraparound and Generation of TIDs" later in this chapter, the issue of generating TIDs is reviewed to account for another subtle but important characteristic of ATP—namely, transactions with infinite retries.

ATP bitmap/sequence number

Every ATP packet includes a bitmap/sequence field in its header. This field is 8 bits wide. ATP handles lost or out-of-sequence response packets by using this field. The significance of this field depends on the type of ATP packet (TReq, TResp, or TRel).

In TReq packets, this field is known as the **transaction bitmap.** The requester indicates to the responder the number of buffers reserved for the TResp by setting a bit in the TReq packet's bitmap for each reserved buffer. The responder can examine the TReq packet's bitmap and determine the number of packets the requester is expecting to receive in the TResp message.

In TResp packets, this field is known as the ATP sequence number. The value of this field in the TResp packet is an integer (in the range 0–7), indicating the sequential position of that response packet in the TResp message. The requester ATP can use this value to put the received response packet in the appropriate response buffer (even if the response packet is received out of sequence) for delivery to the transaction requester (the ATP client). In addition, the requester ATP clears a bit in its copy of the transaction bitmap to indicate that the corresponding response packet has been received.

The actual TResp message may turn out to be smaller than was expected by the requester. Therefore, a provision is made in the response packet's header to signal an **end of message** (EOM). This EOM is set by the responder's ATP in the last response packet of the message. Upon receiving a response packet with the EOM indication, the requester must clear all bits corresponding to higher sequential positions in its copy of the transaction bitmap.

◆ *Note:* This EOM signal is internal to ATP; the responding client tells ATP to set it, but it is not delivered to the requesting client and should not be used for higher-level communications (for example, as an end-of-file indicator).

If the requester's retry timeout expires and the complete TResp has not yet been received (indicated by one or more bits still set to 1 in the requester's transaction bitmap), then a TReq is sent out again with the current value of the transaction bitmap and the same TID as the original request. As a result, only the missing TResp packets need to be sent again by the responder.

The mechanism for requesting only the missing TResp packets is shown in *Figure 9-5*. In *Figure 9-5,* a requester issues a TReq indicating that it has reserved six buffers for the response; the request might be for six blocks of information from a disk device. The TReq packet would have in its ATP data part the pertinent information, such as what file and which six blocks of information are being requested. ATP builds the request packet and sets the least-significant 6 bits in the bitmap. When the responder receives this request packet, it examines the request's ATP data and bitmap and then determines the type and range of the request to be serviced. The six blocks are retrieved from the disk and passed to the ATP layer in the responding node. They are then sent back to the requesting node; each block is in a separate packet with its sequence number indicating the packet's sequential position in the response.

■ **Figure 9-5** Multipacket response example

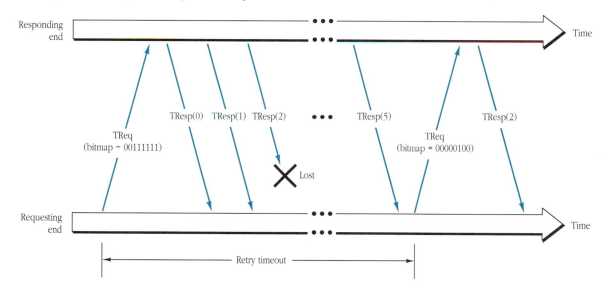

Figure 9-5 shows a case in which the third response packet is lost in the network. Thus, the retry timeout will expire in the requester; this action causes a retransmission of the original request (transparently to the ATP requesting client) but with a bitmap reflecting only the missing third response packet.

◆ *Note:* Single packet request–response transactions are simply the lesser case in which the TReq has 1 bit only set in its bitmap. If two nodes are expected to communicate in this single-packet manner, no extra packet overhead is added by the protocol.

Responders with limited buffer space

A potential difficulty, especially with XO transactions, is that a responder might not have enough buffer space to hold the entire TResp message until the end of the transaction (determined by the receipt of a TRel).

For such responders, ATP provides a mechanism to reuse their buffers through a confirmation of response packet delivery. This reuse is achieved by piggy-backing in a response packet a request to send transaction status (STS). Upon receiving an STS response packet, the requester immediately sends out a TReq with the current bitmap, thus providing the responder a way to determine which response packets have been received. (In other words, the current bitmap indicates which response packets have not yet been received.) The responder can then use this bitmap to free buffers holding already-delivered response packets.

Two client interface issues arise in connection with the **send transaction status (STS) bit.** The retransmitted TReq will be detected by ATP XO as a duplicate and hence will not be delivered to the responding client. Thus, ATP must provide some way of conveying the updated bitmap to the user without the delivery of a duplicate request. Also, in an internet, TReqs can be received out of order; if a duplicate TReq is received whose bitmap indicates that fewer responses have been received than indicated in a previous TReq, then the duplicate TReq should be ignored as a delayed duplicate and should not be delivered to the user.

Figure 9-6 shows the use of STS in an example in which a responder with only two buffers services a request for a seven-packet response. TReq packets sent in response to an STS do not consume the retry count, but do reset the retry timeout.

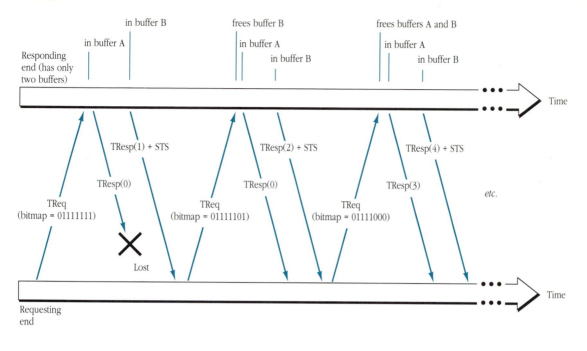

■ **Figure 9-6** Use of STS

ATP packet format

The format of an ATP packet is shown in *Figure 9-7*. An ATP packet consists of an 8-byte ATP header plus up to 578 ATP data bytes. The first byte of the ATP header is used for **control information** (CI). The 2 high-order bits of the CI contain the packet's function code. These bits are encoded in the following way:

- 01 = TReq
- 10 = TResp
- 11 = TRel

The XO bit must be set in all TReq packets that pertain to the XO mode of operation of the protocol. The EOM bit is set in a TResp packet to signal that this packet is the last packet in the transaction's response message. The STS bit is set in TResp packets to force the requester to retransmit a TReq immediately.

■ Figure 9-7 ATP packet format

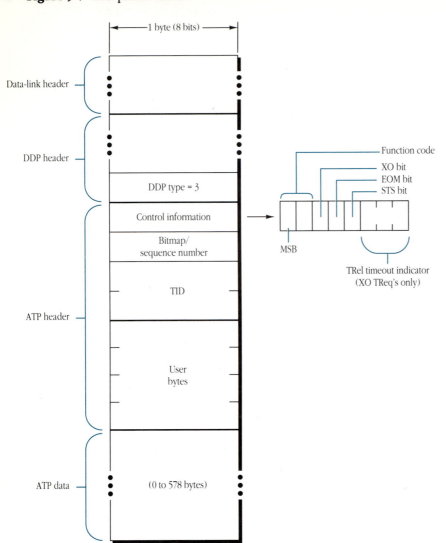

The remaining 3 bits of the CI should always be set to zero, except in the case of an XO TReq packet. In this case, these three bits are an indicator as to the value of the release timer to use for the transaction. These bits are encoded in the following way:

- 000 = 30 second TRel timer
- 001 = 1 minute TRel timer
- 010 = 2 minute TRel timer
- 011 = 4 minute TRel timer
- 100 = 8 minute TRel timer

Other values are reserved and should not be used.

◆ *Note:*AppleTalk Phase 1 nodes will not honor the TRel timer indicator field in XO TReq packets and will always use a TRel timer value of 30 seconds.

The 8 bits immediately following the control field comprise the ATP bitmap or sequence number field. The packets comprising the TResp message are assigned sequence numbers 0–7. The sequence number (encoded as an integer) is sent in the ATP sequence number field of the corresponding response packet.

In the case of a TReq packet, a bit of the bitmap is set to 1 for each expected response packet. The least-significant bit corresponds to the response packet with sequence number 0, up through the most-significant bit that corresponds to the response packet with sequence number 7.

The third and fourth bytes of the ATP header contain the 16-bit TID. TIDs are generated by the ATP requester and are incremented from transaction to transaction as unsigned 16-bit integers (a 0 value is permitted).

The last 4 bytes of the ATP header are not examined by ATP and are used to send client data. Strictly speaking, they should not be considered part of the ATP header. However, they can be used by an ATP client to build a simple header for a higher-level protocol. These bytes have been separated out to allow an implementation of ATP that handles an ATP request or response message's data in an assembled, contiguous form, without interposed higher-level headers. ATP client interfaces should build appropriate mechanisms for exchanging these 4 user bytes independent of the data.

◆ *Note:* The ATP user bytes contained in a TRel packet are not significant, and clients should not use them.

ATP interface

The ATP interface, shown in *Figure 9-1,* is made up of five calls described later in this chapter.

Developers can visualize the ATP package (an implementation of ATP) as consisting of two parts, one each at the requester and the responder ends. The calls to the ATP interface are discussed in the context of both the ATP requesting end and the ATP responding end of *Figure 9-1.*

In the following description of the protocol, various details of the interface are not specified because they are implementation-dependent. The description is adequate for defining the characteristics of the ATP service provided to the next higher layer.

The availability of multiprocessing in the network node is not required. Descriptions of the various interface calls have been written in a generic form indicating parameters passed by the caller to the ATP implementation as well as results returned by the ATP implementation to the caller. The result codes and their interpretation depend on the specifics of the implementation of a call. If the call is issued synchronously, the caller is blocked until the call's operation has been completed or aborted. The returned parameters then become available when the caller is unblocked. In the case of asynchronous calls, a call completion mechanism is activated when the operation completes or aborts. Then the returned parameters become available through the completion routine mechanism.

At least two kinds of interfaces are anticipated:

- a packet-by-packet passing of response buffers to and from ATP

- a response message (in other words, the message is in a contiguous buffer)

The two kinds of interfaces are analogous to the familiar packet stream and byte stream interfaces available for data stream protocols. However, implementers are completely free to provide any type of interface they consider appropriate.

Sending a request

The transaction requester (ATP client) issues a call to send a TReq. The transaction requester must supply several parameters with the call. These parameters include the address of the destination socket, the ATP data part, user bytes of the request packet, buffer space for the expected response packets, and information as to whether the XO mode of service is required. In addition, the transaction requester specifies the duration of the retry timeout to be used and the maximum number of retries. A provision must be made in the interface for the transaction requester to indicate infinite retries—in other words, retransmitting the request until a response is obtained. The transaction requester may be provided with the ability to specify the socket through which the request should be sent. (Alternatively, ATP could pick the socket for the requester.) In addition, if the request is XO, the caller should pass an indicator as to the value to be used for the transaction release timer.

Call parameters

transaction mode (XO or ALO)

transaction responder's address (network number, node ID, and socket number)

ATP request packet's data part and its length

ATP user bytes

expected number of response packets

buffer space for the TResp message

retry timeout

maximum number of retries

TRel timeout indicator (XO requests only)

socket through which to send the request (optional)

Returned parameters

result code: success; failure

number of response packets received

user bytes from responses

A result code of failure is returned if ATP has exhausted all retries and a complete response has not been received.

◆ *Note:* No error is returned if the caller requests XO service and the responder does not support it; in this case, the request will be executed at least once.

A result code of success is returned whenever a complete response message has been received. A complete response is received if either of the following occurs:

- All response packets originally requested have been received.

- All response packets with sequence number 0 to an integer n have been received, and packet n had the EOM indication set.

In either case, the actual number of response packets received is returned to the requesting client. A count of 0 should indicate that the other end did not respond at all. In the case of a count that is not 0, the client can examine the response buffers to determine which portions of the response message were actually received and, if appropriate, detect missing pieces for higher-level recovery.

Opening a responding socket

An ATP client uses this call to instruct ATP to open a socket (either statically or dynamically assigned) for receiving TReqs. If the socket is statically assigned, the client passes the socket number to ATP; otherwise, the dynamically assigned socket number is returned to the caller.

When opening this socket, the client is, in effect, opening a transaction listening socket. The call allows the socket to be set up so that requests are accepted only from a specified network address (provided in the call). This address can include a 0 in the network number, node ID, or socket number field to indicate that any value is acceptable for that field.

Call parameters   transaction listening socket number (if statically assigned)

admissible transaction requester address (network number, node ID, and socket number)

Returned parameters   result code: success; failure

local socket number (if dynamically assigned)

◆ *Note:* This call does not set up any buffers for the reception of TReqs. Clients must use the call for receiving a request to set up buffers.

Closing a responding socket

This call is used to close a previously opened responding socket.

Call parameter   transaction listening socket number

Returned   result code: success; failure
parameter

Receiving a request

A transaction responder issues this call to set up the mechanism for reception of a TReq through an already-opened transaction responding socket.

Call parameters   local socket number on which to listen
buffer for receiving the request

Returned   result code: success; failure (buffer overflow)
parameters   the received request's ATP data
received request's user bytes
TID
transaction requester's address (network number, node ID, and socket number)
bitmap
XO indication

Sending a response

When a transaction responder has finished servicing a transaction request, it issues this call in order to send out one or more response packets. ATP will send out each response buffer with the indicated TID and a sequence number indicating the position of the particular response packet in the response message.

Call parameters   local socket number (the responding socket)

TID

transaction requester's address (network number, node ID, and socket number)

TResp message packets (ATP data part)

transaction user bytes (up to eight sets of 4 bytes each)

descriptors to determine the sequence numbers of the response packets

EOM and STS control

Returned parameter   result code: success; failure

ATP state model

The following description is not a formal specification but an aid for protocol implementers. The appropriate actions to respond to all possible events are presented in this model.

The ATP requester must maintain all information necessary for retransmitting an ATP request and for receiving its responses. This information is referred to as the **transaction control block** (TCB). More specifically, the TCB should contain all the information provided by the transaction requester in a call for sending a request, plus the TID, the request's bitmap, and a response-packets-received counter. A retry timer is associated with each transaction request and TCB. The retry timer is used to retransmit the request packet in order to recover from the loss of request or response packets.

The ATP responder must maintain for each call a **request control block** (RqCB) for receiving a request issued by a client in that node. This block contains the information provided by that call, including all data pertinent to the buffers and to the implementation-dependent client delivery mechanism.

The **response control block** (RspCB) is needed only in nodes implementing the XO mode of operation. It holds the information required to filter duplicate requests and to retransmit packets in response to these duplicates. A release timer is associated with each RspCB. This timer is used to release the RspCB if the release packet sent by the requester is lost. The transactions list mentioned in "Exactly-Once (XO) Transactions" earlier in this chapter consists of these RspCBs. The release timer is set to the value indicated in the TReq packet.

◆ *Note:* The release timer is started as soon as a RspCB is set up (in other words, when the responder's socket receives the TReq). The timer is reset every time a TResp is sent by the responder. This implies that the responding client must send the first TResp within one TRel timer interval of the TReq's arrival and then send subsequent TResps at a maximum separation of one TRel timer from each other. Failure to do so can result in the RspCB being destroyed, making it possible for a duplicate request to be delivered to the responding client.

ATP requester

The ATP requester maintains all information for retransmitting an ATP request and for receiving its responses. A list of events specific to the ATP requester follows and includes step-by-step actions for responding to the events.

Event: Call to send a request issued by a transaction requester in the node

1. Validate the following call parameters:
   □ The number of response packets should be a maximum of eight.
   □ The ATP request's data should be a maximum of 578 bytes long.
   If either parameter is invalid, then reject the call.

2. Create a TCB:
   □ Insert the call parameters into the TCB.
   □ Clear the response-packets-received counter.
   □ Insert the retry count into the TCB.

3. Generate a TID:
   □ This TID must be generated so that the packets of the new transaction will be correctly distinguished from those of other transactions (details of TID generation are discussed at the end of this chapter).
   □ Save the TID in the TCB.

4. Generate the bitmap for the TReq packet and save a copy of it in the TCB.

5. Prepare the ATP header:
   □ Insert the TID and the bitmap.
   □ Set the function code bits to binary 01.
   □ *Only if XO mode is implemented:* If the caller requested XO mode, then set the XO bit and the indicated value of the TRel timer bits.

6. Call DDP to send the TReq packet (ignore any error returned by DDP).

7. Start the request's retry timer.

Event: Retry timer expires

1. If retry count = 0, then:
   □ Set the result code to failure.
   □ Notify the transaction requester (the client in the node) of the outcome.
   □ Remove the TCB.

2. If retry count <> 0, then:

  □ Decrement the retry count (if not infinite).

  □ Change the bitmap in the ATP request's header to the current value in the TCB.

  □ Call DDP to retransmit the request packet (ignore any errors returned by DDP).

  □ Start the retry timer.

Event: TResp packet received from DDP

1. Use the packet's TID and source address to search for the TCB.

2. If a matching TCB is not found, then ignore the packet and exit.

3. If a matching TCB is found, then check the packet's sequence number against the TCB's bitmap to determine whether this response packet is expected. The packet is expected if the bit corresponding to the response packet's sequence number is set in the TCB's bitmap. If the packet is not expected, then ignore it and exit.

4. If the response packet is expected, then:

  □ Clear the corresponding bit in the TCB bitmap.

  □ Set up the response packet's ATP data and user bytes for delivery to the transaction requester.

  □ Increment the response packet's counter in the TCB.

5. If the packet's EOM bit is set, then clear all higher bits in the TCB bitmap.

6. If the packet's STS bit is set, then:

  □ Call DDP to send the TReq with the current TCB information.

  □ Reset the retry timer for the request.

7. If the TCB bitmap = 0 (a complete response has been received), then:

  □ Cancel the retry timer.

  □ Set the result code to success.

  □ *Only if XO mode is implemented:* If the transaction is of XO mode (determined by examining the TCB), then call DDP to send a TRel packet to the responder.

  □ Notify the transaction requester.

  □ Remove the TCB.

ATP responder

The ATP responder must maintain a RqCB for each call to recieve a request issued by a client in that node. A list of events specific to the ATP responder follows and includes specific step-by-step actions for responding to the events.

Event: Call to open a responding socket issued by a client

1. If the caller specifies a statically assigned socket, then call DDP to open that socket; otherwise, call DDP to open a dynamically assigned socket.

2. If DDP returns with an error, then set the result code to equal the error.

3. If DDP returns without an error, then:
   □ Set the result code to success.
   □ Save the socket number and the acceptable transaction requester address in an ATP responding sockets table.

Event: Call issued to close a responding socket in the node

1. Call DDP to close the socket.

2. Release all RqCBs for that socket; for systems supporting the XO mode, release all RspCBs (and cancel all release timers), if any, associated with the socket.

3. Delete the socket from the ATP responding sockets table.

Event: Call to receive a request issued by a transaction responder

1. If the specified local socket is not open, then return to the caller with an error.

2. Create a RqCB and attach it to the socket.

3. Save the call's parameters in the RqCB.

Event: Call to send a response issued by a transaction responder

1. If the local socket is invalid or if the response data length is invalid, then return to the caller with an error.

2. *Only if XO mode is implemented:* Search for a RspCB matching the call's local socket number, TID, and transaction requester address. If a match is found, attach a copy of the response to the RspCB (for potential retransmission in response to duplicate TReqs received subsequently), and restart the release timer.

3. Send the response packets through DDP, setting the ATP header of each with the function code binary 10, the caller-supplied TID, the correct sequence number for the packet's sequential position in the response message, the EOM flag set in the last response packet, and the STS flag, if requested. Ignore any error returned by DDP.

Event: Release timer expires, only if XO mode is implemented

1. Remove the RspCB and release all associated data structures.

Event: TReq packet received from DDP

1. *Only if XO mode is implemented:* If the packet's XO bit is set and a matching RspCB exists (the packet's source, destination addresses, and TID are the same as those saved in the RspCB), then:

   □ Retransmit all response packets requested in the transaction bitmap.

   □ Restart the release timer.

   □ Return the bitmap to the client if the STS bit was set during a previous response.

   □ Exit.

2. If a RqCB does not exist for the local socket or if the packet's source address does not match the admissible requester address in the RqCB, then ignore the packet and exit.

3. *Only if XO mode is implemented:* If the packet's XO bit is set, then create a RspCB, save the request's source and destination addresses, TID, and TRel timer indicator, and start its release timer.

4. Notify the client about the arrival of the request and remove the corresponding RqCB.

Event: TRel packet received from DDP, only if XO mode is implemented

1. Search for a RspCB that matches the packet's TID, source address, and destination address; if not found, then ignore the release packet and exit.

2. If a matching RspCB is found, then:

   □ Remove the RspCB and release all associated data structures.

   □ Cancel the RspCB's release timer.

Optional ATP interface calls

In certain cases, the clients of ATP might use contextual information to enhance their use of ATP through additional interface calls. Examples are calls to release a RspCB and to release a TCB. These calls are useful in implementing certain higher-level protocols but are optional in an ATP implementation.

Releasing a RspCB

The RspCB is used to hold information required to filter duplicate requests and to retransmit response packets for these duplicates. If the ATP client is aware that such filtering is no longer necessary, the client can indicate this to ATP through a call to release the RspCB.

For example, two clients of ATP communicate with each other using the XO mode, and they decide to have, at most, one outstanding transaction at a time. Client A calls ATP to send a TReq packet to client B. Client B sends back the response. Client A, upon receiving the response, sends out a second request (but no release packet). The second request packet, upon being received by B, signals that the response to the previous request has been received by A. Now B could simply call its ATP responder and ask it to release the previous transaction's RspCB. Arguments to this call include the requester's address and the TID of the associated transaction.

Another case in which the call would be useful is when the ATP client decides that it does not want to process the request at the current time but would rather receive a duplicate of that request at a later time.

Releasing a TCB

The TCB contains information for retransmitting an ATP request and for receiving its responses, including an associated timer. If the ATP client is aware that such retransmission is no longer necessary, it can indicate this through a call to release the TCB.

For example, if client A needs to send data to client B, client A must first inform B of its intention and allow B to request the data. Client A can then send a TReq to B to signal "I want to write *n* bytes of data to you; please ask me for it on my socket number *s*." Instead of sending a TResp to this packet, B could just send a TReq to A's socket *s* asking for the data. The reception by A, on socket *s*, of B's request implies that A's original request has been received by B. Client A could call its ATP requester and ask it to eliminate the previous transaction's TCB. This call could also be used by the requesting-end client to cancel an outstanding ATP request at any time (for example, to abort an infinite retry request).

Wraparound and generation of TIDs

In "Transaction Identifiers" earlier in this chapter, TIDs were described as being of finite size. Since TIDs can wrap around, an old packet stored in some internet router may arrive late and be accepted as a valid packet in a later transaction using the same identifier value. Based on an MPL estimate of 30 seconds, this problem can be avoided if the TIDs are 16 bits long (in which case, wraparound takes an estimated 1 minute or more).

A related problem occurs when completion of a particular transaction takes more than 1 minute. For example, a request that searches through an encyclopedia for all references to a particular piece of information might take several minutes. In this case, in the presence of other requests, the transaction ID could wrap around and another transaction could then be issued with the same TID, leading to an equivalent problem as described earlier. ATP does not prohibit operations of this sort. In fact, it is precisely because such transactions are possible that specification of the length of the ATP retry timer and maximum retry count is left up to ATP's transaction requesting client.

Similarly, ATP allows the requester to issue an ATP transaction with maximum retry count set to infinite. In this case, ATP continues to retransmit the TReq until a reply is received. If a reply is not sent, then the transaction will be continually retransmitted. This retransmission leads to the same TID wraparound problem.

A properly implemented ATP will function correctly in the face of these wraparound scenarios. Two key aspects of proper implementation are the use of TIDs to distinguish between transactions and the generation of TIDs.

When asked by a client to send a TReq, the ATP requesting end generates the TID for the request. At the same time, the ATP requesting end creates a TCB, and several pieces of information are saved in the TCB. These pieces of information include the number of the local socket through which the transaction is being sent, the complete internet address of the responding socket to which the transaction is being sent, and the TID. This information is saved to ensure a correct match of the response packets with the transaction. When the ATP requesting end receives a TResp, the requesting end identifies the corresponding request by looking for a TCB whose saved information matches the response packet's TID and the packet's source and destination socket addresses.

Therefore, TID wraparound by itself does not pose a problem unless it causes the simultaneous existence of two or more transactions (TCBs) with the same TID *and* the same requesting and responding socket addresses. This observation allows the specification of the following algorithm for generating TIDs:

```
{ Algorithm used by ATP Requesting end to generate TID for a new transaction }
new_TID := last_used_TID;
Not_In_Use := TRUE;
REPEAT
        new_TID := (new_TID + 1) modulo 2^16;
        Search all TCBs on the local requesting socket, and if any one of these
            has (new_TID = TCB's TID) then set Not_In_Use := FALSE;
UNTIL Not_In_Use;
{ At this point new_TID has the newly generated TID }
last_used_TID := new_TID;
```

◆ *Note:* This algorithm ignores the TCB's destination socket address (that is, the algorithm does not further distinguish on the basis of the destination address for the request). This simplification of the algorithm does not reduce its effectiveness in preventing the wraparound problem.

Chapter 10 **Printer Access Protocol**

CONTENTS

■

THE APPLETALK PRINTER ACCESS PROTOCOL (PAP)
is a session-level protocol that enables communication between workstations
and servers. It is a connection-oriented protocol, which handles

- connection setup

- connection maintenance

- connection closure

- data transfer over the connection

PAP allows multiple connections at both the workstation and server ends.

PAP envisions a server node as containing one or more processes that are
accessible to workstations through PAP. In this chapter, these processes are
referred to as **servers.** A server makes itself visible over the network by
opening a **session listening socket** (SLS) on which it registers its name. ■

The use of the word *printer* in the name of this protocol is purely historical. The protocol was originally designed for the specific purpose of communication with print **servers,** such as the Apple LaserWriter and ImageWriter printers. However, the protocol has no special features for printing and can be used by a wide variety of other kinds of servers. *Figure 10-1* illustrates the protocol architecture used for communication between a user's computer (workstation) and a print server in an AppleTalk network. PAP is a client of the AppleTalk Transaction Protocol (ATP) and the Name Binding Protocol (NBP). Both of these protocols use the Datagram Delivery Protocol (DDP). PAP is an asymmetric protocol; the PAP code in the workstation is different from the PAP code in the printer.

The commands and data sent through the PAP connection are printer-dependent. For the LaserWriter printer, the dialog is in PostScript.

■ **Figure 10-1** Printing architecture

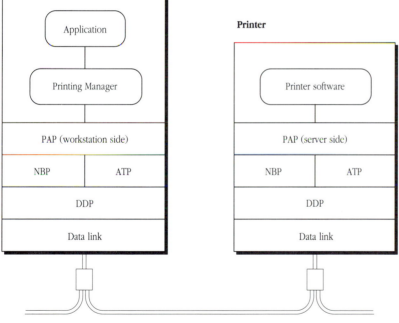

PAP services

In order to establish a connection with a server, a PAP client in a workstation issues a PAPOpen call that results in the initiation of a connection establishment dialog with a server. The client specifies the server by its complete name; in order to initiate a dialog with the server, PAP calls NBP to obtain the address of the server's **session listening socket** (SLS). PAP also allows implementations in which the workstation's PAP client performs the NBP lookup directly (or obtains the server's address through other means) and then makes the PAPOpen call with the address of the server's SLS.

Once a connection has been opened to the server, the PAP client at either end of the connection can receive data from the other end (by issuing PAPRead calls) and can write data to the other end (through PAPWrite calls). PAP uses ATP transactions (in exactly-once mode) to transfer the data. See Chapter 9, "AppleTalk Transaction Protocol," for further details on ATP transactions.

When the data transfer has been completed, the PAP client on either end issues a PAPClose call.

The PAP client in a workstation can, at any time, issue a PAPStatus call to find out the status of a server. PAP does not restrict the syntactic or semantic structure of the returned status information beyond specifying that it is a string of at most 255 bytes preceded by a length byte. The PAPStatus call can be issued even before a connection has been established with the server.

Since PAP is not a symmetric protocol, several PAP calls are used only in server nodes. The first of these is the SLInit call. This call is issued by a server when it starts up and after it has completed its initialization. The SLInit call opens an SLS (an ATP responding socket) in the server node and causes the server's name to be registered on that socket through NBP. Multiple SLInit calls can be issued to the PAP code in the same server node; each SLInit call opens a new SLS and registers the server name provided on that socket.

A second call, the GetNextJob call, is used by the PAP client in the server to indicate to the PAP connection arbitration code that this client is ready to accept a new connection through a particular SLS opened via a prior SLInit call. The GetNextJob call primes the connection arbitration code to accept another connection establishment request from a workstation.

A server client can issue an SLClose call in order to close the SLS and to shut down any active connections on that socket.

A PAP client in the server node can use two calls, PAPRegName and PAPRemName, to register and remove (deregister), respectively, a server name for a specified SLS. For instance, PAPRegName can be used to assign more than one name to the server on a particular SLS. These calls could also be used at server setup time to change the name associated with a particular SLS.

PAP must be able to handle cases of **half-open connections,** which occur when one of the connection ends goes down or otherwise terminates the connection without informing the other end. Half-open connections must be detected by PAP and torn down. For this purpose, PAP maintains a connection timer at each end. In addition, each end of an open connection must send *tickling* packets to the other end on a periodic basis (determined by the tickle timer). The purpose of these packets is to inform the other end that the sender's end is open and "alive." The receipt of any packet on a connection resets the connection timer at the receiving end. If the connection timer expires without a packet having been received, then PAP determines that the other end is unreachable, and the connection end is torn down.

The protocol

The basic model of a PAP-based server is that it processes a specific maximum number of jobs from workstations at the same time. The number of jobs that a server can process at once depends on the server's implementation and is not defined by PAP. While the server is processing this maximum number of jobs, it does not accept requests for initiating additional jobs; instead, it informs requesting workstations that it is busy. While a server is processing a job, a connection is said to be open between the workstation being served and the server. A one-to-one correspondence exists between the number of open connections and the number of jobs being processed by the server. When the server completes a particular job, the corresponding connection is closed, and the server can notify its PAP that it is able to accept another connection from a workstation.

When a server process is first started, it goes through its internal initialization and then issues an SLInit call to its PAP code. This causes PAP to call ATP to open an ATP responding socket, which is the SLS for that server. Then, PAP calls NBP to register the server's name and to bind it to the SLS. Next, PAP issues an ATP call to receive a request on this socket, so that the server can respond to PAPOpen or PAPStatus request packets. However, the PAP client may still not be ready to accept a job. Therefore, PAP will still refuse connection-opening requests through this SLS. In this case, the server is said to be in a blocked state. *Figure 10-2* shows the server states.

After the SLInit call is completed, the server process issues a series of GetNextJob calls to indicate that it is ready to accept jobs. One such call is issued for each job that the server can accept at the time. The server is now in the waiting state and is ready to open connections and accept jobs.

As previously stated, PAP can support multiple servers within one node. Each of these servers is made available on a unique SLS, which is set up through a corresponding SLInit call.

■ **Figure 10-2** Server states

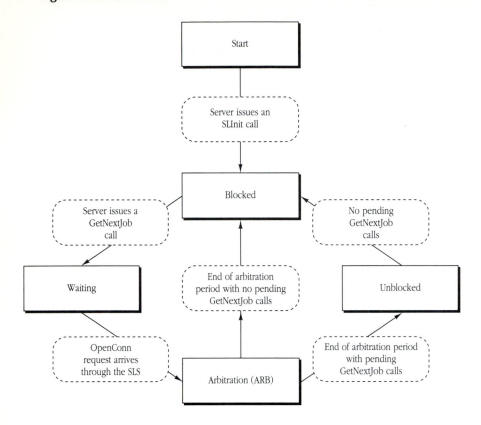

PAP uses NBP to name (in a server) and find (from a workstation) a server's SLS. Apart from these operations, all packets exchanged by PAP are sent through ATP. Each such PAP packet contains a 1-byte quantity in the ATP user bytes that indicates the packet's PAP function.

Connection establishment phase

A **connection** is a logical relationship between two PAP entities, one in the workstation node and the other in the server node. Data can be exchanged by two PAP clients only after a connection has been established (opened). Since PAP uses ATP to transfer data, the two communicating PAPs must accomplish the following during the connection establishment phase:

- discover the address of the ATP responding socket for the other connection end

- determine the maximum amount of data that can be transferred in an ATP transaction, based on the buffer space available at the data receiving end (This maximum size, called the **flow quantum,** is sent by each end to the other end during the connection establishment phase.)

A PAP client in a workstation initiates connection establishment by issuing a PAPOpen call. Such a client provides the complete name of the server as a call parameter. The PAP code obtains the internet socket address of the server's SLS by issuing an NBP Lookup call. The PAP code then opens an ATP responding socket (R_W), generates an 8-bit PAP **connection identifier (ConnID),** and then sends a Transaction Request (TReq), with PAP function OpenConn, to the server's SLS. This packet contains the ConnID, the address of socket R_W, the flow quantum for the workstation, and a wait period used by the server for arbitration. All packets related to this connection that are sent by either end must contain this ConnID. PAP should ignore packets with different ConnIDs that are received through sockets associated with the connection. The workstation must generate the ConnIDs in such a way as to minimize the likelihood that any two connections opened by the workstation will have the same ConnID. (This precaution is especially necessary for connections that are established at about the same time.)

When an ATP TReq of PAP function OpenConn is received at the server's SLS, PAP executes a connection-acceptance algorithm as shown in *Figure 10-2.* If the server is blocked (that is, if there are no outstanding GetNextJob calls), then the server's PAP responds to the OpenConn transaction with an ATP response of PAP function OpenConnReply, indicating "server busy." Included in the OpenConnReply is a status string that is passed back to the workstation client and that can contain further details about the busy state.

If, however, the server is in the waiting state (that is, if one or more GetNextJob calls are pending), then upon receiving an OpenConn (the first one since the server went into the waiting state), the server's PAP goes into an arbitration (ARB) state for a fixed length of time (2 seconds). In the ARB state, PAP receives all incoming OpenConn requests and tries to find the ones corresponding to workstations that have been waiting the longest time for a connection. The ARB interval allows the server to implement a fairness scheme that accepts requests generated by the workstations that have been waiting the longest before accepting those from more recent entrants to the contest.

The length of time in seconds that a workstation has been waiting for a connection (called the WaitTime) is sent with the OpenConn request. When the first OpenConn request since the server went into the waiting state is received, the WaitTime value from that request is loaded into a variable associated with one of the pending GetNextJob calls. This GetNextJob call is marked as having a WaitTime associated with it. If, during the ARB interval, a new OpenConn request is received, the server examines all pending GetNextJob calls to see if any one of them does not have a WaitTime associated with it. If such a free, pending GetNextJob call is found, then the WaitTime of the just-received OpenConn request is saved with this GetNextJob. If no free GetNextJob call is found among the pending calls, then PAP compares the just-received OpenConn request's WaitTime with the values saved in the pending GetNextJobs. If the WaitTime value for the just-received OpenConn request is less than all of the WaitTime values for the pending GetNextJob calls, then PAP responds to the just-received request with an OpenConnReply that indicates "server busy." If, on the other hand, the WaitTime is greater than one or more of the WaitTimes in GetNextJob, PAP associates the new request with the GetNextJob that has the smallest saved WaitTime, replacing that WaitTime with the one from the new request.

At the end of the ARB interval, the server's PAP opens ATP responding socket R_S for each connection request still associated with a GetNextJob and sends ATP responses of PAP function OpenConnReply indicating "connection accepted" to the selected (but still pending) ATP requests. These ATP responses carry the ConnID received in the OpenConn request, the address of socket R_S, and the flow quantum of the server end (which is set by the SLInit call that is issued when the server is initialized). The corresponding PAP connections are now open, and the jobs from the corresponding workstations can be processed.

At the end of the ARB interval, if no GetNextJobs are pending, then the server enters the blocked state; if there are pending GetNextJobs, then the server enters the unblocked state. In the blocked state, the server cannot accept incoming OpenConn requests. However, in the unblocked state there are pending GetNextJob calls, and the server can accept additional connections (jobs).

Note that if the server is in the unblocked state, it has just been through the ARB state and has already opened connections to all workstations that have been waiting for a connection. Therefore, when the server is in the unblocked state and receives an OpenConn request, it need not enter the ARB state; the server accepts incoming OpenConn requests and sets up connections immediately. As soon as the server runs out of pending GetNextJob calls, it enters the blocked state. Then when a GetNextJob call is issued, the server again enters the waiting state.

If the workstation's PAP receives an OpenConnReply indicating that the server is busy (that is, in the blocked state), then PAP waits a specified time period (approximately 2 seconds) and issues another connection-opening transaction. Each time the workstation end repeats this process, it updates its WaitTime value. The current value of this WaitTime is sent with each OpenConn packet. Each of these OpenConn ATP transaction requests is issued with a retry count of 5 and a retry interval of 2 seconds. The workstation's PAP should provide some way for its client to abort a PAPOpen call but should otherwise keep trying until the connection is opened.

Data transfer phase

The opening of a connection initiates PAP's data transfer phase. In this phase, PAP performs the following two functions:

- It transfers data over the connection.

- It detects and tears down half-open connections.

PAP maintains a connection timer (of 2-minute duration) at each end of a connection. This timer, used in detecting half-open connections, is started as soon as the connection is opened. Whenever a packet of any sort is received from the other end of the connection, the timer is reset. If the timer expires (if, for example, no packets are received from the other end during the 2-minute time period), the connection is torn down. This indicates to PAP that the other end has gone down, has closed its connection, or has become otherwise unreachable (if, for example, an internet has become partitioned).

For the timer mechanism to work properly, it is important that, although no client data is being transferred on the connection, PAP exchange control packets to signal that the connection ends are alive. This process is referred to as tickling, and the control packets are called tickling packets. For this purpose, as soon as a connection is established, each end starts an ATP transaction with PAP function Tickle. This transaction, known as a Tickle transaction, has a retry count of infinite and a retry time interval equal to half the connection timeout period. Tickle transactions must be at-least-once (ALO) ATP transactions. Tickle packets are sent to the other end's ATP responding socket (that is, the R_S or R_W socket). The receiver of such a TReq packet must reset its connection timer but must not send a transaction response. Tickle transactions are canceled by each end when the connection is closed.

The data transfer model used by PAP is read-driven. When the PAP client at either end of the connection wants to read data from the other end, it issues a PAPRead call. This call provides PAP with a read buffer into which the data is read; the size of the read buffer must be equal to the end's flow quantum. In response to the PAPRead call, PAP calls ATP to send an ATP transaction request with PAP function SendData and with an ATP bitmap that reflects the size of the call's read buffer. This transaction is issued with a retry count of infinite and a retry time interval of 15 seconds. The call is sent to the other end's ATP responding socket. To prevent duplicate delivery of data to PAP's clients, all ATP data transfer transactions use ATP's exactly-once (XO) mode and a sequence number. This technique of preventing duplicate delivery is described in detail in the following section, "Duplicate Filtration."

The receipt of an ATP TReq packet with PAP function SendData implies that a pending PAPRead is at the other end. This send credit can be remembered by the PAP code and used to service any pending or future PAPWrite calls issued by its client.

When a PAP client (at either end) issues a PAPWrite call, PAP examines its internal data structures to see if it has received a send credit. If it has, then the client takes the data from the PAPWrite call and sends this data in ATP response packets with at most 512 bytes of ATP data in each. The packets are of PAP function Data, and have the end-of-message (EOM) bit set in the last one. If no send credit has been received, then PAP queues the PAPWrite call and awaits a send credit from the other end. (That is, it awaits the receipt of an ATP request of PAP function SendData from the other end.) The amount of data to be sent in a PAPWrite call cannot exceed the flow quantum of the other end; PAPWrite calls that violate this restriction return immediately with an error message.

When a PAP client issues the last PAPWrite call for a particular job, it should ask PAP to send an end-of-file (EOF) indication with that call's data. The EOF indication is delivered to the PAP client at the other end as part of the received information for a PAPRead call; this indication notifies the client that the other end is finished sending data on this connection. In order to specify the end of data, the client can issue a PAPWrite call with no data to be sent; in this case, just an EOF indication is sent to the client at the other end.

Duplicate filtration

As described in Chapter 9, "AppleTalk Transaction Protocol," in the case of internets, ATP XO mode does not guarantee XO delivery of requests—it guarantees only that if a duplicate request is delivered to an ATP client, the request can be ignored because all responses to it have been successfully received by the other side. PAP uses a sequence number in SendData requests to enable it to detect these duplicates and to ignore them. Furthermore, since PAP maintains only one outstanding read request at a time, duplicate filtration can be accomplished in a fairly simple manner.

All SendData requests contain a sequence number in the last 2 ATP user bytes. The sequence number starts at 1 with the first such request and takes on successive values up to 65,535 before wrapping around to 1 again. The value 0 is reserved to mean unsequenced. Any SendData request received with a sequence number of 0 should be accepted by PAP without checking for duplication. This use of 0 is for compatibility with previous versions of PAP. If the sequence number is not 0, PAP should verify that the sequence number is equal to the highest sequence number of the last SendData request received. If this is not the case, the packet should be ignored as a duplicate of a previous, already-completed request. Each side of the PAP connection must maintain independently both a sequence number for its SendData requests and a sequence number for the last SendData request accepted from the other end.

Connection termination phase

When the PAP client at either end issues a PAPClose call, PAP closes the connection. Typically, after the workstation's PAP client has completed sending all data to the server and has received an EOF in return, the client will issue the PAPClose call. An ATP transaction request is sent to the other end with PAP function CloseConn. An end receiving a CloseConn request should immediately send back, as a courtesy, an ATP transaction response of PAP function CloseConnReply. To close a connection's end, it is important to cancel any pending ATP transactions issued by that end, including Tickle transactions. An end receiving a CloseConn packet must cancel its pending ATP transactions for that connection as soon as it is able to do so.

At the server end, the receipt of the CloseConn causes the connection to be torn down, but the server may continue to process data for the ongoing job. When this data has been processed, the PAP client in the server can then issue a GetNextJob call in order to accept another job. In fact, the server can issue a GetNextJob call at any time in order to signal to its PAP code that it is willing to accept another job. These GetNextJob calls are queued up by PAP and used to accept incoming OpenConn requests as discussed in "Connection Establishment Phase" earlier in this chapter.

A server can also close all open connections by issuing an SLClose call, which deregisters all names and closes the server's SLS.

Status gathering

PAP supports status querying of the server through the PAPStatus call. A workstation client need not open a connection with the server in order to issue this call; this call can be issued at any time. The PAPStatus call results in a SendStatus request packet being sent to the server specified in the call (the server can be specified by name, in which case, PAP calls NBP to determine the server's address). The request is sent to the server's SLS. The server's PAP responds with a Status reply packet that contains a Pascal-format string (length byte first) specifying the server's status. This response is made without delivering the request to the PAP client in the server. The PAP client in the server must have previously provided the status string to PAP through an SLInit or HeresStatus call. The HeresStatus call, details of which are implementation-dependent, should be made by the PAP server client whenever the server's status changes. This status string is also returned by PAP in OpenConnReply packets.

PAP packet formats

As previously stated, PAP uses both NBP and ATP. NBP is used by the server's PAP to register or remove a name on the server's SLS. A workstation's PAP uses NBP to determine the address of a server's SLS from the server's name.

Packets sent by ATP in response to PAP calls include a PAP header. The header is built by using the user bytes of the ATP header and, in some cases, by sending 4 or more bytes of the PAP header in the data part of the ATP packet.

The first ATP user byte of the PAP header is the ConnID (except in SendStatus requests and Status replies, whose first byte must be 0). The second ATP user byte is the PAP function of the packet (see the following section for a list of the PAP function values). For packets of PAP function equal to Data, the third ATP user byte is the EOF indication (a number other than 0 indicates EOF). For packets of function SendData, the third and fourth bytes are the sequence number (high byte first). OpenConn and OpenConnReply packets contain, as part of the ATP data, the ATP responding socket numbers and the flow quantum to be used for the connection. The OpenConn request additionally contains the WaitTime; the OpenConn reply contains the open result and the status string. Status replies contain just the status string.

Figures 10-3 through 10-6 illustrate the PAP headers for the various types of PAP packets. For simplicity, the DDP and data-link headers are not included.

■ **Figure 10-3** PAP OpenConn and OpenConnReply packet formats

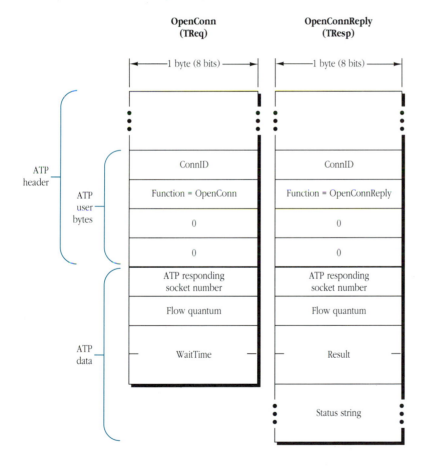

- **Figure 10-4** PAP SendData, Data, and Tickle packet formats

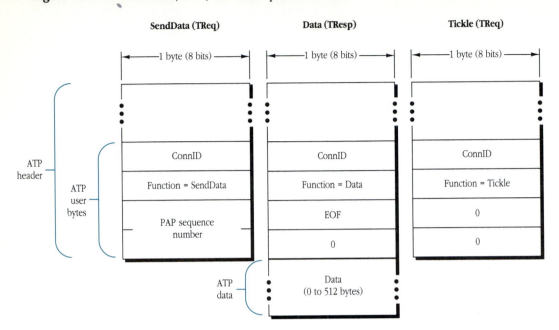

- **Figure 10-5** PAP CloseConn and CloseConnReply packet formats

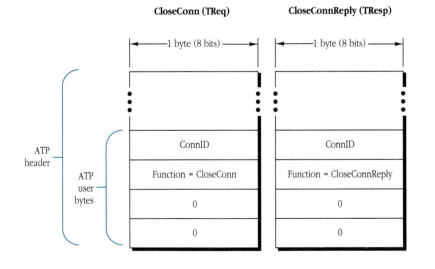

■ Figure 10-6 PAP SendStatus and Status packet formats

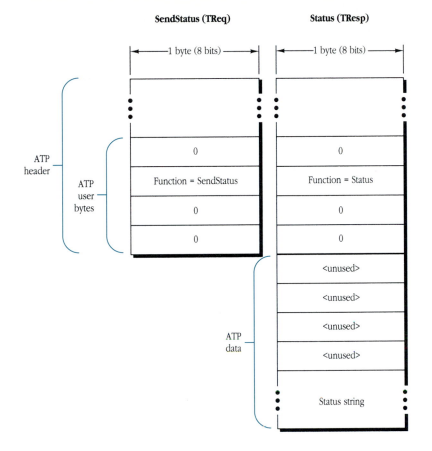

PAP function and result values

The permissible PAP function field values are as follows:

Function	Value
OpenConn	1
OpenConnReply	2
SendData	3
Data	4
Tickle	5
CloseConn	6
CloseConnReply	7
SendStatus	8
Status	9

The values that can be returned in the result code field of a OpenConnReply are as follows:

Result	Value	Meaning
NoError	0	No error—connection opened
PrinterBusy	$FFFF	Printer busy

PAP client interface

This section describes the PAP calls. It lists the parameters that the client must include and provides the significant interface-level aspects of each call. Some of these calls are available only in workstations, others only in servers, and others in both workstations and servers. The call definitions specify which devices can use the calls.

PAPOpen call

A PAP client in a workstation issues the PAPOpen call in order to initiate a connection-opening dialog with the specified server.

Call parameters   specification of the server to which a connection should be opened (either the server's NBP name or the server's SLS address)

flow quantum (the number of 512-byte buffers available for each read)

buffer in which the open status string is to be returned

Returned parameters   result code

connection refnum (a local number assigned by the workstation's PAP to uniquely identify the connection within the workstation)

The open status string should be returned by PAP each time it is received in an OpenConnReply and not just upon call completion. The client must use the connection reference number (refnum) in order to refer to this connection in subsequent calls in the workstation.

PAPClose call

A PAP client in a workstation or a server must issue the PAPClose call in order to close the connection specified by the connection refnum.

Call parameter   connection refnum

Returned parameter   result code

PAPRead call

The PAP client at either end issues a PAPRead call in order to read data from the other end over the connection specified by the connection refnum.

Call parameters   connection refnum

buffer in which to read the data

Returned parameters   result code

size of the data read

EOF indication

◆ *Note:* PAP assumes that the buffer into which the reply data is to be read is no smaller than the flow quantum specified in the PAPOpen or the SLInit call.

PAPWrite call

The PAP client at either end issues a PAPWrite call in order to write data to the other end over the connection specified by the connection refnum.

Call parameters   connection refnum

buffer with the data to be written

size of the data to be written

EOF indication

Returned parameter   result code

If the data size is larger than the flow quantum of the other end, the call returns with an error.

PAPStatus call

A PAP client in the workstation issues a PAPStatus call in order to determine the current status of the server. This call can be used at any time, regardless of whether a connection has been opened by the PAP client to the server. Upon completion, this call returns a string that contains the status message sent by the server.

Call parameters specifications of the server from which status is being requested (either the server's NBP name or the server's SLS address)

buffer in which the status string is to be returned

Returned parameter result code

SLInit call

The PAP client in the server issues an SLInit call in order to open an SLS and to register the server's name on this socket. The client can also include an initial status string in this call.

Call parameters NBP name of the server

flow quantum for all connections to the server (the number of 512-byte buffers available for reads)

status string

Returned parameters result code

server refnum

The server refnum must be used by the server when issuing subsequent GetNextJob calls in order to identify the SLS for which the GetNextJob call is being made. The PAP code in the server node must return a unique server refnum for each SLInit call.

GetNextJob call

The PAP client in the server issues a GetNextJob call whenever it is ready to accept a new job through the SLS specified by a server refnum.

Call parameter   server refnum

Returned   result code
parameters   connection refnum (a number assigned by PAP to uniquely identify the connection)

SLClose call

The PAP client in the server issues an SLClose call in order to close down a server process.

Call parameter   server refnum

Returned   result code
parameter

PAPRegName call

The PAPRegName call is used only in server nodes. This call registers a name (as an NBP entity name for the server) on the SLS corresponding to the specified server refnum.

Call parameters   server refnum

                         server name to register

Returned   result code
parameter

PAPRemName call

The PAPRemName call is used only in server nodes. This call deregisters a name from the SLS corresponding to the specified server refnum.

Call parameters   server refnum

server name to deregister

Returned   result code
parameter

HeresStatus call

The PAP client in the server issues a HeresStatus call in order to provide PAP with a new status string. This call should be issued any time the status string has changed.

Call parameters   server refnum

status string

Returned   result code
parameter

PAP specifications for the Apple LaserWriter printer

The following specifications detail the PAP-client implementation on the Apple LaserWriter printer.

- The flow quantum used by the LaserWriter is 8.

- The LaserWriter printer can handle only one job at a time, so it never has more than one GetNextJob outstanding. Essentially, the unblocked state does not exist on the LaserWriter; the LaserWriter printer can be in only a waiting, arbitration, or blocked state.

Chapter 11 **AppleTalk Session Protocol**

CONTENTS

■

A WIDE VARIETY of higher-level network services are built using the model of a workstation issuing a sequence of commands to a server. The server then carries out these commands and reports the results to the workstation. For example, in a filing service, file system commands are transported to a file server and are executed there; the results are then returned to the workstation.

At the transport layer, the AppleTalk protocol architecture provides a reliable transaction service, via the AppleTalk Transaction Protocol (ATP), that can be used for transporting workstation commands to servers. However, ATP does not provide the full range of transport functions needed by many higher-level network services. This chapter describes the AppleTalk Session Protocol (ASP) designed specifically for the use of these higher-level services.

ASP is a client of ATP; it adds value to ATP to provide the level of transport service needed for higher-level workstation-to-server interaction. ■

What ASP does

The concept of a session is central to ASP. Two network entities, one in a workstation and the other in a server, can set up an ASP session between themselves. A **session** is a logical relationship (connection) between two network entities; it is identified by a unique session identifier. For the duration of the session, the workstation entity can (through ASP) send a sequence of commands to the server entity. ASP ensures that the commands are delivered without duplication in the same order as they were sent and conveys the results of these commands (known as a command reply or reply) back to the workstation entity.

ASP sessions are inherently asymmetrical. The process of setting up a session is always initiated by the workstation entity (when it wishes to use the server entity's advertised service). Once the session is established, the workstation client of ASP sends commands, and the server client of ASP replies to the commands. ASP does not allow its server client to send commands to the workstation client. However, ASP provides an attention mechanism by which the server can inform the workstation of a need for attention.

More than one workstation can establish a session with the same server at the same time. ASP uses the **session identifier** (session ID) to distinguish between commands received during these various sessions. The session ID is unique among all the sessions established with the same server.

What ASP does not do

ASP does not enforce the syntax or interpret the semantics of the commands sent by its workstation clients. Commands are conveyed as blocks of bytes to be interpreted by the server-end client of ASP. Similarly, command replies are sent back over the session to the workstation client without any syntactic or semantic interpretation by ASP.

Although ASP guarantees that commands issued by the workstation end of a session are delivered to its server end in the same order as they were issued, ASP does not ensure that the commands are executed and completed in the specified order by the server end. This proper execution and completion of commands is the responsibility of the ASP client at the server end.

An important goal in the design of ASP was to make its client interface independent of the lower-level transport protocols. Therefore, the higher-level clients of ASP can be moved from one network to another with a minimum of modification. To achieve this, it is necessary to separate from ASP both the mechanism by which a server advertises its service and the manner in which a workstation looks for this advertised service. The way these procedures are accomplished depends primarily upon the transport and naming mechanisms of a particular network; these procedures are the responsibility of the ASP clients, not of ASP itself.

For example, a server entity that needs to make its service known on the AppleTalk network calls ATP to open an ATP responding socket and then calls the Name Binding Protocol (NBP) to register a unique name on this socket. Once that is done, the server entity calls ASP to give to it the address of the ATP responding socket. ASP then starts listening on the socket for session-opening commands coming over the network. A workstation wishing to utilize this advertised service uses NBP to identify the service's socket address. Then the workstation client calls ASP to open a session.

Setting up a responding socket and looking for the socket's address through NBP are done outside the scope of ASP. The participation of ASP starts with the process of setting up a session.

ASP does not provide a user authentication mechanism. If needed, this mechanism must be supplied by a higher-level protocol than ASP. In addition, ASP does not provide any mechanism to allow the use of a particular session by more than one server entity. Such multiplexing of a session can be done by the ASP clients if higher-level protocols divide the function codes into ranges and manage them completely outside the scope of ASP. The use of a single session to gain access to various services on the same node is not recommended.

ASP services and features

ASP provides the following services to its clients:

- setting up (opening) and tearing down (closing) sessions
- sending commands on an open session to the server and returning command replies (which might include a block of data)
- writing blocks of data from the workstation to the server end of the session
- sending an attention from the server to the workstation
- retrieving service status information from the server without opening a session

Opening and closing sessions

Before any sessions are opened, both the workstation ASP client and the server ASP client should interrogate ASP to identify the maximum sizes of commands and replies allowed by the underlying transport mechanism. Both ends of the session can use these sizes to determine whether the underlying transport services are adequate to their needs and to optimize the size of their commands and replies.

The server entity makes itself known on the network by calling ATP to open an ATP responding socket, known as the session listening socket (SLS), and by registering its name on this socket. Then ASP begins listening on the SLS for session-opening requests coming in over the network.

After identifying the internet address (the **entity identifier**) of the intended service's SLS, the workstation client calls ASP to open a session to this service. ASP sends a special OpenSess packet (an ATP request) to the SLS; this packet carries the address of a workstation socket to which session maintenance packets (discussed later in this chapter) are to be sent (see *Figure 11-1*).

■ **Figure 11-1** ASP session-opening dialog

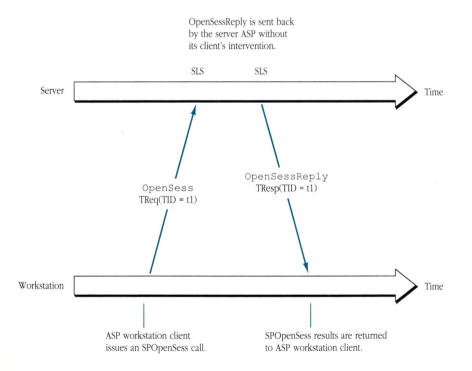

This socket is referred to as the **workstation session socket** (WSS). If the server is able to establish a session, it returns a session acceptance indication, a session ID, and the number of the session's server-end socket, referred to as the **server session socket** (SSS). In all further communication over this session, all packets sent from the workstation must carry this session ID and must be sent to the SSS.

ASP allows protocol version verification in this session-opening dialog. ASP in the workstation sends an ASP protocol version number in the OpenSess packet (to identify the version of ASP that the workstation is using). If the server's ASP is unable to handle this version, it returns an error, and the session is not opened.

A session can be closed by the ASP client at either end by issuing the appropriate command to the client's ASP. That node's ASP notifies the other end and then immediately closes the session. If the session termination was initiated by the workstation client, then a session termination notification is sent to the SSS. If the session termination was initiated by the server client, then the notification is sent to the WSS. See *Figure 11-2* and *Figure 11-3*.

■ **Figure 11-2** Session-closing dialog initiated by the workstation

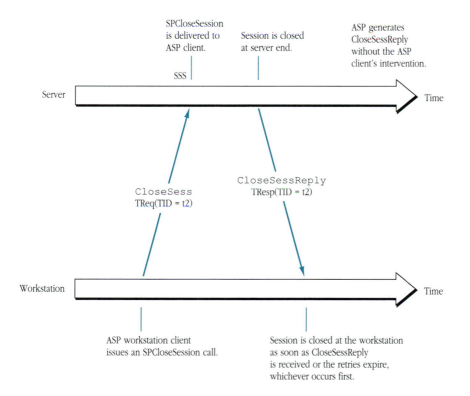

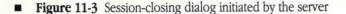

■ **Figure 11-3** Session-closing dialog initiated by the server

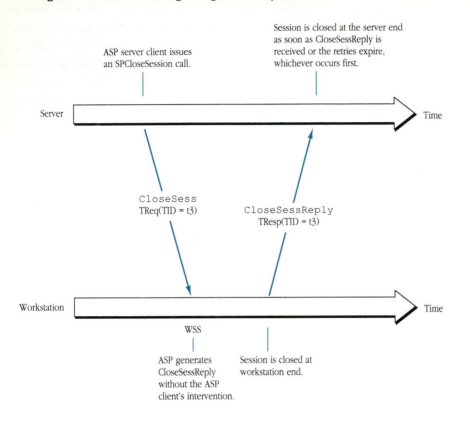

Whenever a session is terminated, the ASP clients at both ends must be notified so that appropriate higher-level action can be taken. This notification is easily done at the server end since it is generally listening for incoming commands on the session. But at the workstation end (if the server end closed the session), the workstation ASP client may not be notified until the next time it tries to issue a command on that session. The actions taken by an ASP client, upon being informed of the closing of a session, vary depending on the higher-level function. For example, the server end might choose to free resources allocated for that session; or, if the higher-level service is a filing service, it might decide to **flush** and close all files opened during that session.

Session maintenance

A session remains open until it is explicitly terminated by the ASP client at either end or until one end of the session goes down or becomes unreachable. ASP provides a mechanism known as session tickling that is initiated as soon as a session is opened. In session tickling, each end of the session periodically sends a packet to the WSS or SLS to inform the other end that it is functioning properly (see *Figure 11-4*). The packet sent by either end of the session is known as a tickle packet. If either end fails to receive any packets (tickles, requests, or replies) on a session for a certain predefined **session maintenance timeout,** it assumes that the other end has gone down or has become unreachable. When the session maintenance timeout occurs, the session times out and closes. Tickle packets are no longer sent out.

■ **Figure 11-4** Tickle packet dialog

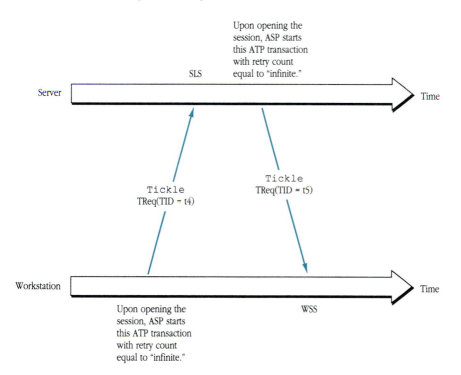

Commands on an open session

Once a session has been opened, the workstation client of ASP can send a sequence of commands to the server end. These commands are delivered in the same order as they were issued at the workstation end, and replies to the commands are returned to the workstation end by ASP. The two types of commands, SPCommands and SPWrites, differ in the direction of the primary flow of data. In addition, the server end can send an SPAttention call to the workstation end to inform the workstation of some server need. The following sections describe how ASP uses ATP to perform these commands.

SPCommands

SPCommands are very similar to ATP requests. The ASP workstation client sends a command (encoded in a variable-length command block) to the server-end client requesting the server to perform a particular function and to send back a variable-length command reply. Examples of such commands are requests to open a particular file on a file server or to read a certain range of bytes from an already opened file. In the first case, a small amount of reply data is returned; in the second case, a multipacket reply might be generated. Each SPCommand translates into an ATP request sent to the SSS, and the command reply is received as one or more ATP response packets, as shown in *Figure 11-5*.

In any case, ASP does not interpret the command block or in any way participate in the command's function. ASP simply conveys the command block to the server end of the session and returns the command reply to the workstation-end client. The command reply consists of a 4-byte command result (CmdResult) and a variable-length command reply data block (CmdBlock).

■ **Figure 11-5** SPCommand dialog

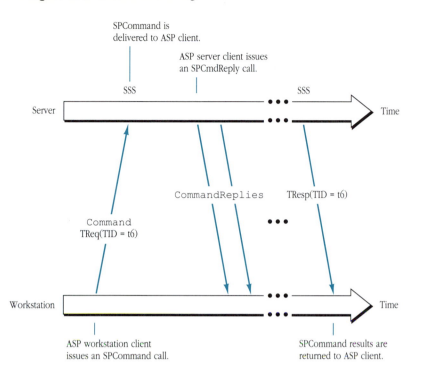

SPWrites

When using an SPWrite call, the ASP client in the workstation intends to convey a variable-length block of data to the server end of a session and expects a reply. Since ASP uses ATP as its underlying transport protocol and since ATP is a protocol in which a requesting end essentially *reads* a multipacket block of data from the responding end, for efficiency it is necessary to translate the SPWrite into two transactions. Essentially, a write to the server end is accomplished by having the server initiate a transaction request to read the data from the workstation end.

In the first transaction, ASP sends an ATP request to the SSS carrying the SPWrite's control information, known as the write command block. The server end examines this information to determine whether to proceed with reading the data from the workstation end. If it does not wish to proceed, the server returns an error in the ATP response packet. (This error is conveyed to the workstation client as the 4-byte command result.) Along with the error, up to eight ATP response packets can be sent back to the workstation. This transaction is illustrated in *Figure 11-6*.

■ **Figure 11-6** SPWrite dialog (error condition)

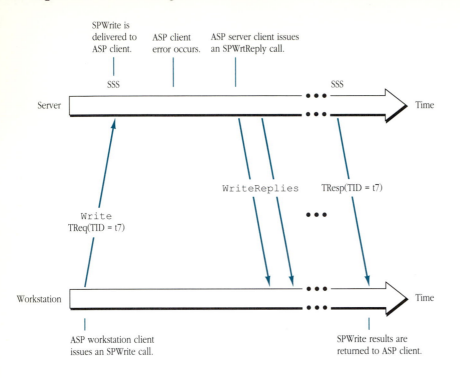

If the server decides to read the data, then the server's ASP sends an SPWrtContinue command, which is an ATP request to the WSS to read the data from the workstation end (see *Figure 11-7*). This ATP request could generate a multipacket ATP response carrying the write data to the server. Upon receiving the write data and performing the particular function requested in the SPWrite call, the server end then responds to the first ATP request (the Write command block) with the appropriate error message (this error message is conveyed to the workstation client as the 4-byte CmdResult) and up to eight WriteReply packets.

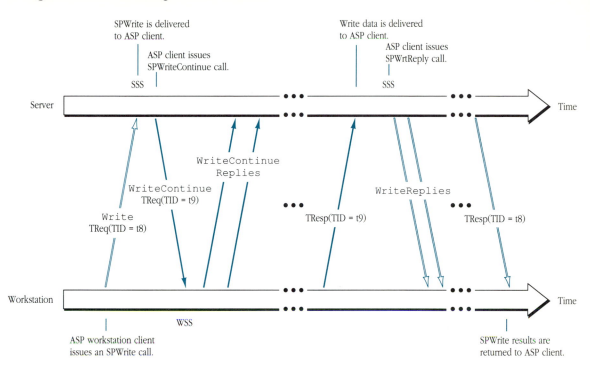

SPAttentions

When a session is open, the server client can send an attention command to the workstation client (see *Figure 11-8*). The sole purpose of this command is to alert the workstation client of the server's need for attention. ASP delivers 2 bytes of attention data (from the command ATP user bytes) to the workstation client and acknowledges the attention command (with an ATP response), but the workstation client has the responsibility to act on the command. An example of the use of the attention mechanism might be for a server to notify a workstation of a change in the server's status. Upon receiving the attention command, the workstation could then issue an SPCommand to the server to find out the details of the status change.

■ **Figure 11-8** SPAttention dialog

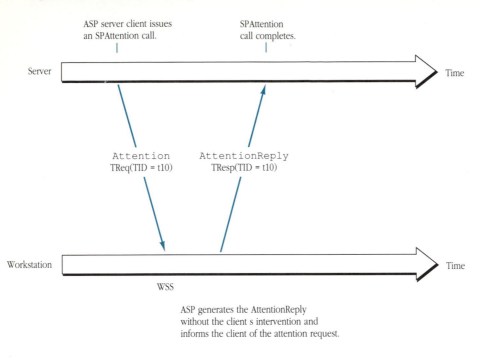

ASP server client issues
an SPAttention call.

SPAttention
call completes.

Server ───▷ Time

Attention
TReq(TID = t10)

AttentionReply
TResp(TID = t10)

Workstation ───▷ Time

WSS

ASP generates the AttentionReply
without the client s intervention and
informs the client of the attention request.

Sequencing and duplicate filtration

By including a sequence number in the appropriate packets exchanged by ASP, ASP ensures that commands are delivered to the server end in the same order as they were issued at the workstation end.

The use of sequence numbers also allows ASP to make the ATP exactly-once (ATP-XO) service more robust. ATP-XO service guarantees that a request is delivered to the ATP client exactly once if the source and destination nodes are on the same AppleTalk network. Over an AppleTalk internet, however, a copy of the ATP request could be delayed in a router node and then delivered as a duplicate after the original transaction has been completed. As a result, a duplicate transaction would be delivered by ATP. This inherent problem of transaction protocols can be eliminated by giving sequence numbers to the transactions belonging to a session in order to filter delayed duplicates.

Getting service status information

ASP provides an out-of-band service to allow its workstation clients to obtain a block of service status information from the SLS without opening a session. In the server, the status block is provided to ASP by the server-end ASP client and is returned in response to SPGetStatus commands received at the SLS (see *Figure 11-9*).

■ **Figure 11-9** SPGetStatus dialog

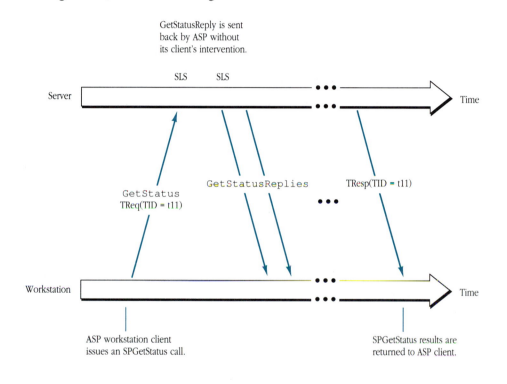

ASP client interface

ASP's service interface is designed to be as independent as possible of the underlying AppleTalk transport mechanisms to allow easy porting of the higher-level protocols (ASP clients) to networks other than AppleTalk and to simplify some of the problems in the design of internet gateways. Regardless of the design, the internal specifications of ASP are very closely related to ATP, and so ASP itself may not be directly portable to other networks.

Server-end calls

This section describes the calls that can be issued by the server-end ASP client.

SPGetParms call

Before any sessions are allowed to be opened, the server's ASP client should first issue an SPGetParms call to retrieve the maximum values of command block size and quantum size. The MaxCmdSize is the maximum size command block that can be sent to the server. The QuantumSize returned by this call is the maximum size reply block that can be sent to an SPCommand or SPGetStatus call, and the maximum size of data that can be transferred in an SPWrtContinue transaction. On an AppleTalk network, since ASP is built on top of ATP, the value of MaxCmdSize returned will be 578 bytes and QuantumSize will be 4624 bytes (eight ATP response packets with 578 data bytes each). For client-compatible session protocols implemented on other networks, these values may be different.

Call parameters   none

Returned parameters   *MaxCmdSize*   maximum size of a command block

QuantumSize   maximum size of a reply block or SPWrtContinue write data

SPInit call

Once it has opened a socket (SLS) and registered its name, the ASP client in the server must issue an SPInit call, passing the network-dependent SLSEntityIdentifier as well as a ServiceStatusBlock to ASP. This block is used to hold the service status information to be returned in reply to SPGetStatus commands received at the SLS. The SLSEntityIdentifier is the complete internet address of the SLS.

SPInit returns the SLSRefNum (unique among all SLSs on the same server node), which is used in the SPGetSession call to refer to the SLS passed in the SPInit call.

Call parameters	*SLSEntityIdentifier*	SLS internet address (network-dependent)
	ServiceStatusBlock	block with status information
	ServiceStatusBlockSize	size of status information block
Returned parameters	*SLSRefNum*	reference number for the SLS
	SPError	error code returned by ASP
		TooManyClients: Server implementation cannot support another client.
		SizeErr: ServiceStatusBlockSize is greater than QuantumSize.

SPGetSession call

The SPGetSession call is issued by the ASP server-end client to allow ASP to accept an SPOpenSession command received on the SLS identified by the SLSRefNum. Each SPGetSession call authorizes ASP to accept one more SPOpenSession command. The SPGetSession call completes when the SPOpenSession command is received on the SLS and a corresponding session has been opened. The SessRefNum is returned to the server ASP client and must be used in all further calls to ASP that refer to that session. This number must be unique among all sessions managed by ASP in the server end.

Call parameters	*SLSRefNum*	reference number for the SLS
Returned parameters	*SessRefNum*	session reference number
	SPError	error code returned by ASP
		ParamErr: SLSRefNum is unknown.
		NoMoreSessions: Server implementation cannot support another session.

SPCloseSession call

The SPCloseSession call is issued by the ASP client to close the session identified by SessRefNum. As a result of the SPCloseSession call, the value of SessRefNum is invalidated and cannot be used in any further calls. In addition, all pending activity on the session is immediately canceled.

Call parameters	*SessRefNum*	session reference number
Returned parameters	*SPError*	error code returned by ASP
		ParamErr: SessRefNum is unknown.

SPGetRequest call

After a session has been opened, the ASP client in the server end must issue SPGetRequest calls to provide buffer space (ReqBuff) for the receipt of requests (workstation commands) on that session. The size (ReqBuffSize) of the buffer for receiving the command block sent with the request depends on the higher-level protocol but need not be greater than QuantumSize.

When a request has been received, the SPGetRequest call completes and returns a unique request identifier (ReqRefNum) and a 1-byte quantity (SPReqType) that identifies the type of ASP request. The permissible values of SPReqType are Command, Write, and CloseSession. If the received command block does not fit in the ReqBuff, ASP returns as much of the command block as will fit, along with a BufTooSmall error.

When the SPGetRequest call completes, the server-end client is given the size of the received command block in the parameter ActRcvdReqLen.

If the session times out and an SPGetRequest call is pending, the call will complete with an SPError value of SessClosed. If no SPGetRequest call is pending, the next SPGetRequest call issued on the session will complete immediately with an error.

Call parameters	*SessRefNum*	session reference number
	ReqBuff	buffer for receiving the command block
	ReqBuffSize	buffer size
Returned parameters	*ReqRefNum*	request identifier
	SPReqType	ASP-level request type
	ActRcvdReqLen	actual size of the received request
	SPError	error code returned by ASP
		ParamErr: SessRefNum is unknown.
		BufTooSmall: ReqBuff cannot hold the entire command block.
		SessClosed: Session has been closed.

SPCmdReply call

If the request returned by the SPGetRequest call has SPReqType equal to Command, then the server-end client must respond to the request with an SPCmdReply call to ASP. The value of ReqRefNum passed with this call must be the same as that returned by the corresponding SPGetRequest call. The following two items must be conveyed to the workstation end of the session:

- a 4-byte command result (CmdResult)
- a variable-length command reply data block (CmdReplyData)

The actual values, format, and meaning of the CmdResult and of the CmdReplyData are not interpreted by ASP.

◆ *Note:* CmdReplyDataSize must be no greater than QuantumSize; otherwise, a SizeErr will be returned and no CmdReplyData will be sent to the workstation.

Call parameters	SessRefNum	session reference number
	ReqRefNum	request identifier
	CmdResult	4-byte command result
	CmdReplyData	command reply data block
	CmdReplyDataSize	size of command reply data block

Returned parameters — SPError — error code returned by ASP

ParamErr: SessRefNum or ReqRefNum is unknown. CmdReplyDataSize is bad (negative value).

SizeErr: CmdReplyDataSize is greater than QuantumSize.

SessClosed: Session has been closed.

SPWrtContinue call

If the request returned by the SPGetRequest call has SPReqType equal to Write, then the server-end client must respond to the request with either an SPWrtContinue or an SPWrtReply call to ASP. The value of ReqRefNum passed with these calls must be the same as that returned by the corresponding SPGetRequest call.

The ASP client decides which of these calls to make, depending on the higher-level protocol; however, the following general description is provided. Upon receiving a request that has SPReqType equal to Write, the ASP client examines the command block received with the request. This block should contain, in the format appropriate to the higher-level protocol, a description of the type and parameters of the higher-level write operation being requested. The ASP client should use this command block information to decide if the requested operation can be carried out successfully. If the operation cannot be carried out, the ASP client should issue the SPWrtReply call with the appropriate higher-level protocol result code value in CmdResult indicating the failure and the reason for it. If the operation can be carried out, however, then the ASP client in the server should initiate the process of transferring the data to be written from the workstation end of the session by issuing the SPWrtContinue call. An SPWrtReply call should also be issued upon completion of the SPWrtContinue call and the ensuing write.

For example, the higher-level client could be a filing protocol requesting the server-end client to write a certain number of bytes to a particular file. If no such file exists, the server end should send back a *no such file* indication by issuing an SPWrtReply call. Otherwise, the server end issues an SPWrtContinue call with a buffer into which the write data can be brought from the workstation, followed by an SPWrtReply once it has finished the write request.

The maximum size of the write data that will be transferred is equal to QuantumSize.

Call parameters	SessRefNum	session reference number
	ReqRefNum	request identifier
	Buffer	buffer for receiving the data to be written
	BufferSize	size of the buffer
Returned parameters	ActLenRcvd	actual amount of data received into buffer
	SPError	error code returned by ASP
		ParamErr: SessRefNum or ReqRefNum is unknown. BufferSize is bad (negative value).
		SessClosed: Session has been closed.

SPWrtReply call

The SPWrtReply call is issued by the ASP client in the server in order to terminate, either successfully or unsuccessfully, an SPWrite call received through SPGetRequest. With this SPWrtReply call, the ASP client provides ASP with the 4-byte command result and the variable-length command reply data block (maximum size equal to QuantumSize) to be conveyed to the workstation-end client. If a SizeErr is returned, no CmdReplyData will be sent to the workstation.

Call parameters	SessRefNum	session reference number
	ReqRefNum	request identifier
	CmdResult	4-byte command result
	CmdReplyData	command reply data block
	CmdReplyDataSize	size of command reply data block
Returned parameters	SPError	error code returned by ASP
		ParamErr: SessRefNum or ReqRefNum is unknown. CmdReplyDataSize is bad (negative value).
		SizeErr: CmdReplyDataSize is greater than QuantumSize.
		SessClosed: Session has been closed.

SPNewStatus call

The SPNewStatus call is used by the ASP client to update the ServiceStatusBlock first supplied in the SPInit call. The previous status information is lost. All subsequent SPGetStatus calls issued by workstations will retrieve the new status block.

Call parameters	*SLSRefNum*	reference number for the SLS
	ServiceStatusBlock	block with status information
	ServiceStatusBlockSize	size of status information block
Returned parameters	*SPError*	error code returned by ASP
		ParamErr: SLSRefNum is unknown
		SizeErr: ServiceStatusBlockSize is greater than QuantumSize.

SPAttention call

The SPAttention call sends the attention code to the workstation and waits for an acknowledgment. The only restriction placed on the value of the attention code is that it must not be 0.

Call parameters	*SessRefNum*	session reference number
	AttentionCode	2-byte attention code (must be a number other than 0)
Returned parameters	*SPError*	error code returned by ASP
		ParamErr: SessRefNum is unknown; AttentionCode cannot be 0.
		NoAck: No acknowledgment received from workstation end.

Workstation-end calls

This section describes the calls that can be issued to the server end by the workstation-end ASP client.

SPGetParms call

The SPGetParms call retrieves the maximum value of the command block size and the quantum size. This call is the same as the SPGetParms call for the server end.

Call parameters   none

Returned parameters	*MaxCmdSize*	maximum size of a command block
	QuantumSize	maximum data size for a command reply or a write

SPGetStatus call

The SPGetStatus call is used by a workstation ASP client to obtain status information for a particular server. If the status information received is too large to fit into the StatusBuffer provided with the call, then ASP returns a BufTooSmall error and as much of the status information as will fit in the StatusBuffer.

Call parameters	*SLSEntityIdentifier*	SLS internet address (network-dependent)
	StatusBuffer	buffer for receiving the status information
	StatusBufferSize	size of status information buffer

Returned parameters	*ActRcvdStatusLen*	size of status information received
	SPError	error code returned by ASP
		NoServer: Server is not responding.
		BufTooSmall: StatusBuffer cannot hold entire status.

SPOpenSession call

The SPOpenSession call is issued by an ASP client after obtaining the internet address of the SLS through an NBP Lookup call. If a session is successfully opened, then a SessRefNum is returned to the caller and should be used on all subsequent calls referring to this session. If a session cannot be opened, an appropriate SPError value is returned. AttnRoutine specifies a routine (part of the workstation-end ASP client) to be invoked upon receipt of an attention request from the server. The exact form that this parameter takes is implementation-dependent.

Call parameters	*SLSEntityIdentifier*	SLS internet address (network-dependent)
	AttnRoutine	attention routine indicator
Returned parameters	*SessRefNum*	session reference number
	SPError	error code returned by ASP
		NoServer: Server is not responding.
		ServerBusy: Server cannot open another session.
		BadVersNum: Server cannot support the offered version number.
		NoMoreSessions: Workstation implementation cannot support another session.

SPCloseSession call

The SPCloseSession call can be issued at any time by the ASP client to close a session previously opened through an SPOpenSession call. As a result of this call, the SessRefNum is invalidated and cannot be used in any further calls. In addition, all pending activity on the session is immediately canceled.

Call parameters	*SessRefNum*	session reference number
Returned parameters	*SPError*	error code returned by ASP
		ParamErr: SessRefNum is unknown.

SPCommand call

Once a session has been opened, the workstation-end client can send a command to the server end by issuing an SPCommand call to ASP. A command block of maximum size (MaxCmdSize) can be sent with the command. If CmdBlockSize is larger than this maximum allowable size, the call completes with SPError equal to SizeErr; in this case, no effort is made to send anything to the server end.

In response to an SPCommand, the server end returns the following two quantities:

- a 4-byte command result
- a variable-length command reply that is returned in the ReplyBuffer. The size of the command reply received is returned in ActRcvdReplyLen. Since this size can be no larger than QuantumSize, it is possible that only part of the reply will be returned in this call. If this happens, an SPError code of *no error* will be returned; the ASP workstation-end client is responsible for generating another command to retrieve the rest of the reply.

Call parameters	*SessRefNum*	session reference number
	CmdBlock	command block to be sent
	CmdBlockSize	size of command block
	ReplyBuffer	buffer for receiving the command reply data
	ReplyBufferSize	size of the reply buffer
Returned parameters	*CmdResult*	4-byte command result
	ActRcvdReplyLen	actual length of command reply data received
	SPError	error code returned by ASP
		ParamErr: SessRefNum is unknown.
		SizeErr: CmdBlockSize is larger than MaxCmdSize.
		SessClosed: Session has been closed.
		BufTooSmall: ReplyBuffer cannot hold the whole reply.

SPWrite call

The SPWrite call is made by the ASP client in order to write a block of data to the server end of the session. The call first delivers the CmdBlock (no larger than MaxCmdSize) to the server-end client of ASP and, as previously described, the server end can then transfer the write data or return an error (delivered in the CmdResult).

The actual amount of data sent will be less than or equal to WriteDataSize and will never be larger than QuantumSize. The amount of write data actually transferred is returned in ActLenWritten.

In response to an SPWrite, the server end returns two quantities: a 4-byte command result and a variable-length command reply that is returned in the ReplyBuffer. The size of the command reply actually received is returned in ActRcvdReplyLen. Note that this size can be no larger than QuantumSize.

Call parameters	SessRefNum	session reference number
	CmdBlock	command block to be sent
	CmdBlockSize	size of command block
	WriteData	data block to be written
	WriteDataSize	size of data block to be written
	ReplyBuffer	buffer for receiving the command reply data
	ReplyBufferSize	size of the reply buffer
Returned parameters	CmdResult	4-byte command result
	ActLenWritten	actual number of bytes of data written
	ActRcvdReplyLen	actual length of command reply data received
	SPError	error code returned by ASP
		ParamErr: SessRefNum is unknown.
		SizeErr: CmdBlockSize is larger than MaxCmdSize.
		SessClosed: Session has been closed.
		BufTooSmall: ReplyBuffer cannot hold the whole reply.

Packet formats and algorithms

This section describes the internal details of ASP, including packet formats. For simplicity, the DDP and data-link headers are omitted from the packets shown in the figures.

Opening a session

When the workstation client issues an SPOpenSession call, ASP issues an ATP-XO transaction request addressed to the SLS, as shown in *Figure 11-1*. This ATP transaction request packet is known as an ASP OpenSess packet. The server's ASP returns an ATP transaction response packet known as an OpenSessReply packet.

The OpenSess packet is shown in *Figure 11-10* and carries the following in its ASP header (the ASP header is contained entirely in the ATP user bytes):

- a 1-byte SPFunction field equal to OpenSess
- a 1-byte field containing the WSS socket number
- a 2-byte ASP version number field

Upon receiving an OpenSess packet, the server's ASP checks to see if an SPGetSession is pending on that SLS. If no such call is pending, then the server's ASP returns a ServerBusy error in the OpenSessReply packet, and the session is not opened. If an SPGetSession is pending, then ASP checks the ASP version number in the OpenSess packet. If the version number is unacceptable, a BadVersNum error is returned. Otherwise, ASP opens an ATP responding socket (SSS) and generates a unique (per SLS) 1-byte session ID. ASP then creates its internal session management data structures in which the WSS is saved together with the session ID, the SLS, and related items. The OpenSessReply packet is then sent back to the workstation. This packet contains, in its ASP header (contained entirely in the ATP user bytes), a 2-byte error code (returned to the client as SPError), the 1-byte session ID, and the SSS. The server end of the session is now active. The tickling process at this time is initiated from the server end.

Upon receiving the OpenSessReply, the workstation-end ASP examines the packet's error code field. If this field indicates no error, then the session ID and the SSS are taken from the packet and, together with other control information, are saved in a session management data structure. At this point, the workstation end of the session is active, and the tickling process is initiated from the workstation end.

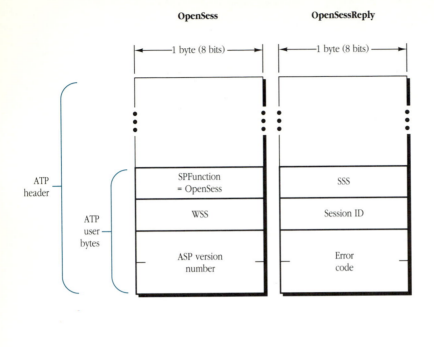

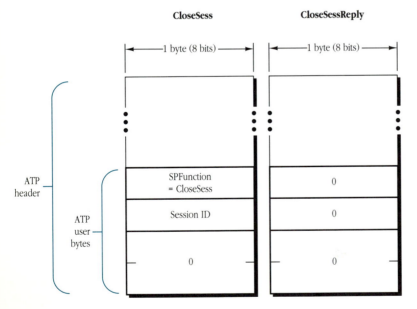

The session management data structure must contain the session ID, the socket number of the other end of the session (the WSS or the SSS), and a 2-byte sequence number (LastReqNum). When the session is opened, the LastReqNum is initialized to 0.

Getting server status

Because an SPGetStatus call can be made and serviced without opening a session, the corresponding packets do not carry a session ID and do not have a sequence number field. The workstation-end ASP issues an ATP at-least-once transaction request addressed to the SLS. This request, known as a GetStatus packet, is sent to the SLS, as shown in *Figure 11-9*.

The GetStatus packet has SPFunction equal to GetStatus, with the rest of the 3 ATP user bytes being unused and therefore set to 0, as shown in *Figure 11-11*.

Upon receiving a GetStatus packet, the ASP at the server end returns up to eight GetStatusReply packets as the multipacket ATP response. Each of these packets has its 4 ATP user bytes equal to 0.

The status information block provided in the SPInit or SPNewStatus call is sent as the ATP data of the GetStatusReply packets. The status information is packed into the reply packets with as many bytes as will fit (in other words, each GetStatusReply packet will contain 578 bytes of status information except for the last packet, which may contain less).

■ **Figure 11-11** ASP packet formats for GetStatus

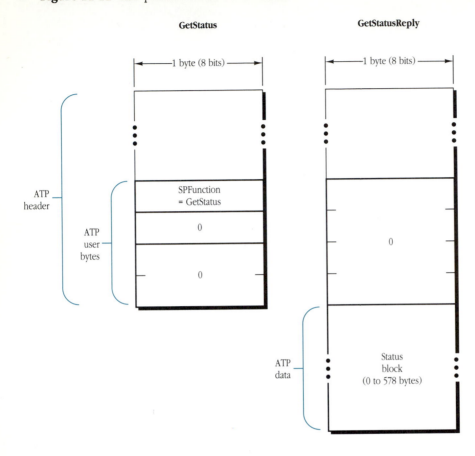

Sending a command request

When the ASP client in the workstation makes an SPCommand call, ASP sends an ATP-XO request to the SSS of the indicated session, as shown in *Figure 11-5*. This packet has SPFunction equal to Command. The packet contains the session ID and a 2-byte sequence number, as shown in *Figure 11-12*. The sequence number must be generated using the following algorithm:

```
If LastReqNum = 65536 then LastReqNum := 0
     else LastReqNum := LastReqNum+1;
Sequence Number := LastReqNum;
```

■ **Figure 11-12** ASP packet formats for Command

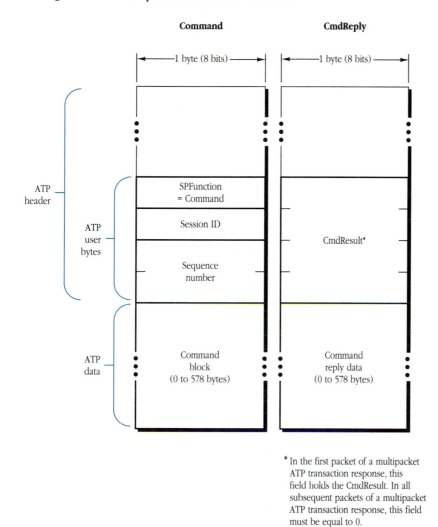

* In the first packet of a multipacket
ATP transaction response, this
field holds the CmdResult. In all
subsequent packets of a multipacket
ATP transaction response, this field
must be equal to 0.

In effect, the sequence number will be 1 greater than the sequence number of the last command sent on the session. LastReqNum is initially set to 0 when the session is opened.

The CmdBlock provided in the SPCommand call is sent in the ATP data part of the packet. Therefore, CmdBlock cannot be larger than 578 bytes.

At the server end, ASP delivers the CmdBlock to the ASP client (if an SPGetRequest was pending; otherwise the packet is ignored). The ASP client in the server then makes an SPCmdReply call that is used to pass a 4-byte command result and a variable-length command reply data block to ASP. ASP generates from one to eight ATP response packets, which ASP sends back to the source of the Command packet. These CmdReply packets have the 4 ATP user bytes set to 0 except for the first CmdReply, which carries the command result in its user bytes. The command reply data block is broken up into eight or fewer pieces and sent in the ATP data part of these packets, as shown in *Figure 11-12*.

Sending a write request

When the ASP client in the workstation makes an SPWrite call, ASP sends an ATP-XO request to the SSS of the indicated session (shown in *Figure 11-7*). This packet has SPFunction equal to Write, and it contains the session ID of the session and a 2-byte sequence number, as shown in *Figure 11-13*. The sequence number must be generated using the algorithm described previously in "Sending a Command Request."

The command block provided in the SPWrite call is sent in the ATP data part of the Write packet. Therefore, CmdBlock cannot be larger than 578 bytes.

At the server end, ASP delivers the Write packet to the ASP client (if an SPGetRequest was pending; otherwise, the packet is ignored). The ASP client in the server determines if it can process the request, presumably by examining the contents of the command block.

If the ASP client in the server cannot process the request, it encodes an appropriate higher-level protocol error message in the 4-byte command result or in the command reply data block or in both and makes an SPWrtReply call to ASP. An ATP response packet known as a WriteReply is then sent back to the source of the SPWrite, as shown in *Figure 11-6*.

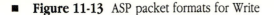
Figure 11-13 ASP packet formats for Write

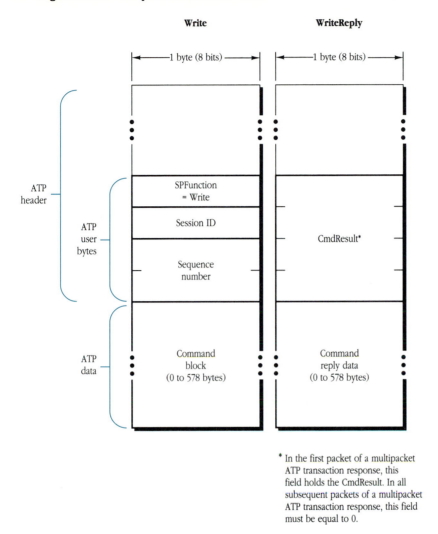

* In the first packet of a multipacket
ATP transaction response, this
field holds the CmdResult. In all
subsequent packets of a multipacket
ATP transaction response, this field
must be equal to 0.

If, however, the ASP client in the server can process the request, it reserves a buffer for the data and makes an SPWrtContinue call to ASP. The SPWrtContinue call causes ASP in the server to send an ATP-XO transaction request to the WSS. This call carries the session ID and the sequence number taken from the SPWrite packet (used by ASP to match the WriteContinue with the corresponding Write), as shown in *Figure 11-14*.

■ **Figure 11-14** ASP packet formats for WriteContinue

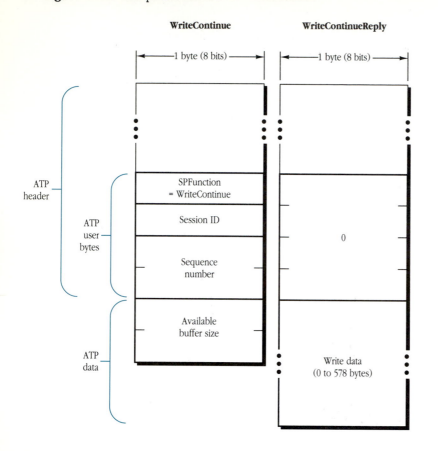

The WriteContinue packet contains a 2-byte ATP data field that contains the size in bytes of the buffer reserved by the server client for the write data. The workstation then returns the write data in the transaction response packets (WriteContinueReply packets). The data is then delivered to the server-end ASP client. The server-end ASP client then issues an SPWrtReply call to ASP that causes ASP to send one to eight WriteReply packets (the ATP response to the original Write packet). The format of the WriteReply packet is shown in *Figure 11-13*.

Maintaining the session

Tickle packets (ATP transaction request packets with SPFunction equal to Tickle) must be sent by each end while a session is open, as shown in *Figure 11-4*.

Tickle packets are sent by the workstation to the SLS and by the server to the WSS. These packets contain the following information in their ASP header (the ATP user bytes), as shown in *Figure 11-15*:

- 1-byte SPFunction equal to Tickle

- SessionID

- two unused bytes

Tickle packets are sent by starting an ATP-ALO transaction with retry count equal to infinite and timeout equal to 30 seconds.

Session maintenance at each end is done by starting a session maintenance timeout of 2 minutes. Whenever any packet (tickle or otherwise) is received on the session, this timer is restarted. If the timer expires (in other words, if no packet is received for 2 minutes), then the other end of the session is assumed to have gone down or become unreachable, and the session is closed.

- **Figure 11-15** ASP packet formats for Attention and Tickle

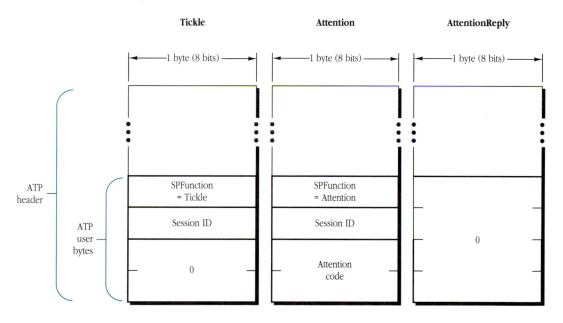

Sending an attention request

When the ASP client in the server makes an SPAttention call, ASP sends an ATP-ALO request to the WSS of the indicated session, as shown in *Figure 11-8*.

This Attention packet requests one response and has SPFunction equal to Attention. It contains the session ID and a 2-byte attention code, as shown in *Figure 11-15*. This attention code is passed by the server client to ASP to be delivered to the workstation client along with the attention request. The attention code is not interpreted by ASP, except that ASP requires the code to be a number other than 0.

Upon receiving an Attention packet, the workstation-end ASP should immediately respond with an AttentionReply. The AttentionReply serves as an acknowledgment of the request, and it completes the SPAttention call on the server end. The workstation ASP should then, in an implementation-dependent manner, alert its client as to the attention request and pass the attention code to the client.

Closing a session

When the ASP client at either end makes an SPCloseSession call, a session-closing ATP-ALO transaction is initiated, as shown in *Figure 11-2* and *Figure 11-3*.

If the session closing was initiated by the workstation client, then a CloseSess packet (an ATP transaction request) is sent to the SSS in the server. The CloseSess packet is then delivered to the ASP client as part of the SPGetRequest mechanism. The server's ASP generates a transaction response (a CloseSessReply packet) without the ASP client's intervention. Immediately upon sending the CloseSessReply packet, the server end of the session is closed, all pending activity (including tickles) is canceled at that end, and no further server-end calls to this session are accepted. Immediately upon receiving the SPCloseSession command reply, the workstation end of ASP cancels all pending activity (including tickles) on the session and does not accept any more calls from its client. Although implementation-dependent, the workstation end can choose to retransmit the CloseSess packet several times; the workstation will close its end of the session either as soon as the CloseSessReply is received or the retries are exhausted.

On the server end, the possibility exists that no SPGetRequest call was pending when the close request was received. In this case, no further calls on the server end should be accepted from the server-end ASP client, and the session should be marked as closed. When the server client issues the next SPGetRequest call for that session, ASP should return a SessClosed result code or other error.

If the session closing was initiated by the server end, then a CloseSess packet is sent to the WSS. The workstation's ASP closes the session immediately upon receipt of the CloseSess packet, and it generates the CloseSessReply packet without client intervention. The ASP client in the workstation can be informed of the session being closed in some implementation-dependent manner or can be informed the next time it makes a call to ASP and refers to that session. The server can choose to retransmit the CloseSess packet several times; the server end will close its end of the session when the CloseSessReply is received or the retries are exhausted. The formats of the CloseSess and CloseSessReply packets are shown in *Figure 11-10*.

◆ *Note:* The CloseSess packet does not include a sequence number and therefore must be accepted by the receiving end without sequence number verification. Also, the receipt of the CloseSess packet by the receiving end should immediately lead to the cancellation of all pending activity (including tickles) on the session.

CloseSess packets are sent as a courtesy to the other end of the session and are used to speed up the process of closing a session at both ends.

The possibility exists that the CloseSess packet or the CloseSessReply sent by either end can get lost; then the end initiating the session-closing activity may not receive an acknowledgment to its request and will close the session and stop tickles when its retries are exhausted. If the other end did not receive the CloseSess packet at all, however, that end will not know the session has been closed. This half-open session will be detected when the session maintenance timer at the still active end expires, at which time the active end will close its own end of the half-open session.

Checking for reply size errors

In the SPGetStatus, SPCommand, and SPWrite requests, the ASP workstation client presents ASP with a buffer that will hold the server's reply. When the reply is received, ASP must check that the reply was not too large to fit into the buffer. Since the server does not directly return the aggregate size of the reply as a parameter, ASP must infer from information returned by ATP whether or not the server's reply fits into the client's buffer.

ASP will try to fill this buffer by requesting from ATP as many 578-byte response packets as needed to fill the buffer. If the server returns fewer than the expected number of response packets, then the reply will clearly fit into the client's buffer. In general, if the server returns the expected number of response packets, then the workstation ASP need only check if the last expected packet fit into the end of the buffer. ATP will indicate to ASP if this packet did not fit.

A difficulty arises if the client's buffer size was an exact multiple of 578 bytes. If the last expected packet is returned completely filled (contains 578 bytes of data), that might indicate that the buffer was just large enough. However, it could also mean that the reply was larger, yet the workstation ASP did not ask for (and hence could not receive) more response packets. ATP does not indicate to ASP that the server wanted to send additional packets.

To resolve this problem, the workstation ASP must ask ATP for one more response packet than expected if the client's buffer size is a multiple of 578. If the reply size is larger than the client's buffer size, this extra response packet will be returned. ASP can infer from the reception of this extra packet that the reply was too large.

This problem will not occur if the size of the client's buffer is greater than or equal to QuantumSize (a multiple of 578), since this reply is the largest that can be sent. The server's reply can not overflow this buffer.

Timeouts and retry counts

ASP uses ATP transactions as its basic building blocks. For each of these transactions, a retransmission timeout value and maximum retry count need to be provided.

Most transactions used by ASP use a retry count of infinite (exceptions: opening a session, getting service status, requesting attention, and closing a session). The retry count of infinite involves no danger of leading to a deadlock, since half-open connections (in other words, the other end is unreachable) are easily detected through the tickling mechanism and the session maintenance timer.

The ASP client should be able to specify the maximum number of retries used by the session opening, get service status information, and get attention and session-closing transactions, although the exact mechanism for doing so is implementation-dependent.

The timeout value to be used in any of the transactions (with the exception of tickles) and how this value is specified by the client or built into ASP are implementation issues; they are not specified here.

The session maintenance timer is of 2-minute duration. Tickles are retransmitted by each end every 30 seconds.

SPFunction values

The permissible SPFunction values are as follows:

SPFunction	Value
CloseSess	1
Command	2
GetStatus	3
OpenSess	4
Tickle	5
Write	6
WriteContinue	7
Attention	8

Chapter 12 **AppleTalk Data Stream Protocol**

CONTENTS

■

THE APPLETALK DATA STREAM PROTOCOL (ADSP)
is a symmetric, connection-oriented protocol that makes possible the
establishment and maintenance of full-duplex streams of data bytes between
two sockets in an AppleTalk internet. Data flow on an ADSP connection is
reliable; ADSP guarantees that data bytes are delivered in the same order as
they were sent and that they are free of duplicates. In addition, ADSP
includes a flow-control mechanism that uses information supplied by the
intended destination. These features are implemented by using sequence
numbers logically associated with the data bytes. ■

ADSP services

ADSP provides the client with a simple, powerful interface to an AppleTalk network. Using ADSP, the client can open a connection with a remote end, send data to and receive data from the remote end, and close the connection.

The client can either send a continuous stream of data or logically break the data into messages that can be understood by the remote end client. ADSP also provides an attention message mechanism that the client can use for its own internal control. A forward-reset mechanism allows the client to abort the delivery of an outstanding stream of bytes to the remote client.

Connections

This section defines connections, connection ends, and connection identifiers (ConnIDs) and explains the roles that they play in ADSP.

A connection is an association between two sockets that allows reliable, full-duplex flow of data bytes between the sockets. With ADSP, the data bytes are delivered in the same order as they were inserted into the connection. In addition, ADSP includes a flow-control mechanism that regulates data transmission based on the availability of reception buffers at the destination.

At any time, a connection can be set up by either or both of the communicating parties. The connection is torn down when it is no longer required or if either connection end becomes unreachable. In order for the protocol to function correctly, a certain amount of control and state information must be maintained at each end of a connection. Opening a connection involves setting up this information at each end and bringing the two ends of the connection to a synchronized condition. The information at each end is referred to as the state of that connection end; the term **connection state** refers collectively to the information at both ends. **Connection end** is a general term that covers both the communicating socket and the connection information associated with it.

Connection states

A connection between two sockets can be either open or closed. When an association is set up between two sockets, the connection is considered an **open connection;** when the association is torn down, the connection is considered a **closed connection.** A connection end can be in one of two states: established or closed. For a connection to be open, both its ends must be established. If one end of a connection is established but the other is closed (or unreachable), the connection is said to be half-open. Data can flow only on an open connection.

ADSP specifies that only one connection at a time can be open between a pair of sockets. However, several connections can be open on the same socket, but the other ends of these various connections must be on different sockets.

A connection end can be closed at any time by the connection end's client. The connection end should inform the remote end that it is going to close. At this time, the connection could become temporarily half-open until the remote end also closes. Once both ends have closed, the connection is closed. See "Connection Opening" and "Connection Closing" later in this chapter for details on the mechanisms used to open and close connections.

Half-open connections and the connection timer

A connection is half-open when one end goes down or becomes unreachable from the other end. In a half-open connection, the end that is still established could needlessly consume network bandwidth. Even in the absence of network traffic, resources (such as timers and buffers) would be tied up at the established end. Therefore, it is important that ADSP detect half-open connections. After detecting a half-open connection, ADSP closes the established end and informs its client that the connection has been closed.

To detect half-open connections, each end maintains a **connection timer** that is started when the connection opens. Whenever an end receives a packet from the remote end, the timer is reset. The timer expires if the end does not receive any packets within 30 seconds. When the timer expires, the end sends a probe and restarts the connection timer. A **probe** is a request for the remote end to acknowledge; the probe itself serves as an acknowledgment to the remote end. Failure to receive any packet from the other end before the timer has expired for the fourth time (that is, after 2 minutes) indicates that the connection is half-open. At that time, ADSP immediately closes the connection end, freeing all associated resources.

Connection identifiers

A connection end is identified by its internet socket address, which consists of a socket number, a node ID, and a network number. In addition, when a connection is set up, each connection end generates a ConnID. A connection can be uniquely identified by using both the internet socket address and the ConnID of the two connection ends.

A sender must include its ConnID in all packets, so that it is clear to which connection the packet belongs. For example, if a connection were set up, closed, and then set up again between the same two sockets, it is possible that undelivered packets from the first connection that remained in internet routers could arrive after the second connection was open. Without the ConnID, the receiving end could mistakenly accept these packets because they would be indistinguishable from packets belonging to the second connection.

An ADSP implementation maintains a variable, LastConnID, that contains the last ConnID used. LastConnID is initially set to some random number. When establishing a new connection end on a particular socket, ADSP generates a new identifier by increasing LastConnID until it reaches a value that is not being used by a currently open connection on the socket. This value becomes the ConnID of the new connection end. ConnIDs are treated as unsigned integers in the range of 1 through ConnIDMax. After reaching the value ConnIDMax, ConnIDs wrap around to 1. A valid ConnID is never equal to 0; in fact, a ConnID of 0 must be interpreted as unknown.

The value of ConnIDMax, and therefore the range of the ConnIDs, is a function of the rate at which connections are expected to be set up and broken down (that is, how quickly the ConnID number wraps around) and of the maximum packet lifetime (MPL) for the internet. If connections are set up and broken down rapidly, then a higher value of ConnIDMax is required. Likewise, the longer the MPL, the higher the value required for ConnIDMax. ADSP uses 16-bit ConnIDs (that is, ConnIDMax equals $FFFF).

Data flow

Either end of an open connection accepts data from its client for delivery to the other end's client. This data is handled as a stream of bytes; the smallest unit of data that can be conveyed over a connection is 1 byte (8 bits). The flow of data between connection ends A and B can be viewed as two unidirectional streams of bytes—one stream from end A to end B and the other stream from end B to end A. Although the following discussion focuses on the data stream from end A to end B, it can be applied equally well to the stream from end B to end A by interchanging A and B in the discussion.

Sequence numbers

ADSP associates a sequence number with each byte that flows over the connection. End B maintains a variable, RecvSeq, which is the sequence number of the next byte that end B expects to receive from end A. End A maintains a corresponding variable, SendSeq, which is the sequence number of the next new byte that end A will send to end B.

End B initially sets the value of its RecvSeq to 0. Upon first establishing itself, end A synchronizes its SendSeq to the initial value of end B's RecvSeq, which is 0. The first byte that is sent by end A over the connection is treated as byte number 0, with subsequent bytes numbered 1, 2, 3, and so on. Sequence numbers are treated as unsigned 32-bit integers that wrap around to 0 when increased by 1 beyond the maximum value $FFFFFFFF.

Since AppleTalk is a packet network, bytes are actually sent over the connection in packets. Each packet carries a field known as PktFirstByteSeq in its ADSP header. PktFirstByteSeq is the sequence number of the first data byte in the packet. Upon receiving a packet from end A, end B compares the value of PktFirstByteSeq in the packet with its own RecvSeq. If these values are equal, end B accepts and delivers the data to its client. End B then updates the value of RecvSeq by adding the number of data bytes in the packet just received to its current value of RecvSeq. Using this process, end B ensures that data bytes are received in the same order as end A accepted them from its client and that no duplicates are received.

When end B receives a packet with a PktFirstByteSeq value that does not equal end B's RecvSeq, end B discards the data as out of sequence. Acceptance of data in only those packets with PktFirstByteSeq values equal to the receiver's RecvSeq values is referred to as in-order data acceptance.

Some ADSP implementations accept and buffer data from early-arriving, out-of-sequence packets, processing the data for client delivery when the intervening data arrives. Such an implementation may also accept packets that contain both duplicate and new data bytes; in this case, the receiving end discards duplicate data and accepts the new data. This approach, which is referred to as in-window data acceptance, can reduce data retransmission and improve throughput. However, because in-window data acceptance adds complexity to implementation, it is an option, rather than a requirement, of ADSP.

Error recovery and acknowledgments

The sequence-number mechanism provides the framework for acknowledging the receipt of data, recovering data packets when they are lost in the network, and filtering duplicate and out-of-sequence packets.

End A maintains a send queue that holds all data sent by it to end B. A variable, FirstRtmtSeq, contains the sequence number of the oldest byte in the send queue.

End B acknowledges receipt of data from end A by sending a sequence number, PktNextRecvSeq, in the ADSP header of any packet going from end B to end A over the connection. This number is equal to end B's RecvSeq at the time that end B sent the packet. When end A receives this packet, the value of PktNextRecvSeq informs end A that end B has already received all data sent by end A up to, but not including, the byte numbered PktNextRecvSeq. End A uses this information to remove all bytes up to, but not including, number PktNextRecvSeq from its send queue. End A must then change its FirstRtmtSeq value to equal the value of PktNextRecvSeq.

Note that the value of PktNextRecvSeq must fall between FirstRtmtSeq and SendSeq (that is, $FirstRtmtSeq \leq PktNextRecvSeq \leq SendSeq$). If the value does not fall in that range, end A should not update FirstRtmtSeq. In addition, even if an incoming packet's data is rejected as out of sequence, the value of PktNextRecvSeq, if in the correct range, is still acceptable and should be used by end A to update FirstRtmtSeq (since end B has received all bytes up to that point).

At times, end A may determine that some data within the stream that it already sent may not have been delivered to end B. In such a case, end A retransmits all data bytes in the send queue whose delivery has not been acknowledged by end B; these data bytes have sequence numbers from FirstRtmtSeq through SendSeq–1.

One of the advantages of using byte-oriented sequence numbers is that they offer flexibility for data retransmission. Previously sent data can be regrouped and retransmitted more efficiently. For example, if end A has sent several small data packets to end B over some period of time, and end A determines that it must retransmit all the data bytes in its send queue, it is possible that all of the data bytes in the previous small packets could fit within one ADSP packet for retransmission. It is also possible for end A to append some new data to the bytes being retransmitted in the packet.

Flow control and windows

ADSP implements a flow-control mechanism to ensure that one end does not send data that the other end does not have enough buffer space to receive (known as choking data flow at its source). In order for this mechanism to work, end B must periodically inform end A of the amount of receive buffer space it has available. This process is referred to as informing end A of end B's **reception window size.**

End B maintains a variable, RecvWdw, which is the number of bytes end B currently has space to receive. When sending a packet to end A, end B always includes the current value of its RecvWdw in a field of its ADSP header known as PktRecvWdw. End A maintains a variable, SendWdwSeq, which represents the sequence number of the last byte for which end B currently has space. End A obtains this value from any packet that it receives from end B by adding the value of PktRecvWdw–1 to the value of PktNextRecvSeq. End A does not send bytes numbered beyond SendWdwSeq because end B does not have enough buffer space to receive them. However, if end B receives a packet whose data would exceed the available buffer space, end B discards the data.

Since ADSP does not support the ability for a client to revoke buffer space, the value of SendWdwSeq should never decrease. If a connection end receives a packet that would cause SendWdwSeq to decrease, this value is not updated.

Note that RecvWdw is a 16-bit field; the window size at either end is limited to 64 Kbytes ($FFFF).

ADSP messages

ADSP allows its clients to break the data stream into client-intelligible messages. A bit can be set in the ADSP packet header to indicate that the last data byte in the packet constitutes the end of a client message. The receiving end must inform its client after delivering the last byte of a message.

An ADSP packet can have its end-of-message (EOM) bit set and must not contain client data. This situation would indicate that the last data byte received in the previous packet was the last in a message. In order to handle this case properly, the EOM indicator is treated as if it were a byte appended to the end of the message in the data stream. Therefore, an EOM always consumes one sequence number in the data stream, just beyond the last byte of the client message. Since no data byte actually corresponds to this EOM sequence number, it is possible that an EOM packet may contain no data.

Forward resets

The forward-reset mechanism allows an ADSP client to abort the delivery of any outstanding data to the remote end's client. A forward reset causes all bytes in the sending end's send queue, all bytes in transit on the network, and all bytes in the remote end's receive queue that have not yet been delivered to the client to be discarded, and it then causes the two ends to be resynchronized.

When a client requests a forward reset, its ADSP connection end first removes any unsent bytes from its send queue and then resets the value of its FirstRtmtSeq to that of its SendSeq. This process effectively flushes all data that has been sent but not yet acknowledged by the remote end. The client's connection end then sends the remote connection end a Forward Reset Control packet with PktFirstByteSeq equal to SendSeq.

Upon receiving a Forward Reset Control packet, ADSP verifies that the value of PktFirstByteSeq falls within the range from RecvSeq to RecvSeq+RecvWdw, inclusive. If the value does not fall within this range, the forward reset is disregarded. If the forward reset is accepted, RecvSeq is synchronized to the value of PktFirstByteSeq, all data in the receive queue up to RecvSeq is removed, and the client is informed that a forward reset was received and processed. The receiver then sends back a Forward Reset Acknowledgment Control packet with PktNextRecvSeq set to the newly synchronized value of RecvSeq. The Forward Reset Acknowledgment Control packet is sent even if the Forward Reset Control packet was disregarded as out of range.

When sending a Forward Reset Control packet, the connection end starts a timer. The timer is removed upon receipt of a valid Forward Reset Acknowledgment Control packet. To be valid, a Forward Reset Acknowledgment Control packet's PktNextRecvSeq must fall within the range SendSeq $\leq$ PktNextRecvSeq $\leq$ SendWdwSeq+1. If the timer expires, the end retransmits the Forward Reset Control packet and restarts the timer. This action continues until either a valid Forward Reset Acknowledgment Control packet is received or until the connection is torn down.

The forward-reset mechanism is nondeterministic from the client's perspective because any or all of the outstanding data could have already been delivered to the remote client. However, the forward-reset mechanism does provide a means for resetting the connection.

Summary of sequencing variables

To summarize, the ADSP header of all ADSP packets includes the following three sequencing variables:

Variable	Description
PktFirstByteSeq	the sequence number of the packet's first data byte
PktNextRecvSeq	the sequence number of the next byte that the packet's sender expects to receive
PktRecvWdw	the number of bytes that the packet's sender currently has buffer space to receive

Each connection end must maintain the following variables as part of its connection-state descriptor:

SendSeq   the sequence number to be assigned to the next new byte that the local end will transmit over the connection

FirstRtmtSeq   the sequence number of the oldest byte in the local end's send queue (Initially, the queue is empty so this number equals SendSeq.)

SendWdwSeq   the sequence number of the last byte that the remote end has buffer space to receive

RecvSeq   the sequence number of the next byte that the local end expects to receive

RecvWdw   the number of bytes that the local end currently has buffer space to receive (Initially, the entire buffer is available.)

Figure 12-1 illustrates how these variables would relate to a connection end's send and receive queues and sequence-number space.

■ **Figure 12-1** Send and receive queues

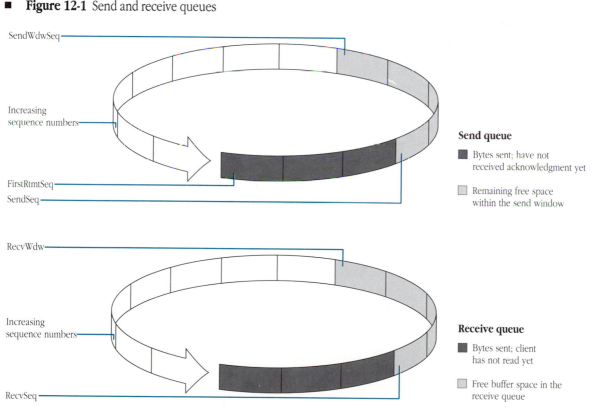

Send queue

■ Bytes sent; have not received acknowledgment yet

☐ Remaining free space within the send window

Receive queue

■ Bytes sent; client has not read yet

☐ Free buffer space in the receive queue

Packet format

Figure 12-2 illustrates an ADSP packet. The packet consists of the data-link and Datagram Delivery Protocol (DDP) headers, followed by a 13-byte ADSP header and up to 572 bytes of ADSP data. To identify an ADSP packet, the DDP type field must equal 7.

The ADSP header contains the following sequence of fields:

- a 16-bit source ConnID
- a 32-bit PktFirstByteSeq
- a 32-bit PktNextRecvSeq
- a 16-bit PktRecvWdw
- an 8-bit ADSP descriptor

If the Control bit in the descriptor field is set, the packet is an ADSP Control packet. Control packets are sent for internal ADSP purposes, and they do not carry any ADSP data bytes. Control packets do not consume sequence numbers.

In sending either a Data packet or a Control packet, the ADSP client can set the Ack Request bit in the descriptor field to indicate that it wants the remote end's ADSP to send back an ADSP packet immediately, with PktNextRecvSeq and PktRecvWdw equal to the current values of its RecvSeq and RecvWdw. Upon receiving a packet whose Ack Request bit is set, an ADSP connection end must respond to the acknowledgment request, even if the packet is to be discarded as out of sequence; the Ack Request bit forces the receiving end's ADSP to send an immediate acknowledgment.

Setting the Attention bit in the ADSP descriptor field designates the packet as an ADSP Attention packet. Attention packets are used to send and acknowledge attention messages. Any Attention packet that contains a client-attention message will have its Control bit clear and its Ack Request bit set. Setting the Ack Request bit forces the receiver to immediately send an acknowledgment of the attention data. An Attention packet with its Control bit set is an attention-control packet for internal ADSP purposes. Attention-control packets are used to acknowledge attention messages and should not have the Ack Request bit set. The Control code in the ADSP descriptor field of an ADSP Attention packet must always be set to 0. An Attention packet received with a Control code number other than 0 should be discarded as invalid. Attention packets are described in detail in "Attention Messages" later in this chapter.

Setting the EOM bit in the ADSP descriptor field indicates a logical end of message in the data stream. This bit applies only to client Data packets, and so neither the Control bit nor the Attention bit can be set in a packet whose EOM bit is set.

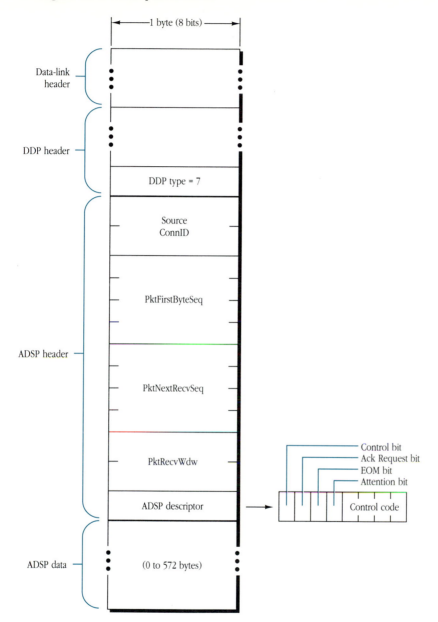

Control packets

ADSP packets are of two broad classes: Data packets and Control packets. Control packets can be distinguished from Data packets by examining the Control bit in the packet's ADSP Descriptor field; when set, this bit identifies a Control packet. Such packets are sent for ADSP's internal operation and do not contain any client-deliverable data.

Control packets are used to open or to close connections, to act as probes, and to send acknowledgment information. The least-significant 4 bits of a Control packet's descriptor field contain a Control code that identifies the type of the ADSP Control packet. The following list shows the Control codes and their corresponding types:

Value	ADSP Control code
0	Probe or Acknowledgment
1	Open Connection Request
2	Open Connection Acknowledgment
3	Open Connection Request and Acknowledgment
4	Open Connection Denial
5	Close Connection Advice
6	Forward Reset
7	Forward Reset Acknowledgment
8	Retransmit Advice

Apple Computer reserves values $9 through $F for potential future use, so these values must be treated as invalid. Control packets with these invalid Control codes are rejected by the receiving end.

A Control code of 0 can have two different meanings, depending on the state of the Ack Request bit. If the Ack Request bit is set, the packet is a Probe packet, so the receiving end should send an acknowledgment immediately. If the Ack Request bit is not set, then the control packet is an Acknowledgment packet. (Note that an acknowledgment is implicit in any valid ADSP packet; also, the Ack Request bit can be set in either a Data packet or a Control packet. Therefore, a Control packet with a Control code of 0 is used only when the sending end has no client data to accompany the acknowledgment or acknowledgment request.)

Open-connection Control codes are sent as part of the open-connection dialog. This dialog is explained in detail in "Connection Opening" later in this chapter. Before being closed by ADSP, a connection end sends a Close Connection Advice Control packet. This packet is purely advisory and requires no reply. Upon receiving such a packet, ADSP closes the connection. For additional details, see "Connection Closing" later in this chapter.

The Forward Reset Control packet provides a mechanism for a client to abort the delivery of all outstanding data that it has sent to the remote client. Upon receiving this packet, the remote end synchronizes its RecvSeq to the value of PktFirstByteSeq in the packet and removes all undelivered bytes from its receive queue. The remote end then returns a Forward Reset Acknowledgment Control packet to the other end and informs its client that it has received and processed a forward reset request.

A connection end may send the Retransmit Advice Control packet in response to receiving several consecutive out-of-sequence Data packets from the remote end. The packet is sent to inform the remote end that it should retransmit the bytes in its send queue beginning with the byte whose sequence number is PktNextRecvSeq.

Data-flow examples

The following figures give examples of data flow on an ADSP connection. In these examples, end A sends Data and Control packets to end B, and end B receives data and sends acknowledgments to end A. However, the examples apply equally well for the opposite situation in which end B sends the Data and Control packets to end A, and end A receives the data and sends acknowledgments to end B.

In the figures, the packets are indicated by arrows that run diagonally between the two connection ends. The bracketed ranges (for example, [0:5]) indicate the range of sequence numbers assigned to data bytes transmitted in the packet. The first number in the range corresponds to PktFirstByteSeq. *Ctl* indicates Control packets. A vertical line above or below the time arrows indicates an event, either the transmission or reception of a packet. The values of variables before an event occurs are shown on the left side of the vertical line; values after the event are shown on the right side. The packet variables of all packets sent by connection end B are listed along end B's time axis.

Figure 12-3 illustrates how the ADSP variables relate to the flow of data. In this example, end A sends an acknowledgment request when it exhausts its known send window. Acknowledgments are implicit in all packets sent from end B, regardless of whether they are Data packets or Control packets.

■ **Figure 12-3** ADSP data flow

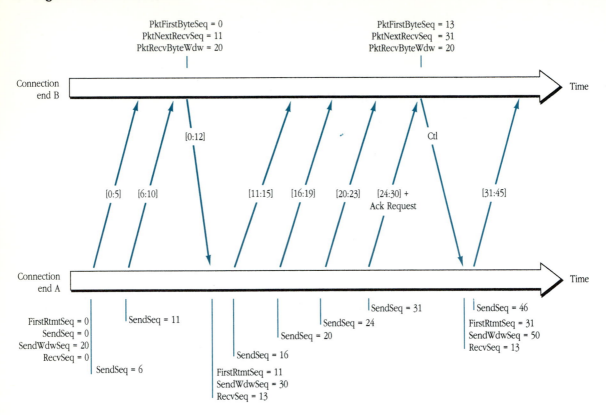

Figure 12-4 shows an example of recovery from a lost packet. In this example, the first packet sent by end A is lost. The receiver discards subsequent packets because they are out of sequence. Some event (a retransmit timer goes off or perhaps the send window is exhausted) causes end A to send an acknowledgment request. End B acknowledges, and end A retransmits all of the lost data.

■ **Figure 12-4** Recovery from a lost packet

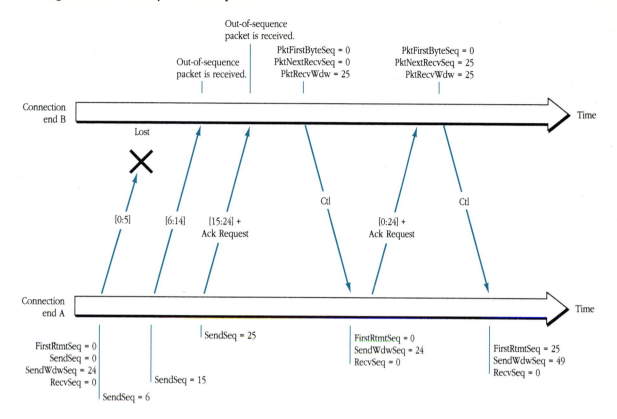

Figure 12-5 gives an example of an idle connection state. Neither client is sending data, so both connection ends periodically send a probe to determine whether the connection is still open.

In *Figure 12-6,* packets from end B are lost, so ADSP eventually tears down the connection.

■ **Figure 12-5** Idle connection state

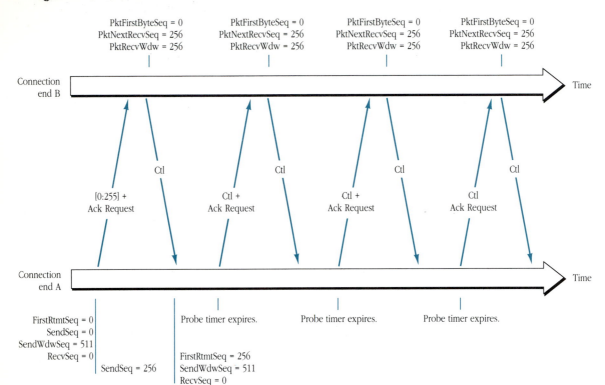

■ **Figure 12-6** Connection torn down due to lost packets

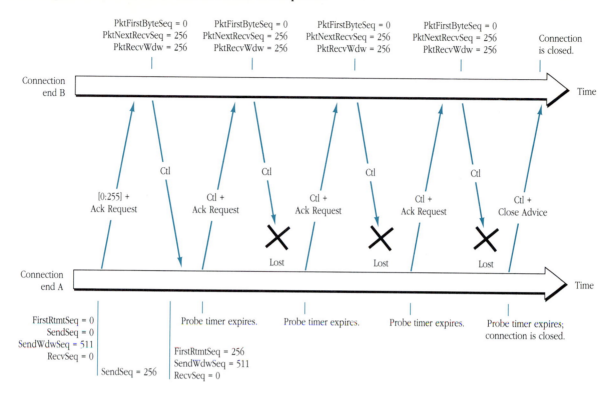

Attention messages

Attention messages provide a method for the clients of the two connection ends to signal each other outside the normal flow of data across the connection. ADSP attention messages are delivered reliably, in order, and free of duplicates.

ADSP Attention packets are used for delivering and acknowledging attention messages. *Figure 12-7* shows an ADSP Attention packet. The Attention bit is set in the packet's ADSP descriptor field to designate an Attention packet. The data part of an Attention packet contains a 2-byte (16-bit) attention code and from 0 to 570 bytes of client attention data.

The 16-bit attention-code field accommodates a range of values from $0000 through $FFFF. Values in the range $0000 through $EFFF are for the client's use. Values in the range $F000 through $FFFF are reserved for potential future expansion of ADSP.

■ **Figure 12-7** ADSP Attention packet format

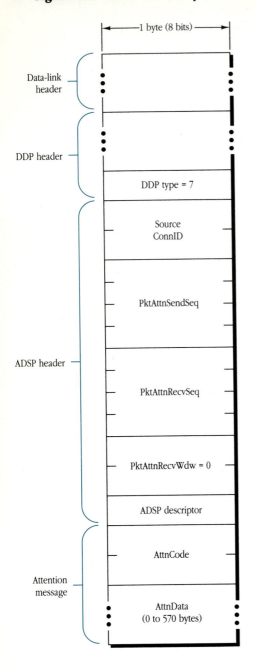

Attention messages use a packet-oriented sequence-number space that is independent of data-stream sequence numbers. The first Attention packet is assigned a sequence number of 0, the second packet is assigned 1, the third packet 2, and so on. Attention sequence numbers are treated as 32-bit unsigned integers that wrap around to 0 when increased by 1 beyond the maximum value $FFFFFFFF.

End B maintains a variable, AttnRecvSeq, which contains the sequence number of the next attention message that end B expects to receive from end A. AttnRecvSeq is initially set to 0 and is increased by 1 with each attention message that end B accepts from end A.

End A maintains a corresponding variable, AttnSendSeq, which contains the sequence number of the next attention message it will send across the connection. When end A is first established, AttnSendSeq is synchronized to the value of end B's AttnRecvSeq.

In any Attention packet sent from end A to end B, the PktAttnSendSeq field of the ADSP packet header contains the current value of end A's AttnSendSeq. In any Attention packet sent from end B to end A, the PktAttnRecvSeq field contains the current value of end B's AttnRecvSeq. Upon receiving an Attention packet, end A uses the value of PktAttnRecvSeq to update its own AttnSendSeq. Before updating AttnSendSeq, end A must ensure that the value of PktAttnRecvSeq equals AttnSendSeq+1. If these values are equal, end A increases AttnSendSeq to equal PktAttnRecvSeq.

Attention data is received into buffer space other than the receive queue in an implementation-dependent manner. End A can send an attention message even if end B's receive window in the regular data stream is closed. However, only one attention message can be outstanding at a time. Once end A sends an attention message to end B, end A cannot send another attention message until it receives an acknowledgment from end B. End B accepts and acknowledges receipt of an attention message if the attention message is properly sequenced and if buffer space is available. If buffer space is not available, end B discards the attention message. Because only one attention message can be sent at a time, the PktAttnRecvWdw field of ADSP attention-packet headers is not used and must always be set to 0.

When sending an attention message, the end starts a timer. If the timer expires, the end retransmits the attention message and restarts the timer. The sending end continues to retransmit the attention message until it receives the appropriate attention-message acknowledgment or until the connection is torn down.

When end A sends an attention message to end B, end A's PktAttnSendSeq field is set to the value of end A's AttnSendSeq. When end B receives the Attention packet, it compares the value of PktAttnSendSeq with its own AttnRecvSeq. If the values are not equal, end B discards the attention message. If the values are equal and buffer space is available, end B accepts the data and increases AttnRecvSeq by 1. Then end B sends end A an attention acknowledgment with the PktAttnRecvSeq field set to the current value of end B's AttnRecvSeq.

An acknowledgment is implicit in any Attention packet sent; that is, acknowledgments are piggybacked on attention messages. The attention acknowledgment itself may be an attention message that end B's client has just asked end B to send, or the acknowledgment may be an ADSP Control packet whose sole purpose is to acknowledge the attention message.

Connection opening

This section describes how connections are opened and explains some of the facilities that ADSP provides for opening connections.

A connection is open when both ends of the connection are established. A connection end is established when it knows the values of all of the following parameters:

Parameter	Description
LocAddr	the internet address of the local end's socket
RemAddr	the internet address of the remote end's socket
LocConnID	the local end's ConnID
RemConnID	the remote end's ConnID
SendSeq	the sequence number to be assigned to the next byte that the local end's ADSP will send over the connection to the remote end
FirstRtmtSeq	the sequence number of the oldest byte in the local end's send queue (Initially, the queue is empty so this number equals SendSeq.)
SendWdwSeq	the sequence number of the last byte that the remote end has buffer space to receive from the local end
RecvSeq	the sequence number of the next byte that the local end expects to receive from the remote end (Initially, this number is set to 0.)
RecvWdw	the number of bytes that the local end currently has buffer space to receive from the remote end (Initially, the local end's entire receive buffer is available.)
AttnSendSeq	the sequence number to be assigned to the next Attention packet that the local end will transmit over the connection
AttnRecvSeq	the sequence number of the next Attention packet that the local end expects to receive from the remote end (Initially, this number is set to 0.)

When attempting to become established, the local end knows the values of LocAddr, LocConnID, RecvSeq, RecvWdw, and AttnRecvSeq. (When a connection is first opened, the values of RecvSeq and AttnRecvSeq will be 0.) The local end must somehow discover the values of RemAddr, RemConnID, SendSeq, SendWdwSeq, and AttnSendSeq. The objective of the connection-opening dialog is for each end to discover these values.

◆ *Note:* A connection can be opened in a variety of ways. ADSP provides one mechanism, but a client can use its own separate, parallel mechanism to discover and provide the required information to ADSP in order to establish either or both connection ends.

In order to open a connection, ADSP provides a type of Control packet known as an Open Connection Request Control packet. Since the Control packet is an ADSP packet, its header contains the sending end's network address and ConnID. In addition, the packet includes the sending end's RecvSeq (PktNextRecvSeq in the packet header) and RecvWdw (PktRecvWdw in the packet header). The end obtains the value of AttnRecvSeq from one of a set of fields in the packet, collectively known as the open-connection parameters.

The end initiating the connection-opening dialog sends an Open Connection Request Control packet to the intended remote end. This packet provides the remote end with the connection parameters it needs to become established. Upon receiving such a packet, the remote end sets its connection parameters as follows:

Parameter	Description
RemAddr	equal to the packet's source network address
RemConnID	equal to the packet's source ConnID
SendSeq	equal to PktNextRecvSeq
SendWdwSeq	equal to PktNextRecvSeq+PktRecvWdw−1
AttnSendSeq	equal to PktAttnRecvSeq

Once the remote end has set these parameters (based on the information in the Open Connection Request Control packet), the end is considered to be established.

In order for a connection to become open, both ends of the connection must be established. Therefore, in the connection-opening dialog, each end must send an Open Connection Request Control packet to the other end (as well as receive an Open Connection Request Control packet from the other end).

Since these packets can be lost during transmission, ADSP provides a mechanism for ensuring that the packets are delivered. When a connection end receives an Open Connection Request Control packet, the receiving end returns an Open Connection Acknowledgment Control packet to the sending end. Upon receiving an Open Connection Acknowledgment Control packet, the receiving end is assured that the other end has become established.

After the two connection ends have exchanged both open-connection requests and acknowledgments, the connection is open and data can safely be sent on it.

Connection-opening dialog

The connection-opening mechanism provided by ADSP requires that a connection end must know the internet socket address of the destination socket to which the end is making a connection request. The client must provide this address to ADSP for the purpose of initiating the connection-opening dialog. How this address is determined is up to the client; generally, the AppleTalk Name Binding Protocol (NBP) is used.

The ADSP connection-opening mechanism is a symmetric operation. Either of two peer clients can initiate the connection-opening dialog. In fact, both peers can attempt to open the connection at the same time; however, only one connection between the two peers should be opened. The following discussion focuses on how end A opens a connection with end B.

When attempting to open a connection with a remote end B, end A first chooses a locally unique ConnID. End A then sends an Open Connection Request Control packet to end B's socket address. This request contains end A's initial connection-state information (its LocConnID, RecvSeq, RecvWdw, and AttnRecvSeq). End B needs this information in order to become established.

Upon receiving the Open Connection Request Control packet, end B extracts the sender's internet socket address and source ConnID and saves them in its RemAddr and RemConnID fields, respectively. The value of the PktNextRecvSeq field is saved as end B's SendSeq. End B then adds the value of PktRecvWdw–1 to PktNextRecvSeq to produce its SendWdwSeq. Finally, the value of PktAttnRecvSeq is saved as end B's AttnSendSeq. Connection end B is now established.

At this point, end A is not established and does not know the state of connection end B. End B responds to end A's Open Connection Request Control packet by sending back an Open Connection Request and Acknowledgment Control packet. End A determines the values of its RemAddr, RemConnID, SendSeq, and SendWdwSeq from the open-connection request, as previously described; then, end A becomes established. The open-connection acknowledgment informs end A that end B has accepted end A's Open Connection Request Control packet and has become established. End A assumes the connection is now open.

End A informs end B of its state by sending an Open Connection Acknowledgment control packet. Upon receiving the acknowledgment, end B assumes the connection is open (see *Figure 12-8*).

Both ends can attempt to open the connection simultaneously. In this case, each ADSP socket receives an Open Connection Request Control packet from the socket to which it has sent an Open Connection Request Control packet. The ADSP implementation identifies end A by matching its RemAddr to the source address of the Open Connection Request Control packet received from end B. End A extracts the required information from the packet and becomes established. End A then sends back an Open Connection Acknowledgment Control packet to inform the remote end that it has become established. This ensures that ADSP establishes only one connection between the two sockets (see *Figure 12-9*).

■ **Figure 12-8** Connection-opening dialog initiated by one end

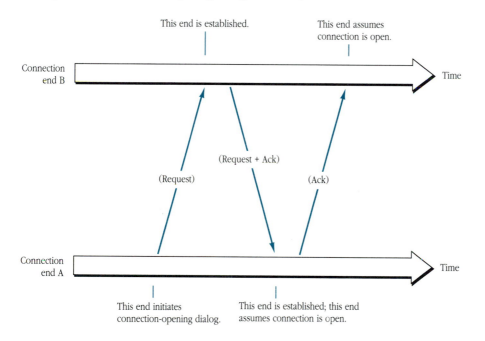

■ **Figure 12-9** Connection-opening dialog initiated by both ends

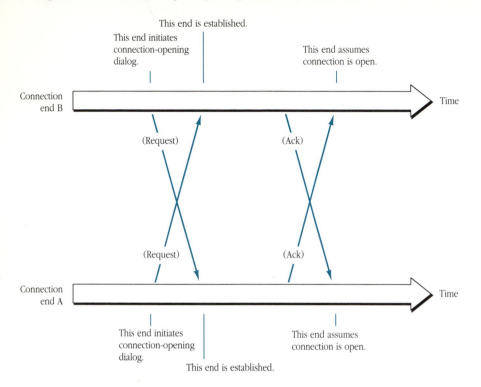

If for any reason an ADSP implementation is unable to fulfill the open-connection request, an open-connection denial is sent back to the requester. In this case, the source ConnID field of the ADSP packet header is 0, while the destination ConnID field of the connection-opening parameters is set to the requester's ConnID (see *Figure 12-10*).

■ **Figure 12-10** Open-connection request denied

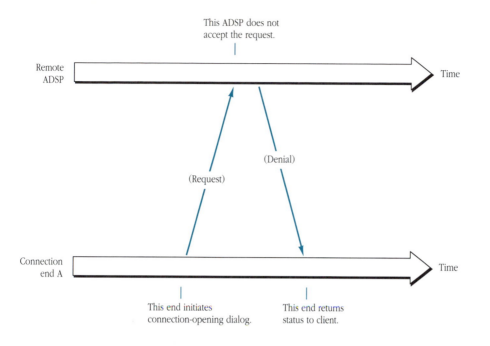

Open-connection Control packet format

An open-connection request is sent as an ADSP Control packet. As such, the request contains all the information required to establish the receiving end. ADSP is a client of the network layer, DDP, which contains the internet address of the sender. (Note that the packet must be sent through the socket on which the connection is to be established.) The ADSP header contains the source ConnID, RecvSeq, and RecvWdw, which are used to determine the receiving end's RemConnID, SendSeq, and SendWdwSeq, respectively. The AttnRecvSeq field of the open-connection parameters following the header is used to set the value of the receiving end's AttnSendSeq.

An ADSP Open Connection Acknowledgment, which is also a Control packet, serves to acknowledge the receipt of an Open Connection Request Control packet. An end can send both an Open Connection Request Control packet and an Open Connection Acknowledgment Control packet at the same time by combining them into one ADSP Control packet. ADSP also provides an Open Connection Denial Control packet for use when a connection request cannot be honored. In the Open Connection Denial Control packet, the source ConnID should be set to 0 in the packet header.

Figure 12-11 shows the format of ADSP packets that are used in the connection-opening dialog. Note the special open-connection parameters that follow the ADSP packet header. These parameters are described in detail after the figure.

The first field of the open-connection parameters is the 16-bit ADSP version field. In any open-connection packet, the ADSP version should be set to the protocol version of the ADSP implementation that sent the packet. An ADSP implementation must deny any open-connection request that has an incompatible ADSP version. This chapter documents ADSP version $0100; all other values are reserved by Apple for potential future expansion of the protocol.

The 16-bit destination ConnID field of the open-connection parameters is used uniquely to associate an open-connection acknowledgment or denial with the appropriate open-connection request. The destination ConnID field of any Open Connection Acknowledgment Control packet or Open Connection Denial Control packet should be set to the source ConnID of the corresponding open-connection request. When an end sending an Open Connection Request Control packet does not know the ConnID of the remote end, the destination ConnID field in the packet must be set to 0.

The 32-bit PktAttnRecvSeq field of the open-connection parameters contains the sequence number of the first Attention packet that the sending end is willing to accept. This value is equal to the sending end's AttnRecvSeq variable.

The following table summarizes the packet-descriptor values and ConnIDs that should be used with each of the open-connection control messages.

Control packet	ADSP packet descriptor	Source ConnID	Destination ConnID
Open Connection Request	$81	LocConnID	0
Open Connection Ack	$82	LocConnID	RemConnID
Open Connection Request+Ack	$83	LocConnID	RemConnID
Open Connection Denial	$84	0	RemConnID

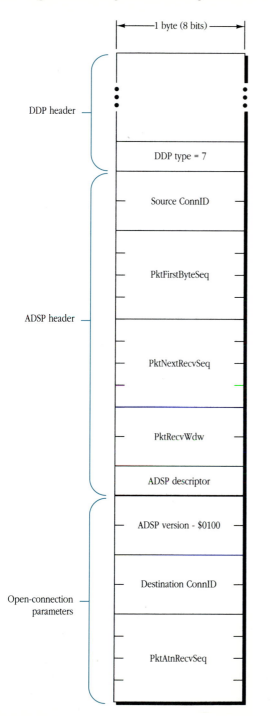

Error recovery in the connection-opening dialog

Since delivery of packets sent by the network layer is not guaranteed, connection-opening packets can be lost or delayed. Therefore, ADSP open-connection requests should be retransmitted at intervals specified by the client (for a maximum number of retries also specified by the client). An end receiving an open-connection request must ensure that it is not a duplicate by comparing the request's source ConnID and address with that of all open or opening connections for the receiving socket. If the request is a duplicate, the appropriate acknowledgment is still sent back. See *Figure 12-12* and *Figure 12-13,* where *X* indicates lost or delayed packets.

■ **Figure 12-12** Connection-opening dialog: packet lost

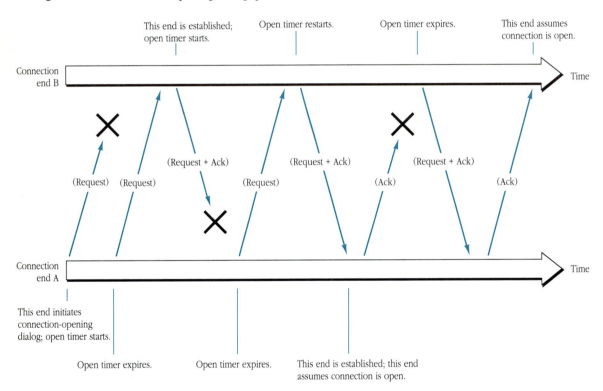

■ Figure 12-13 Simultaneous connection-opening dialog: packet lost

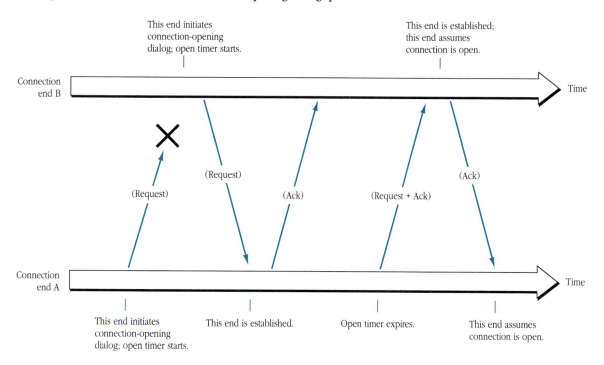

If either end goes down or becomes unreachable during the connection-opening dialog, one end can become established while the other end does not. This results in a half-open connection. When this situation occurs, the open end is closed through normal ADSP mechanisms, as shown in *Figure 12-14*.

- **Figure 12-14** Connection-opening dialog: half-open connection

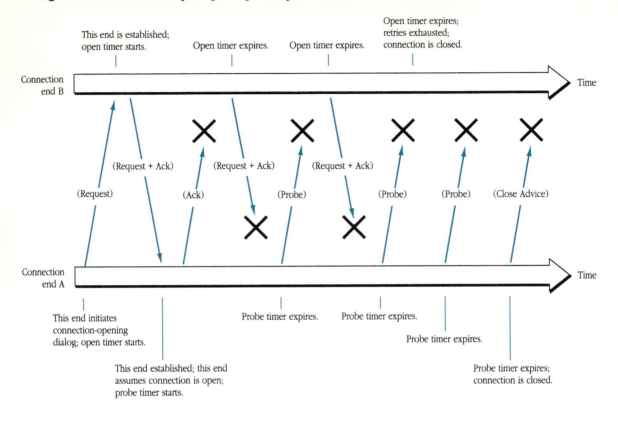

Figure 12-15 shows that it is possible for one end to become established while the other is still opening. In this case, the connection is half open. End A can begin to send Data packets, but end B will discard the packets because the connection is not yet open (end B has not yet received acknowledgment that end A has become established).

End B will retransmit its open-connection request and, upon receiving the request, end A will compare the value of PktFirstByteSeq to its own RecvSeq. If the values are equal, end A has not yet received any data from end B; end A assumes the connection is not yet open, sends back an open-connection acknowledgment with PktFirstByteSeq equal to its FirstRtmtSeq, and then retransmits the data (see *Figure 12-15*).

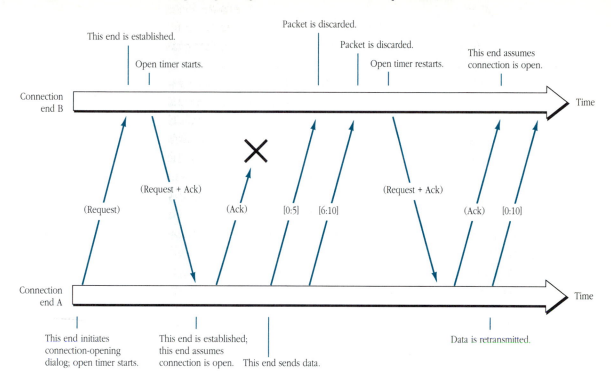

If PktFirstByteSeq does not equal RecvSeq, end A can assume that the connection is open because end A has received data from end B; therefore, the open-connection request must be a late-arriving duplicate and is discarded (see *Figure 12-16*).

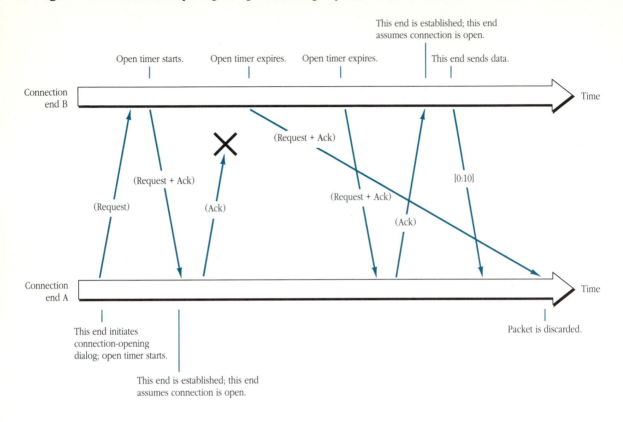

Connection opening outside of ADSP

The preceding discussion focused on one typical connection-opening situation: the opening of a connection between two specific peer sockets. Although this example illustrates and defines the connection-opening concepts and facilities in ADSP, a connection can be opened in other ways. For example, each of the two clients of ADSP may know the connection-opening information of the other end based on an established convention between these clients. In this situation, each client makes a call to its local ADSP to set up the connection, providing the necessary connection-opening parameters. At each end, the ADSP implementation assumes the connection is open.

In a variation of this situation, the two ADSP clients exchange the required connection-opening information via an independent channel, and then each client calls its local ADSP, as previously described, to open the connection.

In both of these cases, ADSP makes no attempt to send any connection-opening packets to the other end; the underlying assumption is that the cooperating clients have adequately synchronized the parameters before calling their respective ADSP implementations.

Connection-listening sockets and servers

A common situation involves one or more clients opening connections to a server. The server sets up a connection-listening socket to which the server's clients send their ADSP open-connection requests.

A **connection-listening socket** is a socket that accepts open-connection requests and passes them along to its client (the server process) for further processing. In general, the client then selects a socket and requests ADSP to establish a connection end on that socket. The client passes to ADSP the information from the received open-connection request (that is, the sender's socket address, source ConnID, RecvSeq, RecvWdw, and AttnRecvSeq). ADSP continues the open-connection dialog, sending an Open Connection Request and Acknowledgment Control packet to the specified remote end.

No restriction defines the socket that the server process picks for the connection end; the socket could be the connection-listening socket itself, another socket on the same node, a socket on another node in the same network, or a socket on a node in another network. If the socket is on a node different from the connection-listening socket, then the server must use its own process (outside of ADSP) to convey the call to the target node's ADSP implementation. The client must be aware of the possibility of duplicate open-connection requests and should forward such requests to ADSP, specifying the same connection end (see *Figure 12-17*).

■ **Figure 12-17** Open-connection request made to connection-listening socket; alternate socket chosen for connection

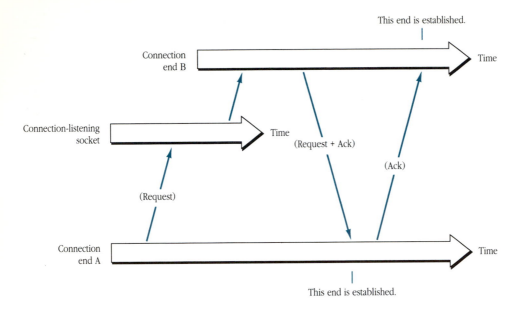

Connection-opening filters

The ADSP client may need to be selective about establishing connections with remote clients; the addresses of some remote clients that make open-connection requests may not be acceptable to the local client. In order to establish a selection criterion, the client can provide ADSP with a filter of valid network addresses with which it is willing to establish connections. This filter could be as simple as specifying "open a connection only with the socket to which you are sending the open-connection request" or "open a connection only with a socket on a particular node." If ADSP receives an open-connection request from an address that does not match the filter, it sends back an open-connection denial and ignores the packet (see *Figure 12-18*).

■ **Figure 12-18** Connection-opening filters: open connection denied

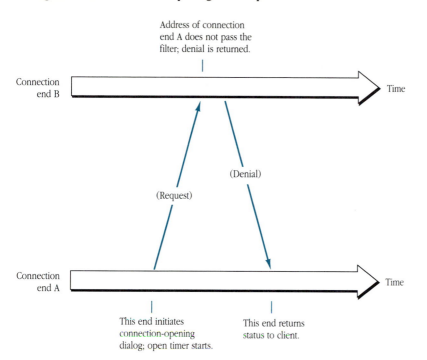

Address of connection
end A does not pass the
filter; denial is returned.

Connection
end B

Time

(Denial)

(Request)

Connection
end A

Time

This end initiates
connection-opening
dialog; open timer starts.

This end returns
status to client.

In the case of a connection-listening socket, the end could conceivably become established with a different network address than the one to which the original open request was sent. The new address may not be acceptable to the original requester. In this case, the original requester can provide ADSP with a filter of network addresses with which it is willing to establish a connection (see *Figure 12-19*).

■ **Figure 12-19** Connection-opening filters with a connection-listening socket

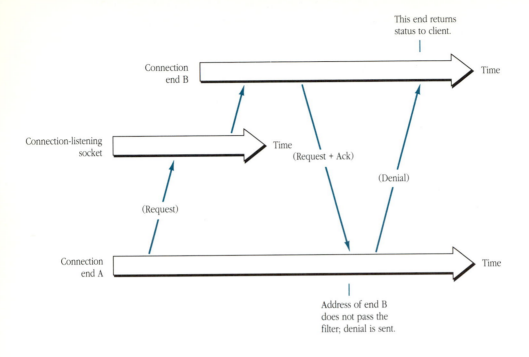

Connection closing

An ADSP connection is closed under one of two circumstances. The first circumstance occurs when either end determines that the other end is not responding to repeated probes. In this event, ADSP immediately closes the remote connection end and notifies the local end's client that the connection is closed.

The second circumstance occurs when either client calls ADSP to close the connection. An ADSP client can make this call at any time. Typically, the local connection end's ADSP awaits acknowledgment of the delivery of any outstanding bytes in its send queue before closing the connection.

Before closing an open connection, ADSP sends a Close Connection Advice Control packet to the remote end. The packet is sent as a courtesy, and its delivery is not guaranteed. If the packet is not successfully delivered to the remote end, the remote end will eventually time out and tear down.

◆ *Note:* Since the close-connection advice message is sent as an ADSP Control packet, no data can accompany it.

Upon receiving a Close Connection Advice Control packet, an ADSP connection end verifies that the packet is sequenced properly. If the packet has arrived early, the receiving end may discard or buffer it until any intervening data packets have arrived. This action avoids prematurely closing the connection while data packets are delayed in internet routers. If the Close Connection Advice Control packet is acceptable, ADSP immediately closes the connection and informs the client of the change in status.

Occasionally, clients need to inform each other reliably that they have completed their conversation and are ready to close the connection. This process can be accomplished if each end sends an attention message to the other end indicating that it has sent and received acknowledgment of all of its data. Upon completing this handshake, each end can safely issue a call to its local ADSP to close the connection.

Part V **End-User Services**

P A R T V of *Inside AppleTalk* describes the protocols that provide end-user services in an AppleTalk network. This part includes a complete description of the AppleTalk Filing Protocol (AFP). It also includes the architectural specification for print spooling in an AppleTalk network. ■

Chapter 13 **AppleTalk Filing Protocol**

CONTENTS

■

THE PURPOSE of the AppleTalk Filing Protocol (AFP) is to allow workstation users to share files. Sharing files across a network requires that the user application know where and how to find a file. This chapter introduces the file access model used by AFP to enable file sharing and discusses the components of AFP software.

The AFP file access model is shown in *Figure 13-1,* which illustrates the discussion that follows. ■

■ **Figure 13-1** The AFP file access model

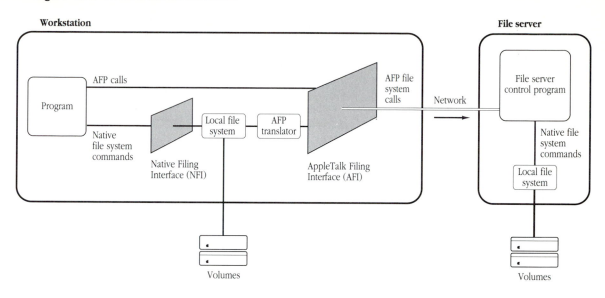

A program running in a workstation (the workstation client or AFP client) requests and manipulates files by using the workstation's **native file system commands.** These commands manipulate files on a diskette or other memory resource that is physically connected to the workstation (a local resource). Through AFP, a workstation program can use the same native file system commands to manipulate files on a shared memory resource that resides on a different node (a remote resource).

A workstation program sends a file system command through the **Native Filing Interface** (NFI) in the workstation. A data structure in local memory indicates whether the volume is managed by the native file system or by some external file system. The native file system discovers whether the requested file resides locally or remotely by looking at this data structure. If the data structure indicates an external file system, the native file system then routes the command to the **AFP translator.**

The translator, as its name implies, translates the native commands into AFP calls and sends them through the **AppleTalk Filing Interface** (AFI) to the file server that manages the remote resource.

The AFP specification defines the AFI part of the file access model. The translator is not defined in the AFP specification; it is up to the applications programmer to design it.

A workstation program may need to gain access to the AFI directly because the program needs to make an AFP call for which no equivalent command exists in the native file system. For example, user authentication might have to be handled through an interface written for that purpose. In *Figure 13-1,* the line leading directly from the program to the AFI illustrates such AFP calls.

Any implementation of AFP must take into account the capabilities of the networked workstation's native file system and simulate its functionality in the shared environment. In other words, the shared file system should duplicate the characteristics of a workstation's local file system. Simulating the functionality of each workstation's native file system becomes increasingly complex as different workstation types share the same file server. Because each workstation type has different characteristics in the way it manipulates files, the shared file system needs to possess the combined capabilities of all workstations on the same network.

Three system components make up AFP:

- a file system structure
- AFP calls
- algorithms associated with the calls

The first component, the AFP file system structure is made up of resources (such as file servers, volumes, directories, files, and forks) that are addressable through the network. These resources are called **AFP-file-system-visible entities** because they are visible through the AFI. In other words, the translator can send commands through AFI to manipulate them.

AFP specifies the relationship between these entities. For example, one directory can be the parent of another. (For descriptions of AFP-file-system-visible entities, see "File System Structure" later in this chapter.)

AFP calls, the second component, are the commands the workstation uses to manipulate the AFP file system structure. As mentioned earlier, the translator sends file system commands to the file server in the form of AFP calls, or the workstation application can make AFP calls directly. (See "AFP Calls" later in this chapter.)

The third software component of AFP is the set of algorithms associated with AFP calls. These algorithms specify the actions performed by the calls.

AFP supports Macintosh computers, Apple II computers running ProDOS®, and personal computers using MS-DOS. AFP can be extended to support additional types of workstations.

Although this chapter distinguishes between workstations and file servers, AFP can support these two functions within the same node. However, AFP does not solve the concurrency problems that can arise in a combined workstation–server node. The software on such combined nodes must be carefully designed to avoid potential conflicts.

AFP does not provide calls that support administration of the file server. Administrative functions, such as registering users and changing passwords, must be handled by separate network-administration software. Additional software must also be provided to add, remove, and find servers within the network.

AFP Version 1.0, which was never released, was developed as a joint effort between Apple Computer, Inc. and Centram Systems West. This chapter describes AFP Versions 1.1 and 2.0. AFP 2.0 provides certain extensions to AFP 1.1; these extensions will be pointed out in the following sections. Unless otherwise noted, all information herein applies to both versions.

Figure 13-2 shows AFP within the AppleTalk protocol architecture.

■ **Figure 13-2** AFP and the AppleTalk protocol architecture

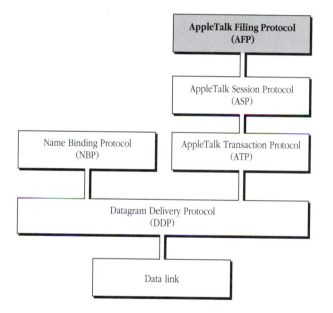

File system structure

This section describes the AFP file system structure and the parameters associated with its AFP-file-system-visible entities. These entities include the file server, its volumes, directories ("folders" in Macintosh terminology), files, and file forks. This section also describes the tree structure, called the **volume catalog,** which is a description of the relationships between directories and files.

By submitting AFP calls, the workstation client can

- obtain information about the file server and other parts of the file system structure
- modify this information
- create and delete files and directories
- retrieve and store information within individual files

The following sections describe the file system structure's AFP-file-system-visible entities.

File server

A **file server** is a computer with at least one large-capacity disk that allows other computers on the network to share the information stored in it. The maximum number of disks is not limited by AFP. Each disk attached to a file server usually contains one volume, although the disk may be subdivided into multiple volumes. Each volume appears as a separate entity to the workstation client.

A file server has a unique name and other identifying parameters. These parameters identify the server's machine type and number of attached volumes, the AFP versions that the server can understand, and the **user authentication methods** (UAMs) that the server supports. AFP file server parameters are listed below.

Parameter	Description
server name	string of up to 32 characters
server machine type	string of up to 16 characters
number of volumes	2-byte integer
AFP version strings	strings of up to 16 characters each
UAM strings	strings of up to 16 characters each
server icon	256 bytes

◆ *Note:* Unless mentioned otherwise, all numerical values are signed numbers. AFP strings can be up to 255 characters long and are case-insensitive and diacritical-sensitive. Strings appear in what is commonly called Pascal format; that is, a length byte followed by the same number of characters. The string "hello" would be encoded as 05 "h" "e" "l" "l" "o". A string of up to 16 characters would require up to 17 bytes to encode (1 byte for the length and up to 16 bytes of characters). The character-code mapping is as defined in Appendix D. All date-time parameters are signed 4-byte integers representing the number of seconds measured from 12:00 A.M. on January 1, 2000.

In this section, strings, file creators, and file types are shown in monospaced font enclosed by single quotes (for example, `'B3   '`). The single quotes are delimiters and are not part of the string, file creator, or file type.

The server machine-type string is purely informative, providing text that describes the file server's hardware and software; it has no significance to AFP.

For descriptions of AFP version strings and UAM strings, see "AFP Login" later in this chapter.

The server icon is optional and is used to customize the appearance of server volumes on a Macintosh Desktop. It consists of a 32-by-32 bit (128 bytes) icon bitmap followed by a 32-by-32 bit (128 bytes) icon mask. The mask usually consists of the icon's outline filled with black (bits that are set). This format fits the specification of icons for a Macintosh (for more information about icons, refer to *Inside Macintosh*).

Figure 13-1 illustrates a file server with two attached volumes.

Volumes

A file server can have one or more volumes that are visible to workstations through the AFI. Each volume has identifying parameters associated with it, as listed below. To provide security at the level of each volume, the server can also maintain an optional password parameter.

Parameter	Description
volume name	string of up to 27 characters
volume signature	2 bytes
volume identifier	2 bytes
volume creation date-time	4 bytes
volume modification date-time	4 bytes
volume backup date-time	4 bytes
volume size (in bytes)	4-byte unsigned long integer
free bytes on volume	4-byte unsigned long integer
volume password (optional)	8 bytes

The volume name identifies a server volume to a workstation user, so it must be unique among all volumes managed by the server. All 8-bit ASCII characters, except null ($00) and colon ($3A), are permitted in a volume name. This name is not used directly to specify files and directories on the volume. Instead, the workstation makes an AFP call to obtain a particular volume identifier, which it then uses in all subsequent AFP calls. (See "Designating a Path to a CNode" later in this chapter.)

The **volume signature** identifies the volume type. Permitted values are discussed in the next section.

For each session between the server and a workstation, the server assigns a **Volume ID** to each of its volumes. This value is unique among the volumes of a given server for that session.

A volume's creation date-time is set by the server when the volume is created. Similarly, the modification date-time is changed by the server each time anything on the volume is modified. These two date-time values are managed solely by the server and cannot be modified by the workstation client. However, the backup date-time can be set by a backup program each time the volume's contents are backed up. When a volume is created, its backup date-time is set to $80000000 (the earliest representable date-time value).

Volume types

An AFP volume is structured in one of two ways: flat or hierarchical. The latter organizes information into containers (**directories**), which in turn contain files. Flat volumes contain only one directory. Directories and files are described in more detail later. This section discusses only directories and their identifiers, **Directory IDs,** as they relate to the structure of volumes.

Of the three types of AFP volumes, one is flat and two are hierarchical. A flat volume contains only one directory, called the **root,** which in turn contains files. If a user tries to create a directory on a flat volume, the server returns an error message. Hierarchical volumes contain directories arranged in a branching hierarchy, also known as a tree structure. AFP allows two types of hierarchical volumes: fixed Directory ID and variable Directory ID.

A fixed Directory ID volume is hierarchical and contains multiple directories. Each directory has its own permanent Directory ID, which is determined when the directory is created. The Directory ID is not used for any other directory during the lifetime of the volume, even if the corresponding directory is deleted from the volume.

A variable Directory ID volume also maintains the uniqueness of its Directory IDs. However, it differs from a fixed Directory ID volume in that it does not associate a permanent Directory ID with each directory. For variable Directory ID volumes, the file server creates a unique Directory ID for a directory whenever the workstation client issues an FPOpenDir call (see the FPOpenDir call under "AFP Calls" later in this chapter). The file server then maintains this Directory ID until either the client issues a FPCloseDir call or the AFP session is terminated. A Directory ID obtained through an FPOpenDir call to a variable Directory ID volume must be used only for that session. If the Directory ID is stored and used to reference the directory in a later session, the call might either fail, reach the wrong directory, or coincidentally reach the correct directory; the results of such a call are unpredictable.

The three AFP volume types are identified by a 2-byte integer field called the volume signature. This field contains one of the following values:

Value	Volume type
1	flat
2	fixed Directory ID
3	variable Directory ID

The volume types have the following support capabilities and constraints. Apple II computers and personal computers using MS-DOS can gain access to any of the three types of server volumes because the concept of Directory IDs is foreign to their file systems. However, Macintosh computers using either the early (flat) file system or the hierarchical file system (HFS) cannot directly use variable Directory ID volumes. Macintosh HFS volumes are fixed Directory ID volumes, and hierarchical volumes on the file server can be handled by HFS only if they are fixed Directory ID volumes. Macintosh applications, such as the Finder™, save Directory IDs and do not expect them to vary.

An application can be written that allows a workstation with a flat local file system to use parts of a variable Directory ID volume. Such an application would mount selected directories of a variable Directory ID volume as flat volumes. (To **mount** a volume is to make it available to a workstation. The volume is not physically mounted on a local disk drive; it only appears that way.) Each corresponding "virtual" volume would appear flat, because only one directory and its offspring files would be visible through the AFI. However, writing such applications is not recommended. This view of the volume is very limited; if the directory contained other directories, they would not be available to the workstation.

Variable Directory ID volumes are included in this definition of AFP to accommodate non-Macintosh machines with file systems that are unable to implement the fixed Directory ID feature. Variable Directory ID volumes allow such machines to function as file servers and to make their files and directories accessible through AFP.

Volume catalog

The volume catalog is the structure that describes the branching tree arrangement of files and directories on a hierarchical volume (fixed and variable Directory ID volumes). The catalog does not span multiple volumes; the workstation client sees a separate volume catalog for each server volume that is visible through the AFI. *Figure 13-3* shows an example of a volume catalog and illustrates its elements.

The volume catalog contains directories and files branching from a base directory known as the root. These directories and files are referred to as **catalog nodes** or **CNodes** (not to be confused with devices on a network, which are also called nodes). Within the tree structure, CNodes can be positioned in two ways; either at the end of a limb, in which case it is called a leaf, or connected from above and below to other CNodes, in which case it is called internal. Internal CNodes are always directories; leaf CNodes can be either files or empty directories.

CNodes have a parent/offspring relationship: A given CNode is the **offspring** of the CNode above it in the catalog tree, and the higher CNode is considered its **parent** or **parent directory.** Offspring are contained within the parent directory. The only CNode without a true parent is the root directory.

When an AFP call makes its way through the volume catalog, it can take only one shortest path from the root to a specific CNode. The CNodes along that path are said to be **ancestors** of the destination node, which in turn is called the **descendent** of each of its ancestors.

■ **Figure 13-3** The volume catalog

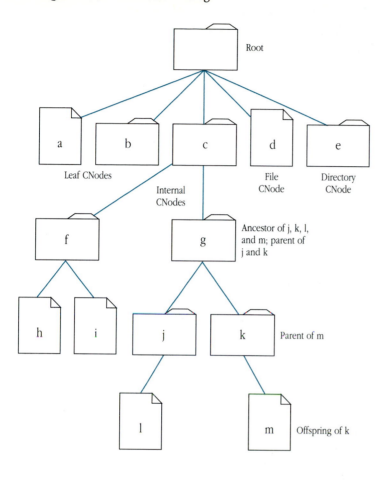

Catalog node names

CNode names identify every file and directory in a volume catalog, and each file or directory has both a **long name** and a **short name.** The root directory of a volume catalog represents the volume, and the root's long name is the same as the volume name. The volume essentially has a short name, which is the short name of the root directory, although AFP does not allow its use. Neither the root nor the volume can be deleted or renamed through AFP.

Long names and short names correspond to two of the native file systems that AFP supports: Macintosh workstations refer to files and directories by long names; MS-DOS workstations use the short-name format. To allow these dissimilar workstations to share resources, the file server provides CNode names in both formats. When creating or renaming files and directories, the workstation user provides a name consistent with the native file system. The server then uses an algorithm to generate the other name (long or short). This section describes the rules for forming CNode names and the algorithm used for creating and maintaining dual names.

The syntax for forming AFP long names is the same as the naming syntax used by the Macintosh HFS, with one exception: Null ($00) is not a permissible character in AFP long names. Otherwise, the mapping of character code to character is the same for AFP as it is for the Macintosh (see Appendix D). AFP long names are made up of at most 31 characters; valid characters are any printable ASCII code except colon ($3A) and null ($00). The volume name, and by inference the root's long name, cannot be longer than 27 bytes.

The syntax for forming AFP short names is the same as the naming syntax used by MS-DOS, which is more restrictive than the naming syntax used in the Macintosh: Names may be up to eight alphanumeric characters, optionally followed by a period ($2E) and a one-to-three alphanumeric character extension.

To ensure that a CNode can be uniquely specified by either name, AFP defines the following rules:

■ No two offspring of a given directory can have the same short name or the same long name.

■ A short name can match a long name if they both belong to the same file or directory.

Therefore, either name, long or short, uniquely identifies CNodes within a parent directory.

AFP naming rules are such that any MS-DOS name can be used directly as a CNode short name, and any Macintosh name can be used directly as a long name. The file server generates the other name for each CNode, deriving it from the first name specified and matching the second name as closely as possible. The long-name format is a superset of the short-name format. The name management algorithm mandates that whenever a CNode is created or renamed with a short name, the long name will always match. Deriving a short name from a long name is not so simple, and AFP does not stipulate an exact algorithm for this derivation. Therefore, different servers may perform this short-name creation differently.

When a CNode is created, the caller supplies the node's name and a name type that indicates whether the name is in short or long format. The server then checks the name to verify that it conforms to the accepted format. The algorithm that follows describes how servers assign short and long names to a CNode (referred to as an object in this algorithm).

```
IF name type is short OR name is in short format
THEN check for new name in list of short names
     IF name already exists
     THEN return ObjectExists result
     ELSE set object's short and long names to new name

ELSE { name type is long OR name is in long format }
     check for new name in list of long names
     IF name already exists
     THEN return ObjectExists result
     ELSE set object's long name to new name
          derive short name from long name
```

This algorithm is used for renaming as well as for creating new names. When a user renames an object, its other name is changed using the above algorithm.

One limitation of this algorithm is that it does not prevent a user from specifying a long name that matches a short name generated by the file server for another file. A server-generated short name is normally not visible to a workstation that sees only long names. If a user inadvertently specifies a long name that matches a preexisting short name, the call fails and the server returns an ObjectExists result code.

For example, for a Macintosh file created with the long name `MacFileLongName`, a file server can generate a short name of `MacFile`. When the user tries to create a new file with the long name `MacFile` in the same directory, the call fails, since the above algorithm stipulates that the long name and short name would both have to be set to `MacFile`.

Directories and files

Directories and files are stored in volumes and constitute the next level of the file system structure visible through the AFI. As was shown in *Figure 13-3,* directories branch to files and other directories. Each directory has an identifier through which it and its offspring can be addressed. Therefore, directories can be thought of as logically containing their offspring directories and files with the parameters described below.

Directory IDs

Each directory in the volume catalog is identified by a 4-byte long integer known as its Directory ID. Because two directories on the same volume cannot have the same Directory ID, the Directory ID uniquely identifies a directory within a volume.

Within the volume catalog, as mentioned earlier, directories have ancestor, parent, and offspring relationships with each other. The Directory ID of a CNode's parent is called the CNode's Parent ID.

A CNode can have only one parent, so a given CNode has a unique Parent ID. However, a CNode can have several ancestor directory identifiers, one for each ancestor. The parent directory is considered an ancestor.

The Directory ID of the root is always 2. The root's Parent ID is always 1. (The root does not really have a parent; this value is returned only if a call asks for the root's Parent ID.) Zero (0) is not a valid Directory ID.

Directory parameters

In AFP Versions 1.1 and 2.0, a server must maintain the following parameters for each directory:

Directory parameter (1.1 and 2.0)	Description
long name	string of up to 31 characters
short name	string of up to 12 characters
Directory ID	4 bytes
Parent ID	4 bytes
attributes	2 bytes
Finder information	32 bytes
offspring count (number of files and directories contained in the directory)	2 bytes
creation date-time	4 bytes
modification date-time	4 bytes
backup date-time	4 bytes
owner ID	4 bytes
group ID	4 bytes
owner access rights	1 byte
group access rights	1 byte
world access rights	1 byte

The Finder information parameter accompanies directories that are used by workstations with HFS. This parameter is maintained by the workstation client and is not examined by AFP. The last five directory parameters listed above relate to directory access controls, discussed later in this chapter.

In AFP Version 2.0, the server must maintain one more parameter in addition to those just listed; the ProDOS information parameter is discussed later in this section.

Directory parameter (2.0)	Description
ProDOS information	6 bytes

The attributes parameter is a bitmap indicating various attributes of the directory. One directory attribute is defined in AFP Version 1.1. (The other attribute bits must be set to 0.)

Directory attribute (1.1)	Description
Invisible	directory should not be made visible to the workstation user

The following directory attributes are defined in AFP Version 2.0:

Directory attribute (2.0)	Description
Invisible	directory should not be made visible to the workstation user
System	directory is a system directory
BackupNeeded	directory needs to be backed up
RenameInhibit	directory cannot be renamed
DeleteInhibit	directory cannot be deleted

The definition of system directory is left up to the workstation.

The BackupNeeded bit is set whenever the directory's modification date-time changes.

No specific bit exists to inhibit moving a directory, but directory movement is constrained by the RenameInhibit bit when a directory is moved or moved and renamed. This is true whether the workstation is using AFP Version 1.1 or 2.0.

File parameters

In Versions 1.1 and 2.0, a server must maintain the following parameters for each file:

File parameter (1.1 and 2.0)	Description
long name	string of up to 31 characters
short name	string of up to 12 characters
Parent ID	4 bytes
file number	4 bytes

(continued) ➡

File parameter (1.1 and 2.0)	Description (continued)
attributes	2 bytes
Finder information	32 bytes
data fork length	4-byte unsigned integer
resource fork length	4-byte unsigned integer
creation date-time	4-bytes
modification date-time	4-bytes
backup date-time	4-bytes

In AFP Version 2.0, the server must maintain one more parameter:

File parameter (2.0)	Description
ProDOS information	6 bytes

The ProDOS information parameter contains a 2-byte File Type and a 4-byte Aux Type intended for use by ProDOS workstations. Note that ProDOS-8 defines the File Type field to be 1 byte and the Aux Type field to be 2 bytes. The extra bytes are reserved for future expansion. The type fields are arranged in the ProDOS information parameter as shown in *Figure 13-4*.

For directories, the ProDOS File Type is always set to $0F. The server will return an afpAccessDenied error if the user attempts to set the ProDOS File Type of a directory to anything other than $0F. No restriction is made on the value of the directory's Aux Type, although it is initially set to $0200 when the directory is created.

■ **Figure 13-4** ProDOS information format

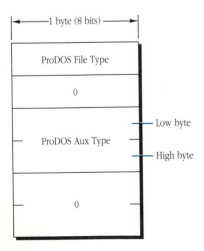

For files, the ProDOS File Type is analogous to the Macintosh Finder Info `fdType` field. In an FPSetFileDirParms or FPSetFileParms call, if either field is set without setting the other, the server will derive an appropriate value for the other field. For example, if a ProDOS workstation sets a file's ProDOS File Type to `$04` and the Aux Type to `$0000` without setting the Finder Info, the server will set the Finder Info `fdCreator to 'pdos'` and the `fdType to 'TEXT'`. The following ProDOS-to-Finder Info mappings are defined in AFP Version 2.0:

Description	ProDOS Info		Finder Info	
	File Type	Aux Type	fdCreator	fdType
ProDOS text	$04	$0000	'pdos'	'TEXT'
ProDOS-8 application	$FF	any	'pdos'	'PSYS'
ProDOS-16 application	$B3	any	'pdos'	'PS16'
Unknown	$00	any	'pdos'	'BINA'
All others	any	any	'pdos'	'p'XYY

If ProDOS Info does not fall into any of the above special categories, the server sets the `fdCreator` field to `'pdos'` and the `fdType` field to `'p'XYY`, where X is equal to the ProDOS File Type and YY is equal to the ProDOS Aux Type. For example, a ProDOS File Type of $32 and Aux Type of $5775 will map to an `fdType` field of `'p2Wu'`. Some values of File Type and Aux Type will map to unprintable characters.

The above mapping is performed only if the Finder Info (`fdCreator` or `fdType`) is actually changed. In other words, if a workstation sets the Finder Info to its current value, the ProDOS Info field will be left untouched.

The ProDOS Info field is derived from Finder Info when a workstation client makes a call specifying new Finder Info without specifying new ProDOS Info. The following Finder-to-ProDOS Info mappings are defined in AFP Version 2.0:

Description	Finder Info		ProDOS Info	
	fdCreator	fdType	File Type	Aux Type
ProDOS text	any	'TEXT'	$04	$0000
ProDOS-8 application	'pdos'	'PSYS'	$FF	unchanged
ProDOS-16 application	'pdos'	'PS16'	$B3	unchanged
Unknown	'pdos'	'BINA'	$00	unchanged
Special format #1	'pdos'	'p'XYY	$X	$YY
Special format #2	'pdos'	'XX '	$XX	unchanged
All others	any	any	$00	$0000

Two special formats are designed to encode ProDOS Info. The first is denoted by an fdType made up of the letter 'p' followed by a 1-byte ProDOS File Type and a 2-byte ProDOS Aux Type (high order byte first). The ProDOS File Type and Aux Type are simply unpacked from the fdType field. The second special format is denoted by an fdType field consisting of a two-character hexadecimal number followed by two spaces (for example, 'B3 '). In this format, the 2-character string is converted to its numerical value and stored as the ProDOS File Type field. The Aux Type field is left unchanged.

If the Finder Info does not fall into any of the above specific mappings, the server sets the ProDOS File Type to $00 and the Aux Type to $0000.

The file number is a unique number associated with each file on the volume. This number is purely informative; AFP does not allow the specification of a file by its file number.

The attributes parameter is a bitmap indicating various attributes of the file. Five file attributes are defined in AFP Version 1.1, and the rest of the 11 bits must be equal to 0. The 5 attributes are:

File attribute (1.1)	Description
Invisible	file should not be made visible to the workstation user
MultiUser	file is an application that has been written for simultaneous use by more than one user
RAlreadyOpen	file's resource fork is currently open by a user
DAlreadyOpen	file's data fork is currently open by a user
ReadOnly	user cannot write to the file's forks

In AFP Version 2.0, 10 file attributes are defined; the other bits must be equal to 0. The 10 attributes are:

File attribute (2.0)	Description
Invisible	file should not be made visible to the workstation user
MultiUser	file is an application that has been written for simultaneous use by more than one user
RAlreadyOpen	file's resource fork is currently open by a user
DAlreadyOpen	file's data fork is currently open by a user
WriteInhibit	user cannot write to the file's forks
System	file is a system file
BackupNeeded	file needs to be backed up
RenameInhibit	file cannot be renamed

File attribute (2.0)	Description *(continued)*
DeleteInhibit	file cannot be deleted
CopyProtect	file should not be copied

The ReadOnly bit is named WriteInhibit in AFP 2.0.

For servers that support both AFP Version 1.1 and 2.0, the following rules will maintain consistency among the file attributes: If a workstation using Version 1.1 sets or clears the ReadOnly bit, the server sets or clears the WriteInhibit, RenameInhibit, and DeleteInhibit bits. Likewise, when this workstation tries to read the state of the ReadOnly bit, the server logically-ORs the Write-, Rename-, and DeleteInhibit bits together and returns the result as the state of the ReadOnly bit.

A workstation using Version 2.0 must be able to set and clear the Write-, Rename-, and DeleteInhibit bits individually, but the server enforces the actions specified by each bit, even for 1.1 workstations. For example, if a 2.0 workstation set a file's RenameInhibit bit, then a 1.1 workstation would not be able to rename the file. It would appear as a ReadOnly file to the latter workstation, and clearing the ReadOnly bit would clear the RenameInhibit bit and therefore allow the file to be renamed.

No specific bit exists to inhibit moving a file, but file movement is constrained by the RenameInhibit bit only when a file is moved and renamed, not when it is simply moved. This constraint occurs whether the workstation is using AFP Version 1.1 or 2.0.

The Macintosh Finder will not copy a file whose CopyProtect bit is set. An attempt to copy the file using the FPCopyFile command will result in an error. This bit may be read, but not set, using AFP. It is to be set by some administrative program, whose specification is beyond the scope of this chapter.

The BackupNeeded bit is set whenever the file's modification date-time changes.

The data fork length and resource fork length are equal to the number of bytes in the corresponding fork.

The creation, backup, and modification date-time parameters are described next.

Date-time values

All date-time quantities used by AFP specify values of the server's clock. These values correspond to the number of seconds measured from 12:00 A.M. on January 1, 2000. In other words, the start of the next century corresponds to a date-time of 0. AFP represents date-time values with 4-byte signed integers.

One of the AFP calls allows the workstation to obtain the current value of the server's clock. At login time, the workstation should read this value (s) and the value of the workstation's clock (w) and compute the offset between these values: $s - w$. All subsequent date-time values read from the server should be adjusted by subtracting this offset from the date-time. All subsequent date-time values sent to the server should be adjusted by adding this offset to the date-time. This adjustment will correct for differences between the two clocks and will ensure that all workstations see a consistent time base.

The creation date-time of a directory or a file is set to the server's system clock when the file or directory is created. The backup date-time is set by backup programs. When a file or directory is created, the server sets the backup date-time to $80000000, which is the earliest representable time.

The server changes the modification date-time of a file that has been written to in a particular session when either of the file's forks is closed or flushed for that session (see the FPCloseFork call under "AFP Calls" later in this chapter).

The server changes the modification date-time of a directory each time the directory's contents are modified. Therefore, any of the following actions will cause the server to assign a new modification date-time to the directory: renaming the directory; creating or deleting a CNode in the directory; moving the directory; changing its access privileges, Finder Info, or ProDOS Info; or changing the Invisible attributes of one of its offspring.

An AFP client with the appropriate access rights can set the creation and modification date-time parameters to any value.

File forks

As in the Macintosh file system, a file consists of two **forks**: a data fork and a resource fork. The bytes in a file fork are sequentially numbered starting with 0. The data fork is an unstructured finite sequence of bytes. The resource fork is used to hold Macintosh operating system resources, such as icons and drivers, and a data structure for mapping them within the fork. AFP is designed to consider both forks as finite-length byte sequences; however, AFP contains no rules relating to the structure of the resource fork. For more information about resource forks, refer to *Inside Macintosh*.

Either or both forks of a given file can be empty. Non-Macintosh AFP clients that need only one file fork must use the data fork. Files created by a workstation with an MS-DOS operating system will have an empty resource fork, because a resource fork is unintelligible to that operating system. Consequently, an MS-DOS workstation that has gained access to a server file created by a Macintosh may not be aware of the existence of the file's resource fork.

Although AFP allows the creation of MS-DOS applications that can understand and manipulate resource forks, such applications would have to preserve the internal structure of the forks. Users of workstations that cannot manage the internal structure of the resource fork should never alter its contents because Macintosh workstations expect a specific format in the resource fork of any file.

To read from or write to the contents of a file's data or resource fork, the workstation client first issues a call to open the particular fork of the file, creating an access path to that file fork. The access path is not to be confused with the paths and pathnames described in the next section.

Once the workstation client creates this access path, all subsequent read and write calls refer to it for the duration of the session.

For each access path, the server maintains the following parameters:

Parameter	Description
OForkRefNum	2 bytes (0 is invalid)
AccessMode	2-byte bitmap
Rsrc/DataFlag	1 bit

The OForkRefNum uniquely identifies the access path among all access paths within a given session. The AccessMode indicates to the server whether this access path allows reading or writing. It is maintained by the server and is inaccessible to workstation clients of AFP. Rsrc/DataFlag indicates to the server that the access path belongs to the data or resource fork.

In addition to the above parameters, the server must provide a way to gain access to the parameters of the file to which this open fork belongs (see the FPGetForkParms call under "AFP Calls" later in this chapter).

Designating a path to a CNode

In order to perform any action on a CNode, the workstation must designate a path to the CNode. AFP provides rules for specifying a path to any CNode in the volume catalog. A CNode (file or directory) can be unambiguously specified to the server by the identifiers shown in *Figure 13-5*.

■ **Figure 13-5** CNode specification

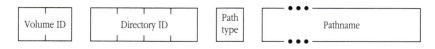

The Volume ID specifies the volume on which the destination CNode resides. The Directory ID can belong to the destination CNode (if the CNode is a directory) or to any one of its ancestor directories, up to and including the root directory and the root's parent directory.

An AFP **pathname** is formatted as a Pascal string (length byte followed by that number of characters). It is made up of CNode names, concatenated with intervening null-byte separators. Each element of a pathname must be the name of a directory, except for the last one, which can be the name of a directory or a file.

The elements of a pathname can be long or short names. However, a given pathname cannot contain a mixture of long and short names. A **path type** byte, which indicates whether the elements of the pathname are all short or all long names, is associated with each pathname. A pathname consisting of short names has a path type of 1. A pathname consisting of long names has a path type of 2.

A pathname can be up to 255 characters long. A single null byte as the length byte indicates that no pathname is supplied. Because the length byte is included at the beginning of the string, each pathname element (CNode name) does not include a length indicator.

The syntax of an AFP pathname follows this paragraph. The asterisk (*) represents a sequence of 0 or more of the preceding elements of the pathname; the plus (+) represents a sequence of 1 or more of the preceding elements; <Sep> represents the separators in the pathname; the vertical bar (|) is an OR operator; and the term on the left side of the ::= symbol is defined as the term(s) on the right side.

```
<Sep>  ::=  <null-byte>+
<Pathname>  ::=  empty-string  |
      <Sep>*<CNode  name>(<Sep><Pathname>)*
```

This syntax represents a concatenation of CNode names separated by one or more null bytes. Pathnames can also start or end with a string of null bytes.

A pathname can be used to traverse the volume catalog in any direction. The pathname syntax allows paths either to descend from a particular CNode through its offspring or to ascend from a CNode to its ancestors. In either case, the directory that is the starting point of this path is defined separately from the pathname by its Directory ID. The first element of the pathname is an offspring of the starting point directory. The pathname must be parsed from left to right to obtain each element that is used as the next node on the path.

To descend through a volume, a valid pathname must proceed in order from parent to offspring. A single null-byte separator preceding this first element is ignored.

To ascend through a volume, a valid pathname must proceed from a particular CNode to its ancestor. To ascend one level in the catalog tree, two consecutive null bytes should follow the offspring CNode name. To ascend two levels in the catalog tree, three consecutive null bytes are used as the separator, and so on.

A particular pathname may descend and ascend through the volume catalog. Because of this, many valid pathnames may refer to the same CNode.

A complete path specification can take a number of forms. The table that follows summarizes the different kinds of path specifications that can be used to traverse the volume catalog illustrated in *Figure 13-6.* A zero in square brackets [0] represents a null-byte separator.

The descriptions and examples that follow refer to this table and the corresponding volume catalog illustrated in *Figure 13-6.* To simplify these examples, the CNodes in this catalog are named *a* through *j,* except the root, which is named *x.* The path type will be ignored in this example. The letter *v* represents the volume's 2-byte Volume ID. Lines connect the CNodes; the unconnected lines indicate that other CNodes in this volume are not shown here.

■ **Figure 13-6** Example 1 of a volume catalog

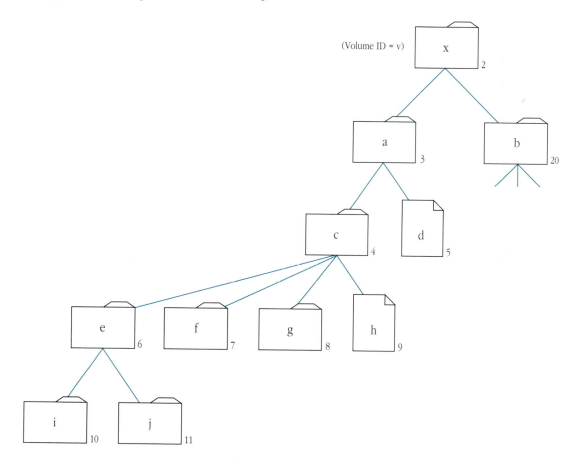

Examples	Volume ID	Directory ID	Pathname
First	v	2	a [0] c [0] e [0] j [0]
Second	v	4	e [0] j
Third	v	6	[0] j
Fourth	v	6	j
Fifth	v	6	[0]
Sixth	v	4	e [0][0] g [0][0] h
Seventh	v	4	e [0][0][0]
Eighth	v	1	x [0] a [0] c [0] h

The *first* example path specification in the table above contains the Volume ID, the root directory's Directory ID, which is always a value of 2, and a pathname. In this case, the pathname must contain the names of all the destination file's ancestors, except the root, and it must end with the name of the file itself. The single trailing null-byte is ignored.

The *second* path specification contains the Volume ID, the Directory ID of an ancestor, and a pathname.

The *third* path is essentially the same as the second. The single leading null-byte is ignored.

In the *fourth* path specification, the Directory ID is the Parent ID of the destination file. In this case, the pathname need contain only the name of the destination file itself.

The *fifth* path specification illustrates another way to uniquely specify a descending path to a directory. It includes the CNode's Volume ID, its Directory ID, and a null pathname. This path specification is used to specify the directory *e*.

The *sixth* path specification is an example of an ascending path. The first CNode in the pathname is the offspring of the starting-point Directory ID. Then the pathname ascends through *e*'s parent *(c)* down to directory *g*, back up to *g*'s parent *(c)*, and down again to *h*.

The *seventh* example shows an ascending pathname that starts at directory *c* (whose Directory ID is 4), moves down to *e*, and then ascends two levels to *e*'s parent's parent *(a)*.

The *eighth* example is a special case in which the starting point of the path is Directory ID 1, the parent of the root. The first name of the pathname must be the volume name or root directory name corresponding to Volume ID *v;* beyond that, pathname traversal is performed as in the other examples.

AFP login

In order to make use of any resource managed by a file server, the workstation must first log in to the server. This section provides an overview of the AFP login process. (AFP login is described in relation to specific calls in "An Overview of AFP Calls" later in this chapter.)

During the AFP login process, the workstation performs the following steps:

1. It finds the server.

2. It determines which AFP versions the server understands.

3. It determines which UAMs the server recognizes.

4. It indicates the AFP version it will use for the session.

5. It tells the server which UAM to use.

6. It prompts the user to provide authentication information. (This step is optional.)

Before a session can be established, the file server must have a session listening socket (SLS). When a server first becomes active on the network, it calls the AppleTalk Session Protocol (ASP) to open an SLS. AFP uses the Name Binding Protocol (NBP) to register the file server's name and type on the socket. For the file server, the NBP type is `'AFPServer'`. When the SLS has been opened and the file server's name has been registered, the file server is available to workstations.

To find the file server, the workstation submits a lookup call to NBP. NBP returns the addresses of all network-visible entities that match the lookup request within the zone specified by the workstation.

The string used to find the names of all file servers is case-insensitive and diacritical-sensitive, and has the following form:

```
=:AFPServer@<zone name>
```

NBP responds to this lookup string with a list of all active file servers in the zone, including the internet addresses of their SLSs. The workstation must then choose a server from among those listed. The way it does this is implementation-dependent.

Another way a workstation can find a file server is to request it by name using the following form:

```
<server's name>:AFPServer@<zone name>
```

If the server is running, NBP will return the internet address of its SLS.

After the workstation picks a server, it uses the FPGetSrvrInfo call to request information about that server. The server returns information that includes which AFP versions and UAMs the server recognizes. Each AFP version is uniquely described by a string of up to 16 characters called the AFPVersion string. The AFPVersion strings for the two protocol versions described in this chapter are 'AFPVersion 1.1' and 'AFPVersion 2.0'. Each UAM is described by a UAM string. (See "User Authentication Methods" later in this chapter for information about this string.)

From the list returned by the server, the workstation chooses which AFP versions and UAM strings the workstation and the server will use for the session that is about to begin.

The workstation initiates the login process by submitting an FPLogin call to the server. This call includes the AFPVersion string, the UAM string, and the internet address of the SLS. The UAM string describes only the UAM; it does not include user login information. Depending on the UAM method used, the FPLogin call can include user login information (such as a user name or password), or subsequent FPLoginCont calls may be required to complete authentication of the user, as described in the next section.

If the user authentication method succeeds, an AFP session between the workstation and the server will begin.

File server security

Information stored in a shared resource sometimes needs protection from unauthorized users. The role of file server security is to provide varying amounts and kinds of protection, depending on what users feel is necessary.

AFP provides security in three ways:

- user authentication when the user logs in to the server
- an optional volume-level password when the user first attempts to gain access to a volume
- directory access control

User authentication methods

AFP provides the capability for servers and workstations to use a variety of methods to authenticate users. Three user authentication methods are already defined: no user authentication, cleartext password, and random number exchange. (Others can be easily added later.)

The workstation indicates its choice of UAM by giving the server a UAM string. These strings are intended to be case-insensitive and diacritical-sensitive.

Some of these methods require additional user authentication information to be passed to the server in the FPLogin call. The following paragraphs describe the three user authentication methods and the kinds of information they require as User Auth Info (user authentication information).

No user authentication

The first of these methods, no user authentication, needs no specification. No user name or password information is required in the FPLogin call. The call, therefore, has no User Auth Info field. The corresponding UAM string is 'No User Authent'.

In order to implement the directory access control described later in this section, the server must assign a user ID and group ID to the user for that session. In this UAM, the server assigns to the user world access rights for every directory in every server volume. World access rights are described in "Directory Access Control" later in this chapter.

Cleartext password

The second method, cleartext password, uses the corresponding UAM string of 'Cleartxt Passwrd'. This method transmits the password as clear, rather than encoded, text along with the user name. The User Auth Info part of the FPLogin call consists of the user name (a string of up to 31 characters) followed by the user's password. In order to ensure that the user's password is aligned on an even byte boundary in the packet, the workstation may have to insert a null byte ($00) between the user name and the password. The user's password is an 8-byte quantity. If the user provides a shorter password, it must be padded on the end with null bytes to make it 8 bytes long. The permissible set of characters in passwords consists of all 7-bit ASCII characters.

User name comparison must be case-insensitive, but password comparison is intended to be case-sensitive in this user authentication method.

The cleartext password method should be used by workstations only if the intervening network is secure against eavesdropping. Otherwise, the password information can be read from FPLogin call packets by anyone listening to the network.

Random number exchange

In environments in which the network is not secure against eavesdropping, random number exchange is a more secure user authentication method. This method corresponds to the UAM string 'Randnum Exchange'. With random number exchange, the user's password is never sent over the network and cannot be picked up by eavesdropping. Deriving the password from the information sent over the network is essentially impossible.

In this UAM method, the server provides a random number to the workstation. The user then enters a password that the workstation uses as an encryption key applied to the random number. The encrypted random number is sent to the server. The server takes the same random number and encrypts it with what the server believes is the user's password. If both encrypted numbers match, the user is authenticated. This method provides network security that is as secure as the basic encryption method.

The random number exchange UAM consists of the following steps:

1. The workstation client sends the FPLogin call with the UAM string and the User Auth Info field containing the user name string.

2. Upon receiving this call, the server examines its user database to determine whether the user name is valid.

3. If the server does not find the user name in the user database, it sends an error code to the workstation indicating that the user name is not valid and then denies the login request. If the server finds the name in the user database, it generates an 8-byte random number and sends it back to the workstation, along with an ID number and an AuthContinue result code. The AuthContinue indicates that all is well at this point, but the user is not yet authenticated.

4. Both the workstation and the server use the National Bureau of Standards Data Encryption Standard (NBS DES) algorithm to encrypt the random number. The user's case-sensitive password is applied as the encryption key to generate an 8-byte value. The server applies the same algorithm to the password it finds associated with the user name in its database.

5. The workstation sends the encrypted value back to the server in the User Auth Info field of the FPLoginCont call, along with the ID number it received from the server. The server uses this ID number to associate the two calls, FPLogin and FPLoginCont.

6. The server compares the workstation's encrypted value with the encrypted value obtained using the password from its user database. If the two encrypted values match, the authentication process is complete and the login succeeds. The server returns a NoErr result code to the workstation. If the two encrypted values do not match, the server returns the UserNotAuth result code.

Volume passwords

AFP provides an optional second level of access control through volume passwords. A server can associate a fixed-length 8-character password with each volume it makes visible through the AFI.

The workstation can issue an FPGetSrvrParms call to the server to discover the names of each volume and to get an indication of whether each of them is password-protected.

To make AFP calls that refer to a server volume, the workstation uses a volume identifier called the Volume ID. The workstation obtains this ID by sending an FPOpenVol call to the server. This call contains the name of the volume as one of its parameters. If a password is associated with the volume, the call must also include the password as another parameter.

Volume passwords constitute a simple protection mechanism for servers that do not need to implement the directory access control described in the next section. However, volume passwords are not as secure as directory access control.

Directory access control

The directory access control method provides the greatest degree of network security in AFP. This method assigns access rights to users. Once the user has logged in to the file server, access rights allow users varying degrees of freedom for performing actions within the directory structure.

AFP defines three directory access rights: search, read, and write:

- A user with *search* access to a directory can list the parameters of directories contained within the directory.

- A user with *read* access to a directory can list the parameters of files contained within the directory, in addition to being able to read the contents of a file.

- A user with *write* access to a directory can modify the contents of a directory, including the parameters of files and directories contained within the directory. Write access allows the user to add and delete directories and files as well as modify the data contained within a file.

Each directory on a server volume has an *owner* and a *group* affiliation. Initially, the owner is the user who created the directory, although ownership of a directory may be transferred to another user. Only the owner of a directory can change its access rights. The server uses a name of up to 31 characters and a 4-byte ID number to represent owners of directories. Owner name and owner ID are synonymous with user name and user ID.

The group affiliation is used to assign a different set of access rights for the directory to a group of users. For each group, the server maintains a name of up to 31 characters, a 4-byte ID number, and a list of users belonging to that group. Assigning group access rights to a directory gives those rights to that set of users.

Each user may belong to any number of groups or to no group. One of the user's group affiliations may be designated as the user's primary group. This group will be assigned initially to each new directory created by the user. The directory's group affiliation may be removed or changed later by the owner of the directory.

The term *world* is used to indicate every user that is able to log on to the server. A directory may be assigned certain world access rights that would be granted to a user who is neither the directory's owner nor a member of the group with which the directory is affiliated.

With each directory, the file server stores three access rights bytes, which correspond to the owner of the directory, its group affiliation, and the world. Each of these bytes is a bitmap that encodes the access rights (search, read, or write) that correspond to each category. The most significant 5 bits of each access rights byte must be 0.

To perform directory access control, AFP associates the following five parameters with each directory:

Parameter	Description
owner ID	4 bytes
group ID	4 bytes
owner access rights	1 byte
group access rights	1 byte
world access rights	1 byte

The owner ID is the same as the owner's user ID. The group ID is the ID number of the group with which the directory is affiliated, or 0. The file server maintains a one-to-one mapping between the owner ID and the user name and between the group ID and the group name. As a result, each name is associated with a unique ID. AFP includes calls that allow users to map IDs to names and vice versa. Assignment of user IDs, group IDs, and primary groups is an administrative function and is outside the scope of this protocol.

A group ID of 0 means that the directory has no group affiliation; the group's access rights (search, read, and write) are ignored.

When a user logs on to a server, identifiers are retrieved from a user database maintained on the server. These identifiers include the user ID (a 4-byte number unique among all server users) and one or more 4-byte group IDs, which indicate the user's group affiliations. The exact number of group affiliations is implementation-dependent. One of these group IDs may represent the user's primary group.

The server must be able to derive what access rights a particular user has to a certain directory. The user access rights (UARights) contain a summary of what the rights are, regardless of the category (owner, group, world) from which they were obtained. In addition, the user access rights contain a flag indicating whether the user owns the directory.

The following algorithm is used by the server to extract the user access rights. The OR in this algorithm indicates inclusive OR operations.

```
UARights := world's access rights;
clear UARights owner flag
If (owner ID = 0) then
      set UARights owner flag
If (user ID = owner ID) then
      UARights := UARights OR owner's access rights;
      set UARights owner flag
If (any of user's group IDs = directory's group ID) then
      UARights := UARights OR directory's group's access rights
```

An owner ID of 0 means that the directory is unowned or is owned by any user. The owner bit of the access rights byte is always set for such a directory.

The access rights required by the user to perform most file management functions are explained in the following paragraphs according to the following notation:

Symbol	Meaning
SA	search access to all ancestors down to, but not including, the parent directory
WA	search or write access to all ancestors down to, but not including, the parent directory
SP	search access to the parent directory
RP	read access to the parent directory
WP	write access to the parent directory

Almost all operations require *SA*. To perform any action within a given directory, the user must have permission to search every directory in the path from the root to the parent's parent directory. Access to files and directories within the parent directory is then determined by *SP, RP,* and *WP*.

Specific file management functions and the access rights needed to perform them are:

Function	Required access rights
Create a file or a directory	The user must have *WA* plus *WP*. A hard create (delete first if file exists) requires the same rights as deleting a file.
Enumerate a directory	To **enumerate** a directory is to list in numerical order the offspring of the directory and selected parameters of those offspring. The user must have search access to all directories down to but not necessarily including the directory being enumerated *(SA)*. In addition, to view its directory offspring, the user must have search access to the directory being enumerated *(SP)*. To view its file offspring, search access to the directory is not required, but the user must have read access to the directory *(RP)*.

(continued) ➡

Function	Required access rights *(continued)*
Delete a file	The user must have *SA, RP,* and *WP.* A file can be deleted only if it is not open at that time.
Delete a directory	The user must have *SA, SP,* and *WP.* A directory can be deleted only if it is empty.
Rename a file	The user must have *SA, RP,* and *WP.*
Rename a directory	The user must have *SA, SP,* and *WP.*
Read directory parameters	The user must have *SA* and *SP.*
Read file parameters	The user must have *SA* and *RP.*
Open a file to read its contents	A file's fork must be opened in read mode before its contents can be read. To open a file in read mode, the user must have *SA* and *RP.* Read mode and other access modes are described in the next section.
Open a file to write to its contents	A file's fork must be opened in write mode in order to write to it. To open an empty fork to write to it, the user must have *WA* and *WP.* (The empty fork must belong to a file that has both forks of 0 length.) To open an existing fork (when either fork is not empty) to write to it, *SA, RP,* and *WP* are required.
Write file parameters	The user must have *WA* plus *WP* to set the parameters of an empty file (when both forks are 0 length). To set the file parameters of a file with an existing fork (when either fork is not empty), *SA, RP,* and *WP* are required.
Write directory parameters	The user must have *SA, SP,* and *WP* to change a directory's parameters if the directory contains offspring. If the directory is empty, the user must have *WA* plus *WP* to change its parameters.
Move a directory or a file	Through AFP, a directory or a file can be moved from its parent directory to a destination parent directory on the same volume. To move a directory, the user must have *SA* and *SP* access to the source parent directory, *WA* to the destination parent directory, plus *WP* to both source and destination parents. To move a file, the user needs *SA* plus *RP* to the source parent directory, *WA* to the destination parent directory, plus *WP* to both source and destination parents.

Function	Required access rights *(continued)*
Modify a directory's access rights information	A directory's owner ID, group ID, and the three access rights bytes can be modified only if the user is the directory's owner and then only if the user has *WA* plus *WP* or *SP* access to the parent directory.
Copy a file (FPCopyFile)	To copy a file, on a single volume or across volumes managed by the server, the user must have *SA* plus *RP* access to the source parent directory and *WA* plus *WP* to the destination parent directory.

File sharing modes

AFP controls user access to shared files in two ways. The first, described in the previous section, provides security by controlling user access to specific directories. The second preserves data integrity by controlling a user's access to a file while it is being used by another user. This section describes the second way, in which files are shared concurrently.

To control simultaneous file access, the file server must enforce **synchronization rules.** These rules prevent applications from damaging each other's files by modifying the same version simultaneously. They also prevent users from obtaining access to information while it is being changed.

Synchronization rules are built from the mode in which a first user and subsequent users open a file. AFP provides two classes of modes: access modes, also know as permissions, and deny modes.

Access modes and deny modes

Most file systems use a set of **permissions** to regulate the opening of files. This set includes permission to modify the contents of a file (read-write) and permission to see the file's contents (read only). In a stand-alone system, these two file-access modes are sufficient.

In the shared environment of a file server, this set of permissions, or **access modes,** is expanded. In addition to this set, a set of restrictions is provided by **deny modes.**

A user application can specify an access mode and a deny mode upon opening a file on the file server. AFP supports the access modes: read, write, read-write, or none. None access allows no further access to the fork, except to close it, and may be useful in implementing synchronization. In addition to one of these access modes, the user indicates a deny mode to the server to specify which rights should be denied to others trying to open the fork while the first user has it open. Users that subsequently try to open that fork can be denied read, write, read-write, or none access.

A user submitting an FPOpenFork call can be denied file access for the following reasons:

- The user does not possess the rights (as owner, group, or world) to open the file with the requested access mode. An AccessDenied result code is returned.

- The fork is already open with a deny mode that prohibits the second user's requested access. For example, the first user opened the fork with a deny mode of DenyWrite, and the second user tries to open the fork in the write mode. A DenyConflict error is returned to the second user.

- The fork is already open with an access mode that conflicts with the second user's requested deny mode. For example, the first user opened the fork for Write access and a deny mode of DenyNone. The second user tries to open the fork with a deny mode indicating DenyWrite. This request is not granted because the fork is already open for Write access. A DenyConflict error is returned to the second user.

Deny modes are cumulative in that each successful opening of a fork combines its deny mode with previous deny modes. Therefore, if the first user opening a file specifies a deny mode of DenyRead, and the second user specifies DenyWrite, the fork's current deny mode (CDM) is Deny Read-Write. DenyNone and DenyRead combine to form a CDM of Deny Read.

Similarly, access modes are cumulative; if the first user opening a file has Read access and the second has Write access, the current access mode (CAM) is Read-Write.

Synchronization rules

Synchronization rules, as previously discussed, allow or deny simultaneous access to a file fork. They are based on the CDM and the CAM of the fork and on the new deny and access modes being requested in a new FPOpenFork call. Synchronization rules are summarized in *Table 13-1*. A dot indicates that a new open call has succeeded; otherwise, it has failed.

■ Table 13-1 Synchronization rules

Current deny mode and current access mode — New open attempt deny mode and new open attempt access mode

		Deny R/W				DenyWrite				DenyRead				DenyNone			
		-	R	RW	W	-	R	RW	W	-	R	RW	W	-	R	RW	W
Deny R/W	-	•				•				•				•			
	R	•				•								•			
	RW													•			
	W									•				•			
DenyWrite	-	•	•			•	•			•	•			•	•		
	R					•	•							•	•		
	RW													•	•		
	W									•	•			•	•		
DenyRead	-	•			•	•			•	•			•	•			•
	R					•			•					•			•
	RW													•			•
	W									•			•	•			•
DenyNone	-	•	•	•	•	•	•	•	•	•	•	•	•	•	•	•	•
	R					•	•	•	•					•	•	•	•
	RW													•	•	•	•
	W									•	•	•	•	•	•	•	•

Desktop database

For file server volumes, AFP provides an interface that replaces the Macintosh Finder's direct use of the **Desktop file.** This interface is necessary because the Desktop file was designed for a stand-alone environment and could not be shared by multiple users. The AFP interface to the **Desktop database** replaces the Desktop file and can be used transparently for both local and remote volumes.

The Desktop database is used by a file server to hold information needed specifically by the Finder to build its unique user interface, in which icons are used to represent objects on a disk volume. To create certain parts of this interface, the Finder uses the Desktop database to perform three functions:

■ to associate documents and applications with particular icons and store the icon bitmaps

■ to locate the corresponding application when a user opens a document

■ to hold text comments associated with files and directories

Macintosh applications usually contain an icon that is to be displayed for the application itself as well as other icons to be displayed for documents that the application creates. These icons are stored in the application's resource fork and in the Desktop database. The Desktop database associates these icons with each file's creator (the `fdCreator` field of the `FInfo` record) and type (the `fdType` field of the `FInfo` record), which are stored as part of the file's Finder information.

The Finder allows a Macintosh user to open a document, that is, to select a file and implicitly start the application that created the file. To do this, the Desktop database maintains a mapping between the file creator and a list of the locations of each application that has that file creator associated with it. This mapping is referred to as an APPL mapping, since all Macintosh applications have a file creator of `'APPL'`. The Finder obtains the first item in the list and tries to start the application. If for some reason the application cannot be started (for example, if it is currently in use), the Finder will obtain the next application from the Desktop database's list and try that one. This list is dynamically filtered to present to the Finder only those applications for which the workstation user has the proper access rights.

The Desktop database is also a repository for the text of comments associated with files and directories on the volume. The Finder will make calls to the Desktop database to read or write these comments, which can be viewed and modified by selecting the Get Info item in the Finder's File menu. Comments are completely uninterpreted by the Desktop database.

For more information about the Macintosh Finder and the use of the Desktop file, refer to *Inside Macintosh*.

AFP's use of ASP

The AppleTalk Filing Protocol requires a basic level of transport services for conveying its request and reply blocks between workstation and server. This section describes how AFP can be built on the AppleTalk Session Protocol (ASP). However, it should not be inferred that AFP must be built on ASP. This section is meant to be a reference for those developers who are implementing AFP on ASP.

- The AFP variable *FPError* is transmitted in ASP's *CmdResult* field, and AFP's Request Blocks are transmitted in the ASP Command Block field.

- The FPGetSrvrInfo request is transmitted to the server as an ASP SPGetStatus call. All other AFP requests, with the exception of FPWrite and FPAddIcon, are transmitted as ASP SPCommand calls. FPWrite and FPAddIcon are transmitted as ASP SPWrite calls.

- When a user wishes to log on to an AFP file server, the workstation must first issue an SPOpenSession call to create an ASP session between workstation and server. The first AFP request sent on that session should be FPLogin. When the log-on procedure has been successfully completed, an AFP session exists between workstation and server. If the log-on procedure fails, the workstation should issue an SPCloseSession call to tear down the ASP session.

- When a user wishes to terminate the AFP session, the workstation must first issue an FPLogout request to the server. When the reply to that request has been received, the workstation should issue an SPCloseSession call to tear down the ASP session.

- Note that FPRead, FPWrite, and FPEnumerate requests can succeed partially. That is to say, the request may return no error, but read, write, or enumerate less than was specified in the request. This can occur with FPRead and FPWrite if the request encounters a range of bytes that were locked by another user.

  These requests may, however, attempt to read, write, or enumerate more bytes than are allowed by ASP's QuantumSize. In such cases, the amount of data transferred may be truncated to QuantumSize or less. If no FPError was returned in the reply, the workstation can issue an additional FPRead, FPWrite, or FPEnumerate request to augment the original request.

  Although the workstation AFP client may have to issue several ASP calls to complete a single AFP request, the first ASP command should convey the actual size of the original AFP request, even if it is greater than QuantumSize. This allows a server to optimize its operation. Subsequent ASP commands should include sizes adjusted to reflect how much of the original request has been completed.

An overview of AFP calls

This section provides an overview of AFP calls and how they are used. Each call obtains access to an AFP-file-system-visible entity; this section groups the calls in relation to the entity they address. These groups include server, volume, directory, file, combined directory-file, fork, and Desktop database calls.

Each AFP call is listed alphabetically and described in detail in "AFP Calls" later in this chapter.

Server calls

A workstation client of AFP uses the following calls to get information about a file server and to open and close a session with it:

- FPGetSrvrInfo

- FPGetSrvrParms

- FPLogin

- FPLoginCont

- FPLogout

- FPMapID

- FPMapName

- FPChangePassword (AFP Version 2.0 only—optional)

- FPGetUserInfo (AFP Version 2.0 only)

Before becoming a client of AFP, a workstation uses NBP to find the internet address of the file server's session listening socket. This address is called the SAddr.

Next, the workstation uses the AFP call FPGetSrvrInfo to obtain server information. At this point, a session is still not open between the workstation and the server. The FPGetSrvrInfo call returns a block of server information containing the following server parameters: server name, machine type, AFP version strings, UAM strings, Macintosh volume icon and mask, and a bitmap of flags. These parameters are described in "AFP Calls" later in this chapter.

The workstation client selects one AFP version string and one UAM string from the lists returned by this call. The workstation then includes these strings in an FPLogin call to establish a session with the file server. A session is needed before any other AFP calls can be made to the server.

In response to the FPLogin call, the server performs user authentication and returns a session reference number (SRefNum), which is used in all calls made over this session. Depending on the chosen UAM, the entire user authentication process can involve FPLoginCont (login continue) calls to continue the authentication process with the server.

After a session is established, the workstation must obtain a list of the server's volumes. To obtain the list, the workstation sends the FPGetSrvrParms call, which returns information about the number of volumes on the server, the names of these volumes, and an indication of whether they are password-protected.

When the workstation user no longer needs to communicate with the server, the workstation client of AFP issues an FPLogout call to terminate the session.

The FPMapID and FPMapName calls are used for directory access control. The FPMapID call obtains the user or group name corresponding to a given user or group ID. The FPMapName call provides the opposite, converting a user or group name to the corresponding user or group ID.

The FPChangePassword call is used to change a user's password. The FPGetUserInfo call retrieves information about a user.

Volume calls

AFP provides five volume-level calls:

- FPOpenVol
- FPCloseVol
- FPGetVolParms
- FPSetVolParms
- FPFlush

After obtaining the volume names through the FPGetSrvrParms call, the workstation client of AFP makes an FPOpenVol call for each volume to which it wants to gain access. If the volume has a password, it must be supplied at this time. The call returns the volume parameters asked for in the call, including the Volume ID.

The Volume ID is used in all subsequent calls to identify the volume to which the calls apply. The Volume ID remains a valid identifier either until the session is terminated with the FPLogout call or until an FPCloseVol call is made.

After obtaining a volume's Volume ID, the workstation client can obtain the volume's parameters by making an FPGetVolParms call. The workstation client can also change the volume's parameters by issuing an FPSetVolParms call. (Volume parameters are described in "File System Structure" earlier in this chapter.)

The FPFlush call requests that the server flush (write to its disk) any data associated with a particular volume.

Directory calls

AFP provides five directory-level calls:

- FPSetDirParms
- FPOpenDir
- FPCloseDir
- FPEnumerate
- FPCreateDir

The FPSetDirParms call allows the workstation client to modify a directory's parameters. To obtain a directory's parameters from the file server, the workstation client uses the FPGetFileDirParms call, which is described under "Combined Directory-File Calls" later in this chapter. (For a list and description of directory parameters, see "Directories and Files" earlier in this chapter.)

The workstation client uses the FPOpenDir call to open a directory on a variable Directory ID volume and to retrieve its Directory ID. The Directory ID is used in subsequent calls to enumerate the directory or to obtain access to its offspring. For variable Directory ID volumes, the FPOpenDir call is the only way to retrieve the Directory ID. Using an FPGetFileDirParms or an FPEnumerate call to retrieve the Directory ID on such volumes returns an error.

On a fixed Directory ID volume, using the FPGetFileDirParms or an the FPEnumerate call is the preferred way to obtain a Directory ID, although using the FPOpenDir call also works.

The workstation client can close directories on variable Directory ID volumes by making an FPCloseDir call, which invalidates the corresponding Directory ID.

The workstation client uses the FPEnumerate call to list, or enumerate, the files and directories contained within a specified directory. In reply to this call, the server returns a list of directory or file parameters corresponding to these offspring.

Directories are created with the FPCreateDir call.

File calls

AFP provides three file-level calls:

- FPSetFileParms
- FPCreateFile
- FPCopyFile (optional)

The workstation client of AFP uses the FPSetFileParms call to modify a specified file's parameters, the FPCreateFile call to create a file, and the FPCopyFile call to copy a file that exists on a volume managed by a server to any other volume managed by that server. To obtain a specified file's parameters, the workstation client uses the FPGetFileDirParms call, discussed next.

Combined directory-file calls

AFP provides five calls that operate on both files and directories:

- FPGetFileDirParms
- FPSetFileDirParms
- FPRename
- FPDelete
- FPMoveAndRename

The workstation client of AFP uses the FPGetFileDirParms call to retrieve the parameters associated with a given file or directory. When it uses this call, the workstation does not need to specify whether the CNode is a file or a directory; the file server indicates the CNode's type in response to this call.

The FPSetFileDirParms call is used to set the parameters of a file or directory. When the workstation client uses this call, it need not specify whether the object is a file or directory. This call allows the workstation to set only those parameters that are common to both types of CNodes.

The FPRename call is used to rename files and directories.

The FPDelete call is used to delete a file or directory. A file can be deleted only if it is not open; a directory can be deleted only if it is empty.

The FPMoveAndRename call is used to move a file or a directory from one parent directory to another on the same volume. The moved CNode can be renamed at the same time.

Fork calls

AFP provides eight fork-level calls:

- FPGetForkParms
- FPSetForkParms
- FPOpenFork
- FPRead
- FPWrite
- FPFlushFork
- FPByteRangeLock
- FPCloseFork

The workstation client of AFP uses the FPGetForkParms call to read a fork's parameters.

The FPSetForkParms call is used to modify a fork's parameters.

The FPOpenFork call is used to open either of an existing file's forks. This call returns an open fork reference number (OForkRefNum), which is used in subsequent calls to this open fork.

The FPRead call is used to read the contents of the fork.

The FPWrite call is used to write to a fork.

The FPFlushFork call is used to request that the server write to its disk any of the fork's data that is in the server's internal buffers.

The FPByteRangeLock call is used to lock ranges of bytes in the fork. Locking a range of bytes prevents other workstation clients from reading or writing data in that part of the fork. Locks allow multiple users to share a file's open fork. If a workstation client locks a byte range, that range is reserved for exclusive manipulation by the client placing the lock.

The FPCloseFork call is used to close an open fork. This call invalidates the OForkRefNum that was assigned when the fork was opened.

Desktop database calls

A workstation client of AFP uses the following calls to read and write information stored in the server's Desktop database.

- FPOpenDT
- FPCloseDT
- FPAddIcon
- FPGetIcon
- FPGetIconInfo
- FPAddAPPL
- FPRemoveAPPL
- FPGetAPPL
- FPAddComment
- FPRemoveComment
- FPGetComment

Before any other Desktop database calls can be made, the workstation client of AFP must make an FPOpenDT call. This call returns a reference number to be used in all subsequent calls.

When access to the Desktop database is no longer needed, the workstation client makes an FPCloseDT call.

FPAddIcon adds a new icon bitmap to the Desktop database.

FPGetIcon retrieves the bitmap for a given icon as specified by its file creator and type.

FPGetIconInfo retrieves a description of an icon. This call can be used to determine the set of icons associated with a given application. Successive FPGetIconInfo calls will return information on all icons associated with a given file creator.

FPAddAPPL adds an APPL mapping for the specified application and its file creator.

FPRemoveAPPL removes the specified application from the list of APPL mappings corresponding to its file creator. It is the workstation client's responsibility to add and remove APPL mappings for applications that are added to or removed from the volume, respectively. For applications that are moved or renamed, the workstation client should remove the old APPL mapping before the operation and add a new APPL mapping with the updated information after the operation has been completed successfully.

FPGetAPPL returns the next APPL mapping in the Desktop database's list of applications corresponding to a given file creator.

FPAddComment stores a comment string associated with a particular file or directory on the volume. When adding a comment for a file or directory that already has an associated comment, the existing comment is replaced.

FPRemoveComment removes the comment associated with a particular file or directory.

FPGetComment retrieves the comment associated with a particular file or directory.

AFP calls

This section describes AFP calls, which are listed alphabetically. This section is intended as a reference source, allowing the reader to look up call descriptions as necessary.

Each call description contains the following information:

- a list of the input and output parameters
- the result codes provided by the call
- an explanation of how the call works
- the access rights required to use the call
- an illustration of the call's block format

The workstation client of AFP sends each AFP call to the server in the form of a **request block,** to which the server responds with the 4-byte FPError result code plus a **reply block.**

The FPWrite and FPAddIcon calls are exceptions in that the data to be written is not included in the command block but is passed by the underlying transport mechanism (ASP or its equivalent) as a separate block.

For every AFP call, the underlying transport mechanism must return an FPError result code. The FPError values for each call are listed and explained.

Some result codes can be returned by all AFP calls; the following result codes are not included in the descriptions of AFP calls.

Result code	Description
NoErr	file server returns this value for every call that is successfully completed
UserNotAuth	server returns this value to indicate that the user has not yet been properly authenticated
MiscErr	server uses this value to map errors and message codes that don't have an equivalent AFP result code (for example, an error reading a disk sector)

For calls that return an empty reply block, the reply block is not shown.

Many AFP calls require a bitmap to be passed along with a block of parameters packed in bitmap order. **Bitmap order** means that the parameter corresponding to the least-significant bit that is set in the bitmap is packed first, followed by the parameter corresponding to the next most-significant bit that is set, and ending with the parameter corresponding to the most-significant bit that is set.

AFP call descriptions use the following abbreviations and definitions to describe call parameters:

Abbreviation	Description
bit	a single binary digit
byte	an 8-bit quantity
EntityAddr	a network-visible entity's internet address; its size and format are network-dependent
int	a 2-byte quantity
long	a 4-byte quantity
ResType	a 4-byte signature used in a Macintosh Finder information field to specify a file creator or file type
string	a group of up to 255 bytes, each representing an ASCII character; this group is preceded by a string-length byte, which is a value representing the number of characters in the string not including the string-length byte

All numerical fields represent signed numbers unless otherwise indicated.

The next page describes the format of the rest of the chapter.

FPCall

A one-sentence, concise description of the call is given here.

Inputs   All input parameters are listed here, with a description of each. Numbers next to a list of parameters indicate the bit number of a corresponding bit in a multibyte field.

Outputs   All output parameters are listed here, with a description of each. Numbers next to a list of parameters indicate the bit number of a corresponding bit in a multibyte field.

Result codes   The values of FPError that might be returned are listed here, with an explanation of each. For brevity, some values of FPError (those that are common to most or all calls) are not shown here.

Algorithm   A detailed description of the algorithm used to service this request is given here.

Rights   The access privileges required to make this request are listed here. The absence of this section signifies that no special access privileges are required.

Notes   This section provides additional notes about what is required to make this request, certain actions that the call does not do, or side effects. It is a catch-all for any information that does not belong in any other section. Not all call descriptions include this section.

Block format   A pictorial description of the Command block and Reply block is displayed here. If the call returns only an FPError parameter, no Reply block will be shown. In some cases, this section will also include pictorial descriptions of some of the fields or parameters relevant to this call.

FPAddAPPL

This request adds an APPL mapping to the Desktop database.

Inputs

SRefNum (int)	session refnum
DTRefNum (int)	Desktop database refnum
Directory ID (long)	ancestor directory identifier
FileCreator (ResType)	file creator of application corresponding to APPL mapping being added
APPL Tag (long)	a user-defined tag stored with the APPL mapping
PathType (byte)	indicates whether Pathname is composed of long names or short names:
	1 = short names
	2 = long names
Pathname (string)	pathname to the application corresponding to APPL mapping being added

Outputs

FPError (long)

Result codes

ParamErr	Session refnum or Desktop database refnum is unknown; pathname is bad.
ObjectNotFound	Input parameters do not point to an existing file.
AccessDenied	User does not have the rights listed below.
ObjectTypeErr	Input parameters point to a directory.

Algorithm

An APPL mapping is added to the volume's Desktop database for the specified application and its location and its file creator. If an APPL mapping for the same application (same filename, same directory, and same FileCreator) already exists, it is replaced.

Rights

The user must have search or write access to all ancestors except the application's parent directory, as well as write access to the parent directory.

Notes

There may be more than one application in the Desktop database's list of APPL mappings for the given FileCreator. To distinguish among them, the APPL Tag parameter is stored with each APPL mapping. The tag information might be used to decide among these multiple applications. It is not interpreted by the Desktop database.

(continued) ➡

The user must have previously called FPOpenDT for the corresponding volume. In addition, the application must be present in the specified directory before this request is issued.

Block format

Request

```
|◄──────1 byte (8 bits)──────►|

┌─────────────────────────────┐
│       AddAPPL function       │
├─────────────────────────────┤
│              0               │
├─────────────────────────────┤
│                              │
│          DTRefNum            │
│                              │
├─────────────────────────────┤
│                              │
│                              │
│         Directory ID         │
│                              │
│                              │
├─────────────────────────────┤
│                              │
│                              │
│         FileCreator          │
│                              │
│                              │
├─────────────────────────────┤
│                              │
│                              │
│          APPL Tag            │
│                              │
│                              │
├─────────────────────────────┤
│          PathType            │
├─────────────────────────────┤
┊          Pathname            ┊
└─────────────────────────────┘
```

FPAddComment

This request adds a comment for a file or directory to the volume's Desktop database.

Inputs

	SRefNum (int)	session refnum
	DTRefNum (int)	Desktop database refnum
	Directory ID (long)	directory identifier
	PathType (byte)	indicates whether Pathname is composed of long names or short names:
		1 = short names
		2 = long names
	Pathname (string)	pathname to the file or directory to which the comment will be associated
	Comment (string)	comment data to be associated with specified file or directory

Outputs   *FPError (long)*

Result codes

	ParamErr	Session refnum or Desktop database refnum is unknown; pathname is bad.
	ObjectNotFound	Input parameters do not point to an existing file or directory.
	AccessDenied	User does not have the rights listed below.

Algorithm   The comment data is stored in the Desktop database and associated with the specified file or directory. If the comment length is greater than 199 bytes, the comment will be truncated to 199 bytes and no error will be returned.

Rights   To add a comment for a directory that is not empty, the user needs search access to all ancestors including the parent directory, as well as write access to the parent directory. To add a comment for an empty directory, the user needs search or write access to all ancestors except the parent directory, as well as write access to the parent directory.

To add a comment for a file that is not empty, the user needs search access to all ancestors except the parent directory, as well as read and write access to the parent. To add a comment for an empty file, the user needs search or write access to all ancestors except the parent directory, as well as write access to the parent.

Notes   The user must have previously called FPOpenDT for the corresponding volume. In addition, the specified file or directory must be present before this request is issued.

(continued) ➡

Block format

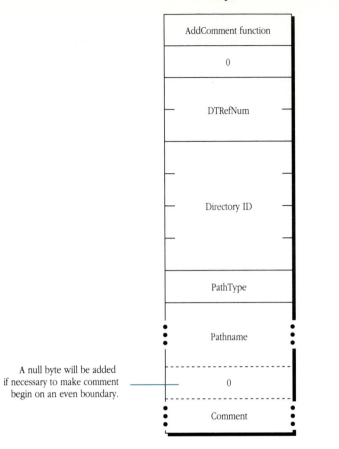

AddComment function

0

DTRefNum

Directory ID

PathType

Pathname

A null byte will be added
if necessary to make comment
begin on an even boundary.

0

Comment

FPAddIcon

This request adds an icon bitmap to the volume's Desktop database.

Inputs

SRefNum (int)	session refnum
DTRefNum (int)	Desktop database refnum
FileCreator (ResType)	file creator associated with icon
FileType (ResType)	file type associated with icon
IconType (byte)	type of icon being added
IconTag (long)	tag information to be stored with the icon
BitmapSize (int)	size of the bitmap for this icon

Outputs *FPError (long)*

Result codes

ParamErr	Session refnum or Desktop database refnum is unknown.
IconTypeError	New icon size is different from existing icon's size.

Algorithm A new icon is added to the Desktop database for the specified FileCreator and FileType. If an icon of the same FileCreator, FileType, and IconType already exists, the icon is replaced. However, if the new icon's size is different from the old icon, the server returns an IconTypeError result code.

Notes The user must have previously called FPOpenDT for the corresponding volume. The command block includes all input parameters except for the icon bitmap, which is sent to the server in an intermediate exchange of ASP packets.

(continued) ➡

Block format

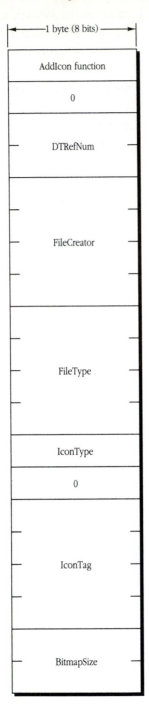

← 1 byte (8 bits) →

AddIcon function
0
DTRefNum
FileCreator
FileType
IconType
0
IconTag
BitmapSize

FPByteRangeLock

This request locks or unlocks a specified range of bytes within an open fork.

Inputs	SRefNum (int)	session refnum
	OForkRefNum (int)	open fork refnum
	Offset (long)	offset to the first byte of the range to be locked or unlocked (can be negative if Start/EndFlag equals End)
	Length (long)	number of bytes to be locked or unlocked (a signed, positive long integer; cannot be negative except for the special value $FFFFFFFF).
	UnlockFlag (bit)	flag to indicate whether to lock or unlock range: 0 = lock 1 = unlock
	Start/EndFlag (bit)	flag indicating whether the Offset field is relative to the beginning or end of the fork (this flag is valid only when locking a range): 0 = Start (relative to beginning of fork) 1 = End (relative to end of fork)
Outputs	FPError (long)	
	RangeStart (long)	number of the first byte of the range just locked; this number is valid only when returned from a successful lock command
Result codes	ParamErr	Session refnum or open fork refnum is unknown; a combination of Start/EndFlag and Offset specifies a range starting before the 0th byte.
	LockErr	Some or all of the requested range is locked by another user.
	NoMoreLocks	Server's maximum lock count has been reached.
	RangeOverlap	User tried to lock some or all of a range that the user already locked.
	RangeNotLocked	User tried to unlock a range that was locked by another user or not locked at all.

(continued) ➡

Algorithm   FPByteRangeLock locks or unlocks a range of bytes for use by a user application. Bytes are numbered from 0 to $7FFFFFFF. The latter value is the maximum size of the fork. The end of fork (end of file in Macintosh terminology) is 1 greater than the number of the last byte in the fork.

Lock conflicts are determined by OForkRefNum. That is, if a fork is opened twice, the two OForkRefNums are considered two different "users" in the discussion below, regardless of whether they were performed on the same or different sessions.

If no user holds a lock on any part of the requested range, the server locks the range specified by this call. A user can hold multiple locks within the same open fork, up to a server-specific limit. Locks cannot overlap. A locked range can start or extend past the end of fork; this does not move the end of fork or prevent another user from writing to the fork past the locked range. An Offset of 0, a Start/EndFlag set to Start, and a Length of $FFFFFFFF lock the entire fork to the maximum size of the fork. Specifying an offset other than 0, a Start/EndFlag set to Start, and a Length of $FFFFFFFF will lock a range beginning at Offset and extending to the maximum size of the fork.

All locks held by a user are unlocked when the user closes the fork. Unlocking a range makes it available to other users for reading and writing. The server returns a RangeNotLocked result code if a user tries to unlock a range that was locked by another user or not locked at all.

Part of a range cannot be unlocked. To unlock a range, the Start/EndFlag must be set to Start, the Length parameter must match the size of the range that was locked, and the Offset parameter must match the number of the first byte in the locked range. If the range was locked with the Start/EndFlag set to Start, use the same Offset to unlock the range. If the range was locked with the Start/EndFlag set to End, set Offset to the value of RangeStart that was returned by the server.

The Start/EndFlag allows a lock to be offset relative to the end of fork. This enables a user to set a lock when the user does not know the exact end of fork, as can happen when multiple writers are concurrently modifying the fork. The server returns the number of the first locked byte.

Block format

Request

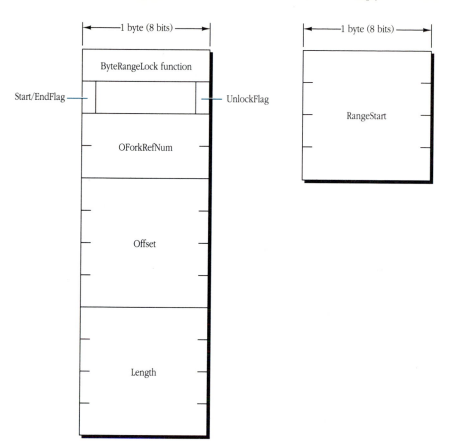

1 byte (8 bits)

ByteRangeLock function

Start/EndFlag ——

—— UnlockFlag

OForkRefNum

Offset

Length

Reply

1 byte (8 bits)

RangeStart

FPChangePassword

This request allows users to change their passwords. **It is new in AFP Version 2.0, and it is optional and may not be supported by all servers.**

Inputs		
	SRefNum (int)	session refnum
	UAM (string)	a string indicating which user authentication method to use

Outputs   *FPError (long)*

Result codes		
	UserNotAuth	UAM failed (specified old password doesn't match), or no user logged in yet on this session.
	BadUAM	UAM specified is not one supported with FPChangePassword.
	CallNotSupported	Workstation is using AFP Version 1.1; call is not supported by this server.
	AccessDenied	FPChangePassword is not enabled for this user.
	ParamErr	User name is null, is greater than 31 characters, or does not exist.

Algorithm

If the UAM specified is `'Cleartxt Passwrd'`, the workstation sends the server its user name plus its old and new passwords in cleartext. The server looks up the password for that user; if it matches the old password sent in the packet, the new password will be saved for that user.

If the UAM specified is `'Randnum Exchange'`, the workstation sends the server its user name, its old password encrypted with its new password, and its new password encrypted with its old password. The server looks up the password for that user, uses that password as a key to decrypt the new password, and uses the result as a key to decrypt the old password. If the final result matches what the server knew to be the old password, then the new password will be saved for that user.

Any password less than 8 bytes long will be padded (suffixed) with null bytes to its full 8-byte length.

Rights

The server need not support this call (see the FPGetSrvrInfo call). In addition, the user may not have been given the ability to change a password.

Notes

The granting of the ability to change a password is an administrative function and is outside the scope of this protocol specification.

As in FPLogin, DES is used to encrypt and decrypt passwords if the specified UAM is `'Randnum Exchange'`.

Block format

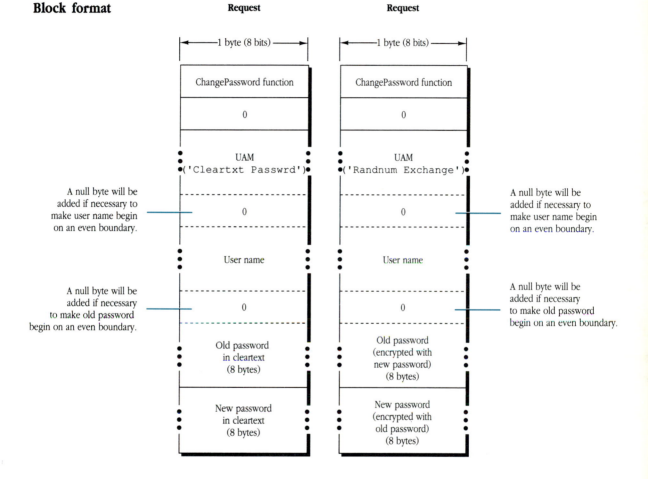

A null byte will be added if necessary to make user name begin on an even boundary.

A null byte will be added if necessary to make old password begin on an even boundary.

A null byte will be added if necessary to make user name begin on an even boundary.

A null byte will be added if necessary to make old password begin on an even boundary.

FPCloseDir

This request closes a directory and invalidates its directory identifier.

Inputs   *SRefNum (int)*   session refnum
                    Volume ID (int)   volume identifier
                    Directory ID (long)   directory identifier

Outputs   *FPError (long)*

Result codes   *ParamErr*   Session refnum, volume identifier, or directory identifier is
                                             unknown.

Algorithm   The FPCloseDir request invalidates the Directory ID.

Notes   This request should be used only for variable Directory ID volumes. The user must have
                    previously called FPOpenVol for this volume and FPOpenDir for this directory.

Block format   **Request**

```
            |◄——————1 byte (8 bits)——————►|
            ┌─────────────────────────────┐
            │      CloseDir function       │
            ├─────────────────────────────┤
            │              0               │
            ├─────────────────────────────┤
            │                              │
            │          Volume ID           │
            │                              │
            ├─────────────────────────────┤
            │                              │
            │                              │
            │         Directory ID         │
            │                              │
            │                              │
            └─────────────────────────────┘
```

FPCloseDT

This request informs the server that the workstation no longer needs the volume's Desktop database.

Inputs	*SRefNum (int)*	session refnum
	DTRefNum (int)	Desktop database refnum
Outputs	*FPError (long)*	
Result codes	*ParamErr*	Session refnum or Desktop database refnum is unknown.
Algorithm	The server invalidates the DTRefNum.	
Notes	The user must first have made a successful FPOpenDT call.	

Block format

Request

```
|←——— 1 byte (8 bits) ———→|

┌─────────────────────────┐
│     CloseDT function     │
├─────────────────────────┤
│            0             │
├─────────────────────────┤
│                          │
│        DTRefNum          │
│                          │
└─────────────────────────┘
```

FPCloseFork

This request closes a fork that was opened by FPOpenFork.

Inputs   *SRefNum (int)*   session refnum
              OForkRefNum (int)   open fork refnum

Outputs   *FPError (long)*

Result codes   *ParamErr*   Session refnum or open fork refnum is unknown.

Algorithm   The server flushes and then closes the open fork, invalidating the OForkRefNum. If the fork had been written to, the file's modification date will be set to the server's clock at this time.

Block format

Request

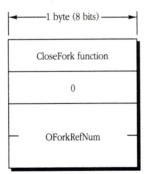

—— 1 byte (8 bits) ——

| CloseFork function |
| 0 |
| OForkRefNum |

FPCloseVol

This request informs the server that the workstation no longer needs the volume.

Inputs   *SRefNum (int)*   session refnum
                    Volume ID (int)   volume identifier

Outputs   *FPError (long)*

Result codes   *ParamErr*   Session refnum or volume identifier is unknown.

Algorithm   The FPCloseVol request invalidates the volume identifier. After making this call, the user can make no further calls to this volume without first making another FPOpenVol call.

Notes   The user must have previously issued an FPOpenVol call for this volume.

Block format   **Request**

```
         |◄──── 1 byte (8 bits) ────►|

         ┌───────────────────────────┐
         │     CloseVol function      │
         ├───────────────────────────┤
         │             0              │
         ├───────────────────────────┤
         │                            │
         ─        Volume ID          ─
         │                            │
         └───────────────────────────┘
```

FPCopyFile

This request copies a file from one location to another on the same file server. It is optional and may not be supported by all servers. Text in **boldface** applies to **AFP Version 2.0 only.**

Inputs	*SRefNum (int)*	session refnum
	Source Volume ID (int)	source volume identifier
	Source Directory ID (long)	source ancestor directory identifier
	Source PathType (byte)	indicates whether Source Pathname is composed of long names or short names:
		1 = short names
		2 = long names
	Source Pathname (string)	pathname of the file to be copied (cannot be null)
	Dest Volume ID (int)	destination volume identifier
	Dest Directory ID (long)	destination ancestor directory identifier
	Dest PathType (byte)	indicates whether Dest Pathname is composed of long names or short names (same values as Source PathType)
	Dest Pathname (string)	pathname to the destination parent directory (may be null)
	NewType (byte)	indicates whether NewName is a long name or a short name (same values as Source PathType)
	NewName (string)	name to be given to the copy (may be null)
Outputs	*FPError (long)*	

Result codes	*ParamErr*	Session refnum, volume identifier, or pathname type is unknown; pathname or NewName is bad.
	ObjectNotFound	The source file does not exist; ancestor directory is unknown.
	ObjectExists	A file or directory by the name NewName already exists in the destination parent directory.
	AccessDenied	User does not have the right to read the file or to write to the destination; in AFP 1.1, the destination volume is ReadOnly.
	VolLocked	**In AFP 2.0, the destination volume is ReadOnly.**
	CallNotSupported	Call is not supported by this server.
	DenyConflict	The file cannot be opened for Read, DenyWrite.
	DiskFull	No more space exists on the destination volume.
	ObjectTypeErr	Source parameters point to a directory.

Algorithm   FPCopyFile copies a file to a new location on the server. The source and destination can be on the same or on different volumes.

The server tries to open the source file for Read, DenyWrite access. If this fails, the server returns a DenyConflict result code to the workstation. If the server successfully opens the file, it copies the file to the directory specified by the destination parameters.

The copy is given the name specified by the NewName parameter. If NewName is null, the server gives the copy the same name as the original. The file's other name (long or short) is generated as described in "Catalog Node Names" earlier in this chapter. A unique file number is assigned to the file. The server also sets the file's Parent ID to the Directory ID of the destination parent directory. All other file parameters remain the same as the source file's parameters. The modification date of the destination parent directory is set to the server's clock.

Rights   The user must have search access to all ancestors of the source file, except the source parent directory, and read access to the source parent directory. Further, the user must have search or write access to all ancestors of the destination file, except the destination parent directory, and write access to the destination parent directory.

Notes   The user must have previously issued the FPOpenVol request for both the source and destination volumes.

(continued) ➡

Block format

|---- 1 byte (8 bits) ----|

CopyFile function
0
Source Volume ID
Source Directory ID
Dest Volume ID
Dest Directory ID
Source PathType
Source Pathname
Dest PathType
Dest Pathname
NewType
NewName

FPCreateDir

This request creates a new directory. Text in **boldface** applies to **AFP Version 2.0 only.**

Inputs

SRefNum (int)	session refnum
Volume ID (int)	volume identifier
Directory ID (long)	ancestor directory identifier
PathType (byte)	indicates whether Pathname is composed of long names or short names:
	1 = short names
	2 = long names
Pathname (string)	pathname, including name of new directory (cannot be null)

Outputs

FPError (long)	
New Directory ID (long)	identifier of new directory

Result codes

ParamErr	Session refnum, volume identifier, or pathname type is unknown; pathname is null or bad.
ObjectNotFound	Ancestor directory is unknown
ObjectExists	A file or directory already exists by that name.
AccessDenied	User does not have the rights listed below; in AFP 1.1, the volume is ReadOnly.
VolLocked	**In AFP 2.0, the destination volume is ReadOnly.**
FlatVol	The volume is flat and does not support directories.
DiskFull	No more space exists on the volume.

Algorithm

If the volume is hierarchical, an empty directory is created with the name specified in Pathname. The file server assigns the directory a unique (per volume) New Directory ID. Its owner ID is set to the user ID of the user making the call, and its group ID is set to the ID of the user's primary group, if one has been specified for the user.

(continued) ➡

Access rights for the directory are initially set to read, write, and search for the owner, with no rights for the group or world. Finder information is set to 0, and all directory attributes are initially cleared. The directory's creation date and modification date, and the modification date of the parent directory, are set to the server's clock. The directory's backup date is set to $80000000, signifying that this directory has never been backed up.

The directory's other name (long or short) is generated as described in "Catalog Node Names" earlier in this chapter.

Rights   The user must have search or write access to all ancestors, except this directory's parent directory, as well as write access to the parent directory.

Notes   The user must have previously called FPOpenVol for this volume.

Block format

Request   Reply

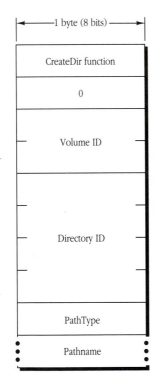

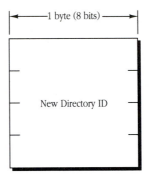

FPCreateFile

This request creates a file. Text in **boldface** applies to **AFP Version 2.0 only.**

Inputs	*SRefNum (int)*	session refnum
	Volume ID (int)	volume identifier
	Directory ID (long)	ancestor directory identifier
	CreateFlag (bit)	a flag that specifies a hard or soft create:
		0 = soft create
		1 = hard create
	PathType (byte)	indicates whether Pathname is composed of long names or short names:
		1 = short names
		2 = long names
	Pathname (string)	pathname, including name of new file (cannot be null)
Outputs	*FPError (long)*	
Result codes	*ParamErr*	Session refnum, volume identifier, or pathname type is unknown; pathname is null or bad.
	ObjectNotFound	Ancestor directory is unknown.
	ObjectExists	If attempting a soft create, a file by that name already exists.
	ObjectTypeErr	A directory by that name already exists.
	AccessDenied	User does not have the rights listed below; in AFP 1.1, the volume is ReadOnly.
	VolLocked	**In AFP 2.0, the destination volume is ReadOnly.**
	FileBusy	If attempting a hard create, the file already exists and is open.
	DiskFull	No more space exists on the volume.

(continued) ➡

Algorithm   For a soft create, if a file by that name already exists, the server returns an ObjectExists result code. Otherwise, it creates a new file and assigns it the name specified in Pathname. A unique file number is assigned to the file. Finder information is set to 0, and all file attributes are initially cleared. The file's creation and modification dates, and the modification date of the file's parent directory, are set to the server's clock. The file's backup date is set to $80000000, signifying that this file has never been backed up. The file's other name (long or short) is generated as described in "Catalog Node Names" earlier in this chapter. The lengths of both of the file's forks are set to 0.

In a hard create, if the file already exists and is not open, it is deleted and then recreated. All file parameters (including the creation date) are reinitialized as described above.

Rights   For a soft create, the user must have search or write access to all ancestors, except this file's parent directory, as well as write access to the parent directory. For a hard create, the user must have search access to all ancestors, except the parent directory, as well as read and write access to the parent directory.

Notes   The user must have previously called FPOpenVol for this volume.

Block format

Request

FPDelete

This request deletes a file or directory. Text in **boldface** applies to **AFP Version 2.0 only.**

Inputs

SRefNum (int)	session refnum
Volume ID (int)	volume identifier
Directory ID (long)	ancestor directory identifier
PathType (byte)	indicates whether Pathname is composed of long names or short names:
	1 = short names
	2 = long names
Pathname (string)	pathname of file or directory to be deleted (may be null if a directory is to be deleted)

Outputs

FPError (long)

Result codes

ParamErr	Session refnum, volume identifier, or pathname type is unknown; pathname is bad.
ObjectNotFound	Input parameters do not point to an existing file or directory.
DirNotEmpty	The directory is not empty.
FileBusy	The file is open.
AccessDenied	User does not have the rights listed below; in AFP 1.1, the file or directory is marked DeleteInhibit; in AFP 1.1, the volume is ReadOnly.
ObjectLocked	**In AFP 2.0, the file or directory is marked DeleteInhibit.**
VolLocked	**In AFP 2.0, the volume is ReadOnly.**

Algorithm

If the CNode to be deleted is a directory, the server checks to see if it contains any offspring. If it contains offspring, the server returns a DirNotEmpty result code. If a file is to be deleted, it must not be currently open by any user or a FileBusy result code is returned. The modification date of the deleted file or directory's parent directory is set to the server's clock.

(continued) ➡

Rights The user must have search access to all ancestors, except the file or directory's parent directory, as well as write access to the parent directory. If a directory is being deleted, the user must also have search access to the parent directory; for a file, the user must also have read access to the parent directory.

Notes The user must have previously called FPOpenVol for this volume.

Block format Request

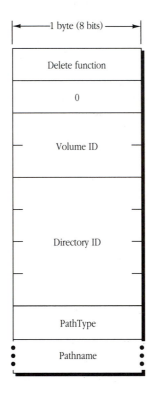

FPEnumerate

This request lists the contents of a directory.

Inputs

SRefNum (int)	session refnum
Volume ID (int)	volume identifier
Directory ID (long)	ancestor directory identifier
File Bitmap (int)	bitmap describing which parameters are to be returned if the enumerated offspring is a file (the bit corresponding to each desired parameter should be set); this field is the same as that in the FPGetFileDirParms call and can be null
Directory Bitmap (int)	bitmap describing which parameters are to be returned if the enumerated offspring is a directory (the bit corresponding to each desired parameter should be set); this field is the same as that in the FPGetFileDirParms call and can be null
ReqCount (int)	maximum number of offspring structures to be returned
Start Index (int)	directory offspring index
MaxReplySize (int)	maximum size of reply block
PathType (byte)	indicates whether Pathname is composed of long names or short names:
	1 = short names
	2 = long names
Pathname (string)	pathname to desired directory

Outputs

FPError (long)	
File Bitmap (int)	copy of input parameter
Directory Bitmap (int)	copy of input parameter

(continued) ➡

Outputs	ActCount (int)	actual number of structures returned	
	ActCount structures containing a 2-byte header and parameters in the form:	Struct Length (byte)	unsigned length of this structure, including these two header bytes, and rounded up to the nearest even number
		File/DirFlag (bit)	flag indicating whether offspring is a file or directory: 0 = file 1 = directory
		Offspring parameters	packed in bitmap order, with a trailing null byte if necessary to make the length of the entire structure even

Result codes	ParamErr	Session refnum, volume identifier, or pathname type is unknown; pathname is bad; MaxReplySize is too small to hold a single offspring structure.
	DirNotFound	Input parameters do not point to an existing directory.
	BitmapErr	An attempt was made to retrieve a parameter that cannot be retrieved with this call; an attempt was made to retrieve the Directory ID for a directory on a variable Directory ID volume; both bitmaps are empty.
	AccessDenied	User does not have the rights listed below.
	ObjectNotFound	No more offspring exist to be enumerated.
	ObjectTypeErr	Input parameters pointed to a file.

Algorithm

The FPEnumerate call enumerates a directory as specified by the input parameters. If the File Bitmap is empty, only directory offspring are enumerated, and the Start Index can range from 1 to the total number of directory offspring. Similarly, if the Directory Bitmap is empty, only file offspring are enumerated, and the Start Index can range from 1 to the total number of file offspring. If both bitmaps have bits set, the Start Index can range from 1 to the total number of offspring. In this case, offspring structures for both files and directories are returned. These structures are not returned in any particular order.

This call is completed when the number of structures specified by ReqCount has been inserted into the reply block, when the reply block is full, or when no more offspring exist to be enumerated. No partial offspring structures are returned.

The server retrieves the specified parameters for each enumerated offspring and packs them, in bitmap order, in structures in the reply block. The server inserts one copy of the input bitmaps before all the structures.

The server needs to keep variable-length parameters, such as Long Name and Short Name, at the end of each structure. In order to do this, the server represents variable-length parameters in the bitmap order as fixed-length offsets (integers). Each offset is measured from the start of the parameters in each structure (not from the start of the bitmap or the start of the header bytes) to the start of the variable-length field. Each structure will be padded (suffixed) with a null byte if necessary to make its length even.

If NoErr is returned, all the structures in the reply block are valid. If any error result code is returned, no valid offspring structures exist in the reply block.

If the Offspring Count bit of the Directory Bitmap is set, the server will adjust the Offspring Count of each directory to reflect what access rights the user has to that directory. For example, if a particular directory contains three file and two directory offspring, the server will return its Offspring Count as *2* if the user has only search access to the directory, *3* if the user has only read access to the directory, or *5* if the user has both search and read access to the directory.

Rights   The user must have search access to all ancestors except this directory. In addition, the user needs search access to this directory in order to enumerate directory offspring and read access in order to enumerate file offspring.

Notes   The user must have previously called FPOpenVol for this volume.

Because enumerating a large directory can take several calls and other users may be adding to or deleting from the directory, enumeration can miss offspring or return duplicate offspring. To enumerate a directory accurately, the user must enumerate until an ObjectNotFound result code is returned and then filter out duplicate entries.

A given offspring is not guaranteed to occupy the same index number in the parent directory from one enumeration to the next.

(continued) ➡

Block format

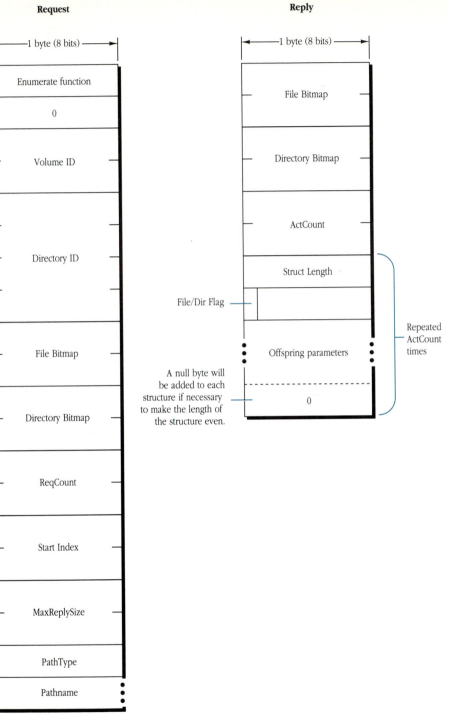

Request

1 byte (8 bits)

- Enumerate function
- 0
- Volume ID
- Directory ID
- File Bitmap
- Directory Bitmap
- ReqCount
- Start Index
- MaxReplySize
- PathType
- Pathname

Reply

1 byte (8 bits)

- File Bitmap
- Directory Bitmap
- ActCount
- Struct Length
- File/Dir Flag
- Offspring parameters
- 0

A null byte will be added to each structure if necessary to make the length of the structure even.

Repeated ActCount times

FPFlush

This request writes to a disk any volume data that has been modified.

Inputs

	SRefNum (int)	session refnum
	Volume ID (int)	volume identifier

Outputs *FPError (long)*

Result codes *ParamErr* Session refnum or volume identifier is unknown.

Algorithm The FPFlush call flushes (writes to disk) as much changed information as possible. This may include flushing

- all forks opened by the user

- volume catalog information changed by the user

- any updated volume data structures

AFP does not specify that the server must perform all of these functions. Therefore, users should not rely on the server to perform any particular function.

The volume's modification date may change as a result of this call, but users should not rely on it; updating of the date is implementation-dependent. If no volume information was changed since the last FPFlush call, the date may or may not change.

Notes The user must have previously called FPOpenVol for this volume.

Block format

Request

```
|——1 byte (8 bits)——|

┌─────────────────────┐
│   Flush function    │
├─────────────────────┤
│          0          │
├─────────────────────┤
│                     │
│      Volume ID      │
│                     │
└─────────────────────┘
```

FPFlushFork

This request writes to a disk any data buffered from previous FPWrite calls.

Inputs   *SRefNum (int)*   session refnum

                    OForkRefNum (int)   open fork refnum

Outputs   *FPError (long)*

Result codes   *ParamErr*   Session refnum or open fork refnum is unknown.

Algorithm   The FPFlushFork call writes to a disk any data buffered by the server from previous
                    FPWrite calls. If the fork has been modified, the server sets the file's modification date to
                    the server's clock.

Notes   In order to optimize disk access, the server may buffer FPWrite calls made to a particular
                    file fork. Within the constraints of performance, the server flushes each fork as soon as
                    possible. The workstation client can force the server to flush any buffered data issuing
                    this call.

Block format   **Request**

                          |◄——— 1 byte (8 bits) ———►|

                          | FlushFork function |
                          | 0 |
                          | OForkRefNum |

FPGetAPPL

This request retrieves an APPL mapping from the volume's Desktop database.

Inputs

SRefNum (int)	session refnum
DTRefNum (int)	Desktop database refnum
FileCreator (ResType)	file creator of application corresponding to the APPL mapping
APPL Index (int)	index of the APPL mapping to be retrieved
Bitmap (int)	bitmap describing which parameters of the application file are to be returned; this field is the same as File Bitmap in the FPGetFileDirParms call

Outputs

FPError (long)	
APPL Tag (long)	tag information associated with the APPL mapping
File parameters requested	

Result codes

ParamErr	Session refnum or Desktop database refnum is unknown.
ItemNotFound	No files in the Desktop database match the input parameters.
BitmapErr	An attempt was made to retrieve a parameter that cannot be obtained with this call.

Algorithm

For each FileCreator, the Desktop database contains a list of APPL mappings. Each APPL mapping contains the parent Directory ID and CNode name of an application associated with the FileCreator, as well as an APPL Tag that can be used to distinguish among the APPL mappings (the APPL Tag is left uninterpreted by the Desktop database).

Information about the application file associated with each APPL mapping can be obtained by making successive FPGetAPPL requests with APPL Index varying from 1 to the total number of APPL mappings stored in the Desktop database for that FileCreator. If APPL Index is greater than the number of APPL mappings in the Desktop database for the specified FileCreator, an ItemNotFound result code is returned. An APPL index of 0 returns the first APPL mapping, if one exists in the Desktop database.

The server retrieves the specified parameters for the application file and packs them, in bitmap order, in the reply block.

(continued) ➡

Rights   The user must have search access to all ancestors except the parent directory and read access to the parent directory of the application about which information will be returned.

Notes   The user must have previously called FPOpenDT for the corresponding volume.

Block format

Request

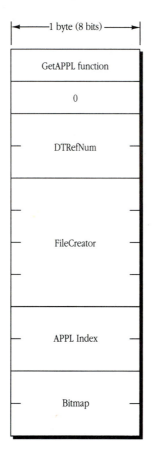

Reply

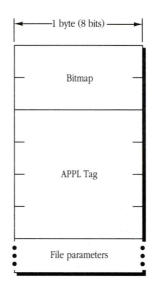

FPGetComment

This request retrieves a comment associated with a specified file or directory from the volume's Desktop database.

Inputs

SRefNum (int)	session refnum
DTRefNum (int)	Desktop database refnum
Directory ID (long)	directory identifier
PathType (byte)	indicates whether Pathname is composed of long names or short names:
	1 = short names
	2 = long names
Pathname (string)	pathname to desired file or directory

Outputs

FPError (long)	
Comment (string)	comment text

Result codes

ParamErr	Session refnum or Desktop database refnum is unknown.
ObjectNotFound	Input parameters do not point to an existing file or directory.
AccessDenied	User does not have the rights listed below.
ItemNotFound	No comment was found in the Desktop database.

Algorithm
The comment for the specified file or directory, if it is found in the volume's Desktop database, is returned in the reply block.

Rights
If the comment is associated with a directory, the user must have search access to all ancestors, including the parent directory. If the comment is associated with a file, the user must have search access to all ancestors, except the parent directory, and read access to the parent directory.

Notes
The user must previously have called FPOpenDT for the corresponding volume. In addition, the file or directory must exist before this call is issued.

(continued) ➡

Block format

Request

Reply

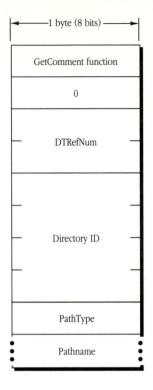

FPGetFileDirParms

This request retrieves parameters for a CNode (either a file or a directory). Text in **boldface** applies to **AFP Version 2.0 only.**

Inputs		
SRefNum (int)	session refnum	
Volume ID (int)	volume identifier	
Directory ID (long)	ancestor directory identifier	
File Bitmap (int)	bitmap describing which parameters are to be returned if the CNode is a file (the bit corresponding to each desired parameter should be set)	

    0   *Attributes (int),* consisting of the following flags:

          0   *Invisible*

          1   *MultiUser*

          2   System

          3   *DAlreadyOpen*

          4   *RAlreadyOpen*

          5   *ReadOnly* **(called WriteInhibit in AFP 2.0)**

          6   BackupNeeded

          7   RenameInhibit

          8   DeleteInhibit

          10 CopyProtect

          15 *Set/Clear (used in FPSetFileDirParms)*

    1   *Parent Directory ID (long)*

    2   *Creation Date (long)*

    3   *Modification Date (long)*

    4   *Backup Date (long)*

    5   *Finder Info (32 bytes)*

    6   *Long Name (int)*

    7   *Short Name (int)*

    8   *File Number (long)*

    9   *Data Fork Length (long)*

    10   *Resource Fork Length (long)*

    13   ProDOS Info (6 bytes)

(continued) ➡

Directory Bitmap (int)		bitmap describing which parameters are to be returned if the CNode is a directory (the bit corresponding to each desired parameter should be set)

0   *Attributes (int),* consisting of the following flags:

      0   *Invisible*

      2   ***System***

      6   ***BackupNeeded***

      7   ***RenameInhibit***

      8   ***DeleteInhibit***

1   *Parent Directory ID (long)*

2   *Creation Date (long)*

3   *Modification Date (long)*

4   *Backup Date (long)*

5   *Finder Info (32 bytes)*

6   *Long Name (int)*

7   *Short Name (int)*

8   *Directory ID (long)*

9   *Offspring Count (int)*

10   *Owner ID (long)*

11   *Group ID (long)*

12   *Access Rights (long),* composed of the access rights for owner, group, and world, and a User Access Rights Summary byte *(UARights)*

13 **ProDOS Info (6 bytes)**

PathType (byte)		indicates whether Pathname is composed of long names or short names:

1 = short names

2 = long names

Pathname (string)		pathname to desired file or directory

Outputs	*FPError (long)*	
	File Bitmap (int)	copy of input parameter
	Directory Bitmap (int)	copy of input parameter
	File/DirFlag (bit)	flag that indicates whether CNode is a file or a directory:
		0 = file
		1 = directory
	Parameters requested	
Result codes	*ParamErr*	Session refnum, volume identifier, or pathname type is unknown; pathname is bad.
	ObjectNotFound	Input parameters do not point to an existing file or directory.
	BitmapErr	An attempt was made to retrieve a parameter that cannot be obtained with this call.
	AccessDenied	User does not have the rights listed below.

Algorithm
The server packs the requested parameters in the reply block in the order specified by the appropriate bitmap and includes a File/DirFlag indicating whether the CNode was a file or a directory. A copy of the input bitmaps is inserted before the parameters.

The server needs to keep variable-length parameters, such as Long Name and Short Name, at the end of the block. In order to do this, the server represents variable-length parameters in the bitmap order as fixed-length offsets (integers). Each offset is measured from the start of the parameters (not from the start of the bitmap) to the start of the variable-length field. The actual variable-length fields are then packed after all fixed-length fields.

If the CNode exists and both bitmaps are null, no error is returned; the File Bitmap, Directory Bitmap, and File/DirFlag are returned with no other parameters.

If a directory's access rights are requested, the server returns an Access Rights long (4-byte quantity) containing the read, write, and search access privileges corresponding to owner, group, and world. The upper byte of the Access Rights long is the User Access Rights Summary byte, which indicates what privileges the user has to this directory. The most-significant bit in the User Access Rights Summary byte is the Owner bit. This bit indicates whether or not the user is the owner of the directory. It is also set if the directory is not owned by any registered user.

(continued) ➡

If the Offspring Count bit of the Directory Bitmap is set, the server will adjust the Offspring Count of each directory to reflect what access rights the user has to that directory. For example, if a particular directory contains three file and two directory offspring, the server will return its Offspring Count as *2* if the user has only search access to the directory, *3* if the user has only read access to the directory, or *5* if the user has both search and read access to the directory.

Rights

The user must have search access to all ancestors except this CNode's parent directory. If the CNode is a directory, the user also needs search access to the parent directory. If the CNode is a file, the user needs read access to the parent directory.

Notes

The user must have previously called FPOpenVol for this volume.

Most of the Attributes requested by this call are stored in corresponding flags within the CNode's Finder Info record.

Block format

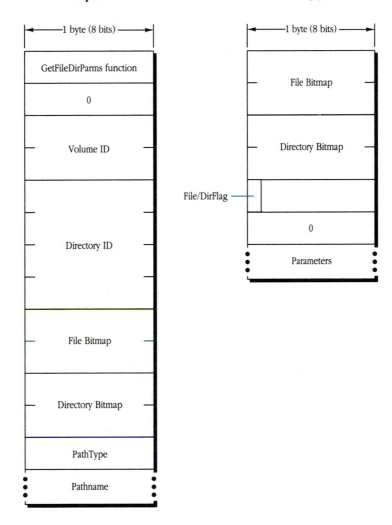

Request

←——1 byte (8 bits) ——→

| GetFileDirParms function |
| 0 |
| Volume ID |
| Directory ID |
| File Bitmap |
| Directory Bitmap |
| PathType |
| Pathname |

Reply

←——1 byte (8 bits) ——→

| File Bitmap |
| Directory Bitmap |
| File/DirFlag | |
| 0 |
| Parameters |

(continued) ➡

File Bitmap

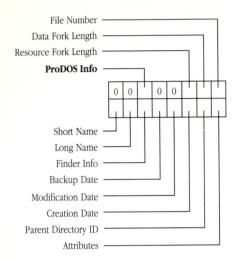

File Number
Data Fork Length
Resource Fork Length
ProDOS Info

Short Name
Long Name
Finder Info
Backup Date
Modification Date
Creation Date
Parent Directory ID
Attributes

Directory Bitmap

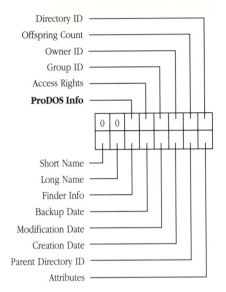

Directory ID
Offspring Count
Owner ID
Group ID
Access Rights
ProDOS Info

Short Name
Long Name
Finder Info
Backup Date
Modification Date
Creation Date
Parent Directory ID
Attributes

File Attributes

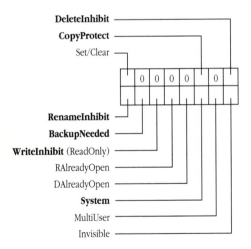

DeleteInhibit
CopyProtect
Set/Clear

RenameInhibit
BackupNeeded
WriteInhibit (ReadOnly)
RAlreadyOpen
DAlreadyOpen
System
MultiUser
Invisible

Directory Attributes

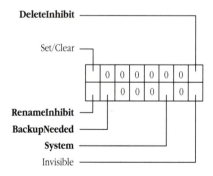

DeleteInhibit

Set/Clear

RenameInhibit
BackupNeeded
System
Invisible

Access Rights

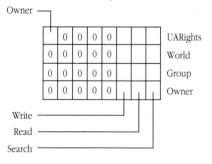

Owner

UARights
World
Group
Owner

Write
Read
Search

FPGetForkParms

This request retrieves parameters for a file associated with a particular open fork. Text in **boldface** applies to **AFP Version 2.0 only.**

Inputs	*SRefNum (int)*	session refnum
	OForkRefNum (int)	open fork refnum
	Bitmap (int)	bitmap describing which parameters are to be retrieved (the bit corresponding to each desired parameter should be set); this field is the same as File Bitmap in the FPGetFileDirParms call
Outputs	*FPError (long)*	
	Bitmap (int)	copy of the input parameter
	File parameters requested	
Result codes	*ParamErr*	Session refnum or open fork refnum is unknown.
	BitmapErr	An attempt was made to retrieve a parameter that cannot be obtained with this call; bitmap is null.
	AccessDenied	Fork was not opened for read **(this code is never returned in AFP Version 2.0).**

Algorithm

The FPGetForkParms call retrieves the specified parameters for the file. The server packs the parameters, in bitmap order, in the reply block.

Variable-length parameters are kept at the end of the block. In order to do this, the server represents variable-length parameters in the bitmap order as fixed-length offsets (integers). These offsets are measured from the start of the parameters to the start of the variable-length fields. The actual variable-length fields are then packed after all fixed-length fields.

This call retrieves the length of the fork indicated by OForkRefNum; a BitmapErr result code is returned if an attempt is made to retrieve the length of the file's other fork.

Rights

In AFP Version 1.1, the fork must be open for read by the user. **In AFP Version 2.0, the fork need not be open for read to retrieve a file's parameters.**

(continued) ➡

Block format

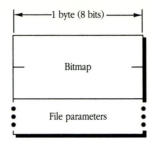

Request

├─── 1 byte (8 bits) ───┤

| GetForkParms function |
| 0 |
| OForkRefNum |
| Bitmap |

Reply

├─── 1 byte (8 bits) ───┤

| Bitmap |
| File parameters |

FPGetIcon

This request retrieves an icon from the volume's Desktop database.

Inputs		
	SRefNum (int)	session refnum
	DTRefNum (int)	Desktop database refnum
	FileCreator (ResType)	file creator of files with which the icon is associated
	FileType (ResType)	file type of files with which the icon is associated
	IconType (byte)	preferred icon type
	Length (int)	the number of bytes reserved for icon bitmap

Outputs		
	FPError (long)	
	Icon Bitmap (bytes)	the actual bitmap for the icon

Result codes		
	ParamErr	Session refnum or Desktop database refnum is unknown.
	ItemNotFound	No icon corresponding to the input specification was found in the Desktop database.

Algorithm

The server retrieves an icon bitmap from the Desktop database, as specified by its FileCreator, FileType, and IconType. If the server does not find a matching icon, it returns an ItemNotFound result code.

An input Length value of 0 is acceptable to test for the presence or absence of a particular icon. If Length is less than the actual size of the icon bitmap, only Length bytes will be returned.

Notes

The user must have previously called FPOpenDT for the corresponding volume.

(continued) ➡

Block format

Request	Reply

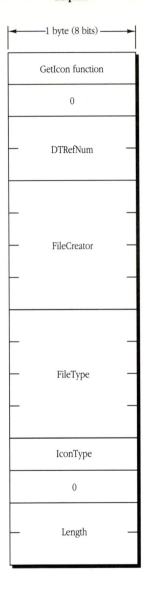

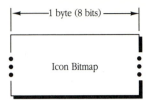

FPGetIconInfo

This request retrieves icon information from the volume's Desktop database.

Inputs	*SRefNum (int)*	session refnum
	DTRefNum (int)	Desktop database refnum
	FileCreator (ResType)	file creator of files with which the icon is associated
	IconIndex (int)	index of requested icon
Outputs	*FPError (long)*	
	IconTag (long)	tag information associated with the requested icon
	FileType (ResType)	the file type of the requested icon
	IconType (byte)	the type of the requested icon
	Size (int)	the size of the icon bitmap
Result codes	*ParamErr*	Session refnum or Desktop database refnum is unknown.
	ItemNotFound	No icon corresponding to the input specification was found in the Desktop database.

Algorithm The server retrieves information about an icon in the volume's Desktop database, as specified by its FileCreator and IconIndex.

For each FileCreator, the Desktop database contains a list of icons. Information about each icon can be obtained by making successive FPGetIconInfo calls with IconIndex varying from 1 to the total number of icons stored in the Desktop database for that FileCreator. If IconIndex is greater than the number of icons in the Desktop database for the specified FileCreator, an ItemNotFound result code is returned.

Notes The user must have previously called FPOpenDT for the corresponding volume.

(continued) ➡

Block format

Request

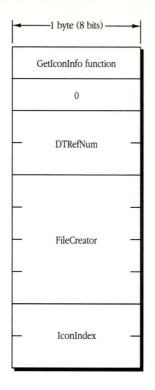

Reply

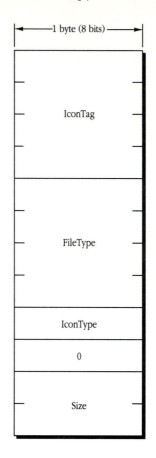

FPGetSrvrInfo

This request obtains a block of descriptive information from the server, without requiring a session to be opened. Text in **boldface** applies to **AFP Version 2.0 only.**

Inputs   *SAddr (EntityAddr)*   internet address of the server

Outputs   *FPError (long)*

                Flags (int)   flags, consisting of:

                                            0   *SupportsCopyFile*   set if server supports the
                                                                     FPCopyFile call

                                            1   **SupportsChgPwd**   **set if server supports the**
                                                                     FPChangePassword call

                Server Name (string)   the name of the server

                Machine Type (string)   string describing the server's hardware and/or operating system

                AFP Versions (strings)   versions of AFP that the server uses

                UAMs (strings)   user authentication methods supported by the server

                Volume Icon and Mask
                (256 bytes)

Result codes *NoServer*   Server is not responding.

Algorithm   The FPGetSrvrInfo call retrieves information about the server in the form of an information block.

To facilitate access to all the fields of the information block, the block begins with a header containing the offset to each field of information: first an offset to the Machine Type, followed by the offset to the AFP Versions strings, the offset to the UAM strings, and the offset to the Volume Icon and Mask. These offsets are measured relative to the start of the information block. The Volume Icon and Mask field is optional; if it is not included, the offset to the Volume Icon and Mask will be 0.

The AFP versions and the UAMs are formatted as a 1-byte count followed by that number of strings packed back-to-back without padding.

(continued) ➡

Notes   This is the only AFP call that can be made without first setting up a session between the workstation and server.

The server can pack fields in the reply block in any order, and each field should be accessible only through the use of offsets. In other words, the workstation client should make no assumptions about how the fields are packed relative to one another. The exception is the Server Name field, which always begins immediately after the Flags field.

This call should be implemented using the ASP GetStatus mechanism.

Block format

Request

—1 byte (8 bits)—

GetSrvrInfo function

Flags

0	0	0	0	0	0	0	0
0	0	0	0	0	0		

SupportsChgPwd
SupportsCopyFile

Reply

—1 byte (8 bits)—

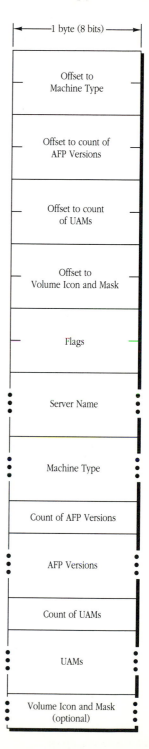

Offset to
Machine Type

Offset to count of
AFP Versions

Offset to count
of UAMs

Offset to
Volume Icon and Mask

Flags

Server Name

Machine Type

Count of AFP Versions

AFP Versions

Count of UAMs

UAMs

Volume Icon and Mask
(optional)

FPGetSrvrParms

This request retrieves server parameters. Text in **boldface** applies to **AFP Version 2.0 only.**

Inputs	*SRefNum (int)*	session refnum
Outputs	*FPError (long)*	
	Server Time (long)	current date-time on the server's clock
	NumVols (byte)	number of volumes managed by the server
	NumVols structures containing a 1-byte header and volume name in the form:	*HasPassword (bit)* flag indicating whether or not this volume is password-protected: 0 = not protected 1 = has password
		HasConfigInfo (bit) **flag indicating whether or not this volume contains Apple II configuration information**
		VolName (string) character string name of volume
Result codes	*ParamErr*	Session refnum is unknown.

Algorithm The VolNames strings and HasPassword **(and HasConfigInfo)** flag are packed together without padding in the reply block. **In AFP 2.0, the HasConfigInfo flag will be set for one of the volumes to indicate which volume contains Apple II configuration information.**

Block format

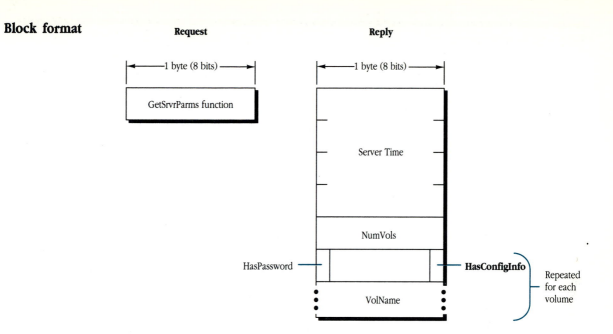

FPGetUserInfo

This request is used to retrieve information about a user. **It is new in AFP Version 2.0.**

Inputs	*SRefNum (int)*	session refnum
	ThisUser (bit)	flag indicating whether information is to be returned for the user who is the client of the session (if set, the User ID field is ignored)
	User ID (long)	ID of user for whom information is to be retrieved (not valid if ThisUser bit is set)
	Bitmap (int)	bitmap describing which parameters are to be retrieved (the bit corresponding to each desired parameter should be set):
		0 *User ID (long)*
		1 *Primary Group ID (long)*
Outputs	*FPError (long)*	
	Bitmap (int)	copy of input parameter
	User Info parameters requested	
Result codes	*ParamErr*	ThisUser bit is not set (it must be set in AFP Version 2.0).
	ItemNotFound	User ID is unknown.
	BitmapErr	An attempt was made to retrieve a parameter that cannot be obtained with this call.
	AccessDenied	User not authorized to retrieve user information for this user.
	CallNotSupported	Workstation is using AFP Version 1.1.

Algorithm   The server retrieves the specified parameters for the specified user and packs them, in bitmap order, in the reply packet.

Notes   This call can be used only to retrieve the User ID and Primary Group ID of the user who is the client of this session, thus requiring that the ThisUser bit be set. The User ID parameter is intended for future expansion.

Block format

Request

Reply

Bitmap

Primary Group ID

User ID

FPGetVolParms

This request retrieves parameters for a particular volume.

Inputs

SRefNum (int)	session refnum
Volume ID (int)	volume identifier
Bitmap (int)	bitmap describing which parameters are to be returned (the bit corresponding to each desired parameter should be set); cannot be null:

0   *Attributes (int)*, consisting of the following flag:

    0   *ReadOnly*

1   *Signature (int)*

2   *Creation Date (long)*

3   *Modification Date (long)*

4   *Backup Date (long)*

5   *Volume ID (int)*

6   *Bytes Free (long) unsigned*

7   *Bytes Total (long) unsigned*

8   *Volume Name (int)*

Outputs

FPError (long)	
Bitmap (int)	copy of input parameter
Volume parameters requested	

Result codes

ParamErr	Session refnum or volume identifier is unknown.
BitmapErr	An attempt was made to retrieve a parameter that cannot be obtained with this call; bitmap is null.

Algorithm

The FPGetVolParms call retrieves parameters that describe a specified volume. The volume is specified by its Volume ID as returned from the FPOpenVol call. In response to this call, the server packs the volume parameters in bitmap order in the reply block, along with a copy of the Bitmap inserted before the parameters.

The server needs to keep all variable-length parameters, such as the Volume Name field, at the end of the block. In order to do this, the server represents variable-length parameters in bitmap order as fixed-length offsets (integers). These offsets are measured from the start of the parameters (not from the start of the Bitmap) to the start of the variable-length fields. The variable-length fields are then packed after all fixed-length fields.

Notes   The user must have previously called FPOpenVol for this volume.

The ReadOnly attribute must be set by some administrative function.

Block format

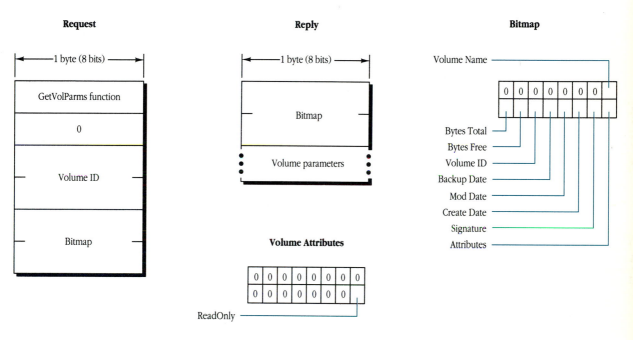

FPLogin

This request establishes an AFP session with a server.

Inputs

SAddr (EntityAddr)	internet address of the file server
AFP Version (string)	a string indicating which AFP version to use
UAM (string)	a string indicating which user authentication method to use
User Auth Info	information required to authenticate the user; dependent on the UAM used (can be null)

Outputs

FPError (long)	
SRefNum (int)	session refnum used to refer to this session in all subsequent calls (valid if no error or AuthContinue result code is returned)
ID Number (int)	an ID to be used for certain UAMs by the FPLoginCont call (valid only if AuthContinue result code is returned)
User Auth Info	a buffer returned for certain UAMs (valid only if AuthContinue result code is returned)

Result codes

NoServer	Server is not responding.
BadVersNum	Server cannot use the specified AFP version.
BadUAM	UAM is unknown.
ParamErr	User is unknown.
UserNotAuth	UAM failed.
AuthContinue	Authentication not yet complete.
ServerGoingDown	Server is shutting down.
MiscErr	User is already authenticated.

Algorithm

The workstation sends the server an AFP Version string, which indicates the AFP version to use, and a UAM string, which indicates the user authentication method to use. These strings are packed into the request block with no padding. User Auth Info, if used, follows the UAM string without padding.

If the server cannot use the requested AFP Version, a BadVersNum result code will be returned. Otherwise, that version will be used for the duration of the session.

In the 'Cleartxt Passwrd' UAM, the user's name and password are sent in the User Auth Info field. The password is transmitted in cleartext and must be padded (suffixed) with null bytes if necessary to make its length 8 bytes. If necessary, a null byte will be inserted after the user name to make the password begin on an even boundary. The server looks up the password for that user and compares it to the password in the request block. If the two passwords match, then the user has been authenticated and the login succeeds. If they do not match, a UserNotAuth result code is returned.

In the 'Randnum Exchange' UAM, only the user name is sent in the User Auth Info field. If the user name is valid, the server generates an 8-byte random number and sends it back to the workstation, along with an ID number and an AuthContinue result code. The AuthContinue indicates that all is well at this point and that the user is not yet authenticated.

The workstation then uses the password as a key to encrypt the random number and sends the result back to the server in the User Auth Info field of an FPLoginCont request, along with the ID Number returned from the FPLogin request. The server uses this ID Number to associate the two calls, FPLogin and FPLoginCont. The server looks up the password for that user and uses it as a key to encrypt the same random number. If the two encrypted numbers match, then the user has been authenticated and the login succeeds. Otherwise, the server returns a UserNotAuth result code.

If any error result code (other than AuthContinue) is returned, the session is not opened.

Notes   User name comparison is case-insensitive and diacritical-sensitive; password comparison is case-sensitive.

Random-number encryption is performed using DES.

Block format

Request

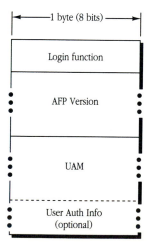

Reply

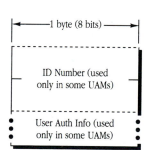

FPLoginCont

This request continues the login and user authentication process started by the FPLogin call.

Inputs	*SRefNum (int)*	session refnum
	ID Number (int)	number returned from the previous FPLogin or FPLoginCont call
	User Auth Info	information required to authenticate the user, depending on the UAM
Outputs	*FPError (long)*	
	ID Number (int)	an ID returned for certain UAMs; used by the subsequent FPLoginCont call (valid only if AuthContinue result code is returned)
	User Auth Info	a buffer returned for certain UAMs (valid only if AuthContinue result code is returned)
Result codes	*NoServer*	Server is not responding.
	UserNotAuth	UAM failed.
	AuthContinue	User authentication not yet complete.

Algorithm   The FPLoginCont call sends the ID Number and User Auth Info parameters to the server, which uses them to execute the next step in the UAM. If an additional exchange of packets is required, the server returns an AuthContinue result code. Otherwise, it returns either no error, meaning the user has been authenticated, or UserNotAuth, meaning the authentication method has failed. If the server returns no error, the SRefNum is validated for use in subsequent calls. If the server returns UserNotAuth, it also closes the session and invalidates the SRefNum.

Block format

Request

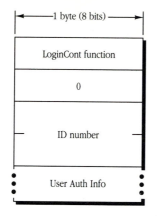

├───── 1 byte (8 bits) ─────┤

| LoginCont function |
| 0 |
| ID number |
| User Auth Info |

Reply

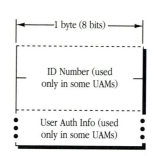

├───── 1 byte (8 bits) ─────┤

| ID Number (used only in some UAMs) |
| User Auth Info (used only in some UAMs) |

FPLogout

This request terminates a session with a server.

Inputs   *SRefNum (int)*   session refnum

Outputs   *FPError (long)*

Result codes   *ParamErr*   Session refnum is unknown.

Algorithm   The server flushes and closes any forks opened by this session, frees all session-related resources, and invalidates the session refnum.

Block format   **Request**

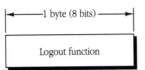

FPMapID

This request maps a user ID to a user name, or a group ID to a group name.

Inputs
    SRefNum (int)   session refnum
    Subfunction (byte)   subfunction code:
                                1 = map user ID to user name
                                2 = map group ID to group name
    ID (long)   item to be mapped, either user ID or group ID

Outputs
    FPError (long)
    Name (string)   name corresponding to ID

Result codes
    ParamErr   Session refnum or subfunction code is unknown; no ID was passed in the request block.
    ItemNotFound   ID was not recognized

Algorithm
The server retrieves a user or group name corresponding to the specified user ID or group ID. An ItemNotFound result code is returned if the ID does not exist in the server's list of valid user or group IDs.

Notes
A user ID or group ID of 0 maps to a null string.

Block format

Request

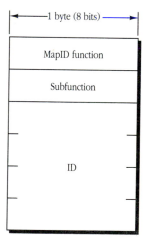

Reply

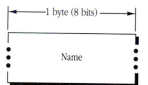

FPMapName

This request maps a user name to a user ID, or a group name to a group ID.

Inputs

SRefNum (int)		session refnum
Subfunction (byte)		subfunction code:
		3 = map user name to user ID
		4 = map group name to group ID
Name (string)		item to be mapped, either user name or group name

Outputs

FPError (long)

ID (long)   ID corresponding to input name

Result codes

ParamErr   Session refnum or function code is unknown.

ItemNotFound   Name is not recognized.

Algorithm

The server retrieves an ID number corresponding to a user or group name or returns an ItemNotFound result code if it does not find the name in its list of valid names.

Notes

A null user or group name maps to an ID of 0.

Block format

Request

Reply

1 byte (8 bits)

MapName function

Subfunction

Name

1 byte (8 bits)

ID

FPMoveAndRename

This request moves a directory or file to another location on the same volume. It can also be used to rename the directory or file. Text in **boldface** applies to **AFP Version 2.0 only.**

Inputs

SRefNum (int)	session refnum
Volume ID (int)	volume identifier
Source Directory ID (long)	source ancestor directory identifier
Source PathType (byte)	indicates whether Source Pathname is composed of long names or short names:
	1 = short names
	2 = long names
Source Pathname (string)	pathname of file or directory to be moved (may be null if a directory is to be moved)
Dest Directory ID (long)	destination ancestor directory identifier
Dest PathType (byte)	indicates whether Dest Pathname is composed of long names or short names (same values as Source PathType)
Dest Pathname (string)	pathname to the destination parent directory (may be null)
NewType (byte)	indicates whether NewName is a long name or a short name (same values as Source PathType)
NewName (string)	new name of file or directory (may be null)

Outputs *FPError (long)*

(continued) ➡

Result codes	ParamErr	Session refnum, volume identifier, or pathname type is unknown; pathname or NewName is bad.
	ObjectNotFound	Input parameters do not point to an existing file or directory.
	ObjectExists	A file or directory with the name NewName already exists.
	CantMove	An attempt was made to move a directory into one of its descendent directories.
	AccessDenied	User does not have the rights listed below; in AFP 1.1, the volume is ReadOnly; in AFP 1.1, the directory being moved (and/or renamed) is marked RenameInhibit; in AFP 1.1, the file being moved and renamed is marked RenameInhibit.
	ObjectLocked	**In AFP 2.0, the directory being moved (and/or renamed) is marked RenameInhibit; in AFP 2.0, the file being moved and renamed is marked RenameInhibit.**
	VolLocked	**In AFP 2.0, the volume is ReadOnly.**

Algorithm

This call does not just copy the CNode; it deletes it from the original parent directory. If the NewName parameter is null, the moved CNode retains its original name. Otherwise, the server moves the CNode, creating the long or short names as described in the "Catalog Node Names" earlier in this chapter. The CNode's modification date and the modification date of the source and destination parent directories are set to the server's clock. The CNode's Parent ID is set to the destination Parent ID. All other parameters remain unchanged, and if the CNode is a directory, the parameters of all descendent directories and files remain unchanged.

The FPMoveAndRename call indicates the destination of the move by specifying the ancestor Directory ID and pathname to the CNode's destination parent directory.

If the CNode being moved is a directory, all its descendents are moved as well.

Rights

To move a directory, the user must have search access to all ancestors, down to and including the source and destination parent directories, as well as write access to those directories. To move a file, the user must have search access to all ancestors, except the source and destination parent, as well as read and write access to the source parent directory and write access to the destination parent directory.

Notes

The user must have previously called FPOpenVol for this volume.

A CNode cannot be moved from one volume to another with this call, even if both volumes are managed by the same server.

Block format

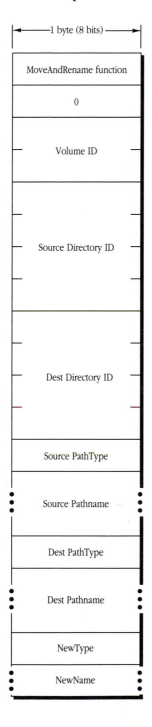

FPOpenDir

This request opens a directory on a variable Directory ID volume and returns its Directory ID.

Inputs	*SRefNum (int)*	session refnum
	Volume ID (int)	volume identifier
	Directory ID (long)	ancestor directory identifier
	PathType (byte)	indicates whether Pathname is composed of long names or short names:
		1 = short names
		2 = long names
	Pathname (string)	pathname to desired directory (cannot be null)
Outputs	*FPError (long)*	
	Directory ID (long)	identifier of specified directory
Result codes	*ParamErr*	Session refnum, volume identifier, or pathname type is unknown; pathname is bad.
	ObjectNotFound	Input parameters do not point to an existing directory.
	AccessDenied	User does not have the rights listed below.
	ObjectTypeErr	Input parameters point to a file.

Algorithm   If the Volume ID parameter specifies a variable Directory ID volume, the server generates a Directory ID for the specified directory. If the Volume ID parameter specifies a fixed Directory ID type, the server returns the fixed Directory ID belonging to this directory.

Although this call can obtain a Directory ID for a directory on a fixed Directory ID volume, it is not the recommended way to obtain the parameter; use the FPGetFileDirParms or FPEnumerate call instead.

Rights   The user must have search access to all ancestors down to and including this directory's parent directory.

Notes   The user must have previously called FPOpenVol for this volume.

Block format

Request

Reply

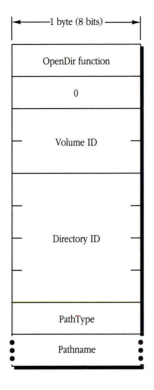

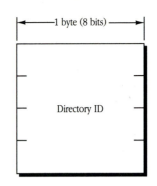

FPOpenDT

This request opens the Desktop database on a particular volume.

Inputs   *Volume ID (int)*   volume identifier

Outputs   *FPError (long)*
                    DTRefNum (int)   Desktop database refnum

Result codes   *ParamErr*   Session refnum or volume identifier is unknown.

Algorithm   The server opens the Desktop database on the selected volume and returns a Desktop database refnum, which is unique among such refnums. The DTRefNum is to be used in all subsequent Desktop database calls relating to this volume.

Block format

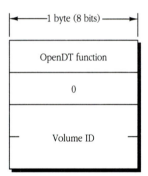

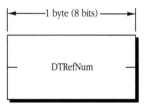

FPOpenFork

This request opens the data or resource fork of an existing file to read from it or write to it. Text in **boldface** applies to **AFP Version 2.0 only.**

Inputs

SRefNum (int)	session refnum
Volume ID (int)	volume identifier
Directory ID (long)	ancestor directory identifier
Bitmap (int)	bitmap describing which parameters are to be returned (the bit corresponding to each desired parameter should be set); this field is the same as File Bitmap in the FPGetFileDirParms call and can be null
AccessMode (int)	desired access and deny modes, specified by any combination of the following bits:

0   *Read*   allows the fork to be read

1   *Write*   allows the fork to be written to

4   *DenyRead*   denies others the right to read the fork while this user has it open

5   *DenyWrite*   denies others the right to write to the fork while this user has it open

(See "File Sharing Modes" earlier in this chapter for an explanation of deny modes.)

PathType (byte)	indicates whether Pathname is composed of long names or short names:

1 = short names

2 = long names

Pathname (string)	pathname to desired file; cannot be null
Rsrc/DataFlag (bit)	flag indicating which fork is to be opened:

0 = data fork

1 = resource fork

Outputs

FPError (long)	
Bitmap (int)	copy of input parameter
OForkRefNum (int)	refnum used to refer to this fork in subsequent calls
File parameters requested	

(continued) ➡

Result codes	ParamErr	Session refnum, volume identifier, or pathname type is unknown; pathname is null or bad.
	ObjectNotFound	Input parameters do not point to an existing file.
	BitmapErr	An attempt was made to retrieve a parameter that cannot be obtained with this call (fork will not be opened).
	DenyConflict	Fork cannot be opened because deny modes conflict (however, the file's parameters will be returned).
	AccessDenied	User does not have the rights listed below; in AFP 1.1, the file is marked WriteInhibit and the user attempted to open it for write; in AFP 1.1, the volume is ReadOnly and the user attempted to open the file for write.
	ObjectLocked	**In AFP 2.0, the file is marked WriteInhibit and the user attempted to open it for write.**
	Vollocked	**In AFP 2.0, the volume is ReadOnly and the user attempted to open the file for write.**
	ObjectTypeErr	Input parameters point to a directory.
	TooManyFilesOpen	The server cannot open another fork.

Algorithm

The server opens the specified fork if the user has the access rights for the requested access mode and if the access mode does not conflict with already-open access paths to this fork.

If the call opens the fork, the server packs the specified parameters, in bitmap order, in the reply block, preceded by Bitmap and OForkRefNum. This OForkRefNum is used in all subsequent calls involving the open fork.

File parameters are returned only if the call is completed with no error or with a DenyConflict result code. In the latter case, the server returns 0 for the OForkRefNum and also returns the requested parameters so that the user can determine whether he or she is the one who has the fork open.

A BitmapErr result code is returned if an attempt is made to retrieve the length of the file's other fork.

The server needs to keep variable-length parameters, such as Long Name and Short Name, at the end of the reply block. In order to do this, the server represents variable-length parameters in bitmap order as fixed-length offsets (integers). Each offset is measured from the start of the parameters (not from the start of the Bitmap) to the start of the variable-length fields. The actual variable-length fields are then packed after all fixed-length fields.

If the fork is opened and the user has requested the file's attributes in the Bitmap, the appropriate DAlreadyOpen or RAlreadyOpen bit is set.

Rights

To open a fork for read or none (when neither read nor write access is requested) access, the user must have search access to all ancestors, except the parent directory, as well as read access to the parent directory. For details about access modes, see "File Sharing Modes" earlier in this chapter.

To open the fork for write, the volume must not be designated for read-only access. If both forks are currently empty, the user must have search or write access to all ancestors, except the parent directory, as well as write access to the parent directory. If either fork is not empty and one of them is being opened for write, the user must have search access to all ancestors, except the parent directory, as well as read and write access to the parent directory.

Notes

The user must have previously called FPOpenVol for this volume. Each fork must be opened separately; a unique OForkRefNum is returned for each.

(continued) ➡

Block format

Request

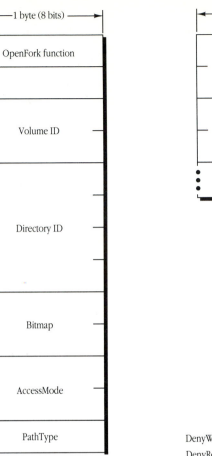

- 1 byte (8 bits)
- OpenFork function
- Rsrc/DataFlag
- Volume ID
- Directory ID
- Bitmap
- AccessMode
- PathType
- Pathname

Reply

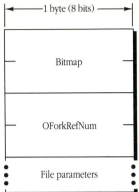

- 1 byte (8 bits)
- Bitmap
- OForkRefNum
- File parameters

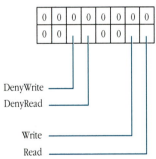

AccessMode

0	0	0	0	0	0	0	0
0	0				0	0		

- DenyWrite
- DenyRead
- Write
- Read

FPOpenVol

This call makes a volume available to the workstation.

Inputs	*SRefNum (int)*	session refnum
	Bitmap (int)	bitmap describing which parameters are to be returned (the bit corresponding to each desired parameter should be set); this field is the same as that in the FPGetVolParms call and cannot be null
	Volume Name (string)	name of the volume as returned by the FPGetSrvrParms call
	Password (8 bytes)	optional password
Outputs	*FPError (long)*	
	Bitmap (int)	copy of input parameter
	Volume parameters requested	
Result codes	*ParamErr*	Session refnum or volume name is unknown.
	BitmapErr	An attempt was made to retrieve a parameter that cannot be obtained with this call; bitmap is null.
	AccessDenied	Password is not supplied or does not match.

Algorithm

The FPOpenVol call indicates that the user of a workstation wants to work with a volume. This call must be submitted before any other call can be made to obtain access to the CNodes on the volume.

If a password is required to gain access to the volume, it is sent as the Password parameter in cleartext, padded (suffixed) with null bytes to its full 8-byte length. Password comparison is case-sensitive. The server checks that the password supplied by the user matches the one kept with the volume. If they do not match, or if no Password parameter was supplied, an AccessDenied result code is returned.

If the passwords match, or if the volume is not password-protected, the server retrieves the requested parameters and packs them into the reply block. The user now has permission to make calls relating to files and directories on the volume.

(continued) ➡

Notes

The FPOpenVol call cannot be made with a null Bitmap parameter. The Bitmap must request that the Volume ID be returned. This parameter cannot be retrieved any other way, and it is needed for most subsequent calls.

FPOpenVol can be called multiple times without an intervening FPCloseVol call; however, a single FPCloseVol call invalidates the Volume ID.

Block format

Request

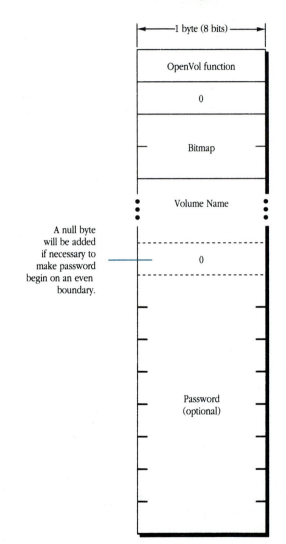

Reply

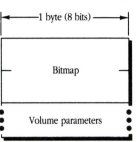

A null byte will be added if necessary to make password begin on an even boundary.

FPRead

This request reads a block of data from an open fork. Text in **boldface** applies to **AFP Version 2.0 only.**

Inputs	*SRefNum (int)*	session refnum
	OForkRefNum (int)	open fork refnum
	Offset (long)	number of the first byte to be read
	ReqCount (long)	number of bytes to be read
	Newline Mask (byte)	mask used to determined where the read should be terminated
	Newline Char (byte)	character used to determine where the read should be terminated
Outputs	*FPError (long)*	
	ActCount (long)	number of bytes actually read from the fork
	Fork data requested	
Result codes	*ParamErr*	Session refnum or open fork refnum is unknown; ReqCount or Offset is negative; Newline Mask is invalid.
	AccessDenied	Fork was not opened for read access.
	EOFErr	End of fork was reached.
	LockErr	Some or all of the requested range is locked by another user.

Algorithm

The FPRead request retrieves a range of bytes from a specified fork. The server begins reading at the byte number specified by the Offset parameter. The server terminates the read for one of the following reasons (whichever comes first):

- It encounters the character specified by the combination of Newline Char and Newline Mask.

- It reaches the end of fork.

- It encounters the start of a range locked by another user.

- It finishes reading the number of bytes specified by the ReqCount parameter.

(continued) ➡

If the server reaches the end of fork or the start of a locked range, it returns all data read up to that point along with an EOFErr or LockErr result code.

Newline Mask is a byte mask that is to be logically ANDed with a copy of each byte read. If the result matches the Newline Char, the read terminates. In AFP 1.1, the only legal values of Newline Mask are $00 and $FF. **In AFP 2.0, all values of Newline Mask are allowed.** Using a Newline Mask of $00 essentially disables the Newline check feature.

If the user reads a byte that was never written to the fork, the result is undefined.

Rights   The fork must be open for read by the user issuing this request.

Notes   Lock the range before submitting this call. The underlying transport mechanism may force the request to be broken into multiple smaller requests. If the range is not locked when this call begins execution, it is possible for another user to lock some or all of the range before this call completes, causing the read to succeed partially.

The ActCount parameter is returned by the underlying transport mechanism and not as a parameter in the reply block.

Block format

Request

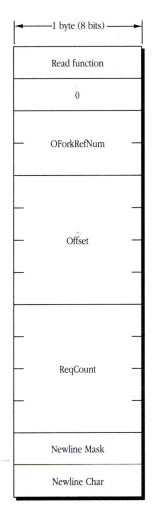

←—— 1 byte (8 bits) ——→

Read function
0
OForkRefNum
Offset
ReqCount
Newline Mask
Newline Char

Reply

←—— 1 byte (8 bits) ——→

Fork data

FPRemoveAPPL

This request removes an APPL mapping from the volume's Desktop database.

Inputs	SRefNum (int)	session refnum
	DTRefNum (int)	Desktop database refnum
	Directory ID (long)	ancestor directory identifier
	FileCreator (ResType)	file creator of application corresponding to the APPL mapping
	PathType (byte)	indicates whether Pathname is composed of long names or short names:
		1 = short names
		2 = long names
	Pathname (string)	pathname to the application corresponding to the APPL mapping being removed

Outputs   FPError (long)

Result codes	ParamErr	Session refnum or Desktop database refnum is unknown.
	ObjectNotFound	Input parameters do not point to an existing file.
	AccessDenied	User does not have the rights listed below.
	ItemNotFound	No APPL mapping corresponding to the input parameters was found in the Desktop database.

Algorithm   The server locates in the Desktop database the APPL mapping corresponding to the specified application and FileCreator. If an APPL mapping is found, it is removed.

Rights   The user must have search access to all ancestors, except the parent directory, as well as read and write access to the parent directory.

Notes   The user must have previously called FPOpenDT for the corresponding volume. In addition, the file must exist in the specified directory before this call is issued.

Block format

|-------- 1 byte (8 bits) --------|

RemoveAPPL function
0
DTRefNum
Directory ID
FileCreator
PathType
Pathname

FPRemoveComment

This request removes a comment from the volume's Desktop database.

Inputs

SRefNum (int)	session refnum
DTRefNum (int)	Desktop database refnum
Directory ID (long)	ancestor directory identifier
PathType (byte)	indicates whether Pathname is composed of long names or short names:
	1 = short names
	2 = long names
Pathname (string)	the pathname to the file or folder associated with the comment

Outputs

FPError (long)

Result codes

ParamErr	Session refnum, Desktop database refnum, or pathname type is unknown; pathname is bad.
ItemNotFound	No comment was found in Desktop database.
AccessDenied	User does not have the rights listed below.
ObjectNotFound	Input parameters do not point to an existing file or directory.

Algorithm

The server removes the comment associated with the specified file or folder from the Desktop database.

Rights

If the comment is associated with a directory that is not empty, the user must have search access to all ancestors, including the parent directory, plus write access to the parent directory. If the comment is associated with an empty directory, the user must have search or write access to all ancestors, including the parent directory, plus write access to the parent directory.

If the comment is associated with a file that is not empty, the user must have search access to all ancestors, except the parent directory, plus read and write access to the parent directory. If the comment is associated with an empty file, the user must have search or write access to all ancestors, except the parent directory, plus write access to the parent directory.

Notes

The user must have previously called FPOpenDT for the corresponding volume.

Block format

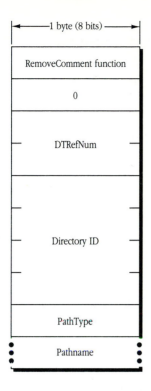

1 byte (8 bits)

RemoveComment function
0
DTRefNum
Directory ID
PathType
Pathname

FPRename

This request renames a directory or file. Text in **boldface** applies to **AFP Version 2.0 only.**

Inputs	SRefNum (int)	session refnum
	Volume ID (int)	volume identifier
	Directory ID (long)	ancestor directory identifier
	PathType (byte)	indicates whether Pathname is composed of long names or short names:
		1 = short names
		2 = long names
	Pathname (string)	pathname to file or directory to be renamed; can be null if a directory is being renamed
	NewType (byte)	indicates whether NewName is a long name or short name (same values as PathType)
	NewName (string)	new name of file or directory (cannot be null)
Outputs	FPError (long)	
Result codes	ParamErr	Session refnum, volume identifier, or pathname type is unknown; pathname or NewName is bad.
	ObjectNotFound	Input parameters do not point to an existing file or directory.
	ObjectExists	A file or directory with the name NewName already exists.
	AccessDenied	User does not have the rights listed below; in AFP 1.1, the volume is ReadOnly; in AFP 1.1, the file or directory is marked RenameInhibit.
	VolLocked	**In AFP 2.0, the volume is ReadOnly.**
	ObjectLocked	**In AFP 2.0, the file or directory is marked RenameInhibit.**
	CantRename	An attempt was made to rename a volume or root directory.

Algorithm   The server assigns a new name to the file or directory. The other name (long or short) is generated as described in "Catalog Node Names" earlier in this chapter. The modification date of the parent directory is set to the server's clock.

Rights

To rename a directory, the user must have search access to all ancestors, including the CNode's parent directory, as well as write access to the parent directory. To rename a file, the user must have search access to all ancestors, except the CNode's parent directory, as well as read and write access to the parent directory.

Notes

The user must have previously called FPOpenVol for this volume.

Block format

Request

FPSetDirParms

This request sets parameters for a specified directory. Text in **boldface** applies to **AFP Version 2.0 only.**

Inputs	SRefNum (int)	session refnum
	Volume ID (int)	volume identifier
	Directory ID (long)	ancestor directory identifier
	Bitmap (int)	bitmap describing which parameters are to be set (the bit corresponding to each desired parameter should be set); this field is the same as Directory Bitmap in the FPGetFileDirParms call
	PathType (byte)	indicates whether Pathname is composed of long names or short names:
		1 = short names
		2 = long names
	Pathname (string)	pathname to desired directory
	Directory parameters to be set	
Outputs	FPError (long)	
Result codes	ParamErr	Session refnum, volume identifier, or pathname type is unknown; pathname is bad; owner or group ID is not valid.
	ObjectNotFound	Input parameters do not point to an existing directory.
	BitmapErr	An attempt was made to set a parameter that cannot be set with this call; bitmap is null.
	AccessDenied	User does not have the rights listed below; in AFP 1.1, the volume is ReadOnly.
	VolLocked	**In AFP 2.0, the volume is ReadOnly.**
	ObjectTypeErr	Input parameters point to a file.

Algorithm   The FPSetDirParms call sets parameters for a directory. The parameters must be packed, in bitmap order, in the request block.

The workstation needs to keep variable-length parameters, such as Long Name and Short Name, at the end of the block. In order to do this, variable-length parameters are represented in bitmap order as fixed-length offsets (integers). These offsets are measured from the start of the parameters to the start of the variable-length fields. The actual variable-length fields are then packed after all fixed-length fields.

A null byte must be added between the Pathname and the Directory Parameters if necessary to make the parameters begin on an even boundary in the request block.

If this call sets the access controls, dates (except modification date), Finder Info, **ProDOS Info,** or changes any attributes, the modification date of the directory will be set to the server's clock. If this call sets the access controls, owner ID, group ID, or Invisible attribute, the modification date of the directory's parent directory will be set to the server's clock.

Changing a directory's access rights immediately affects other currently open sessions. If the user does not have the access rights to set any one of a number of parameters, an AccessDenied result code will be returned and no parameters will be set.

Rights   To set a directory's access rights, owner ID, or group ID, or to change the **DeleteInhibit, RenameInhibit, WriteInhibit,** or Invisible attributes, the user must have search or write access to all ancestors, including this directory's parent directory, and the user must be the owner of the directory. To set any parameter other than the ones mentioned above for an empty directory, the user must have search or write access to all ancestors, except the parent directory, as well as write access to the parent directory. To set any parameter other than the ones mentioned above for a directory that is not empty, the user must have search access to all ancestors, including the parent directory, as well as write access to the parent directory.

Notes   The user must have previously called FPOpenVol for this volume.

This call cannot be used to set a directory's name (use FPRename), parent Directory ID (use FPMoveAndRename), Directory ID, or Offspring Count.

(continued) ➡

Block format

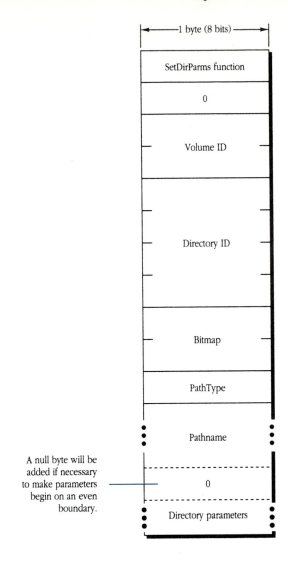

FPSetFileDirParms

This request sets parameters for a file or directory. Text in **boldface** applies to **AFP Version 2.0 only.**

Inputs	*SRefNum (int)*	session refnum
	Volume ID (int)	volume identifier
	Directory ID (long)	ancestor directory identifier
	Bitmap (int)	bitmap describing which parameters are to be set (the bit corresponding to each desired parameter should be set); this field is the same as File Bitmap or Directory Bitmap in the FPGetFileDirParms call (only the parameters that are common to both bitmaps may be set by this call)
	PathType (byte)	indicates whether Pathname is composed of long names or short names:
		1 = short names
		2 = long names
	Pathname (string)	pathname to desired file or directory
	Parameters to be set	
Outputs	*FPError (long)*	
Result codes	*ParamErr*	Session refnum, volume identifier, or pathname type is unknown; pathname is bad.
	ObjectNotFound	Input parameters do not point to an existing file or directory.
	AccessDenied	User does not have the rights listed below; in AFP 1.1, the volume is ReadOnly.
	VolLocked	**In AFP 2.0, the volume is ReadOnly.**
	BitmapErr	An attempt was made to set a parameter that cannot be set with this call; bitmap is null.

(continued) ➡

Algorithm
The parameters that this call can set or clear are the Invisible **and System** attributes, Creation Date, Modification Date, Backup Date, Finder Info, **and ProDOS Info.**

These parameters are common to both files and directories. The parameters must be packed, in bitmap order, in the request block.

The workstation needs to keep variable-length parameters at the end of the block. In order to do this, variable-length parameters are represented in bitmap order as fixed-length offsets (integers). These offsets are measured from the start of the parameters to the start of the variable-length fields. The actual variable-length fields are then packed after all fixed-length fields.

A null byte must be added between the Pathname and the Parameters if necessary to make the Parameters begin on an even boundary in the request block.

If the Attributes field is included, the Set/Clear bit indicates that the specified attributes are to be either set or cleared (0 equals clear the specified attributes; 1 equals set the specified attributes). Therefore, it is not possible to set some attributes and clear others in the same call.

If this call changes the CNodes's Invisible attribute, the modification date of the CNode's parent directory will be set to the server's clock. If this call changes the CNode's attributes or sets the CNode's dates (except modification date), Finder Info, or **ProDOS Info,** the modification date of the CNode will be set to the server's clock.

Rights
To set the parameters for a directory that is not empty, the user needs search access to all ancestors, including the parent directory, as well as write access to the parent directory. To set the parameters for an empty directory, the user needs search or write access to all ancestors, except the parent directory, as well as write access to the parent directory.

To set the parameters for a file that is not empty, the user needs search access to all ancestors, except the parent directory, as well as read and write access to the parent. To set the parameters for an empty file, the user needs search or write access to all ancestors, except the parent directory, as well as write access to the parent.

Notes
The user must have previously called FPOpenVol for this volume.

If it is known whether the CNode is a file or directory, the user can submit the FPSetFileParms or FPSetDirParms calls to set the Creation Date, Modification Date, Backup Date, and Finder Info parameters. To set a directory's Access Rights, Owner ID, or Group ID, use the FPSetDirParms call. To set a file's attributes other than Invisible **and System,** use the FPSetFileParms call.

Block format

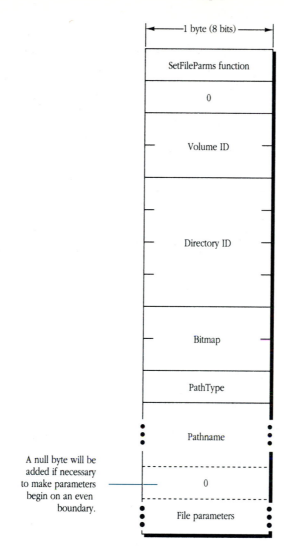

A null byte will be added if necessary to make parameters begin on an even boundary.

FPSetFileParms

This request sets parameters for a specified file. Text in **boldface** applies to **AFP Version 2.0 only.**

Inputs	SRefNum (int)	session refnum
	Volume ID (int)	volume identifier
	Directory ID (long)	ancestor directory identifier
	Bitmap (int)	bitmap describing which parameters are to be set (the bit corresponding to each desired parameter should be set); this field is the same as File Bitmap in the FPGetFileDirParms call
	PathType (byte)	indicates whether Pathname is composed of long names or short names:
		1 = short names
		2 = long names
	Pathname (string)	pathname to desired file
	File parameters to be set	
Outputs	FPError (long)	
Result codes	ParamErr	Session refnum, volume identifier, or pathname type is unknown; pathname is null or bad.
	ObjectNotFound	Input parameters do not point to an existing file.
	AccessDenied	User does not have the rights listed below; in AFP 1.1, the volume is ReadOnly.
	VolLocked	**In AFP 2.0, the volume is ReadOnly.**
	BitmapErr	An attempt was made to set a parameter that cannot be set with this call; bitmap is null.
	ObjectTypeErr	Input parameters point to a directory.

Algorithm	The FPSetFileParms call sets parameters for a file. The parameters must be packed, in bitmap order, in the request block.

The workstation needs to keep variable-length parameters at the end of the block. In order to do this, variable-length parameters are represented in bitmap order as fixed-length offsets (integers). These offsets are measured from the start of the parameters to the start of the variable-length fields. The actual variable-length fields are then packed after all fixed-length fields.

A null byte must be added between the Pathname and the File Parameters if necessary to make the parameters begin on an even boundary in the block.

The following parameters may be set or cleared: the Attributes (all except DAlreadyOpen, RAlreadyOpen, and **CopyProtect**), the Creation Date, Modification Date, Backup Date, Finder Info, **and ProDOS Info.**

If the Attributes parameter is included, the Set/Clear bit indicates that the specified attributes are to be either set or cleared (0 equals clear the specified attributes; 1 equals set the specified attributes). Therefore, it is not possible to set some attributes and clear others in the same call.

If this call changes a file's Invisible attribute, the modification date of the file's parent directory will be set to the server's clock. If this call changes a file's Attributes or sets any dates (except modification date), Finder Info, or **ProDOS Info,** the modification date to the file will be set to the server's clock.

Rights

If the file is empty (both forks are of 0 length), the user must have search or write access to all ancestors, except this file's parent directory, as well as write access to the parent directory. If either fork is not empty, the user must have search access to all ancestors is except the parent directory, as well as read and write access to the parent directory.

Notes

The user must have previously called FPOpenVol for this volume.

This call cannot be used to set a file's name (use FPRename), parent Directory ID (use FPMoveAndRename), file number, or fork lengths.

(continued) ➡

Block format

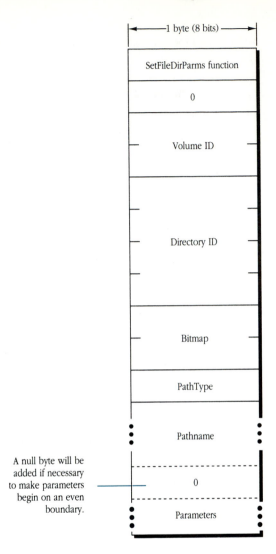

1 byte (8 bits)

SetFileDirParms function

0

Volume ID

Directory ID

Bitmap

PathType

Pathname

A null byte will be added if necessary to make parameters begin on an even boundary.

0

Parameters

FPSetForkParms

This request sets the fork length for a specified open fork. Text in **boldface** applies to **AFP Version 2.0 only.**

Inputs	*SRefNum (int)*	session refnum
	OForkRefNum (int)	open fork refnum
	Bitmap (int)	bitmap describing which parameters are to be set; this field is the same as File Bitmap in the FPGetFileDirParms call; however, only the appropriate Fork Length bit can be set
	Fork Length (long)	new end-of-fork value
Outputs	*FPError (long)*	
Result codes	*ParamErr*	Session refnum or open fork refnum is unknown.
	BitmapErr	An attempt was made to set a parameter that cannot be set with this call; bitmap is null.
	DiskFull	No more space exists on the volume.
	LockErr	Locked range conflict exists.
	AccessDenied	User does not have the rights listed below; in AFP 1.1, the volume is ReadOnly.
	VolLocked	**In AFP 2.0, the volume is ReadOnly.**

Algorithm

The Bitmap and Fork Length are passed to the server, which changes the length of the fork specified by OForkRefNum. The server returns a BitmapErr result code if the call tries to set the length of the file's other fork or if it tries to set any other file parameter.

The server returns a LockErr result code if the fork is truncated to eliminate a range or part of a range locked by another user.

Rights

The fork must be open for write by the user.

Notes

This call cannot be used to set a file's name (use FPRename), parent directory (use FPMoveAndRename), or file number.

(continued) ➡

Block format

```
|←——— 1 byte (8 bits) ———→|

| SetForkParms function |

|           0           |

|      OForkRefNum      |

|        Bitmap         |

|      Fork Length      |
```

FPSetVolParms

This request sets the backup date for a specified volume. Text in **boldface** applies to **AFP Version 2.0 only.**

Inputs	*SRefNum (int)*	session refnum
	Volume ID (int)	volume identifier
	Bitmap (int)	bitmap describing which parameters are to be set; this field is the same as that in the FPGetVolParms call; however, only the Backup Date bit can be set
	Backup Date (long)	new backup date
Outputs	*FPError (long)*	
Result codes	*ParamErr*	Session refnum or volume identifier is unknown.
	BitmapErr	An attempt was made to set a parameter that cannot be set with this call; bitmap is null.
	AccessDenied	In AFP 1.1, the volume is ReadOnly.
	VolLocked	**In AFP 2.0, the volume is ReadOnly.**
Algorithm	The server changes the backup date for the specified volume.	
Notes	The user must have previously called FPOpenVol for this volume.	

(continued) ➡

Block format

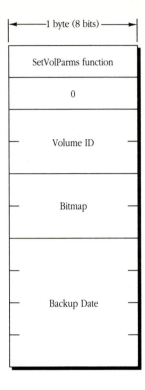

1 byte (8 bits)

SetVolParms function

0

Volume ID

Bitmap

Backup Date

FPWrite

This request writes a block of data to an open fork.

Inputs	SRefNum (int)	session refnum
	OForkRefNum (int)	open fork refnum
	Offset (long)	byte offset from the beginning or end of the fork to where the write is to begin (should be negative to indicate a byte within the fork relative to the end of the fork)
	ReqCount (long)	number of bytes to be written
	Start/EndFlag (bit)	flag indicating whether the Offset field is relative to the beginning or end of the fork:
		0 = Start (relative to the beginning of the fork)
		1 = End (relative to the end of the fork)
	Fork data	
Outputs	FPError (long)	
	ActCount (long)	number of bytes actually written to the fork
	LastWritten (long)	the number of the byte just past the last byte written
Result codes	ParamErr	Session refnum or open fork refnum is unknown.
	AccessDenied	User does not have the rights listed below.
	LockErr	Some or all of requested range is locked by another user.
	DiskFull	No more space exists on the volume.

Algorithm

The Start/EndFlag allows a block of data to be written at an offset relative to the end of the fork. Therefore, data can be written to a fork when the user does not know the exact end of fork, as can happen when multiple writers are concurrently modifying a fork. The server returns the number of the byte just past the last byte written.

The server writes data to the open fork, starting at Offset number of bytes from the beginning or end of the fork. If the block of data to be written extends beyond the end of fork, the fork is extended. If part of the range is locked by another user, the server returns a LockErr result code and does not write any data to the fork.

The file's Modification Date is not changed until the fork is closed.

(continued) ➡

Rights   The fork must be open for write access by the user issuing this request.

Notes   Lock the range before submitting this call. The underlying transport mechanism may force the request to be broken into multiple smaller requests. If the range is not locked when this call begins execution, it is possible for another user to lock some or all of the range before this call completes, causing the write to succeed partially.

The fork data to be written is transmitted to the server in an intermediate exchange of ASP packets.

Block format

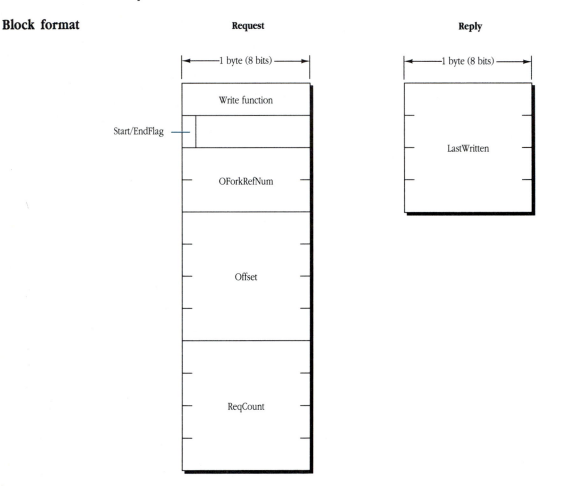

Chapter 14 **Print Spooling Architecture**

CONTENTS

■

THE WORD *SPOOL* is an acronym for Simultaneous Peripheral Operations On Line, and a print spooler is a hardware application or a software application (or both) that is used to store data on a disk temporarily until the printer is ready to process it. Since the print spooler handles the interaction required with the printer in order to accomplish the printing process, use of a spooler frees the originating computer, such as an Apple Macintosh computer, to perform other activities during the printing process. This chapter describes AppleTalk print spooling in general and compares printing with a spooler to printing without a spooler. In addition, since print spooling can be accomplished either by a spooler/server or as a background process on the originating computer, this chapter also compares these two options. ■

Printing without a spooler

In an AppleTalk network, when printing is performed without the benefit of a spooler, the workstation initiating the print job is unavailable for other purposes until the printer has finished processing the print job. This section discusses several factors that affect the length of time that a workstation is tied up for printing.

When a Macintosh workstation user selects a document and invokes a print command, the workstation executes the document-composition application corresponding to that document. The application, in conjunction with the Macintosh Printing Manager, produces the print file information and sends it, in real time, to the printer, as shown in *Figure 14-1*. In this case, the document-composition application has control of the workstation until the print job is completely processed; during this time, a dialog takes place between the workstation and the printer, so the workstation is unavailable for any other purpose. The length of time that the workstation is unavailable to the user is determined by at least the following three factors:

- the speed at which the printer converts the print job into its physical printed form
- the size of the print file being produced
- the type of print file being produced

In an AppleTalk network, when the document-composition application calls the Printing Manager in the Macintosh to send a print job to a LaserWriter (or to an ImageWriter), the Macintosh begins a series of AppleTalk calls in an attempt to establish a connection. These calls perform the following functions in order:

1. Using the Name Binding Protocol (NBP) name-lookup operation, look for the currently selected printer and find its AppleTalk address.

2. Using the Printer Access Protocol (PAP), attempt to open a connection with the printer.

- **Figure 14-1** Configuration for printing without a spooler

Workstation

Printer

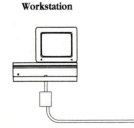
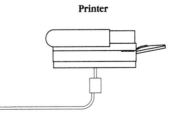

If the printer is busy (that is, if the printer is servicing another job), it refuses to accept a new connection. In this case, the Printing Manager must continue trying to open the connection until the printer finishes processing the current job and breaks the connection established for that job, which frees the printer to establish another connection. During this time, the user's workstation is unavailable for other use. The length of time that the workstation is unavailable to the user is determined not only by the characteristics of the printer and of the user's own print job, but also by the following factors:

- the size and type of job currently being printed
- the number of other workstations contending for the printer

It could be several minutes (on rare occasions, even hours) before the printer accepts the new print job. In the meantime, the user's workstation remains unavailable unless the user cancels the pending print request.

Benefits of printing with a spooler

Since a print spooler stores a printer-ready file on disk and interacts with the printer until the file is printed, introducing a print spooler between the document-composition system and the printer reduces the length of time that a workstation is tied up for printing. As soon as the print job is ready to be printed, the workstation sends the job to the spooler to store on disk, which releases the workstation for other uses. The spooler then establishes and maintains the required dialog with the printer until the print job is finished.

A print spooler can also provide a mechanism for controlling access to a printer. The spooler can include a user authentication system that would force potential users to enter user identification information (such as user names and passwords) before allowing the users to gain access to a specific printer. The authentication function can be extended to include a wide variety of access options. For example, classes of user authorization could be established, and certain classes of print jobs could be given priority over other jobs.

A print spooler also provides a mechanism for gathering statistical information about printer usage. An accounting department can use information about the printing activity of the users for billing purposes. In addition, management can use statistics about printer access to evaluate a site's design and to plan potential modifications.

Background spoolers versus spooler/servers

The following two types of spooler implementations can be used with AppleTalk workstations:

■ background spoolers

■ spooler/servers

A *background spooler* is a software system that runs on a workstation as a background process to spool a print job to the user's local disk (usually a hard disk). With a background spooler, once the print job is ready for printing, the job becomes the spooler's responsibility. The spooler takes charge of storing the print file, establishing a connection with the printer, and interacting with the printer until the job is finished.

When a background spooler is used, although the workstation must remain connected to the network until the job is processed, the user can continue to use the workstation for other operations. However, if the workstation is switched off, or if its connection to the network is otherwise broken, the print job will not be printed. In addition, background spoolers cannot provide mechanisms for controlling printer access or for gathering accounting data about printer usage.

A *spooler/server* is an intermediary (or agent) that is positioned between one or more workstations and one or more printers, as shown in *Figure 14-2*. When a spooler/server is used, the Macintosh Printing Manager produces the print file and sends it over the network to the spooler/server; the spooler/server then interacts with the printer to print the job.

After receiving the print file, the spooler/server can terminate its connection with the workstation. Then, the workstation is free to perform other tasks or can be switched off. A spooler/server also provides an intermediate point between the workstation and the printer for inserting various kinds of access control and for gathering accounting statistics.

Impact of the Macintosh on printing

The Macintosh computer's printing architecture tightly binds a document's print file to the printer on which it is to be printed. When a print job is sent from a Macintosh to a LaserWriter or similar printer, the Printing Manager in the Macintosh queries the printer for various parameters throughout the printing process. Therefore, two-way communication is maintained between the Macintosh and the printer for the duration of the job. The spooler/server must emulate a printer during communication with a workstation by responding to queries in the print stream as it receives the print job.

■ **Figure 14-2** Configuration for printing with a spooler/server

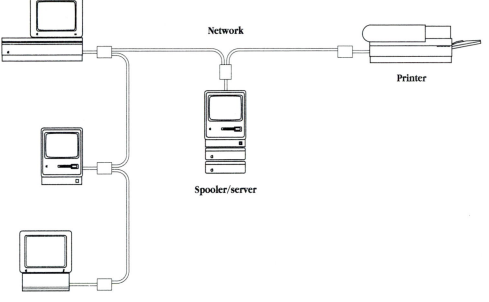

The print stream that a Macintosh sends to a LaserWriter is in PostScript. However, document-structuring conventions have been developed to provide guidelines for embedding comments in PostScript code in order to communicate with document managers (such as print spoolers). These comments allow spoolers to respond to queries without having to interpret actual PostScript code.

Printing without a spooler

Figure 14-3 illustrates the protocol architecture used for printing without a spooler on a LaserWriter (or an ImageWriter) printer from AppleTalk workstations. You can also apply this model to other printers connected to an AppleTalk network.

The Macintosh workstation uses NBP to obtain the AppleTalk address of the printer's listening socket. The Macintosh identifies the printer for NBP by the printer's complete NBP name (if the printer is a LaserWriter, the type field of the entity name is "LaserWriter").

■ Figure 14-3 Protocol architecture for printing without a spooler

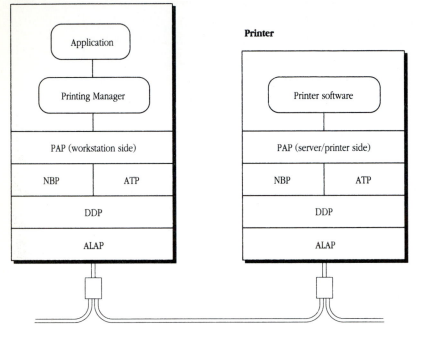

Once the AppleTalk address of the printer's listening socket is determined, the workstation opens a connection to the printer through PAP. When this connection is established, the workstation and the printer interact over the PAP connection.

PAP is a client of the AppleTalk Transaction Protocol (ATP), which in turn uses the Datagram Delivery Protocol (DDP). PAP is an asymmetric protocol; the PAP code in the workstation is different from the PAP code in the printer. *Figure 14-3* illustrates this difference.

The commands and data sent through the PAP connection are printer-dependent. For the LaserWriter, the dialog is in the PostScript programming language.

Printing with a spooler/server

Figure 14-4 illustrates the printing architecture when a spooler/server is introduced between the Macintosh workstation and a printer (such as a LaserWriter or an ImageWriter). The key feature of this architecture is that the spooler/server sets itself up as a surrogate printer. Doing this means that when a workstation looks for a printer of the appropriate type (for example, "LaserWriter"), it views the spooler/server as such a printer. In fact, through this name-lookup process, the workstation cannot distinguish this spooler/server from a printer of the same type. (The spooler/server can set itself up as one or more printers with appropriate names.)

The spooler/server responds to a PAP connection request from the workstation exactly the way a PAP-based printer would. Once the connection is established, the spooler process emulates all of the relevant aspects of a workstation's interaction with a printer, while storing the print files in its internal storage (typically, a hard disk).

■ **Figure 14-4** Protocol architecture for printing with a spooler/server

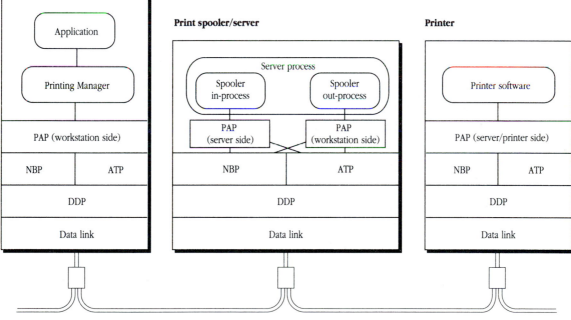

Through PAP, it is possible to establish multiple connections to a printer. The design of the printer determines the number of connections that a printer services simultaneously. LaserWriter and ImageWriter printers accept only one connection (therefore, one job) at a time. Typically, spooler/servers should accept several connections at a time in order to reduce the delay experienced by workstations that are trying to print.

The spooler/server includes a spooler out-process, which functions exactly as a workstation in transmitting jobs to the printer. The spooler out-process picks up spooled print files from its internal storage and prints them on the destination printer in exactly the same way that a workstation would.

Together with the appropriate protocol modules and drivers, the spooler process converts the spooler/server into a two-sided entity, which appears as a printer to the workstations and as a workstation to the printers. Consequently, the spooler/server includes both the server-end PAP and the workstation-end PAP.

A simple modification of the print-spooling architecture makes it possible to include spooling either to printers that are directly plugged into the spooler/server or to printers with which the spooler/server communicates through a protocol other than PAP. In these cases, the in-process side of the spooler/server remains the same as the in-process side shown in *Figure 14-4*. However, the out-process side is modified to provide a mechanism for transmitting the print files from the server's internal storage to the actual printer. If you are designing a spooler for these purposes, while you can tailor the out-process to meet specific needs, the in-process must strictly obey the disciplines for printers dictated by PAP. *Figure 14-5* provides an example of this type of architecture. In this figure, X represents non-PAP modules and drivers.

Controlling printer access

Because a spooler/server is positioned between the workstations and the printers, it can be used to control printer access. When a spooler/server is controlling access to a printer, workstations can communicate with this printer only through the spooler/server.

In this case, the spooler/server provides an intermediary location for

- implementing a user authentication system (see "User Authentication Dialog," next, for details on this implementation)
- gathering and storing global statistics about printer use (for accounting or planning purposes)

■ **Figure 14-5** Protocol architecture for alternate spooling environments

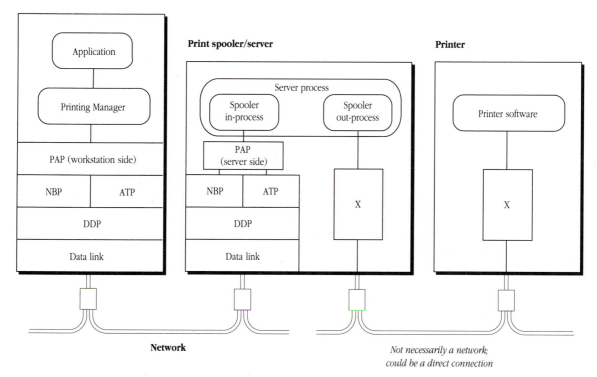

For example, if a network contains three printers, one printer can be dedicated to jobs from the executive staff; the other two printers can be made available to the rest of the staff and used based on which has the least activity. In addition, the number of pages printed on each printer can be recorded so that the activity levels on the three printers can be compared.

To restrict direct access to a particular printer and to force workstations to obtain access to the printer through the spooler/server, the spooler process renames the printer so that other network devices can no longer recognize it as a printer. In this case, the spooler opens a connection to a printer at startup and then sends a command to the printer to change the type field of its name to a string that does not correspond to any type of printer. For example, a spooler/server may change the type field of the name of a LaserWriter printer from "LaserWriter" to an optional new string. Next, the spooler/server opens its own PAP listening socket and assigns itself a name with

"LaserWriter" in the type field (this name may be either a new string or the string that the printer used before it was renamed). As a result, when workstations use the NBP name-lookup process to search for the printer, they find the spooler/server instead of the printer.

This technique of renaming the printer is not mandated by the print spooling architecture. Additionally, if the spooler/server also includes a direct passthrough service, workstations can still print directly to a printer that has been renamed. When direct passthrough is used, rather than spooling files for the printer, the spooler/server passes messages between the workstations and the printer (see "Direct Passthrough" later in this chapter).

User authentication dialog

Just after the workstation opens a PAP connection to the spooler/server (or to a printer), the devices engage in an exchange of messages known as the user authentication dialog. This dialog consists of a series of messages whose format coincides with PostScript comment conventions. The spooler/server must be able to carry on this dialog. Details on using PostScript comments are provided later in this chapter.

◆ *Note:* The discussion that follows applies to printers that implement PostScript (in particular, LaserWriter printers). Other AppleTalk printers (such as ImageWriter printers) require different mechanisms.

The first step of the dialog is to determine whether the device to which the PAP connection has been opened is a spooler/server. To do this, the workstation uses a SpoolerQuery with the following format:

```
%%?BeginQuery: rUaSpooler
false = flush
%%?EndQuery: true
```

If the device is a PostScript device, such as the LaserWriter, and if it does not have the ability to respond to this query, the second line causes the device to send back `false` as a reply. Since a LaserWriter does not interpret comments, it responds with `false`, indicating that it is not a spooler. However, if the device is a spooler/server, when it receives the first line of this query, it skips the second line and sends back `true` as a reply, indicating that it is a spooler.

If the reply to the SpoolerQuery query is `false`, the user authentication dialog is skipped, and the connection is used for printing directly to the printer.

However, if the reply to the SpoolerQuery query is `true`, the user authentication dialog is continued. The next step in this dialog is to query for a list of the user authentication methods (UAMs) that the particular spooler handles. The following is an example of this query:

```
%%?BeginUAMethodsQuery
%%?EndUAMethodsQuery: NoUserLogin
```

The response to this query is a set of one or more strings, with each string identifying a user authentication method that the spooler supports. The response must terminate with either an asterisk (*) or the string `NoUserLogin`. There are three standard user authentication methods specified by Apple:

- `NoUserAuthent`
- `CleartxtPasswrd`
- `RandnumExchange`

If you design other special methods for user authentication, you should define a string to identify each of these methods.

◆ *Note:* There is a fourth reply, `NoUserLogin`, that is used for spoolers that do not support logging in of users. A spooler that does not want to control user access can return the string `NoUserLogin`. In this case, the workstation bypasses the login dialog completely.

The first standard authentication method requires the spooler to receive a login string. The workstation sends the spooler the following:

```
%%Login: NoUserAuthent
```

The spooler must reply with the message `LoginOK`, and the workstation can then continue with the printing phase of the connection.

The second standard authentication method requires that the spooler receive a user name string and a password, which it compares with a user authentication database to verify that the user is valid. The workstation sends the spooler the following:

```
%%Login: CleartxtPasswrd <user name> <password>
```

If the spooler finds a match for the user name and password pair in its user authentication database, then the spooler responds with the message `LoginOK`. The workstation can then continue the printing phase of the connection. However, if the user information does not match an entry in the user authentication database, then the spooler responds with the message `InvalidUser`. In this case, the spooler does not permit further use of the PAP connection by the user and disconnects the workstation after a few seconds. This disconnection interval should be long enough to ensure the delivery of the `InvalidUser` message to the workstation.

To prevent peek programs from being used to spy and read passwords out of network packets, the third standard authentication method does not send the password over the network cable. In this case, the workstation sends the following:

```
%%Login: RandnumExchange <user name>
```

Upon receiving this information, the spooler examines its user authentication database to see if the indicated user name exists. If the user name is not found in the database, the spooler sends back the message `InvalidUser` and disconnects the workstation, as previously described. If the user name is found, the spooler sends back a message that consists of the word `Randnum`, followed by a space and a 16-character hexadecimal ASCII representation of a 64-bit random number that the server generates. Upon receiving the random number, the workstation uses the user password as the key to encrypt this random number by using the National Bureau of Standards Data Encryption Standard (NBS-DES) algorithm. Then, the workstation sends the following reply in which *XXXX...* represents the encrypted random number:

```
%%LoginContinue: RandnumExchange <XXXX...>
```

In the meantime, the spooler uses the user's password from its database as the key to encrypt its random number. The spooler compares the quantity produced by this encryption with the encrypted value sent by the workstation. If the two values are equal, the user is valid, so the spooler returns the `LoginOK` reply and the printing phase of the connection can begin. If the values are unequal, the spooler replies with the message `InvalidUser` and disconnects the workstation.

Direct passthrough

In addition to providing a user authentication service, you can design the spooler/server to allow a workstation to establish a direct (or passthrough) connection to a printer. When a direct passthrough is established, the spooler does not spool files for printing, but simply passes messages back and forth between the workstation and the printer.

Direct passthrough is required when the spooler/server has renamed the printer and when a workstation needs to communicate with the printer directly. For example, certain applications can optimize the use of LaserWriter virtual memory by querying the printer at various stages of the print job and then modifying the print file to conform to the actual situation during printing.

There are two ways of accommodating such applications. The first approach, known as spooler bypass, is to leave the printer's name unaltered, so that it is available for direct access by both the workstations and the spooler/server. In this case, the spooler/server must contend with workstations attempting to gain access to the printer.

The second approach is to allow the spooler/server to rename the printer and to force the spooler/server to provide a passthrough option to a workstation that requests a direct connection to the printer. In this case, the workstation connects to the spooler in the typical manner. After completing the user authentication dialog, the workstation sends a PostScript comment to request a passthrough connection to the printer. This comment takes the following form:

```
%%?BeginPassThroughQuery
%%?EndPassThroughQuery false
```

If the spooler receiving this request does not support passthrough, it responds with `false`; if the spooler does support passthrough, it responds with `true`. After a spooler responds with `true`, it acts as a forwarding agent, passing messages between the workstation and the printer in real time.

If there are other jobs for the specified printer in the spooler's queue, the workstation requesting direct passthrough must wait until the spooler finishes all of the jobs for that printer and succeeds in establishing a new connection to the printer.

Spooler/server queue management

You can design a spooler/server application to offer spool-management functions, such as rearranging the printing order of the jobs in the queue, changing jobs from queue to queue, or deleting jobs from the queue. However, neither PAP nor the Macintosh Printing Manager are designed to accommodate queue-management functions. Therefore, you must provide such functionality through independent means.

Since the design of a mechanism that provides queue management depends on the specific characteristics and functional design of the spooler/server, Apple has not established a standard design for the queue-management functions.

A spooler/server that is implemented on a system with a user interface such as a screen, a mouse, and a keyboard could allow queue management through user input at the spooler/server station. The print spooling architecture does not specify the nature and details of this functionality. Therefore, third-party developers can add value to the spooler/servers that they develop.

For closed spooler/servers (that is, spooler/servers that do not have a user interface), you can develop a printer-queue protocol for queue management. *Figure 14-6* provides an example of a print spooling architecture that incorporates such a protocol. In this figure, *PQP* represents the printer-queue protocol. The example assumes that the user path to this queue-management service will be independent of the path from the application to the Printing Manager to PAP that is used by the actual printing operation. In the case of the Macintosh, one possibility is the use of a desk accessory and a private protocol. This approach leads to different desk accessories and different queue-management protocols for each spooler/server design.

If you are developing applications that generate PostScript code destined for PostScript printers, you should incorporate the Adobe PostScript Document Structuring Conventions in your PostScript code to ensure that the documents will be fully spoolable. If you are developing a spooler/server to pass PostScript document files to a PostScript printer in an AppleTalk network, the spooler/server must be able to interpret and respond to these comments.

Printing on a LaserWriter depends on two-way communication between the LaserWriter and the workstation. Therefore, when emulating a LaserWriter, the print spooler must be able to maintain a dialog with a workstation. The PostScript comment conventions make it possible for a document manager (such as a print spooler, server, or postprocessor) to maintain this type of a dialog without having to interpret actual PostScript code.

The comments, which are interpreted by the print spooler, are ignored by the PostScript interpreter in the printer (just as the spooler ignores the PostScript code because it cannot interpret it). The comment layer in a PostScript program is cooperative rather than enforced; that is, although the PostScript interpreter always ignores the comments, the document manager may or may not interpret them.

■ Figure 14-6 Protocol architecture for spooler/server queue management

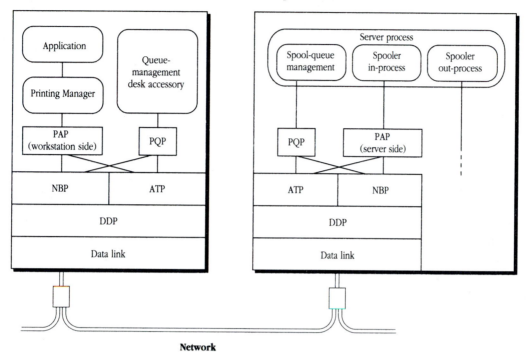

The PostScript comments:

- provide information needed by document managers for merging, editing, spooling, and accounting

- provide user-friendly comments that describe the print job and divide it into sections

- provide summary information about the resources required by the print job

- surround machine-dependent and job-specific PostScript code

- surround PostScript code that significantly changes the state of the printer

- surround PostScript code that requires a response from the printer and define the minimum valid response

About document structuring conventions

Adobe Systems has developed general document structuring conventions for PostScript comments so that they can be used universally with a variety of document managers. These conventions include three general classes of comments:

Comment type	Definition
structure	delimits structural components of a PostScript document file; delimits special text blocks; provides document and page setup information
resource	specifies resources that are required in order to print a PostScript document but that are not included within its text (for example, fonts, specific paper color, collating order, or even printer features such as size of paper trays)
query	checks the status of the printer (for example, availability of fonts, files, and virtual memory)

If a PostScript document file obeys a proper subset of these structuring conventions, it is said to be conforming to the PostScript comment connections. If a file does not follow the structuring conventions, it is said to be nonconforming and cannot be processed by AppleTalk spoolers designed to interface with PostScript printers.

The use of comments is designed to facilitate communication between document-composition systems and document managers. Therefore, the comments that make up the subset to which the document file must conform depend on the installation. For example, the document-composition system can include the resource requirements in the comment subset to ensure that these requirements are handled properly. However, if a document-composition system relies on the printing environment (the spooler and printer) to handle resource requirements appropriately, resource comments need not be included in the comment subset.

About PostScript document files

A conforming PostScript document file includes the following structural features:

■ prologue

■ script

■ pages

The *prologue* is a set of procedure definitions that define operations required by a document-composition system. The PostScript document begins with a prologue, which typically contains application-dependent definitions and which is stored in a place accessible to an application program. The prologue is used as a standard preface to each page and, generally, should not contain executable code.

The *script* is usually generated automatically by an application program. The script, which contains the data that represents a particular document, should not contain any definitions. The script of a multipage document is organized as a sequence of independent single-page descriptions.

The *pages* in a PostScript script are functionally independent of each other, but they are dependent on the definitions in the prologue. The pages can be executed in any order and rearranged without affecting the printed document. This means that the pages can be printed in parallel as long as the prologue definitions are available to each page.

A document file can contain another document file description as part of its script. An illustration embedded in a document is an example of this structure. One benefit of PostScript document descriptions is that they allow documents from different sources to be merged for final printing.

About PostScript print jobs

In understanding PostScript document files, you must understand the difference between a document file and a print job. A document file is a data representation that may be transmitted, edited, stored, spooled, or otherwise processed. A document is transmitted to a printer in a series of print jobs, each of which contains a certain type of code. There are three types of PostScript print jobs with which you should be familiar:

- standard print jobs
- queries
- exit server jobs

Standard print jobs are those jobs destined for the printer. The print spooler passes these jobs to the PostScript printer. They contain the code for the printed document.

Queries are print jobs that check printer status. Queries require a response from the printer. A print spooler must be able to respond to these queries by interpreting query comments.

Exit server jobs bypass the normal server-loop save/restore context. They contain a block of text with resources for the printer (such as fonts that are being downloaded to the printer), rather than an actual printing job. The print spooler generally stores the resources that are contained in an exit server job on its hard disk so that they are permanently available to the printer.

The job type is specified by the Job Identification comment, which is the first line of every print job. Comments consist of a percent sign (%) followed by text and terminated by a newline character. The PostScript interpreter completely ignores the comments. However, comments conforming to the file-structuring conventions can query or convey structural information to document managers. Comments that contain structural information start with %! or %%. Query comments begin with %%?. Comments that do not start with one of these three notations are ignored by document managers (as well as by the PostScript interpreters).

Comment format

The format of a PostScript comment depends on its function. Comments interpreted by document managers must be in one of the following forms. In these examples, angle brackets (< >) designate required portions of the comment, and square brackets ([ ]) indicate optional portions.

This form is used at the beginning of the PostScript job to identify the job type:

```
%!<keyword> [<argument> ...]
```

This form is used to mark a position or event in the print stream or to supply a value for a keyword:

```
%%<keyword> [<argument> ...]
```

This form is used with machine-dependent or job-dependent code and may supply values that define the specific function of the code:

```
%%Begin <keyword> [<argument> ...]
<PostScript code>
%%End <keyword>
```

This form is used for queries requiring a response from the printer:

```
%%?Begin <keyword> [<argument> ...]
<PostScript code>
%%?End <keyword> <response> [<response> ...]
```

Syntax conventions

PostScript comments must adhere to the following syntax conventions:

- The case of letters in a comment is significant.

- Each comment must begin with %.

- No spaces are allowed between the %%, %!, or %%? and the keyword, as shown in the following example:

```
%%keyword
```

- Either a colon, one space, or both a colon and a space can be used to separate a keyword and its first argument; however, the colon, when present, is not optional. These three forms are shown in the following examples:

```
%%keyword:argument
%%keyword: argument
%%keyword argument
```

- When a colon follows a keyword, no space is allowed between the keyword and the colon.

- One space should be used between the colon and the first value.

- One space should be used between values, as shown in the following example:

```
%%keyword argument value1 value2
```

- A newline character must follow immediately after the last value.

- Comments may not exceed 255 characters.

- A comment line can be continued on subsequent lines by beginning the continuation with %%+, as shown in the following example:

```
%%keyword: argument value value value value
%%+ value value value
```

- Either parentheses or double quotations marks can be used to set off values, as shown in the following examples:

```
%%keyword: argument (value)
%%keyword: argument "value"
```

- A string argument can contain spaces, provided it is enclosed in either parentheses or double quotation marks, as shown in the following examples:

```
%%keyword: (string comprising argument)
%%keyword: "string comprising argument"
```

Comments in documents

The first line of every PostScript document file must start with %!, which identifies the program as a PostScript print job. The %! introduces the Job Identification comment, which specifies the Adobe code version and, optionally, the job type, as shown in this example:

```
%!PS-Adobe-2.0
```

The Job Identification comment should be used only once in each print job. If the version is 2.0, the print job conforms to version 2.0 of the Adobe PostScript Document Structuring Conventions.

Following the Job Identification comment is the text of the document itself, interspersed with comment lines that contain structural information and other information about the document. The rest of the comments in a PostScript document file begin with %% (or %? if the file is a query job) and are followed by a keyword. If the comments require one or more values, the keyword is followed by a colon (typically) and the value or values.

Some structure comments and all query comments occur in pairs of beginning and ending comments that surround PostScript code. Comment pairs that enclose PostScript code can also enclose other comments or comment pairs.

All conforming document files must end with %%EOF, which indicates that an End Of File (EOF) message is being sent to the PostScript device.

The following general constraints apply to all document files that conform to version 2.0 of the Adobe PostScript Document Structuring Conventions. If document files do not adhere to these constraints, they are considered nonconforming and may not be handled reliably by document managers.

Prologue and script

A conforming PostScript document should be divided into a prologue and a script. Nothing can be executed in the prologue and no definitions can be included in the script. The prologue should always be designed so that it can be removed from a document file and downloaded permanently into the printer; then, when subsequent document files containing only the script are downloaded, they can depend on the preloaded prologue for definitions. See "About PostScript Document Files" earlier in this chapter for a more detailed discussion of prologues and scripts.

Pages

When the Page Marker comment is used within the body of a document, the pages in the document do not depend on each other. Each page can rely on definitions in the prologue, but a page should not depend on a state set in another page of the document. Keeping pages independent allows document managers to rearrange the document pages without affecting the execution of the document. For more information, see "About PostScript Document Files" earlier in this chapter.

Line length

A PostScript comment can contain a maximum of 255 characters. There are no constraints on the placement of line breaks. When a comment is continued on the next line, the new line should begin with the notation %%+ to indicate that the comment line is continuing. This convention is used most frequently for comments that contain a list of font names, as shown in the following example:

```
%%Document Fonts: Palatino-Roman Palatino-Bold
%%+ Palatino-Italic Palatino-Bold Italic Courier
%%+ Optima Times Geneva Chicago
```

Structure comments

This section describes the structure comments used in a PostScript document file that an AppleTalk print spooler interprets. These comments are the typical structure comments that should be included in PostScript code in order to communicate with an AppleTalk spooler. In addition, if you are creating a spooler to run in an AppleTalk network, the spooler should be able to interpret this subset of structure comments. For additional structure comments that can be included in PostScript document files, refer to *Adobe Document Structuring Conventions, Version 2.0.*

Structure comments serve the following purposes:

- They delimit the structural components of a PostScript page. For example, they mark the prologue, script, and PostScript page breaks.

- They provide document and page setup information (such as the document title, date, and page count).

- They provide a markup convention for noting the beginning and ending of particular pieces of the document file that might need to be identified for further use. For example, structure comments can be used to mark embedded font files or procedure definitions, facilitating their removal from the print job or the restructuring of the print job.

Structure comments are divided into the following three categories, which correspond to the parts of the document file in which the comments are used:

Comment type	Definition
header	precedes any noncomment PostScript program text and provides information about the document as a whole
body	interspersed throughout the PostScript program text; serves mainly to delimit the various parts of the document file
trailer	follows all the noncomment PostScript program text and provides additional information about the document as a whole

The rest of this chapter describes these categories and the comments that they include. Comment definitions are listed alphabetically under each category and include syntax and an example. The structure comments are summarized as follows:

Comment	Description
Header	
`%!PS-Adobe-2.0 [identifier]`	version number/job identifier
`%%CreationDate: text`	date assigned to document
`%%Creator: text`	name of document-composition application
`%%For: text`	person for whom document is being printed
`%%Title: text`	document title

Comment	Description *(continued)*

Body

`%%BeginExitServer: password` `%%EndExitServer`	introduction to text registered outside of normal server loop

`%%BeginProcSet: name version`
`revision`
`%%EndProcSet`
	delimiters of procedure subset

`%%Page: label ordinal`	indication of PostScript page break
`%%Trailer`	indication of boundary between script and trailer

Header comments

Header comments provide general information about the PostScript document file. They include the following types of global information for the print spooler:

- code and job identification
- document title
- document-creation date
- identification of document-composition application
- user name of document originator

◆ *Note:* A PostScript header can also include other general comments that are not needed by a print spooler (and that are not interpreted by Apple's LaserShare print spooler), but that could be used by other types of document managers. This chapter describes only those comments interpreted by LaserShare. Refer to the *Adobe Document Structuring Conventions, Version 2.0,* for other header comments.

Header comments appear at the beginning of a document file, before any executable PostScript code. Every PostScript job must begin with a Job Identification comment. The header comments continue until the first occurrence of a line that does not start with %% or %! (or until an End Comments comment; see the *Adobe Document Structuring Conventions, Version 2.0,* for a description of this comment). Header comments should be contiguous; if the document manager encounters a line that does not begin with %%, it may quit parsing for header comments. In general, header comments make up most of the document prologue, ending immediately before the PostScript document description begins.

After the Job Identification comment, the header comments can be listed in any order. However, if two or more comments contain the same keyword, the first comment (and its corresponding value) is the one that the spooler interprets. In this case, the spooler ignores the other occurrences of the comment. This process makes it possible to insert new comments at the beginning of a file without having to search for and delete the old comments embedded in the file.

Some header comments can be deferred to the trailer at the end of the document file. This practice is common for comments containing information that is not available until the end of the document, such as page counts. In this case, a comment with the same keyword and the value (`atend`) must appear in the header-comments section.

Creation Date comment

The Creation Date comment indicates the date, the time, or both the date and time assigned to the document. The text string for this comment can be in any format because the date and time are used only for informational purposes (for example, on banner pages).

Syntax: `%%CreationDate: text`

Example: `%%CreationDate: Tuesday, July 13, 1987`

Creator comment

The Creator comment identifies the creator of the document file. The creator is usually the document-composition application that was used to generate the document. However, the text string may optionally (or additionally) include the name of the person creating the document.

Syntax: `%%Creator: text`

Example: `%%Creator: Write`

For comment

The For comment specifies for whom the document is being printed. This specification is usually the user name of the person who composed the document. This information can be included in the banner page and can be used for routing the document to the person printing it.

Syntax: %%For: text

Example: %%For: Smith, John

Job Identification comment

The Job Identification comment identifies the PostScript job as a document file that conforms to version 2.0 of the Adobe PostScript Document Structuring Conventions. The Job Identification comment must be the first line of the document file. (To avoid confusion, the file should not contain any lines, other than the Job Identification comment, that begin with %!.)

This comment also identifies the PostScript job type of the document file. If no keyword is included in the comment, the job is a standard PostScript printing job. However, the comment can include a keyword that identifies the job as either a query job or an exit server job. PostScript job types are explained in "About PostScript Print Jobs" earlier in this chapter.

If the Query keyword is included in the comment, the entire job consists of PostScript queries to which the spooler must reply. "Query Comments," later in this chapter, contains a discussion of these comments.

If the ExitServer keyword is included in the comment, the job will execute PostScript exit server commands to register the contents of the file outside of the normal server-loop save/restore context. For example, the file may include code for special type fonts that will be permanently available to the printer. See "Exit Server Comments" later in this chapter for more information.

Syntax: %!PS-Adobe-2.0 [identifier]

Examples: %!PS-Adobe-2.0
          %!PS-Adobe-2.0 Query
          %!PS-Adobe-2.0 ExitServer

Title comment

The Title comment contains a text title for the document. This title can be used to identify the document on the spooler queue, or it may appear on banner pages to help route the documents. The text string used for the title may be derived from an application-level document name or from a filename.

Syntax: `%%Title: text`

Example: `%%Title: Project Status Report`

Body comments

Body comments provide structural information about the PostScript document file's organization. They act as boundary markers between parts of a document file (for example, to separate the prologue from the script or to mark PostScript page breaks). These markers enable an application to extract page subsets or to reverse the order of the pages in a PostScript document file while still maintaining the structure of the document by preserving the prologue at the beginning and the trailer at the end of the file.

Body comments can appear anywhere in a document file. Since body comments frequently delimit a block of text in a PostScript document file, they usually come in pairs, each with a beginning comment and an ending comment.

A print spooler need only interpret those PostScript comments that have a direct effect on document spooling. Therefore, the LaserShare spooler interprets only a subset of the available PostScript body comments. LaserShare ignores any comments that it does not recognize. PostScript document files generated with the Macintosh computer's LaserWriter driver include body comments that do not affect spooling and are therefore ignored by the LaserShare spooler. These comments are not documented here; the following comment descriptions are for those body comments that LaserShare interprets. Refer to the *Adobe Document Structuring Conventions, Version 2.0,* for descriptions of other body comments.

Exit Server comments

The Exit Server comments surround PostScript exit server code. The PostScript exit server code introduces a segment of PostScript code, known as a procedure set, that is to be registered outside of the normal server-loop save/restore context. The Exit Server comments immediately precede the Begin Procedure Set comment, which marks the beginning of the text block that bypasses the server loop. Rather than being an actual printing job, the procedure set introduced by Exit Server comments contains resources for the printer, such as fonts that are being downloaded. See "Procedure Set Comments" later in this chapter for further explanation.

Usually, the Exit Server comments are included only in an exit server job. An exit server job begins with the `%!PS-Adobe-2.0 ExitServer` comment and contains a procedure set with permanent resources for the printer. These resources are generally stored on the spooler's disk. "Sample Print Streams," later in this chapter, provides an example of an exit server job.

◆ *Note:* Although it is not recommended, the Exit Server comments occasionally can appear as part of a standard PostScript printing job. In this case, when LaserShare encounters the Exit Server comments, it strips them out of the print stream; if a procedure set follows the Exit Server comments, LaserShare does not store the procedure set as a permanent resource, but handles it like any standard procedure set included in a document file. See "Procedure Set Comments" and "Include Procedure Set Comment" later in this chapter.

Syntax:
```
%%BeginExitServer: password
%%EndExitServer
```

Examples:
```
%%BeginExitServer: 000000
    serverdict begin
    000000
    exitserver
%%EndExitServer
```

Page Marker comment

The Page Marker comment marks PostScript page boundaries. This comment usually occurs once for each page and provides information about the page's requirements and structure. Page Marker comments are used to preserve the page order in PostScript documents; they act as counters to track the number of pages in the document file.

The Page Marker comment requires two arguments:

Argument	Description
label	optional information to identify the page according to the document's internal numbering scheme (The text string should not contain blank space characters.)
ordinal	a number reflecting the position of the page within the body of the PostScript file (The number must be a positive integer.)

A question mark (?) can be used for either of these arguments if the number is unknown.

The Page Marker comment is used frequently. It is required so that pages do not rely on each other but do rely only on the definitions made in the prologue of the document file. A spooler should be able to physically rearrange the contents of the print file into a different order (or to print pages in parallel) based on the information in the Page Marker comment.

Syntax: `%%Page: label ordinal`

Example: `%%Page: ? 1`

Procedure Set comments

The Procedure Set comments surround a procedure set within the body of a PostScript document file. The procedure set typically represents a subset of the document prologue; the prologue can be broken into several subpackages known as procedure sets. Procedure sets can be used to define groups of routines for different imaging requirements. For example, a procedure set may include the code for generating specialized fonts.

Each procedure set is identified by the following three arguments:

Argument	Description
name	a disk filename or the PostScript name by which the procedure set is identified
version	a sequential number that uniquely identifies a procedure set from earlier or later versions with the same name
revision	a sequential number that uniquely identifies different releases within the same version of a procedure set

Frequently, the `BeginProcSet` comment is preceded by a pair of Exit Server comments indicating that the routines in the procedure set should be made permanently available to the printer. In fact, the Procedure Set comments frequently surround the code in an exit server job. See "About PostScript Print Jobs" and "Exit Server Comments," earlier in this chapter, for more information about this use of procedure sets.

Syntax:
```
%%BeginProcSet: name version revision
%%EndProcSet
```

Examples:
```
%%BeginProcSet: "exampleProcSet" 1 0
    /aSimpleProc
    {newpath 200 350 150 0 360 arc closepath fill}
    def
%%EndProcSet
```

Trailer comment

The document trailer follows the Trailer body comment and contains any postprocessing or cleanup comments, including any header comments that were deferred to the end of the document.

The use of trailer comments in PostScript document files is optional; AppleTalk spoolers are not required to recognize trailer comments. Refer to the *Adobe Document Structuring Conventions, Version 2.0*, for descriptions of the trailer comments that Adobe has defined and for details on using trailer comments.

The Trailer comment should occur once in each document file, at the end of the document script. This comment separates the script from any trailer comments that may be included in the document file. The print spooler uses the Trailer comment to confirm that the printer has received the entire print document (that is, to detect that the print job was not aborted midstream). Any conforming PostScript document file is expected to include a Trailer comment at the end of its script.

Syntax: `%%Trailer`

Example: `%%Trailer`

Resource comments

This section describes the resource comments used in PostScript document files that are interpreted by AppleTalk print spoolers. These comments are the typical resource comments that should be included in PostScript code in order to communicate with an AppleTalk spooler. In addition, if you are creating a spooler to run in an AppleTalk network, the spooler should be able to interpret these resource comments. Refer to the *Adobe Document Structuring Conventions, Version 2.0,* for additional resource comments that can be included in PostScript document files.

Resource comments (or resource requirements) specify resources that are required in order to print the PostScript document but are not embedded within its text. (Prologues, fonts, and included files are examples of such resources.) The resource comments can also specify other document requirements, which can vary from particular paper-stock form, to a specific paper color, to a specific collating order. In addition, resource comments can specify requirements for individual printer features, such as the number or size of paper trays that should be attached to the printer.

Conventions for using resource comments

Resource comments can appear anywhere in a document. They indicate that the named resource should be included in the document at the point at which the comment is inserted. The code included can be for a font, a disk file, or any other resource. If resource comments appear in the body of a document, a corresponding comment should appear in the header of the document to indicate that the entire document requires the files.

The number and types of resource comments included in a document file depend partially on the degree to which the document-composition application relies on the printing environment to provide the required resources. If the document-composition application relies on the printing environment to supply resources, few resource comments are used in the document file; however, if the document-composition application chooses to ensure that resources are available by providing them itself, more resource comments appear in the document file. (Documents with extensive resource requirements are common in large distributed networks that take print spooling for granted and that have centralized resource management.)

Definitions

AppleTalk print spoolers should be able to interpret and respond to the two resource comments summarized below. The *Adobe Document Structuring Conventions, Version 2.0,* describes additional resource comments that can be used for communicating with spoolers.

Comment	Description
`%%EOF`	indication of the end of the file
`%%IncludeProcSet: name version revision`	instruction to include the specified procedure set

End Of File comment

The End Of File comment indicates that an end-of-file message is being inserted into the print stream. Every PostScript job must begin with the Job Identification comment and end with an End Of File comment.

Syntax: `%%EOF`

Example: `%%EOF`

Include Procedure Set comment

The Include Procedure Set comment directs the spooler to insert the specified procedure set into the header of the document file. The procedure set typically represents a subset of the document prologue; the prologue can be broken into several subpackages known as procedure sets. The procedure sets can be used to define groups of routines for different imaging requirements. For example, a procedure set may include the code for generating specialized fonts.

Each procedure set is identified by the following three arguments:

Argument	Description
name	a disk filename or the PostScript name by which the procedure set is identified
version	a sequential number that uniquely identifies a procedure set from earlier or later versions with the same name
revision	a sequential number that uniquely identifies different releases within the same version of a procedure set

Syntax: `%%IncludeProcSet: name version revision`

Example: `%%IncludeProcSet: "exampleProcSet" 1 0`

Query comments

This section describes the Query comments used in a PostScript file. Query comments are incorporated in PostScript code that queries PostScript printers so that a spooler/server or other document manager can respond to the queries without having to interpret the PostScript code. Any document manager that spools to a PostScript printer must be able to interpret and respond to these query comments.

A query is any PostScript code that generates a response that is sent back to the originating computer. The originating computer uses the information in the response for decision-making. Query comments always occur in pairs that contain a beginning query and an ending query, with the keywords indicating the query type. The query pairs enclose PostScript code.

In general, queries are used to determine the current state or characteristics of the printer, including the availability of the following resources:

■ prologues

■ files

■ fonts

■ virtual memory

■ printer-specific features and enhancements

Conventions for using query comments

Any print file that embeds PostScript queries should follow the query conventions in order to be spooled successfully. "Structure Comments," earlier in this chapter, describes general guidelines for using PostScript comment conventions. This section summarizes some guidelines that apply specifically to using query comments that conform to version 2.0 of the Adobe PostScript Document Structuring Conventions.

Every query comment begins with `%%?Begin` followed by a text string of up to 256 characters and an end-of-line indicator. The end-of-line symbol is typically either a linefeed or a carriage return.

The end of a query is delimited (minimally) by the sequence `%%?End` followed by one or more keywords, an optional colon (:), and the default response to the query.

All End Query comments must include a field for a default value. The print spooler should return the default value when it cannot interpret or does not support the query. The value of the default is entirely application-dependent. The application can use the default field to determine specific information about the spooling environment and to take appropriate action.

A PostScript query should be sent as a separate print job in order to guarantee that it will be fully spoolable; that is, query comments are not valid if they are embedded in either a standard print job or an exit server job. Query jobs must begin with the Job Identification comment `%!PS-Adobe-2.0 Query` and end with `%%EOF`. A query job contains only query comments and need not contain any other standard structuring conventions. A query job can include more than one query. However, if query comments are embedded within the body of a standard print job, there is no guarantee that the spooler will handle the print job properly.

Spooler responsibilities

A print spooler should be able to extract query information from any print file that begins with `%!PS-Adobe-2.0 Query`. The spooler should fully parse a query job file until it reaches the EOF indicator.

Document spoolers must perform the following tasks in response to query conventions:

- recognize queries
- remove queries from the print stream
- send back some reply to the originating computer

If a spooler cannot interpret a query, the spooler should return the value provided as the default for the End Query comment. A spooler can minimally recognize a query by the sequence `%%?Begin` and can respond with the default. However, a spooler should make an attempt to recognize the full query keyword if possible and should respond to any query that follows the structuring conventions.

Apple's LaserShare print spooler responds to all query comments. In some cases, however, LaserShare simply returns the default, indicating that it cannot provide the information requested. These cases are noted in the comment definitions that follow.

Definitions

This section contains the query comments defined by version 2.0 of the Adobe PostScript Document Structuring Conventions. The query comments are listed alphabetically in pairs of beginning and ending comments. The descriptions include syntax and an example. Query comments are summarized as follows:

Comment	Query
`%%?BeginFeatureQuery featuretype option` `%%?EndFeatureQuery: default`	state of printer-specific feature
`%%?BeginFileQuery: filename` `%%?EndFileQuery: default`	availability of specified file
`%%?BeginFontListQuery` `%%?EndFontListQuery: default`	list of available fonts
`%%?BeginFontQuery: fontname` `%%?EndFontQuery: default`	availability of specified fonts
`%%?BeginPrinterQuery` `%%?EndPrinterQuery: default`	printer's product name, version number, and revision number
`%%?BeginProcSetQuery: name version revision` `%%?EndProcSetQuery: default`	status of procedure set
`%%?BeginQuery: identifier` `%%?EndQuery: default`	variable based on identifier
`%%?BeginVMStatusQuery` `%%?EndVMStatusQuery: default`	state of PostScript memory

Feature Query comments

The Feature Query comments obtain information about the state of a printer-specific feature, as defined by the printer's Adobe Printer Description (APD) file. LaserShare does not specifically support this query and responds to it with the default.

Syntax:
```
%%?BeginFeatureQuery: featuretype option
%%?EndFeatureQuery: default
```

Examples:
```
%%?BeginFeatureQuery: @InputSlot manualfeed
    statusdict /manualfeed known {
        statusdict /manualfeed get
    } {
        (unknown)
    } ifelse
    = flush
%%?EndFeatureQuery: unknown
```

File Query comments

The File Query comments are used to determine whether the specified file is available to the printer. The standard response consists of a line that contains either 0 or 1, where 0 indicates that the file is not present and 1 indicates that it is present.

When a file system is not available to the spooler, the File Query comments are meaningless to the spooler, which responds to them with the default. Since LaserShare does not support a file system, LaserShare always responds to these comments with the default.

Syntax:
```
%%?BeginFileQuery: filename
%%?EndFileQuery: default
```

Examples:
```
%%?BeginFileQuery: "myFile"
    myDict /myFile known = flush
%%?EndFileQuery: false
```

Font List Query comments

The Font List Query comments return a list of all fonts available to the printer. The standard response consists of a sequence of lines, each of which contains the name of a font. A newline character should terminate each line; an asterisk (*) should terminate the list itself.

LaserShare responds to this query with a list of the fonts available to the printer that it serves.

Syntax: `%%?BeginFontListQuery`
              `%%?EndFontListQuery: default`

Examples: `%%?BeginFontListQuery`
                  `FontDirectory {pop = flush} forall`
                  `/* = flush`
              `%%?EndFontListQuery`

Font Query comments

The Font Query comments are used to determine whether the specified font is available to the printer. The font name used with these comments should be an appropriate PostScript name. The standard response consists of a line that contains either 0 or 1, where 0 indicates that the font is not present and 1 indicates that it is present. LaserShare responds to this query with either 0 or 1, indicating whether the font is available to the printer.

Syntax: `%%?BeginFontQuery: fontname`
              `%%?EndFontQuery: default`

Examples: `%%?BeginFontQuery: Times`
                  `mark`
                  `/Times`
                  `{`
                   `counttomark 0 gt {`
                    `FontDirectory exch known {1} {0}ifelse = flush`
                   `}{`
                    `pop exit`
                   `} ifelse`
                  `} bind loop`
              `%%?EndFontQuery: unknown`

Global Query comments

The Global Query comments provide a general-purpose query that can serve any function not provided by one of the other query comments. For example, this query can be used to determine whether the remote device is a spooler or a printer.

Syntax: `%%?BeginQuery: identifier`
         `%%?EndQuery: default`

Examples: `%%?BeginQuery: rUaSpooler`
             `false == flush`
         `%%?EndQuery: true`

Printer Query comments

The Printer Query comments request status information about the printer, such as the printer's product name, version number, and revision number. The standard response consists of the printer's product name string, version string, and revision string, each of which should be followed by a newline character. The strings should match the information in the printer's APD file.

    LaserShare responds to this query with information about the printer that it serves.

Syntax: `%%?BeginPrinterQuery`
         `%%?EndPrinterQuery: default`

Examples: `%%?BeginPrinterQuery`
             `statusdict begin`
             `revision ==`
             `version ==`
             `product ==`
             `end`
             `flush`
         `%%?EndPrinterQuery: unknown`

Procedure Set Query comments

The Procedure Set comments check whether the specified procedure set is available to the printer. Each procedure set is identified by the following three arguments:

Argument	Description
name	a disk filename or the PostScript name by which the procedure set is identified
version	a sequential number that uniquely identifies a procedure set from earlier or later versions with the same name
revision	a sequential number that uniquely identifies different releases within the same version of a procedure set

The standard response to this query consists of a line that contains one of the following values:

Value	Description
0	indicates that the procedure set is missing
1	indicates that the procedure set is present and usable
2	indicates that the procedure set is present, but that the version does not match the version specified in the query

LaserShare responds to the Procedure Set Query comments with one of the standard responses.

Syntax:
```
%%?BeginProcSetQuery: name version revision
%%?EndProcSetQuery: default
```

Examples:
```
%%?BeginProcSetQuery: "privateDict" 25 0
     userdict /privateDict known
           {privateDict /theVersion get 25 eq
                {1}
                {2} ifelse}
          {0} ifelse
       = flush
%%?EndProcSetQuery: unknown
```

Virtual Memory Status Query comments

The Virtual Memory Status Query comments check the state of the PostScript printer's virtual memory. The standard response consists of a line that contains the results of the PostScript vmstatus operator (refer to the Adobe *PostScript Language Reference Manual, Version 2.0,* for a detailed description of this operator).

Because LaserShare does not specifically support this query, it responds with the default.

Syntax: `%%?BeginVMStatusQuery`
         `%%?EndVMStatusQuery: default`

Examples: `%%?BeginVMStatusQuery`
             `vmstatus = = = flush`
          `%%?EndVMStatusQuery: unknown`

Sample print streams

The following code is an example of the way that structure comments appear in the print stream for a standard PostScript job.

```
%!PS-Adobe-2.0
%%Title: ps test macwrite
%%Creator: MacWrite
%%CreationDate: Monday, July 13, 1987
%%For: Smith, John
%%BeginProcSet: "exampleProcSet" 1 0
       /aSimpleProc
       {newpath 200 350 150 0 360 arc closepath fill}
       def
%%EndProcSet
md begin

T T -31 -30 761 582 100 72 72 1 F F F F T T psu
(Smith, John; document: ps test macwrite)jn
0 mf
od
%%Page: ? 1
op
0 -42 xl
1 1 pen
0 0 gm
(nc 0 0 730 510 6 rc)kp
13 10 gm
(nc 0 5 730 480 6 rc)kp
bu fc
```

(continued) ➡

```
{}mark T /Helvetica-Bold /|_____Helvetica-Bold 0 rf
bn
1 setTxMode
1 fs 12.47991 fz
bu fc
2 F /|_____Helvetica-Bold fnt
bn
(this is to test PostScript)show
F T cp
%%Trailer
cd
end
%%EOF
```

The following code is an example of the way that comments appear in a print stream for a PostScript query job.

```
%!PS-Adobe-2.0 Query
%%Title: Query job to determine font status
%%?BeginFontQuery: Palatino-Roman Palatino-Bold
 mark
  /Palatino-Roman
  /Palatino-Bold
{
   counttomark 0 gt {
    FontDirectory exch known { 1 } { 0 } ifelse = flush
   }{
    pop exit
   } ifelse
 } bind loop
%%?EndFontQuery: 0 0
% send an EOF, depending on protocol
%%EOF
```

The following code is an example of the way that comments appear in a print stream for a PostScript exit server job. Exit server jobs are registered outside of the normal server loop.

```
%!PS-Adobe-2.0 Exitserver
%%Title: ps test write
%%Creator: Write
%%CreationDate: Monday, July 13, 1987
%%BeginExitServer: 000000
      serverdict begin
      000000
      exitserver
%%EndExitServer
%%BeginProcSet: "exampleProcSet" 1 0
      /aSimpleProc
      {newpath 200 350 150 0 360 arc closepath fill}
      def
%%EndProcSet
%%Trailer
%%EOF
```

Appendixes

Appendix A LocalTalk Hardware Specifications

CONTENTS

■

LocalTalk electrical characteristics

LocalTalk uses **Synchronous Data Link Control** (SDLC) frame format and a frequency modulation technique called FM-0. (**FM-0** is a bit-encoding technique that provides self-clocking.) Balanced signaling is achieved using the Electronics Industries Association (EIA) standard RS-422 hardware drivers and receivers in each of the attached devices. The transformer provides ground isolation as well as protection from static discharge. Since devices are passively connected to the trunk cable by means of a drop cable, an individual device may fail without disturbing communication along the rest of the data link's trunk cable. Devices can be added and removed from the link with only minor disruption of service.

The physical layer performs the following functions:

- bit encoding and decoding

- signal transmission and reception

- carrier sense

Bit encoding and decoding

Bits are encoded using a self-clocking technique known as FM-0 (also called biphase space). In FM-0, each bit cell (nominally, 4.34 microseconds) contains a transition at each end that provides timing information known as one bit-time. Zeros are encoded by adding transition at midcell, as shown in *Figure A-1*.

- **Figure A-1** FM-0 encoding

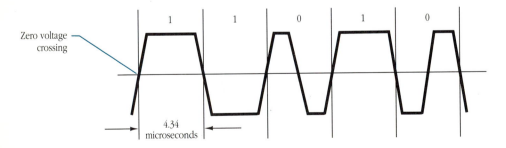

Signal transmission and reception

The use of the EIA RS-422 signaling standard for transmission and reception over LocalTalk provides significantly higher data rates over longer distances than that of the EIA RS-232-C standard. LocalTalk uses differential, balanced voltage signaling at 230.4 Kbits per second over a maximum distance of 300 meters. The balanced configuration provides better isolation from ground noise currents and is not susceptible to fluctuating voltage potentials between system grounds or common-mode electromagnetic interference (EMI).

Carrier sense

The physical layer provides an indication to the LocalTalk Link Access Protocol (LLAP) when activity is sensed on the cable. The following two indications are provided:

- SDLC frame in progress
- missing clock detected

In the preferred hardware implementation of LocalTalk, a **Zilog 8530 Serial Communications Controller** (SCC) is used. This semiconductor device provides both of the above carrier-sensing indications. The SCC chip provides a software-readable hunt bit that is set (equal to 1) while the hardware is searching for the start of the next SDLC frame. When this bit is cleared (equal to 0), the hardware is in the middle of an SDLC frame.

◆ *Note:* A frame cannot be detected until a complete flag has been transmitted on the line and recognized by the hardware. On the other hand, the synchronization pulse sent before frames and the resulting missing clock detected by receivers provide a more immediate indication of an ongoing transmission (see Chapter 1, "LocalTalk Link Access Protocol"). Missing clock indicates the detection and then the absence of a clocking signal on the line.

Electrical/mechanical specification

The following sections provide a detailed electrical/mechanical specification of LocalTalk, as well as cable and connector characteristics (these specifications correspond to Apple document number 062-0190-B).

Connection module

AppleTalk devices are connected to LocalTalk by a connection module that contains a transformer, a DB-9 or DIN-8 connector at the end of a 460-millimeter cable, and two 3-pin miniature DIN connectors, as shown in *Figure A-2*.

■ **Figure A-2** LocalTalk connection module

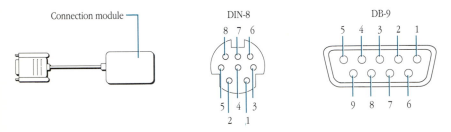
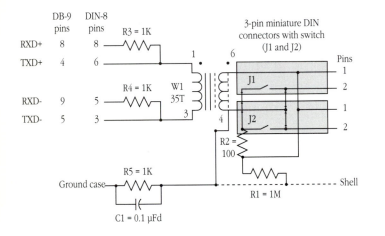

Each 3-pin connector has a coupled switch. If both connectors are used, the switches are open; if one of the connectors is not used, a 100-ohm termination resistor (R2) is connected across the line. The use of the connection module allows devices to be removed from the system by disconnecting them from the module without disturbing the operation of the bus. Resistors R3 and R4 increase the noise immunity of the receivers, while R5 and C1 isolate the frame grounds of devices and prevent ground-loop currents. The resistor (R1) provides static drain for the cable shield to ground.

LocalTalk connector

The LocalTalk connector is a miniature 3-pin connector similar to the Hosiden connector (number TCP8030-01-010). The connector pin assignment is shown in *Figure A-3*.

■ **Figure A-3** Connector pin assignment (looking into the connector)

Cable connection

The interconnecting cable is wired one-to-one to the LocalTalk connector, as shown in *Figure A-4*.

■ **Figure A-4** Interconnecting cable connection

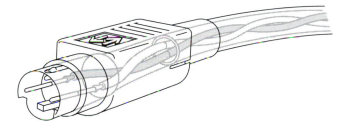

Transformer specifications

The transformer is used in the LocalTalk connection module to provide isolation between the LocalTalk cable and the devices that are connected to the cable.

The transformer is a 1:1 turns ratio transformer with tight coupling between primary and secondary and with electrostatic shielding to give excellent common node isolation, as shown in *Figure A-5*.

- **Figure A-5** Transformer specification

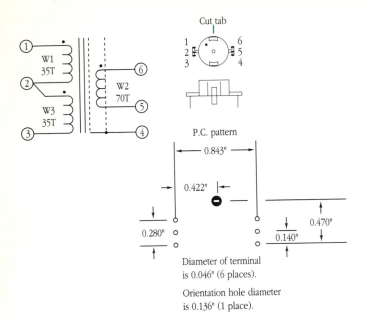

Part/Condition	Specification
core material	Siemens B65651–K000-R030 (or equivalent)
bobbin	Siemens B65652–PC1,L (or equivalent)
retaining clip	Siemens B65653–T (or equivalent)
magnetizing inductance	20 mH minimum
leakage inductance	15 μH maximum
capacitance	5 pF maximum (primary or secondary with electrostatic shield and core guarded)

The primary shielding is wound as two windings of #32 AWG wire in a series with one wound below the secondary and one above it, as shown in *Figure A-6*. The secondary shielding is a single continuous winding of #32 wire.

- **Figure A-6** Schematic and build detail

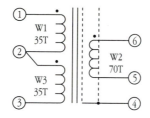

All wire #32 AWG.
Turns counts are typical and may be
adjusted for different core materials.

Environmental conditions

The transformer is designed to operate properly and to meet its specifications under the following environmental conditions:

Condition	Range
operating temperature	0° to 70° C
storage temperature	−40° to 70° C
relative humidity	5 to 95%
altitude	0 to 4572 meters

The transformer must also meet the Apple Computer shock and vibration requirements while mounted on a printed circuit board and tested to Apple specification number 062-0086.

Mechanical strength and workmanship

The transformer winding assembly, pins, mounting plate, core, and clamp must be securely mounted and rigid with respect to each other.

The pins must be easily solderable; solderability must meet the EIA RS-186-9E standard. All components must be free of undue mechanical stresses.

Appendix B LLAP Access Control Algorithms

CONTENTS

The following procedural model is written in a Pascal-like language (pseudo-code) and provided as a specification of the LocalTalk Link Access Protocol (LLAP). Any particular implementation of LLAP must follow this specification.

An equivalent specification is to be found in the following U.S. patents:

■ G. Sidhu, A. Oppenheimer, L. Kenyon, R. Hochsprung: "Local Area Network with Self-Assigned Address Method," *United States Patent No. 4,689,786,* August 25, 1987.

■ R. Hochsprung, L. Kenyon, A. Oppenheimer, G. Sidhu: "Local Area Network with Carrier Sense Collision Avoidance," *United States Patent No. 4,661,902,* April 28, 1987.

Assumptions

The model assumes that the program executes fast enough so as not to introduce any execution delay into the timing of events. Where LLAP specifies a timing delay, it is assumed to be performed by means of references to a global real function, RealTime, which returns the current time in microseconds. All timing constraints are specified as real constants.

The model assumes sequential, single-process execution of the code, especially the TransmitPacket function and the ReceivePacket procedure (and the procedures they call).

In a typical implementation, packet reception is triggered by means of a hardware interrupt. The interrupt routine then executes the ReceiveLinkMgmt function. The interrupt routine must provide a mechanism for saving valid data packets and for informing higher-level protocols of this event. However, such details are implementation-dependent and are outside the scope of *Inside AppleTalk.*

The model assumes that a transmitter continuously listens to the link while waiting for its access to the line.

Global constants, types, and variables

The following global constants, types, and variables are used throughout the model.

```
CONST
        minFrameSize = 3;          { smallest (LAP header only) frame }
        maxFrameSize = 605;        { size of largest LAP frame including FCS }
        maxDataSize = 600;         { size of largest (encapsulated) LLAP data field }
        bitTime = 4.34;            { bit time (μsec) }
        byteTime = 39.0;           { worst case single byte time (μsec) }
        minIDGtime = 400.0;        { minimum interdialog gap (μsec) }
        IDGslottime = 100.0;       { slot time of transmit backoff algorithm (μsec) }
        maxIFGtime = 200.0;        { maximum interframe gap (μsec) }
        maxDefers = 32;            { maximum defers for a single packet }
        maxCollsns = 32;           { maximum collisions for a single packet }
        lapENQ = $81;              { LAP type field value of ENQuiry frame }
        lapACK = $82;              {       ... ACKnowledgment frame }
        lapRTS = $84;              {       ... RequestToSend frame }
        lapCTS = $85;              {       ... ClearToSend frame }
        hdlcFLAG = $7E;            { value of an HDLC FLAG }
        wksTries = 20;             { Number of ENQ sets for a workstation to try }

TYPE
{ global result types from LAP functions }
        TransmitStatus = (transmitOK, excessDefers, excessCollsns, dupAddress);
        ReceiveStatus = (receiveOK, Receiving, nullReceive, frameError);
        FrameStatus = (noFrame, lapDATAframe, lapENQframe, lapACKframe,
                lapRTSframe, lapCTSframe, badframeCRC, badframeSize,
                badframeType, overrunError, underrunError);

{ Data link types and structures }
        bit = 0..1;
        bitVector = packed array [0..7] of bit;
        octet = $00..$FF;
        anAddress = octet;
        aLAPtype = octet;
        aDataField = PACKED ARRAY [1..maxDataSize] of octet;

{ Basic structure of an LLAP frame, not including FLAGs, FCS }
        frameInterpretation = (raw, structured);
        aFrame = PACKED RECORD
        CASE frameInterpretation OF
            raw: rawData : PACKED ARRAY [1..maxFrameSize] of octet;
            structured: (
                dstAddr : anAddress;
                srcAddr : anAddress;
                lapType : aLAPtype;
                dataField : a DataField)
        END;
```

```
VAR
        MyAddress : octet;                              { set during InitializeLAP }
        Backoff : INTEGER;                              { current backoff range }
        fAdrValid,                                      { MyAddress has been validated}
        FAdrInUse,                                      { Another node has same MyAddress }
        fCTSexpected : BOOLEAN;                         { RTS has been sent, CTS is valid }
        deferCount, collsnCount : INTEGER;  { optional, for statistics only }
        deferHistory, collsnHistory : bitVector;
        outgoingLength, incomingLength : INTEGER;
        outgoingPacket, incomingPacket : aFrame;
```

Hardware interface declarations

The following declarations refer to hardware-specific interfaces that are assumed to be available
to the LLAP procedures. The functions are typically bits and/or bytes contained in the relevant
hardware interface chip(s). Similarly, the procedures are expected to be represented in actual
hardware by means of control bits.

A brief description of the assumed attributes of each of these declarations follows:

Declaration	Description
CarrierSense	indicates that the hardware is sensing a frame on the link
RcvDataAvail	indicates that a data byte is available
rxDATA	identifies the next data byte available (when indicated by RcvDataAvail)
EndOfFrame	indicates that a valid closing flag has been detected
CRCok	indicates that the received frame check sequence (FCS) is correct (when EndOfFrame)
OverRun	indicates that the code did not keep up with data reception
MissingClock	indicates that a missing clock has been detected
setAddress	sets the hardware to receive frames directed to MyAddress
enableTxDrivers disableTxDrivers	control the operation of the RS-422 drivers
enableTx disableTx	control the operation of the data transmitter
txFLAG	causes the transmission of a flag

Declaration	Description
txDATA	causes the transmission of a data byte
txFCS	causes the transmission of the FCS
txONEs	causes 12–18 one-bits (1's) to be transmitted
resetRx	control the receiver
enableRx	
disableRx	
resetMissingClock	causes the MissingClock indication to be cleared

The hardware interface functions/procedures are as follows:

```
FUNCTION CarrierSense : BOOLEAN;             EXTERNAL;
FUNCTION RxDataAvail : BOOLEAN;              EXTERNAL;
FUNCTION rxDATA : octet;                     EXTERNAL;
FUNCTION EndOfFrame : BOOLEAN;               EXTERNAL;
FUNCTION CRCok : BOOLEAN;                    EXTERNAL;
FUNCTION OverRun : BOOLEAN;                  EXTERNAL;
FUNCTION MissingClock : BOOLEAN;             EXTERNAL;
PROCEDURE setAddress (addr : octet);         EXTERNAL;
PROCEDURE enableTxDrivers;                   EXTERNAL;
PROCEDURE disableTxDrivers;                  EXTERNAL;
PROCEDURE enableTx;                          EXTERNAL;
PROCEDURE txFLAG;                            EXTERNAL;
PROCEDURE txDATA (data : octet);             EXTERNAL;
PROCEDURE txFCS;                             EXTERNAL;
PROCEDURE txONEs;                            EXTERNAL;
PROCEDURE disableTx;                         EXTERNAL;
PROCEDURE resetRx;                           EXTERNAL;
PROCEDURE enableRx;                          EXTERNAL;
PROCEDURE disableRx;                         EXTERNAL;
PROCEDURE resetMissingClock;                 EXTERNAL;
```

Interface procedures and functions

The LLAP model's interface to the next higher layer (its client) is specified in terms of the following three calls:

```
PROCEDURE InitializeLLAP (hint : octet; server : boolean) ;
```

This call initializes LLAP; it is expected to be called exactly once. The `hint` parameter is a suggested starting value for the node's LocalTalk physical-link address; a value of 0 indicates that LLAP should generate a starting value. Upon return from the call, the station's actual address is available in the global variable MyAddress. If `server` is true, then the internal procedure AcquireAddress will spend extra time to determine if another node is using the selected node address.

```
FUNCTION TransmitPacket (dstParam : anAddress; typeParam : aLAPtype;
        dataField : aDataField; dataLength : INTEGER) : TransmitStatus;
```

This call is provided to transmit a packet. The internal function TransmitLinkMgmt performs the transmission link-access algorithms.

```
Procedure ReceivePacket (var dstParam : anAddress;
        var srcParam : anAddress; var typeParam : aLAPtype;
        var dataField : aDataField; var dataLength : integer);
```

This call is provided to receive a packet. The internal function ReceiveLinkMgmt implements the reception link-access algorithms.

InitializeLLAP procedure

The InitializeLLAP procedure is called to reset LLAP's global variables to known states; it calls AcquireAddress to initialize MyAddress. The following is a procedural model for the InitializeLLAP procedure:

```
PROCEDURE InitializeLLAP (hint : octet; server : BOOLEAN);

VAR
    i : INTEGER;

BEGIN
    Backoff := 0;
    { initialize history data for Backoff calculations }
    FOR i := 0 TO 7 DO BEGIN
        deferHistory[i] := 0;
        collsnHistory[i] := 0;
    END;
    deferCount := 0;   collsnCount := 0;   { optional }
    AcquireAddress (hint, server);
END;   { InitializeLAP }
```

AcquireAddress procedure

The AcquireAddress procedure specifies the dynamic node ID assignment algorithm. AcquireAddress creates and sends a control packet (of type lapENQ). When no node responds after repeated attempts, the current value of MyAddress is assumed to be safe for use by this node; the state of fAdrValid reflects this fact. If the global fAdrInUse ever becomes true after a call to AcquireAddress, another node that is using the same MyAddress has been detected. The following is a procedural model for the AcquireAddress procedure:

```
PROCEDURE AcquireAddress (hint : octet; server : BOOLEAN);

VAR
    maxTrys, trys : INTEGER;
    ENQframe : aFrame;

BEGIN
    IF hint > 0
    THEN myAddress := hint
    ELSE IF server
        THEN MyAddress := Random (127) + 128
        ELSE MyAddress := Random (127) + 1;

    setAddress (MyAddress);
    fAdrValid := FALSE;
    IF server
    THEN maxTrys := wksTries * 6    { servers try 6 times as much as workstations }
    ELSE maxTrys := wksTries;

    trys := 0;  fAdrInUse := FALSE;

    { the main loop of AcquireAddress -- repeatedly check for response to ENQ }
    WHILE trys < maxTrys DO BEGIN
        IF (TransmitPacket (MyAddress, lapENQ, ENQframe.dataField,0)
                = transmitOK) OR fAdrInUse
        THEN BEGIN
            IF server
            THEN MyAddress := Random (127) + 128
            ELSE MyAddress := Random (127) + 1;
            setAddress (MyAddress);
            trys := 0;
        END { IF }
        ELSE trys := trys + 1;
    END; { WHILE }

    fAdrValid := TRUE;
END;    { AcquireAddress }
```

TransmitPacket function

The TransmitPacket function is called by the LLAP client to send a data packet. After constructing (encapsulating) the caller's dataParam, the function calls upon TransmitLinkMgmt to perform the actual link access. A procedural model for the TransmitPacket function follows:

```
FUNCTION TransmitPacket (dstParam : anAddress; typeParam : aLAPtype;
            dataParam : aDataField; dataLength : INTEGER) : TransmitStatus;

BEGIN
    IF fAdrInUse
    THEN TransmitPacket := dupAddress
    ELSE BEGIN

        { copy interface data into frame for TransmitLinkMgmt }
        WITH outgoingPkt DO BEGIN
            dstAddr := dstParam;
            srcAddr := MyAddress;
            lapType := typeParam;
            dataField := dataParam;
        END; { WITH }

        outgoingLength := dataLength + 3;
        TransmitPacket := TransmitLinkMgmt;
    END; { ELSE }
END;    { TransmitPacket }
```

TransmitLinkMgmt function

The TransmitLinkMgmt function implements the Carrier Sense Multiple Access with Collision Avoidance (CSMA/CA) algorithm. LLAP attempts to minimize collisions by requiring transmitters to wait for the duration of the interdialog gap (IDG) plus a random period of time before sending their request-to-send (RTS) packets. Any transmitter that detects that another transmission is in progress while it is waiting must defer.

In order to minimize delays under light loading yet still minimize the probability of collisions under moderate to heavy loading, the random delay or backoff is picked in a range that is constantly adjusted based on the recently observed history of the node's attempts to access the link. Two history bytes or vectors (called deferHistory and collsnHistory in the pseudo-code below) are used to keep track of the number of deferrals and presumed collisions in the last eight link-access attempts. These 2 bytes are used to adjust a **global backoff mask** that can take on particular values between $0 and $F (specifically, binary 0, 01, 011, 0111, and 01111). These values determine the range of the random period to be picked.

The global backoff mask is adjusted at the beginning of a particular request to transmit a data packet, and it is used only the first time a node tries to transmit that data packet. Additionally, a **local backoff mask** is used during the retry attempts of a given data packet. The use of the local backoff mask has the effect of spreading out attempts to a nonlistening node, thus increasing the node's chances of receiving the packet.

The global backoff mask is adjusted as follows:

1. The mask starts with value 0.

2. If the node had to back off more than twice in the last eight attempts, the mask is extended by 1 bit up to a maximum of 4 bits (logical shift left and set the low-order bit). The backoff history byte is then set to all 0s so that further adjustments are inhibited until more history data has accumulated.

3. Else, if the node had to defer less than twice in the last eight attempts, the mask is reduced by 1 bit (logical shift right). The defer history byte is set to all 1s so that further adjustments are inhibited until more history data has accumulated.

4. Else, if neither of these apply, the mask is left unchanged.

Due to collisions and deferrals, LLAP may have to make many attempts to send a packet. The following sequence of operations is performed before making the first attempt:

1. The global backoff mask is adjusted as specified above.

2. The 2 history bytes are shifted left 1 bit, and the low-order bit of each is set to 0.

3. The global backoff mask is copied into a local backoff mask.

During each attempt to send a directed packet, the following sequence of operations is performed:

1. If the line is busy, the node waits until the end of the dialog. The low-order bit of the deferral history byte and the low-order bit of the local backoff mask are set to 1.

2. If the line is not busy, the node waits 400 microseconds. If the line becomes busy during this time, the node defers as previously described in step 1.

3. The random wait period is generated: A random number is picked and masked by (ANDed with) the local backoff mask. The node waits for 100 microseconds (the IDG slot time) multiplied by this random number. If the line becomes busy during this time, the node defers.

4. The node sends a lapRTS. If a lapCTS is received within the maximum interframe gap (IFG) or if the packet is to be broadcast, the data is sent. Otherwise, a collision is presumed; the low-order bit of the collision history byte is set to 1; the local backoff mask is shifted left 1 bit, and its low-order bit is set. The node then tries again.

5. If, during an attempt to send a packet, 32 collisions occur or the node has to defer 32 times, the attempt is aborted, and an error is returned to the LLAP client.

A procedural model for the TransmitLinkMgmt function follows.

◆ *Note:* Although the section above refers to the use of local and global backoff masks, the pseudo-code below achieves the same result by treating the local and global backoff variables as numbers, not masks, in the range 0 to 16. In either case, `Backoff` represents an upper limit of the random number to be picked.

```
FUNCTION TransmitLinkMgmt : TransmitStatus;

    VAR
        LclBackOff, i : INTEGER;
        fBroadcast, fENQ : BOOLEAN;
        xmttimer : REAL;
        rcvdframe : FrameStatus;
        RTSframe : aFrame;

    BEGIN

    WITH RTSframe DO BEGIN
        dstAddr := outgoingPacket.dstAddr;
        srcAddr := MyAddress;
        lapType := lapRTS
    END;
```

```
fBroadcast := (outgoingPacket.dstAddr = $FF);
fENQ := (outgoingPacket.lapType = lapENQ);

{ Adjust Backoff, based upon recent history }
{ Increase Backoff if we've seen a lot of collisions }
IF bitCount (collsnHistory) > 2
THEN BEGIN
    Backoff := min (max (Backoff * 2, 2), 16);
    FOR i := 0 TO 7 DO collsnHistory[i] := 0;
END { IF }

{ Decrease Backoff if we haven't had to defer very much }
ELSE IF bitCount (deferHistory) < 2
    THEN BEGIN
        Backoff := Backoff DIV 2;
        FOR i := 0 TO 7 DO deferHistory[i] := 1;
    END; { ELSE IF }

{ Shift history data }
FOR i := 7 DOWNTO 1 DO BEGIN
    collsnHistory[i] := collsnHistory[i-1];
    deferHistory[i] := deferHistory[i-1];
END; { FOR }
collsnHistory[0] := 0; deferHistory[0] := 0;

{ Initialize main loop }
deferTries := 0;        collsnTries := 0;
LclBackoff := Backoff;   transmitdone := FALSE;

{ Begin main loop }
REPEAT

    { Wait for minimum Inter-Dialog Gap time }
    REPEAT

        { Wait for any packet in progress to pass }
        IF CarrierSense
        THEN BEGIN
            { We're not really deferring, just waiting,
            but ensure minimum backoff anyway }
            LclBackoff := max (LclBackoff, 2);
            deferHistory[0] := 1;
```

(continued) ➡

```
            { Perform watchdog reset of Rx for "stuck" CarrierSense }
            xmttimer := RealTime + 1.5 * maxFrameSize * byteTime;
            REPEAT
            UNTIL ( NOT CarrierSense) OR (RealTime > xmttimer);
            IF CarrierSense THEN ResetRx;{ something's wrong, clear it }
        END; { IF }

{ We could ResetMissingClock anytime, as long as it's not within IDG
slottime of sending our packet }
ResetMissingClock;

        { Wait for minimum IDG after packet (or idle line) }
        xmttimer := RealTime + minIDGtime;
        REPEAT
        UNTIL (RealTime > xmttimer) OR CarrierSense;

UNTIL NOT CarrierSense;

{ Wait our additional backoff time, deferring to others }
{ (LclBackoff - 1) is the upper bound of the random number we pick }
xmttimer := RealTime + Random (LclBackoff) * IDGslottime;
REPEAT
UNTIL (RealTime > xmttimer) OR CarrierSense;

IF CarrierSense OR MissingClock
THEN BEGIN      { defer }
    DeferCount := DeferCount + 1;    { optional }
    LclBackoff := max (LclBackoff, 2);
    deferHistory[0] := 1;
    IF deferTries < maxDefers THEN deferTries := deferTries + 1
    ELSE BEGIN
        TransmitLinkMgmt := excessDefers;
        transmitdone := TRUE;
    END { ELSE }
END { IF }

ELSE BEGIN      { NOT (CarrierSense OR MissingClock) }
    IF fENQ
    THEN transmitFrame (outgoingPacket, 3)
    ELSE transmitFrame (RTSFrame, 3);

    { use common code to detect line state }
    fCTSexpected := TRUE;
    rcvdframe := receiveFrame;
    fCTSexpected := FALSE;
```

```
IF fAdrInUse
THEN BEGIN
    TransmitLinkMgmt := dupAddress;
    transmitDone := TRUE;
END { IF }

ELSE CASE rcvdFrame OF
    noFrame:
    IF fBroadcast
    THEN BEGIN
        transmitFrame (outgoingPacket, outgoingLength);
        TransmitLinkMgmt := transmitOK;
        transmitdone := TRUE;
    END;

    lapCTSframe :
    IF (NOT fENQ) AND (NOT fBroadCast)
    THEN BEGIN
        transmitFrame (outgoingPacket, outgoingLength);
        TransmitLinkMgmt := transmitOK;
        transmitdone := TRUE;
    END;
END; { CASE }

{ Assume collision if we don't receive the expected CTS }
IF NOT transmitdone
THEN BEGIN
    CollsnCount := CollsnCount + 1;     { optional }
    collsnHistory[0] := 1;              { update history data }
    IF collsnTries < maxCollsns
    THEN BEGIN
   ●    LclBackoff := min (max (LclBackoff*2,2),16);
        collsnTries := collsnTries + 1;
    END { IF }
    ELSE BEGIN
        TransmitLinkMgmt := excessCollsns;
        transmitdone := TRUE;
    END { ELSE }
END { IF NOT ... }
END { ELSE NOT ... }

UNTIL transmitdone;

END;   { TransmitLinkMgmt }
```

TransmitFrame procedure

The TransmitFrame procedure is responsible for putting data on the link. Certain details, such as how a flag is sent and a packet terminated, which includes sending the frame check sequence (FCS), are not explicitly stated here since they are hardware-dependent.

```
PROCEDURE TransmitFrame (VAR frame : aFrame; framesize : INTEGER);

VAR
    i : INTEGER;
    bittimer : REAL;

BEGIN

    disableRx;

    { Generate the synchronizing pulse -- really required only before RTS frames}
    bittimer := RealTimer + 1.5 * bitTime;
    enableTxDrivers;
    WHILE RealTime < bittimer DO BEGIN
    END;
    disableTxDrivers;
    bittimer := RealTimer + 1.5 * bitTimer;
    WHILE RealTime < bittimer DO BEGIN
    END;

    { Start the actual frame transmission }
    enableTxDrivers;
    enableTx;
    txFLAG;   txFLAG;        { Output 2 opening FLAG's }
    FOR i := 1 TO framesize DO
        TxData (frame.rawData[i]);
    txFCS;                    { Send the FCS }
    txFLAG;                   { Send the trailing FLAG }
    txONEs;                   { Send 12 1's for extra clocks }
    disableTxDrivers;

    { reestablish default listening mode }
    resetMissingClock;
    enableRx;

END;    { TransmitFrame }
```

ReceivePacket procedure

The ReceivePacket procedure given below is the primary interface routine to higher levels. This procedure is described as if synchronously called by the user. In many implementations, the lower-level ReceiveLinkMgmt function would be invoked by an interrupt routine.

```
PROCEDURE ReceivePacket ( VAR dstParam : anAddress; VAR srcParam : anAddress;
                    VAR typeParam : aLAPtype; VAR dataParam : aDataField;
                    VAR dataLength : INTEGER);

VAR
    status : ReceiveStatus;

BEGIN

    REPEAT
        status := ReceiveLinkMgmt;
        IF status = receiveOK
        THEN BEGIN
            WITH incomingPacket DO BEGIN
                dstParam := dstAddr;
                srcParam := srcAddr;
                typeParam := lapType;
                dataParam := dataField;
            END; { WITH }
            dataLength := incomingLength;
        END; { IF }
    UNTIL status = receiveOK

END;    { ReceivePacket }
```

ReceiveLinkMgmt function

The ReceiveLinkMgmt function implements the receiver side of LLAP; it would typically be called from an interrupt routine rather than from ReceivePacket.

```
FUNCTION ReceiveLinkMgmt : ReceiveStatus;

VAR
    status : ReceiveStatus;
    CTSframe, ACKframe : aFrame;
```

(continued) ➡

```
BEGIN

    status := Receiving;
    WHILE status = Receiving DO
        CASE ReceiveFrame OF
            badframeCRC, badframeSize, badframeType, underrunError, overrunError:
            status := frameError;

            lapENQframe :
            IF fAdrValid
            THEN BEGIN
                ACKframe.dstAddr := incomingPacket.srcAddr;
                ACKframe.srcAddr := MyAddress;
                ACKframe.lapType := lapACK;
                TransmitFrame (ACKframe,3);
                status := nullReceive;
            END { IF }
            ELSE BEGIN
                fAdrInUse := TRUE;
                status := nullReceive;
            END; { ELSE }

            lapRTSframe :
            IF fAdrValid
            THEN BEGIN
                CTSframe.dstAddr := incomingPacket.srcAddr;
                CTSframe.srcAddr := MyAddress;
                CTSframe.lapType := lapCTS;
                TransmitFrame (CTSframe,3);
            END { IF }
            ELSE BEGIN
                fAdrInUse := TRUE;
                status := nullReceive;
            END; { ELSE }

            lapDATAframe :
            IF fAdrValid
            THEN status := receiveOK
            ELSE BEGIN
                fAdrInUse := TRUE;
                status := nullReceive;
            END; { ELSE }

            noFrame:
            status := nullReceive;
```

```
        END; { CASE }
    ReceiveLinkMgmt := status;

END; { ReceiveLinkMgmt }
```

ReceiveFrame function

The ReceiveFrame function is responsible for interacting with the hardware.

```
FUNCTION ReceiveFrame : FrameStatus;

VAR
    rcvtimer : REAL;

BEGIN
    { Provide timeout for idle line }
    rcvtimer := RealTime + maxIDGtime;
    REPEAT
    UNTIL CarrierSense OR (RealTime > rcvtimer);
    IF NOT CarrierSense
    THEN BEGIN
        ReceiveFrame := noFrame;
        EXIT (ReceiveFrame);
    END; { IF }

    { Line is not idle, check if frame is for us }
    rcvtimer := RealTime + maxIFGtime;      {maxIFGtime is a good timeout value}
    REPEAT
    UNTIL RxCharAvail OR (RealTime > rcvtimer);
    IF RxCharAvail
    THEN BEGIN                    { receive frame }
        error := FALSE;   framedone := FALSE;   incomingLength := 0;
        REPEAT
            rcvtimer := RealTime + 1.5 * byteTime;
            REPEAT
            UNTIL RxCharAvail OR (RealTime > rcvtimer);
            IF RxCharAvail
            THEN BEGIN
                IF OverRun
                THEN BEGIN
                    ReceiveFrame := overrunError;
                    error := TRUE;
                END { IF OverRun }
```

(continued) ➡

```
        ELSE IF incomingLength < maxFrameSize
            THEN BEGIN
                incomingLength := incomingLength + 1;
                incomingPacket.rawData[incomingLength] := rxDATA;
            END { ELSE IF }
            ELSE BEGIN
                ReceiveFrame := badframeSize;
                error := TRUE;
            END; { ELSE }

        IF EndOfFrame THEN
            IF CRCok
            THEN BEGIN
                incomingLength := incomingLength - 2;    { account for CRC }
                IF incomingLength < minFrameSize
                THEN BEGIN
                    ReceiveFrame := badframeSize;
                    error := TRUE;
                END { IF incomingLength ... }
                ELSE framedone := TRUE;
            END { IF CRCok }
            ELSE BEGIN        { bad CRC }
                ReceiveFrame := badframeCRC;
                error := TRUE;
            END;
    END { IF RxCharAvail }

    ELSE BEGIN        { RealTime > rcvtimer }
        ReceiveFrame := underrunError;
        error := TRUE;
    END { ELSE }

UNTIL framedone OR error;

{ Check on validity of the frame }
IF framedone THEN
    IF fAdrValid THEN        { if our address if valid, check on actual type }
        IF incomingPacket.lapType < $80
        THEN ReceiveFrame := lapDATAframe;
        ELSE CASE incomingPacket.lapType OF
            lapENQ :
            ReceiveFrame := lapENQframe;

            lapACK :
            BEGIN
                ReceiveFrame := lapACKframe;
                fAdrInUse := TRUE;
            END; { lapACK }
```

```
                    lapRTS :
                    ReceiveFrame := lapRTSframe;

                    lapCTS :
                    IF fCTSexpected
                    THEN ReceiveFrame := lapCTSframe
                    ELSE BEGIN
                        fAdrInUse := TRUE;
                        ReceiveFrame := badframeType
                    END; { ELSE }

                    OTHERWISE
                    ReceiveFrame := badframeType;
                END { CASE }

         ELSE IF incomingPacket.rawData[1] <> $FF
             THEN BEGIN
                 fAdrInUse := TRUE;      { we received something we didn't expect }
                 ReceiveFrame := noFrame;
             END { ELSE IF }
    END { IF RxCharAvail }
    ELSE ReceiveFrame := noFrame;    { no CharAvail }

    resetRx;
    resetMissingClock;

END;    { ReceiveFrame }
```

Miscellaneous functions

The following low-level routines are referenced by the foregoing procedural specification.

```
FUNCTION bitCount (bits : bitVector ) : INTEGER;
VAR
    i, sum : INTEGER;

BEGIN
    sum := 0;
    FOR i := 0 TO 7 DO
        sum := sum + bits[i];
    bitCount := sum
END;    { bitCount }
```

(continued) ➡

```
FUNCTION min (val1, val2 : INTEGER) : INTEGER;
BEGIN
    IF val1 < val2
    THEN min := val1
    ELSE min := val2
END;    { min }

FUNCTION max (val1, val2 : INTEGER) : INTEGER;
BEGIN
    IF val1 > val2
    THEN max:= val1
    ELSE max:= val2
END;    { max }

FUNCTION Random (maxval : INTEGER) : INTEGER;
BEGIN
    { this function is implemented as any "good" pseudorandom number generator
      that produces a result in the range 0..maxval-1 }
END;
```

SCC implementation

One of the integrated circuits used in the implementation of LocalTalk is the Zilog 8530 Serial
Communications Controller (SCC). This section explains how the hardware interface routines
declared in the foregoing sections could be implemented with that device. This explanation does
not imply that the SCC must be used in the implementation of LLAP. Many other devices can be
employed effectively to implement LLAP. All of the following registers and bit names are used by
Zilog in its SCC documentation.

Declaration	Description
CarrierSense	indicates that the hardware is sensing a frame on the link; corresponds to the complement of the SYNC/HUNT bit in RR0
RcvDataAvail	indicates that a data byte is available; corresponds to the Rx Character Available bit in RR0
rxDATA	identifies the next data byte available (RR8)
EndOfFrame	indicates that a valid closing flag has been detected; the EndOfFrame bit in RR1

Declaration	Description *(continued)*
CRCok	indicates that the received frame's FCS is correct (when EndOfFrame is true); the complement of the CRC/Framing Error bit in RR1
OverRun	indicates that the code did not keep up with data reception; the Rx Overrun Error bit in RR1
MissingClock	indicates that the hardware has detected a missing transition on the link; the One Clock Missing bit in RR10
setAddress	sets the hardware to receive frames whose destination address matches MyAddress; sets WR6 in the SCC
enableTxDrivers disableTxDrivers	control the operation of the RS-422 drivers; the drivers would generally be controlled by one of the SCC's output bits (on the Macintosh computer, it's the RTS bit in WR5)
enableTx disable Tx	control the operation of the data transmitter by means of the Tx Enable bit in WR5
txFLAG	causes the automatic transmission of a flag at frame opening when Tx Enable is set; however, code must delay long enough to cause the extra flag; the trailing flag is generated automatically at frame end as part of the Tx Underrun processing
txDATA	causes the transmission of a data byte (WR8)
txFCS	causes the automatic transmission of the FCS by letting Tx Underrun occur
txONEs	causes 12–18 one-bits (1's) to be sent by disabling the SCC transmitter (setting TX Enable to 0) while leaving the RS-422 drivers on and delaying
resetRx enableRx disableRx	control the receiver by means of the Rx Enable bit in WR3; resetRx should also flush the receive FIFO
resetMissingClock	causes the MissingClock indication to be cleared by a Reset Missing Clock command via WR14

CRC-CCITT calculation

The CRC-CCITT (cyclic-redundancy check Consultative Committee on International Telephone & Telegraph) algorithm, used to determine the FCS, uses the standard CRC-CCITT polynomial:

$$G(x) = x^{16} + x^{12} + x^5 + 1$$

The CRC-CCITT FCS value corresponding to a given packet is calculated based on the following polynomial division identity:

$$\frac{M(x)}{G(x)} = Q(x) + \frac{R(x)}{G(x)}$$

where:

$M(x)$ = binary polynomial (corresponding to the packet after complementing its first 16 bits)

$R(x)$ = remainder after dividing $M(x)$ by the generating polynomial (its coefficients are the bits of the CRC)

$Q(x)$ = quotient after dividing $M(x)$ by the generating polynomial (its coefficients are ignored when calculating the CRC)

At the transmitter, the implementation of the CRC for the FCS field computes the CRC starting with the first bit of the destination node ID following the opening flag and stopping at the end of the data field. The FCS field is equal to the 1's complement of the transmitter's remainder. The same calculation is performed at the receiver; however, the FCS bytes themselves are included in the computation. The result of a correctly received transmission is then the binary constant 0001110100001111 ($x^{15}...x^0$). This constant is a characteristic of the divisor.

In addition to the division of the data's binary value by the generating polynomial to yield the remainder for checking, the following manipulations occur:

■ The dividend is initially preset to all 1's before the computation begins, which has the effect of complementing the first 16 bits of the data.

■ The transmitter's remainder is inverted bit-by-bit (FCS field) as it is sent to the receiver. The high-order bit of the FCS field is transmitted first ($x^{15}...x^0$).

If the receiver computation does not yield the binary constant 0001110100001111, the packet is discarded.

Appendix C **AppleTalk Parameters**

CONTENTS

■

This appendix summarizes various numerical quantities used in the AppleTalk protocols. This information is organized into subsections, one for each relevant protocol. A $ symbol is used to denote hexadecimal; a % symbol represents binary numbers. All other numerals are decimal.

LLAP parameters

This section provides values for the LLAP type field, timing constants used by LLAP, and LLAP frame parameters.

LLAP type field values	Description
$00	invalid LLAP type value (do not use)
$01 through $7F	valid LLAP type values for use in LLAP client packets
$01 through $0F	reserved for Apple Computer's use only
$01	DDP short-form header packet
$02	DDP extended-form header packet
$0F	experimental LLAP packet (reserved for Apple Computer's use only)
$80 through $FF	reserved for LLAP control frames
$81	lapENQ packet
$82	lapACK packet
$84	lapRTS packet
$85	lapCTS packet

■ **Figure C-1** LLAP type field values

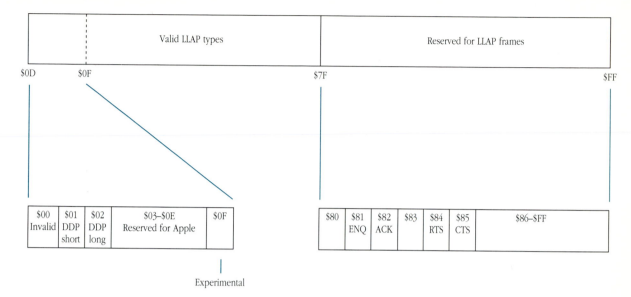

LLAP timing constant	Value
interframe gap (IFG)	less than 200 microseconds
interdialogue gap (IDG)	at least 400 microseconds
IDG slot time	100 microseconds

LLAP frame parameter	Description
flag byte used for framing an LLAP packet	%01111110
number of flag bytes needed at the start of a frame	2 or more flag bytes
number of bits in abort sequence	12–18 bits
maximum number of data bytes in LLAP packet (not including LLAP header, frame preamble, and frame trailer)	600 bytes

AARP parameters

AARP packet parameter	Description
SNAP protocol discriminator for AARP packets	$00000080F3
broadcast destination address for AARP packets on Ethernet	$090007FFFFFF
broadcast destination address for AARP packets on token ring	$C00040000000

AARP command	Value
AARP Request	1
AARP Response	2
AARP Probe	3

EtherTalk and TokenTalk parameters

Packet parameter	Description
SNAP protocol discriminator for AppleTalk packets	$080007809B
broadcast destination address for AppleTalk packets on Ethernet	$090007FFFFFF (EtherTalk) $C00040000000 (TokenTalk)

AARP values as used for EtherTalk	Description
hardware type indicating Ethernet	1
hardware type indicating token ring	2
protocol type indicating AppleTalk	$809B
Ethernet hardware address length	6 bytes
AppleTalk protocol address length	4 bytes (high byte must be 0)
AARP probe retransmission interval	1/5 of a second
AARP probe retry count	10

■ **Figure C-2** Zone multicast addresses

	ELAP	TLAP
AppleTalk broadcast address	$090007FFFFFF	$C00040000000
Zone multicast addresses	$090007000000	$C00000000800
When used with the address		$C00000001000
assignment algorithm described		$C00000002000
in Chapter 8, the first address		$C00000004000
in each list represents a[0].		$C00000008000
		$C00000010000
		$C00000020000
	253 addresses	$C00000040000
		$C00000080000
		$C00000100000
		$C00000200000
		$C00000400000
		$C00000800000
		$C00001000000
		$C00002000000
		$C00004000000
		$C00008000000
		$C00010000000
	$0900070000FC	$C00020000000

DDP parameters

This section provides values for DDP packet parameters, protocol type fields, and socket numbers.

DDP packet parameter	Description
LLAP type value for short-form header DDP packet	1
LLAP type value for extended-form header DDP packet	2
maximum number of data bytes in a DDP packet	586 bytes

DDP type field value	Description
$00	invalid DDP type value (do not use)
$01 through $FF	valid DDP type values for use in DDP client packets
$01 through $0F	reserved for Apple Computer's use only
$01	RTMP Response or Data packet
$02	NBP packet
$03	ATP packet
$04	AEP packet
$05	RTMP Request packet
$06	ZIP packet
$07	ADSP packet

■ **Figure C-3** DDP type field values

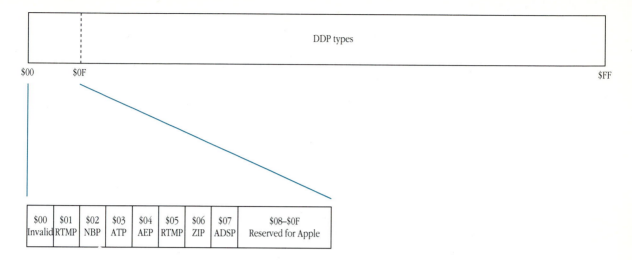

$00 Invalid	$01 RTMP	$02 NBP	$03 ATP	$04 AEP	$05 RTMP	$06 ZIP	$07 ADSP	$08–$0F Reserved for Apple

DDP socket value	Description
$00	invalid (do not use)
$FF	invalid (do not use)
$01 through $FE	valid DDP sockets
$01 through $7F	statically assigned sockets
$01 through $3F	reserved for Apple Computer's use only
$01	RTMP socket
$02	names information socket (NIS)
$04	Echoer socket
$06	zone information socket (ZIS)
$40 through $7F	experimental use only (do not use in released products)

■ **Figure C-4**   DDP socket numbers

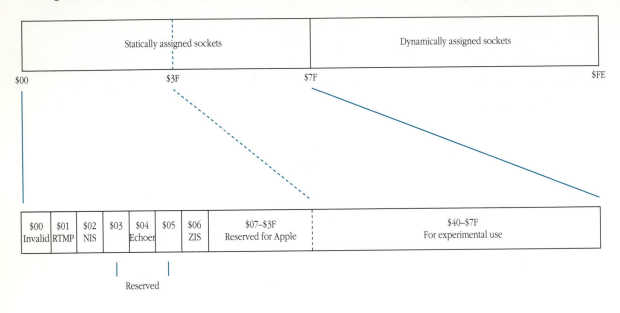

━━

RTMP parameters

RTMP packet parameter	Description
DDP type value for RTMP Response and Data packets	1
DDP type value for RTMP Request packets	5
RTMP Request packet function field value	1
RTMP Route Data Request packet function value	2 (split horizon processed) 3 (no split horizon processing)

RTMP timer value	Description
send-RTMP timer	10 seconds
validity timer	20 seconds
timer for aging A-ROUTER in a nonrouter node	50 seconds

Miscellaneous value	Description
RTMP listening socket	socket 1
maximum number of hops supported	16 hops

AEP parameters

AEP socket parameter	**Number**
AEP socket	socket 4

AEP packet parameter	**Description**
DDP type value for AEP packets	4
Echo function values	1 = Echo Request
	2 = Echo Reply
maximum data size	585 bytes

NBP parameters

NBP socket parameter	**Description**
names information socket (NIS)	socket 2
maximum number of characters in object, type, or zone fields	32 characters

Wildcard symbol	**Description**
*	used only in the zone field of an entity name to mean the zone of the packet's sender
=	used as the object and/or type field of an entity name to mean all objects and/or all types (cannot be used as the zone field)
≈	characters within object and/or type field used to match zero or more characters. Maximum of one per field.

NBP packet parameter	**Description**
DDP type value for NBP packets	2
NBP control field value	1 = BrRq
	2 = LkUp
	3 = LkUp-Reply
	4 = FwdReq

ZIP parameters

ZIP socket parameter	Number
zone information socket	socket 6

ZIP function	Value
ZIP Query	1
ZIP Reply	2
ZIP GetNetInfo	5
ZIP GetNetInfoReply	6
ZIP Extended Reply	8
ZIP Notify	7
ZIP GetMyZone	7 (in ATP user bytes)
ZIP GetZoneList	8 (in ATP user bytes)
ZIP GetLocalZones	9 (in ATP user bytes)

ZIP timer value	Description
Query retransmission time	10 seconds
ZIP bringback time	10 minutes

ATP parameters

ATP packet parameter	Description
DDP type value for ATP packets	3
function code values	%01 = TReq
	%10 = TResp
	%11 = TRel
maximum size of data in ATP packet	578 bytes

ATP TRel timer indicator	Value
000	30 seconds
001	1 minute
100	8 minutes

PAP parameters

PAP type	Value
OpenConn	1
OpenConnReply	2
SendData	3
Data	4
Tickle	5
CloseConn	6
CloseConnReply	7
SendStatus	8
StatusReply	9

PAP packet parameter	Description
maximum data size	512 bytes
maximum length of status string	255 bytes (not including the length byte)

PAP timer value	Description
OpenConn request ATP retry timer	2 seconds
tickle timer	60 seconds
connection timer	2 minutes
SendData request retry timer	15 seconds

PAP retry count value	Description
OpenConn request retry count	5

PAP result code	Description
PrinterBusy	$FFFF

ASP parameters

SPFunction	Value
CloseSession	1
Command	2
GetStatus	3
OpenSess	4
Tickle	5
Write	6
WriteContinue	7
Attention	8

ASP timer value	Description
tickle timer	30 seconds
session maintenance timer	2 minutes

Decimal value	Hex value	SPError
0	($00)	NoError*
–1066	$FBD6	BadVersNum†
–1067	$FBD5	BufTooSmall†
–1068	$FBD4	NoMoreSessions*
–1069	$FBD3	NoServers†
–1070	$FBD2	ParamErr*
–1071	$FBD1	ServerBusy†
–1072	$FBD0	SessClosed*
–1073	$FBCF	SizeErr*
–1074	$FBCE	TooManyClients‡
–1075	$FBCD	NoAck‡

* This error can be returned on both workstation and server ends.

† This error can be returned on the workstation end only.

‡ This error can be returned on the server end only.

The ASP version number described in Chapter 11, "AppleTalk Session Protocol," is version $0100.

The values −1060 to 1065 are reserved for implementation-dependent errors. All other values are invalid in this field. The following error codes are the only ones actually transmitted through ATP (on the OpenSession call): NoError, BadVersNum, and ServerBusy.

ADSP parameters

ADSP control code	Value
Probe or Acknowledgment	0
Open Connection Request	1
Open Connection Acknowledgment	2
Open Connection Request and Acknowledgment	3
Open Connection Denial	4
Close Connection Advice	5
Forward Reset	6
Forward Reset Acknowledgment	7
Retransmit Advice	8

ADSP packet parameter	Description
DDP type value for ZIP packets	7
maximum data size	572 bytes

AFP parameters

Each function code is a 16-bit integer sent in the packet high-byte first.

Decimal value	Hex value	AFP function
1	$01	ByteRangeLock
2	$02	CloseVol
3	$03	CloseDir
4	$04	CloseFork

(continued) ➡

Decimal value	Hex value	AFP function *(continued)*
5	$05	CopyFile
6	$06	CreateDir
7	$07	CreateFile
8	$08	Delete
9	$09	Enumerate
10	$0A	Flush
11	$0B	FlushFork
14	$0E	GetForkParms
15	$0F	GetSrvrInfo
16	$10	GetSrvrParms
17	$11	GetVolParms
18	$12	Login
19	$13	LoginCont
20	$14	Logout
21	$15	MapID
22	$16	MapName
23	$17	MoveAndRename
24	$18	OpenVol
25	$19	OpenDir
26	$1A	OpenFork
27	$1B	Read
28	$1C	Rename
29	$1D	SetDirParms
30	$1E	SetFileParms
31	$1F	SetForkParms
32	$20	SetVolParms
33	$21	Write
34	$22	GetFileDirParms
35	$23	SetFileDirParms
36	$24	ChangePassword
37	$25	GetUserInfo
48	$30	OpenDT
49	$31	CloseDT
51	$33	GetIcon
52	$34	GetIconInfo
53	$35	AddAPPL

Decimal value	Hex value	AFP function *(continued)*
54	$36	RmvAPPL
55	$37	GetAPPL
56	$38	AddComment
57	$39	RmvComment
58	$3A	GetComment
192	$C0	AddIcon

Each call returns a result code, which is a 4-byte integer.

Decimal value	Hex value	FPError
0	$0	NoErr
−5000	$FFFFEC78	AccessDenied
−5001	$FFFFEC77	AuthContinue
−5002	$FFFFEC76	BadUAM
−5003	$FFFFEC75	BadVersNum
−5004	$FFFFEC74	BitmapErr
−5005	$FFFFEC73	CantMove
−5006	$FFFFEC72	DenyConflict
−5007	$FFFFEC71	DirNotEmpty
−5008	$FFFFEC70	DiskFull
−5009	$FFFFEC6F	EOFErr
−5010	$FFFFEC6E	FileBusy
−5011	$FFFFEC6D	FlatVol
−5012	$FFFFEC6C	ItemNotFound
−5013	$FFFFEC6B	LockErr
−5014	$FFFFEC6A	MiscErr
−5015	$FFFFEC69	NoMoreLocks
−5016	$FFFFEC68	NoServer
−5017	$FFFFEC67	ObjectExists
−5018	$FFFFEC66	ObjectNotFound
−5019	$FFFFEC65	ParamErr
−5020	$FFFFEC64	RangeNotLocked
−5021	$FFFFEC63	RangeOverlap
−5022	$FFFFEC62	SessClosed
−5023	$FFFFEC61	UserNotAuth

(continued) ➡

Decimal value	Hex value	FPError *(continued)*
–5024	$FFFFEC60	CallNotSupported
–5025	$FFFFEC5F	ObjectTypeErr
–5026	$FFFFEC5E	TooManyFilesOpen
–5027	$FFFFEC5D	ServerGoingDown
–5028	$FFFFEC5C	CantRename
–5029	$FFFFEC5B	DirNotFound
–5030	$FFFFEC5A	IconTypeError
–5031	$FFFFEC59	VolLocked
–5032	$FFFFEC58	ObjectLocked

Appendix D **Character Codes**

Several AppleTalk protocols utilize character string entity names, which can be composed of any 8-bit characters. Their representations are exactly the same as those used by the Macintosh and are shown in *Table D-1* below.

■ **Table D-1** Character set mapping used in AppleTalk

First digit

Second digit	0	1	2	3	4	5	6	7	8	9	A	B	C	D	E	F
0	NUL	DLE	SPACE	0	@	P	`	p	Ä	ê	†	∞	¿	–		
1	SOH	DC1	!	1	A	Q	a	q	Å	ë	°	±	¡	—		
2	STX	DC2	"	2	B	R	b	r	Ç	í	¢	≤	¬	"		
3	ETX	DC3	#	3	C	S	c	s	É	ì	£	≥	√	"		
4	EOT	DC4	$	4	D	T	d	t	Ñ	î	§	¥	ƒ	'		
5	ENQ	NAK	%	5	E	U	e	u	Ö	ï	•	µ	≈	'		
6	ACK	SYN	&	6	F	V	f	v	Ü	ñ	¶	δ	Δ	÷		
7	BEL	ETB	'	7	G	W	g	w	á	ó	ß	Σ	«	◊		
8	BS	CAN	(	8	H	X	h	x	à	ò	®	∏	»	ÿ		
9	HT	EM	)	9	I	Y	i	y	â	ô	©	π	…			
A	LF	SUB	*	:	J	Z	j	z	ä	ö	™	∫	␣			
B	VT	ESC	+	;	K	[	k	{	ã	õ	´	ª	À			
C	FF	FS	,	<	L	\	l	|	å	ú	¨	º	Ã			
D	CR	GS	-	=	M	]	m	}	ç	ù	≠	Ω	Õ			
E	SO	RS	.	>	N	^	n	~	é	û	Æ	æ	Œ			
F	SI	US	/	?	O	_	o	DEL	è	ü	Ø	ø	œ			

␣ — Stands for a nonbreaking space, the same width as a digit.

An implementation of the AppleTalk protocols such as NBP and ZIP that use character string names must often perform string comparison. Throughout AppleTalk, this comparison is done in a case-insensitive manner (that is, K = k), and it must also be done in a diacritical-sensitive manner (that is, e ≠ é ≠ è). The mapping in *Table D-2* shows the rules for uppercase equivalence of characters in AppleTalk. For example, lowercase ç matches uppercase Ç in a string comparison. Any character that does not appear in this table has no uppercase equivalent in AppleTalk and therefore can only match itself. Note that this mapping does not exactly conform to the standards used in all human languages. In certain languages, the uppercase equivalent of é is E; in other languages (and in AppleTalk), it is É.

■ **Table D-2** Lowercase-to-uppercase mapping in AppleTalk

Lowercase		Uppercase equivalent	
Value	Character	Value	Character
$61	a	$41	A
$62	b	$42	B
⋮	⋮	⋮	⋮
$7A	z	$5A	Z
$88	à	$CB	À
$8A	ä	$80	Ä
$8B	ã	$CC	Ã
$8C	å	$81	Å
$8D	ç	$82	Ç
$8E	é	$83	É
$96	ñ	$84	Ñ
$9A	ö	$85	Ö
$9B	õ	$CD	Õ
$9F	ü	$86	Ü
$BE	æ	$AE	Æ
$BF	ø	$AF	Ø
$CF	œ	$CE	Œ

Glossary

AARP: see AppleTalk Address Resolution Protocol.

abort sequence: 12–18 1's (one bits) at the end of an LLAP frame.

access modes: a set of permissions used by AFP to regulate access to a file; AFP supports four access modes: read, write, read-write, and none.

access privileges: the privileges given to or withheld from users to open and make changes to a directory and its contents. Through the setting of access privileges, you control access to the information that is stored on a file server.

Acknowledge control packet: an LLAP packet sent in response to an Enquiry control packet, indicating that the requested LLAP node number is already in use.

Address Mapping Table (AMT): a collection of protocol-to-hardware address mappings for each protocol stack that a node supports. The AMT is updated by AARP to ensure that current addressing information is available.

address resolution: the translation of node addresses between different node-numbering schemes.

ADSP: see AppleTalk Data Stream Protocol.

AEP: see AppleTalk Echo Protocol.

AFI: see AppleTalk Filing Interface.

AFP: see AppleTalk Filing Protocol.

AFP-file-system-visible entity: a network-visible entity accessible through the AFI.

AFP translator: workstation software that translates native file system commands to AFP calls; the AFP translator obtains the commands from the NFI and translates them to the AFI for transmission over the network to a file server.

ALO transaction: see at-least-once transaction.

AMT: see Address Mapping Table.

ancestor: a directory that is along the path to a destination CNode (file or directory), known as the descendent.

AppleTalk Address Resolution Protocol (AARP): the protocol that reconciles addressing discrepancies in networks that support more than one set of protocols. For example, by resolving the differences between an Ethernet addressing scheme and the AppleTalk addressing scheme, AARP facilitates the transport of DDP packets over a high-speed EtherTalk connection.

AppleTalk Data Stream Protocol (ADSP): a connection-oriented protocol that provides a reliable, full-duplex, byte-stream service between any two sockets in an AppleTalk internet. ADSP ensures in-sequence, duplicate-free delivery of data over its connections.

AppleTalk Echo Protocol (AEP): a simple protocol that allows a node to send a packet to any other node in an AppleTalk internet and to receive an echoed copy of that packet in return.

AppleTalk Filing Interface (AFI): the interface to an AFP file server through which workstations can gain access to server volumes, files, directories, and forks.

AppleTalk Filing Protocol (AFP): the presentation-layer protocol that allows users to share data files and application programs that reside in a shared resource, known as a file server.

AppleTalk Session Protocol (ASP): a general-purpose protocol that uses the services of ATP to provide session establishment, maintenance, and teardown, along with request sequencing.

AppleTalk Transaction Protocol (ATP): a transport protocol that provides a loss-free transaction service between sockets. This service allows exchanges between two socket clients in which one client requests the other to perform a particular task and to report the results; ATP binds the request and response together to ensure the reliable exchange of request–response pairs.

ASP: see AppleTalk Session Protocol.

at-least-once (ALO) transaction: an ATP transaction in which the request is repeated until a response is received by the requester or until a maximum retry count is reached. This recovery mechanism ensures that the transaction request is executed at least one time.

ATP: see AppleTalk Transaction Protocol.

backbone network: a central network to which a number of other smaller, usually lower-speed, networks connect; the backbone (or spine) network is usually constructed with a high-speed communication medium.

backbone router: one in a series of internet routers that are used to interconnect several AppleTalk networks through a backbone network.

background spooler: a print-spooling process that runs in the background on an originating computer.

bitmap order: when data is packed in bitmap order, the parameter corresponding to the least-significant set bit in the bitmap is packed first, followed by the parameter corresponding to the next most-significant set bit; packing continues in this manner, and the packet ends with the parameter corresponding to the most-significant set bit.

bit stuffing: a technique used to ensure that the unique bit pattern used to designate a flag byte (01111110) does not occur within the data packet. When bit stuffing is used, the link-level protocol (such as LLAP) inserts a 0 bit after every string of five consecutive 1 bits detected in the data stream being transmitted (the receiving LAP performs the inverse operation, stripping out each 0 bit that follows five consecutive 1 bits, in order to restore the data to its original state).

broadcast hardware address (broadcast ID): a hardware address common to all nodes on a data link; packets sent to this address will be delivered to every node on the data link. Broadcast hardware addresses facilitate broadcast transmissions.

broadcasting: delivery of a transmission to all active stations at the same time, such as over a bus-type local network.

broadcast packet: a packet intended to be received by all nodes in a network. In a LocalTalk implementation, broadcast packets are assigned a destination node identification number of 255 ($FF).

broadcast protocol address: an address that is accepted by all nodes that support a particular protocol stack; the broadcast protocol address facilitates the directed broadcast of packets to this subset of nodes.

broadcast transmission dialog: in a LocalTalk environment, the transmission of packets intended to be received by all nodes in the network. The source sends a lapRTS packet to the broadcast hardware address and then sends the data packet.

bus: a single, shared communication link. Messages are broadcast along the whole bus, and each network device listens for and receives messages directed to its unique address. The physical medium of a LocalTalk network is a twisted-pair bus.

Carrier Sense Multiple Access with Collision Avoidance (CSMA/CA): a technique that allows multiple stations to gain access to a transmission medium (multiple access) by listening until no signals are detected (carrier sense), and then signaling their intent to transmit before transmitting. When contention occurs, transmission is based on a randomly selected order (collision avoidance). LLAP, used for node-to-node delivery in a LocalTalk environment, uses the CSMA/CA technique.

catalog node (CNode): an entry (either a directory or a file) in a volume catalog of a disk. AFP recognizes two types of CNodes: internal CNodes, which are always directories, and leaf CNodes, which are located at the end of a limb in the tree-structured catalog and which can be either files or empty directories.

CCITT: see Consultative Committee on International Telephone & Telegraph.

clear-to-send (CTS) control packet: an LLAP packet sent in response to an RTS control packet, indicating the sending node's receipt of the RTS and its readiness to receive the data packet.

client: a software process that makes use of the services of another software process. See socket client.

closed connection: a connection that has been torn down. In a closed connection, neither end of the connection is established, so data transmission over the connection is no longer possible.

CNode: see catalog node.

connection: an association between two sockets that facilitates the establishment and maintenance of an exclusive dialog between two entities. See session.

connection end: in a connection, the communicating socket and the connection information associated with it.

connection identifier (ConnID): an identification number associated with each connection; a connection provides a unique identifier by using the socket address and the ConnID of the two connection ends.

connection-listening socket: a socket that accepts open-connection requests and passes them along to its ADSP client for further processing.

connection state: the term used to refer collectively to control and state information that is maintained by the two ends of a connection.

connection timer: a timer that is started when a connection opens. When an end receives a packet from the other end, the timer is reset; the timer expires if the end does not receive any packets within a specified time period (if no data is being transmitted, tickling packets can be sent to keep the connection open). Connection timers are used by the AppleTalk session-layer protocols, such as PAP, ASP, and ADSP.

ConnID: see connection identifier.

Consultative Committee on International Telephone & Telegraph (CCITT): a committee formed in 1938 that sets the international standards for the hardware and communications protocols for data and voice transmissions.

control information (CI): the field in an ATP packet indicating the packet type and various control information, such as the end-of-message flag.

control packets: messages that do not contain data, but that are used for administrative purposes, such as enquiry, acknowledgment, and notification; control packets are also used to open and close connections.

CRC: see cyclic-redundancy check.

CSMA/CA: see Carrier Sense Multiple Access with Collision Avoidance.

CTS: see clear-to-send control packet.

cyclic-redundancy check (CRC): an error-checking control technique that uses a polynomial algorithm to generate a 16-bit FCS based on the content of the frame. The FCS is appended to the end of each frame and is matched by the receiver to determine whether an error has occurred. LLAP uses the standard CRC-CCITT algorithm: $G(x) = x^{16} + x^{12} + x^5 + 1$.

DAS: see dynamically assigned socket.

datagram: a self-contained packet, independent of other packets in a data stream. Since a datagram carries its own routing information, its reliable delivery does not depend on earlier exchanges between the source and destination devices. DDP is responsible for delivering AppleTalk transmissions as datagrams.

Datagram Delivery Protocol (DDP): the network-layer protocol that is responsible for the socket-to-socket delivery of datagrams over an AppleTalk internet.

data packets: messages that contain client data.

data transparency: a technique of data transmission that allows data characters to be sent or received in any form, without regard to their possible interpretation as control characters. For example, to ensure that data containing six consecutive 1 bits is not interpreted as a flag byte, LLAP uses a data transparency mechanism known as bit stuffing. See bit stuffing.

DDP: see Datagram Delivery Protocol.

default zone: the zone to which any node on an extended network will automatically belong until a different zone is explicitly selected for that node.

deny modes: a set of AFP permissions that establishes what rights should be denied to users attempting to open a file fork that has already been opened by another user.

DES: data encryption standard published by the National Bureau of Standards (FIPS publication #46).

descendent: a destination CNode (an entry in a volume catalog of a disk); the directories along the path to the descendent are considered its ancestors.

Desktop database: a database used by a file server to hold information for use by the Macintosh Finder.

Desktop file: an invisible resource file that holds information for use by the Macintosh Finder.

directed broadcast: the transmission of a packet that is intended to be received by all nodes on a network other than the sender's network.

directed packet: a packet intended to be received by a single node.

directed transmission dialog: in a LocalTalk environment, the transmission of packets intended to be received by a single node. The source sends a lapRTS packet to the destination; the destination responds with a lapCTS packet; then the source sends the data packet.

directory: a construct for organizing information stored on a disk; disk directories can contain files and other directories. Each directory for a disk volume has an identifier, through which it and the files and other directories that it contains can be addressed. Sometimes called "folder."

Directory ID: a unique value that is assigned to each directory when it is created.

duplicate transaction-request filtering: an ATP process used to implement XO transaction service; in this process, the responder searches through a transactions list to determine whether the request has already been received. Duplicates are not delivered to ATP's client.

dynamically assigned socket (DAS): a socket assigned dynamically by DDP upon request from clients in the node. In an AppleTalk network, the sockets numbered 128–254 ($80–$FE) are allocated as DASs.

dynamic node address assignment: an addressing scheme that assigns node addresses dynamically, rather than associating a permanent address with each node. Dynamic node address assignment facilitates adding and removing nodes from the network by preventing conflicts between old node addresses and new node addresses.

ELAP: see EtherTalk Link Access Protocol.

end of message (EOM): a signal that indicates the end of a message. When the EOM bit is set in the header of a packet, it indicates that this packet is the last in a multipacket message, such as a multipacket ATP response or an ADSP data stream.

Enquiry control packet: an LLAP packet sent as part of the dynamic node number assignment algorithm, asking if any node on the link is currently using the specified LLAP node number.

entity identifier: the unique address of a network-visible entity's socket in a node within an internet. The specific format of an entity identifier is network-dependent.

entity name: a name that an NVE may assign itself. Although not all NVEs have names, NVEs can possess several names (or aliases). An entity name is made up of three character strings: object, type, and zone.

entity type: the part of an entity name that describes to what class the entity belongs; for example, "LaserWriter" or "AFPServer."

entry state: a variable associated with each entry in a routing table; three possible values for this variable are good, suspect, and bad.

enumerate: to list the offspring (files and directories) of a directory and selected parameters for those offspring.

enumerator value: a number used to distinguish among several entity names that are registered on the same socket. On a given socket, each entity name will have a unique enumerator value.

EOM: see end of message.

EtherTalk: Apple's data-link product that allows an AppleTalk network to be connected by Ethernet cables.

EtherTalk Link Access Protocol (ELAP): the link-access protocol used in an EtherTalk network. ELAP is built on top of the standard Ethernet data-link layer.

exactly-once (XO) transaction: an ATP transaction in which the request is delivered only one time, thus protecting against damage that could result from a duplicate transaction.

extended AppleTalk network: an AppleTalk network that allows addressing of more than 254 nodes and can support multiple zones.

extended DDP header: the DDP header type used for packets that are transmitted from one network to another network within an AppleTalk internet.

FCS: see frame check sequence.

file: a collection of related information that is stored on a disk. A file on a disk has a name through which it is accessible. Related files may be grouped together in a common directory. In the Macintosh file system and the AFI, a file is divided into two forks: a data fork and a resource fork.

file server: a computer running a specialized program that provides network users with access to shared disks or other mass storage devices. Through the implementation of access controls, a file server facilitates controlled access to common files and applications.

Finder: a Macintosh application that allows access to documents and other applications; the Finder uses icons to represent objects on a disk or volume. You use it to manage documents and applications and to get information to and from disks.

flag byte: a special bit pattern that is used in bit-oriented protocols to mark the beginning (and often the end) of a frame. The flag byte used as a frame delimiter in LLAP is the bit sequence 01111110 ($7E).

flow quantum: the maximum amount of data that can be transferred in a PAP transaction based on the buffer space available at the end that is issuing the read request.

flush: to write data from a cache in memory to a disk.

FM-0: a bit-encoding technique that provides self-clocking. LocalTalk implementations use FM-0 encoding.

folder: see directory.

fork: Macintosh files are divided into two parts, known as forks; the data fork is an unstructured finite sequence of data bytes. The resource fork is the part of a file that is accessible through the Macintosh Resource Manager and that contains specialized data used by an application, such as menus, fonts, and icons (as well as the application code for an application file).

frame: a group of bits forming a distinct transmission unit that is sent between data-link-layer entities. Each frame contains its own control information for addressing and error checking. The first several bits in a frame form a header that contains address and other control information, followed by the data (or message) being sent, and ending with a check sequence for error detection.

frame check sequence (FCS): a 16-bit sequence used for error checking that occurs at the end of each frame. In a LocalTalk implementation, the standard CRC-CCITT algorithm is used to compute the FCS. It is computed as a function of the contents of the destination node ID, source node ID, LLAP type, and data fields.

frame preamble: the part of an LLAP frame preceding the LLAP packet; specifically, 2 or more flag bytes.

frame trailer: the part of an LLAP frame following the LLAP packet; specifically, the FCS, trailing flag byte, and an abort sequence.

gateways: nodes that separate and manage communication between different types of networks; for example, a gateway is used to connect an AppleTalk protocol-based network to a non-AppleTalk protocol-based system. The gateway serves as a translator between the protocols of the two connected networks.

global backoff mask: a mask used by LLAP that takes on particular values to adjust the amount of time a node waits before transmitting in order to avoid collisions. The possible values in binary are: 0, 01, 011, 0111, 01111.

guest: a user who is logged on to a file server without a registered user name and password. A guest cannot own a directory. Guests receive whatever access privileges are assigned to "world."

half-open connection: a connection in which one end is established and the other end is closed, unreachable, or not yet open.

half router: an internet router used primarily to connect two remote AppleTalk networks. Each remote network contains an internet router that interconnects to the router attached to the other

network through a long-distance communication link. This combination of two half-routers serves, in effect, as a single routing unit.

hardware address: the unique node address that is determined by the physical and data-link layers of the network.

header: the portion of a message, usually at the beginning of a packet, that contains control information, such as the source and destination addresses, packet-type identifiers, sequence numbers, and priority-level indicators.

HFS: see hierarchical file system.

hierarchical file system (HFS): the file system used on Macintosh hard disks and 800K floppy disks.

history bytes: two 8-bit bytes that are maintained by LLAP and that contain the number of times a node has deferred and the number of times it has sensed a collision in the last eight attempts to gain access to the link. These history bytes are used to determine the value of the random wait period.

hop count: the number of internet routers that a datagram passes through en route to its destination; each internet router is counted as 1 hop.

IDG: see interdialogue gap.

IEEE 802.2: The Institute of Electrical and Electronics Engineers standard defining service interfaces and packet formats for data-link service.

IFG: see interframe gap.

interdialogue gap (IDG): the minimum separation time between dialogues; for LLAP, 400 microseconds.

interframe gap (IFG): the maximum separation time between frames of a single dialogue; for LLAP, 200 microseconds.

International Standards Organization-Open System Interconnection (ISO-OSI) reference model: a seven-layer network architecture reference model established by the ISO and adhered to by the CCITT. The OSI model is intended to provide a common basis for coordinating the development of standards aimed at systems interconnection, while allowing existing standards to be placed in perspective within a common framework. The model represents a network as a hierarchical structure of layers of function; it segments the data communication concept into seven layers and defines the functionality of each layer. Each layer provides a set of functions accessible to the layer above it. In the "open" philosophy, the services provided by one layer to another are strictly defined, but the manner used to provide the services is left open to interpretation.

internet: one or more AppleTalk networks connected by intelligent nodes referred to as internet routers.

internet router (IR): an intelligent node that connects AppleTalk networks and serves as the key component in extending the datagram delivery mechanism to an internet setting. An IR functions as a packet-forwarding agent to allow datagrams to be sent between any two nodes of an internet by using a store-and-forward process. AppleTalk internet routers fall into three categories: local routers, half routers, and backbone routers.

internet socket address: the address of a socket in an AppleTalk internet. This address is made up of the socket number and the node ID and network number of the node in which the socket is located; the internet address provides a unique identifier for any socket in an AppleTalk internet.

IR: see internet router.

ISO-OSI reference model: see International Standards Organization-Open System Interconnection reference model.

LAP: see Link Access Protocol.

link: any data transmission medium shared by a set of nodes and used for communication among these nodes.

Link Access Protocol (LAP): a link-level protocol that is responsible for the transmission of data across the physical link and ensures data integrity on this link. Sometimes called "data-link access protocol." The LocalTalk Link Access Protocol (LLAP) is the LAP protocol used in a LocalTalk environment.

LLAP: see LocalTalk Link Access Protocol.

LLAP type field: a 1-byte LLAP field that indicates packet type. Values in the range 1–127 ($01–$7F) indicate that the packet is a data packet; the type field specifies the LLAP type of the client to whom the packet's data must be delivered. Values in the range 128–255 ($80–$FF) are reserved for control packets.

local backoff mask: similar to the global backoff mask; the local backoff mask is used by LLAP to extend the time period between delivery attempts to a nonlistening node, thereby increasing that node's chances of receiving the packet.

local router: an internet router used to connect AppleTalk networks that are in close proximity to each other; the local router is directly connected to each of the AppleTalk networks that it links.

LocalTalk Link Access Protocol (LLAP): the link-level protocol that manages node-to-node delivery of data in a LocalTalk environment. LLAP manages bus access, provides a node-addressing mechanism, and controls data transmission and reception, ensuring packet length and integrity.

long name: the name used in AFP for a CNode (file or directory on a volume attached to a file server) so that the CNode can be recognized by a Macintosh workstation.

LSB: least-significant bit.

maximum packet lifetime (MPL): the length of time that a packet is allowed to exist in the internet (for AppleTalk, approximately 30 seconds).

missing clock: the detection and then absence of clocking information. Used by LLAP transmitters to synchronize their access to the bus.

mount: the process of making a disk volume that is attached to a file server available to a workstation.

MSB: most-significant bit.

multicast hardware address: a destination hardware address common to a designated subset of nodes in a network; a packet with a multicast address as a destination is sent to all network nodes that can be identified by the multicast address. Multicast addresses facilitate directed broadcasts to a group of nodes.

Name Binding Protocol (NBP): the AppleTalk transport-level protocol that translates a character string name into the internet address of the corresponding socket client; NBP enables AppleTalk protocols to understand user-defined zones and device names by providing and maintaining translation tables that map these names to corresponding socket addresses.

name-lookup process: the NBP process that binds the entity's name to its internet address.

names directory (ND): a distributed database of entity-name to entity-internet-address mappings; the ND is the union of the individual names tables in all the nodes of an internet.

names information socket (NIS): the NBP socket through which name lookup requests are received.

names table: a table in each node that contains entity-name to entity-internet-address mappings (known as NBP tuples) of all named NVEs in the node.

native file system commands: commands used to manipulate files on a diskette or other memory resource that is physically connected to a workstation.

Native Filing Interface (NFI): the interface through which native file system commands are made; the NFI defines the nature and format of parameters passed in and returned by the command.

NBP: see Name Binding Protocol.

ND: see names directory.

network number: a 16-bit number used to indicate the AppleTalk network a node is connected to. Nodes choose their network number from within the network number range assigned to their network.

network number range: the range of network numbers that are valid for use by nodes on a given AppleTalk network.

network-specific broadcast: a broadcast intended only for those nodes with the indicated network number.

network-visible entity (NVE): resources that are addressable through a network. Typically, the NVE is a socket client for a service available in a node.

network-wide broadcast: a broadcast intended for all nodes on a given network.

NFI: see Native Filing Interface.

NIS: see names information socket.

node: a data-link addressable entity on a network.

node ID: see node identifier.

node identifier (node ID): an 8-bit number that, when combined with the AppleTalk network number of a node, is used to uniquely identify each node on a network.

nonextended network: an AppleTalk network that supports addressing of up to 254 nodes and supports only one zone.

nonrouter node: a network node that does not function as an internet router.

NVE: see network-visible entity.

offspring: each CNode (file or directory in a volume catalog) is considered the offspring of the CNode directly above it in the catalog tree; the higher CNode is called the parent (or parent directory).

open connection: an association that is set up between two sockets in which both ends have been established so that data can flow over the connection.

open systems architecture: a hardware or software architecture that is well defined and whose specifications are publicly available, allowing others to substitute component parts or form interconnections to other architectures.

packet: a group of bits, including data and control elements, that is transmitted together as a unit

within a frame; the control elements include a source address, a destination address, and possibly error-control information.

PAP: see Printer Access Protocol.

parent (or parent directory): a directory is considered a parent to the CNode (file or directory) directly below it in the catalog tree; the lower CNode is called an offspring. The Parent ID is the Directory ID of the parent directory.

password: a unique string of characters that a user (or program) must supply in order to gain access to a network (or to a specific resource within the network); passwords are frequently encrypted prior to transmission to ensure network security.

pathname: the name of a CNode (file or directory) that specifies where the CNode belongs in the catalog tree. The pathname is formed by concatenating the directory names of all ancestor directories that make up the path.

path type: indicates whether the elements of the associated AFP pathname are all short names or all long names.

permissions: AFP access and deny modes that are used to regulate access to files. The AFP permission modes contribute to the synchronization rules that can prevent applications from damaging files through simultaneous access attempts.

port descriptor: information fields used to describe a router port; these fields include a flag that indicates whether the port is connected to an AppleTalk network, the port number, the router's address corresponding to the port, and the network number range for the network to which the port is connected.

Printer Access Protocol (PAP): the AppleTalk protocol that manages interaction between workstations and print servers; PAP handles connection setup, maintenance, and termination, as well as data transfer.

print spooler: a hardware application or a software application (or both) that intercepts printable document files and that interacts with a printer to print the document, freeing the originating computer of this responsibility.

probe: a packet sent requesting acknowledgment from the remote end of a connection; the probe itself serves as an acknowledgment to the remote end.

protocol: a set of procedural rules for information exchange over a communication medium; these rules govern the content, format, timing, sequencing, and error control of messages exchanged in a network.

protocol address: the unique address that a node assigns to identify the protocol client that is to receive a packet for a particular protocol stack. An example of a protocol address is the 16-bit AppleTalk network number and 8-bit node ID protocol address that DDP and AARP use to verify that an incoming packet is intended for the particular DDP node.

protocol family: a collection of related protocols that correspond to the layers of the ISO-OSI reference model and that together enable transmission and reception of packets over a network. The combination of all AppleTalk protocols is an example of a protocol family.

protocol stack: a particular implementation of a protocol family within a node.

provisional node address: the address used by a node in the process of selecting its network number.

pseudorandom numbers: numbers picked via a mathematical process that approximates a truly random process.

reception window size: the amount of buffer space that a connection end has available for receiving incoming data.

reply block: the format of an AFP call that is sent from the file server to an AFP workstation client; the response to a command block.

request block: the format of an AFP call that is sent from the AFP workstation client to the file server.

request control block (RqCB): an information block that an ATP responder maintains for each call for receiving a request issued by its client; the RqCB contains information provided by the call, including all data pertinent to the buffers and to the client delivery mechanism.

request-to-send (RTS) control packet: an LLAP packet sent to inform all nodes on the link of a node's desire to transmit a data packet and to request the destination node to send back a CTS control packet.

response control block (RspCB): an information block that an ATP responder maintains in nodes implementing the exactly-once mode of operation; the RspCB holds the information required to filter duplicate requests and to retransmit response packets.

root: the base or topmost directory in a volume catalog.

router: see internet router.

routing seed: the initial routing table set up by an internet router after it is first switched on.

routing table: a table, resident in each AppleTalk internet router, that serves as a mapping of the internet, specifying the path and distance (in hops) between the internet router and other networks. Routing tables are used to determine whether and where a router will forward a data packet. RTMP is used to update the routing tables.

Routing Table Maintenance Protocol (RTMP): the AppleTalk protocol used to establish and maintain the routing information that is required by internet routers in order to route datagrams from any source socket to any destination socket in the internet. Using RTMP, internet routers dynamically maintain routing tables to reflect changes in internet topology.

routing tuple: the last part of an RTMP Data packet; routing tuples consist of two values: the destination network number or range and the distance, in hop counts, from the sending internet router to the destination network.

RqCB: see request control block.

RspCB: see response control block.

RTMP: see Routing Table Maintenance Protocol.

RTMP Stub: a process that listens on the RTMP socket in nonrouter nodes and that, upon receiving an RTMP Data packet, copies the packet's origination network number range and node address into two variables associated with the nonrouter node; the network number range is copied to THIS-NET-RANGE, and the node address (network number and node ID) is copied to A-ROUTER.

RTS: see request-to-send.

SAS: see statically assigned socket.

SCC: see Zilog 8530 Serial Communications Controller.

SDLC: see Synchronous Data Link Control.

seed router: an internet router in an AppleTalk network that has the network number range built into its port descriptor. Each AppleTalk network must have at least one seed router. This router will define the network number range for the other routers in that network.

send transaction status (STS) bit: a bit in the header of an ATP TResp packet, requesting the receiver of that packet to resend the ATP TReq with the current bitmap.

Serial Communications Controller (SCC): see Zilog 8530 Serial Communications Controller.

server node IDs: one of two classes of node ID numbers; server node IDs fall within the range 128–254 ($80–$FE) and are used by network servers (such as printers, spoolers, and file servers).

servers: network nodes that provide a service to the other nodes in the network, such as shared access to a file system (a file server), control of a printer (a printer server), or storage of messages in a mail system (a mail server).

server session socket (SSS): a socket in a server to which all session-related packets are sent.

session: a logical connection between two network entities (typically, a workstation and a server) that facilitates establishment and maintenance of an exclusive dialog between the two entities. In an AppleTalk network, ASP can be used to establish, maintain, and tear down sessions; ASP also ensures that the commands transmitted during a session are delivered in the same order as they were sent and that the results of the commands are conveyed back to the originating entity. See connection.

session identifier (session ID): an identification number associated with each session; the session ID is unique among all the sessions to the same server; since multiple workstations can have sessions to the same server simultaneously, ASP uses session IDs to distinguish between commands received in these various sessions.

session listening socket (SLS): a socket in a server on which the server registers its name and listens for requests to open a session.

session maintenance timeout: a timeout period that occurs when one end of a session determines that the other end is unreachable because it has been unresponsive; when the session maintenance timeout occurs, ASP closes the session.

short DDP header: the DDP header type often used for packets whose source and destination sockets are within the boundaries of a single AppleTalk network. (An extended header is required for packets that are transmitted across network boundaries within an internet.)

short name: the name used in AFP for a CNode (file or directory on a volume attached to a file server) so that the CNode can be recognized by an MS-DOS workstation.

SLS: see session listening socket.

SNAP: Sub-Network Access Protocol; used to distinguish between different protocol families using IEEE 802.2 packets.

socket: an addressable entity within a node connected to an AppleTalk network; sockets are owned by software processes known as socket clients. AppleTalk sockets are divided into two groups, statically assigned sockets (SASs), which are reserved for clients such as AppleTalk core protocols,

and dynamically assigned sockets (DASs), which are assigned dynamically by DDP upon request from clients in the node.

socket client: a software process or function implemented in a network node.

socket listener: code provided by a socket client to receive datagrams addressed to the socket.

socket number: an 8-bit number that identifies a socket. A maximum of 254 different socket numbers can be assigned in a node.

sockets table: a table that maintains an appropriate descriptor of each active socket listener in a node; the data structure for the sockets table is built and maintained by the code that implements DDP in the node.

spooler/server: a combination of hardware and software that stores documents sent to it over a network and manages the printing of those documents on a printer.

SSS: see server session socket.

startup range: the range from which a node selects the network number part of its provisional address if it has no other network number saved.

statically assigned socket (SAS): a socket that is permanently reserved for use by a designated process. In an AppleTalk network, SASs are the sockets numbered 1–127 ($01–$7F); they are reserved for use by specific socket clients and for low-level built-in network services.

STS: see send transaction status bit.

synchronization pulse: in LLAP, a transition period on the link that is followed by an idle period greater than 2 bit-times, resulting in a missing clock indication in all receiving nodes. Used to synchronize access to the link.

synchronization rules: rules used by file servers to control simultaneous file access. The synchronization rules used by AFP are based on a set of file-opening permissions: an access mode and a deny mode.

Synchronous Data Link Control (SDLC): a data-link layer protocol for managing synchronous, code-transparent, serial-by-bit information transfer. SDLC transmission exchanges may be full duplex or half duplex over either a switched or nonswitched link. The configuration of the link may be point-to-point, multipoint, or loop. SDLC frame format is used in LocalTalk implementations.

TCB: see transaction control block.

TID: see transaction identifier.

TokenTalk: Apple's data-link product that allows an AppleTalk network to be connected by token ring cables.

TokenTalk Link Access Protocol (TLAP): the link-access protocol used in a TokenTalk network. TLAP is built on top of the standard token ring data-link layer.

transaction: an exchange of information between a source and a destination client that accomplishes a particular action or result. In an AppleTalk environment, ATP provides a transaction service that enables a source client's request to be bound to the destination client's response.

transaction bitmap: the field in an ATP TReq packet indicating which ATP TResp packets are being requested.

transaction control block (TCB): an information block that the ATP requester must maintain for

retransmitting an ATP request and for receiving its responses.

transaction identifier (TID): an identification number provided by ATP to bind together the request and response portions of a transaction.

Transaction Release (TRel): an ATP packet sent in response to XO TResp, specifying that the entire response message was received; upon receiving the TRel, the transaction responder removes the RspCB.

Transaction Request (TReq): an ATP packet sent to ask an ATP client to perform an action and to return a response.

Transaction Response (TResp): an ATP packet sent in response to a TReq, specifying the results of the requested operation.

transactions list: a list that the ATP responder maintains of all the recently received transactions; this list is used to implement XO transaction service.

TRel: see Transaction Release.

TReq: see Transaction Request.

TResp: see Transaction Response.

UAM: see user authentication method.

user authentication method (UAM): any procedure used by a server and workstation by which the server is convinced of the user's identity.

user name: a string of characters that uniquely identifies a user for login purposes; the user name is entered by the user and confirmed in a user-authentication database before the user is permitted to gain access to the network resource.

user node IDs: one of two classes of node ID numbers; user node IDs fall within the range 1–127 ($01–$7F) and are generally used by workstations.

volume: a file storage unit. Each disk attached to an AppleTalk file server is considered a volume, although some disks may contain multiple volumes.

volume catalog: a tree-structured catalog of the files and directories on a volume.

Volume ID: a session-unique value assigned by a file server to each of its volumes; AFP calls use the Volume ID to specify the desired volume.

volume signature: a 2-byte field in AFP calls that identifies the volume type; volumes are of three possible types: flat, fixed Directory ID, or variable Directory ID.

workstation session socket (WSS): a socket in a workstation to which all session-related packets are sent.

WSS: workstation session socket.

XO transaction: see exactly-once transaction.

Zilog 8530 Serial Communications Controller (SCC): an integrated circuit commonly used to provide controller services in an LLAP implementation.

ZIP: see Zone Information Protocol.

ZIP bringback time: a specified amount of time after a network is brought down in which the network can be brought up again with a new zone name.

ZIS: see zone information socket.

ZIT: see zone information table.

zone: an arbitrary subset of the nodes within an internet.

Zone Information Protocol (ZIP): the AppleTalk session-layer protocol that is used to maintain and discover the internet-wide mapping of network number ranges to zone names; ZIP is used by NBP to determine which networks contain nodes which belong to a zone.

zone information socket (ZIS): the statically assigned socket (SAS) in each internet router to which nodes address requests for zone information and through which the internet router responds to those requests.

zone information table (ZIT): a complete network-range-to-zones-list mapping of the internet maintained by each internet router in an AppleTalk internet.

zone multicast address: a data-link-dependent multicast address at which a node receives the NBP broadcasts directed to its zone.

zones list: specifies the zone names that can be chosen by nodes on the network.

Index

The Apple Publishing System

Inside AppleTalk, Second Edition, was written, edited, and composed on a desktop publishing system using Apple® Macintosh® computers and Microsoft® Word. Proof pages were created on the Apple LaserWriter® printers; final pages were printed on a Varityper® VT600™. Line art was created using Adobe Illustrator™ and typeset on a Linotronic® 300. PostScript®, the LaserWriter page-description language, was developed by Adobe Systems Incorporated.

Text type and display type are Apple's corporate font, a condensed version of ITC Garamond®. Bullets are ITC Zapf Dingbats®. Some elements, such as program listings, are set in Apple Courier, a fixed-width font.